CULTURE AND HORTICULTURE

Also by Wolf D. Storl

Healing Lyme Disease Naturally: History, Analysis, and Treatments

The Herbal Lore of Wise Women and Wortcunners:
The Healing Power of Medicinal Plants

CULTURE AND HORTICULTURE

The Classic Guide to Organic and Biodynamic Gardening

WOLF D. STORL

North Atlantic Books
Berkeley, California

Published by
North Atlantic Books
P.O. Box 12327
Berkeley, California 94712

Cover photo © Istockphoto.com/cjp
Illustrations by Wolf D. Storl
Cover and book design by Suzanne Albertson

Printed in the United States of America

Culture and Horticulture: The Classic Guide to Organic and Biodynamic Gardening is sponsored by the Society for the Study of Native Arts and Sciences, a nonprofit educational corporation whose goals are to develop an educational and cross-cultural perspective linking various scientific, social, and artistic fields; to nurture a holistic view of arts, sciences, humanities, and healing; and to publish and distribute literature on the relationship of mind, body, and nature.

North Atlantic Books' publications are available through most bookstores. For further information, visit our website at www.northatlanticbooks.com or call 800-733-3000.

Library of Congress Cataloging-in-Publication Data

Storl, Wolf-Dieter.
    Culture and horticulture : classic guide to organic and biodynamic gardening / Wolf D. Storl.
        p. cm.
    Classic guide to biodynamic gardening
    Summary: "First published in 1979, this work is a classic of organic gardening, exploring soil fertility, harvesting and storage, and many other aspects of biodynamic gardening"—Provided by publisher.
    Includes bibliographical references and index.
    ISBN 978-1-58394-550-6
1. Organic gardening. I. Title. II. Title: Classic guide to organic and biodynamic gardening.
SB453.5.S86 2013
635'.0484—dc23   2012026214

1 2 3 4 5 6 7 8 9 United 18 17 16 15 14 13
Printed on recycled paper

To the memory of Robert Elbers of Warmonderhof, Holland

The rushes daily grow taller,
Apricot blossoms daily more lush.
As an old farmer, I enjoy the view;
Everything I do according to the seasons.
I rise early to feed the cows,
Then yoke a pair to farm in eastern acres.
Earthworms crawl in and out of the ground,
Field crows follow me around.
In flocks they peck and cry,
as if to tell me of their hunger.
My heart is full of compassion
Looking at this, I pity both them and myself.
I give my food to the crows;
At dusk I return with an empty basket.
My family greets me with mocking smiles;
But never would I have changed my mind.

Ch'u Kuang-hsi, sixth century

CONTENTS

ILLUSTRATIONS

FOREWORD BY LARRY BERGER

Our small Oregon campus was all abuzz with the rumor that the school had hired a "Hell's Angel" to teach anthropology. On first meeting Wolf I expected such, but as he approached me I could see his beard waving in the wind yet he sported no black leather jacket or wild tattoos. Although he may have looked to be a natural riding a Harley, Wolf seemed more like a large, wise and gentle gnome than a "biker."

It so happened that Wolf lived close to the campus and often he would be seen out digging up his yard. Soon several rows of raised beds were formed and out burst an array of vegetables, some of which had never been seen before in these parts. Interest quickly spiked in Wolf's unique garden and a Saturday morning class at the college was arranged. The class became so popular that if you didn't arrive soon enough you either had to sit on the floor or stand because the chairs were all taken. It was through these classes that this book came to be.

While most of us were there for the basic info like the "where," "when," and "how" to plant "what," there were excursions to Wolf's garden a short walk away for that. We were given plenty of practical hands-on experience through turning compost piles, making manure teas, and thinning rows of witlof and fennel. We relished working in the deep dark tilth of the garden beds. This was not often experienced in the mountainous terrain of southern Oregon. We learned that the fertility of the soil did not have to be measured with lab tests but could be intuitively felt through one's fingers and that if you give the soil the proper blend of organic compost your garden will flourish.

Besides giving us a plethora of practical information, Wolf drew us into his world of German mystics, nature spirits, and the cosmic influences on plants. Rudolf Steiner, the father of the agricultural system named *biodynamics*, first used the term in a series of lectures given to farmers to improve their faltering crops. Wolf brought these lectures alive through his gardening experiences in Switzerland. His stories brought us back to the time when nature was enthused with spirit. Planting by the moon and companion planting were novel (and preposterous) ideas to most of us then; yet with Wolf's patient clarity it all started to come together and make sense. Gardening was more a method of communing with nature than having dominion over it.

I inherited Wolf's garden when he returned to Europe. Before leaving he counseled me that "Just as a cow mourns the loss of the farmer when he is gone, a garden will mourn the loss of its gardener." I tried my best to keep the garden happy but we all mourned the loss of Wolf Storl. He was a huge source of inspiration for gardeners throughout the valley. With much demand from the students the school published the first printing of these lectures. I have referenced my dog-eared first copy many times over the decades. It has stood the test of time as one of the best primers on organic and in particular biodynamic gardening. I look forward to sharing this newly revised edition with future generations of avid gardeners.

Larry Berger
January 2013

# ACKNOWLEDGMENTS

For many hours spent at the typewriter, I want to thank John Kehoe. I am grateful to Christine Storl, without whose help this book would not have been possible. Special thanks to Lutz Kramer of Rogue Community College, Oregon, for reading the manuscript, and to the students who prompted the writing.

PART I
History and Philosophy

It is, you see—though people seem to find the idea amusing—the garden that makes the gardener.
>   —Alan Chadwick, master gardener and student of
>   Rudolf Steiner

Search the World, and there's not to be found
A book so good as this for Garden Ground
>   —Stephen Blake, *The Compleat Gardeners Practice,* 1664

Introduction to Part I

This book is written as an introduction to gardening in its wider aspects, linking it into historical, philosophical, and cosmological contexts, taking horticulture from the microscope to the wider cosmos. Surely such vistas are involved when one takes a shovel to hand to turn the soil: eons have formed it; life permeates it in manifold forms; cosmic cycles of sun and moon warm it, circulate water through it, lure out of it the season's vegetation; and man shapes it according to his thinking and willing, plants and husbands it according to his cultural tradition, and finds mental and physical sustenance through it. All of that is gardening!

This book is not just a collection of garden facts and practices, for there are enough good books of this kind on the market. It is not written primarily for the seasoned biodynamic agriculturist versed in anthroposophical lore, nor for the academic biologist and college-trained horticulturist, who, while dealing with the relevant and irrelevant variables, test tubes, and statistics, loses the total picture. I do not mean to amass detail after detail, hoping to eventually emerge with the larger concept. Unlike the archeologist who matches potsherds hoping to find and finally reconstruct the complete pattern of the vessel, we hope to approach the subject as one who has glimpsed into the potter's workshop having caught sight of the overall shape of the vessel, while lacking knowledge of most of the details. Thus we start with the holistic concept of the archetypal image of the garden, trying to outline, sketch, and accentuate this image by the use of various observed facts, details, and useful analogies. For this reason, if it becomes evident that some of the minor details are obscure, it should not detract from the overall concept, the archetypal garden, which is central to our

3

concern. This methodology is a surer way of avoiding the truncations and Frankensteinian distortions that have come about by a blind amassing of facts and details without regard to the holistic aspects, and which have, in my opinion, eventually been translated into our social and environmental crises.

The first part of the book is concerned with a philosophical, historical, and epistemological setting, and the second part deals with the more practical, down-to-earth aspects of gardening.

I first came into contact with organic gardening, and the biodynamic method in particular, while I was studying ethnology in Switzerland and doing "participant observation research" in a community where *biodynamic agriculture* provided the subsistence basis. I had gardened before, helping a proverbial "old neighbor" for years to earn pocket money as a boy and learning many tricks of the trade, including the use of pesticides and ammonia sulfate. Eventually I enrolled at Ohio State University School of Agriculture to learn forestry. In the first year of general introduction to agriculture, I learned that the old family subsistence farm must come to an end, that the farm should be a production unit like a factory, that work processes must be specialized and technologized so that the farmer can go into his barn wearing a business suit and just push buttons . . . otherwise humanity's exploding population would starve. More or less, that is what one was told.

While strolling through the experimental fields of the college and mentally comparing them to the other soils I had seen in the small Ohio farming community where I had grown up, I noticed their lack of a certain living quality. When I saw more of the research equipment and procedure, when a professor received an award for a starling-killing machine, when I heard of placing windows in the stomachs of experimental animals in order to watch their digestion, I became upset. I could not think of trees as renewable capital or mere, albeit complicated, chemical processes. Though I had been part of a group of honor students, candidates for a technocratic elite that was meant to implement these concepts (as part of the technocratic

"Green Revolution") later, I gave up forestry and studied anthropology instead. For the most part, I forgot about my early contact with agriculture until my later research in a rural community in Switzerland, where I discovered a better way of farming and gardening.

The community, Village Aigues-Vertes, near Geneva, was interesting anthropologically because it was not a traditional Swiss village but a newly founded community that dedicated itself to providing good homes and a sheltered environment for people with disabilities, of which there were about fifty at the time I was there. At the time of my study, the community's social structure consisted of ten households, averaging about eight persons each, workshops (pottery, enameling, weaving, doll making, carpentry, repair shop, etc.), and a basis of biodynamic farming and gardening. Committees, such as the housewives' committee, produce committee, machine and equipment committee, and so forth, organized the village. A weekly general village meeting was held at which the committees reported problems and discussed and decided upon projects by—ideally— unanimous agreement. Except for personal items, major means of production and resources were held in common. The village was one of several "Camphill Villages," founded in the 1940s by the Viennese child pedagogue and pioneer in curative education, Dr. Karl Koenig. Koenig conceptualized the villages as alternatives to the social arrangements that brought about the excesses of mass society, whether of capitalism, fascism, or communism. He utilized the philosophies of the Bruderhof (Hutterian brethren), of the Bohemian philosopher Comenius, of Robert Owen, and of the Three-fold Social Order of Rudolf Steiner. The villagers were happy and secure and I experienced this as one of the few communal efforts that seemed to be working successfully.

Agriculturally, the community had access to about eighty acres of land, of which only thirty-two acres (thirteen hectares) were in direct production, the rest being occupied by woodland and structures. The garden was a little bit more than two acres at the time of the study. All the food for everyone who lived there was produced from this amount of land, plus some surplus to sell to city people, who literally came begging for fresh organic produce. The garden yielded a most varied assortment of vegetables year-round. In the winter, the selection narrowed to carrots, leeks, witlof (or witloof), endives, oyster plants, parsnips, turnips, beets, and onions. If there was a good harvest, the cabbage, celeriac, squash, and fennel could last well into the spring. Five gardeners, three of them somewhat mentally disabled, and occasional student helpers worked in the garden year-round. In the summer, the work was intense from dawn to dusk; in the winter, the work was easier, consisting of cleaning vegetables, fixing tools, working on manure composts, picking up wheelbarrow loads of stones that kept growing like spuds in the moraine soil, planting witlof roots in warmer indoor boxes for sprouting, watering the lamb's lettuce, endives, and sugarloaf under the plastic foliage tunnels, and so on. In February, the hot beds were prepared from horse manure and liquid manure, the first sowings were put in, and the constant watering, airing, and watching out for frosts kept the gardeners on their toes.

Two farmers and four or five disabled assistants who were skilled milkers and accustomed to a variety of work courses operated the farm. Eight milk cows, a bull, some heifers, calves, a workhorse sometimes with a foal, pigs, chickens, ducks, sheep, and rabbits made up the animal helpers. The number of animals was carefully suited to the land and available pasture, so that the whole worked like a self-contained organism. The farm produced all the milk that was needed and all the grain that was baked into bread at the village bakery. Excess milk was turned into cheese, cottage cheese, etc. Eggs, butter, and cheese were sometimes in short supply. Red and black currants, gooseberries, strawberries, elderberries, roan berries, and raspberries were produced in their season, requiring the workers from the workshops to help with the plentiful harvests. In the village, juices and preserves were made from the berries, plumbs, cherries, apricots, pears, and apples; villagers also partook in pickling and sauerkraut making. Similarly, during the haying season, potato harvesting, or the beet-seedling-thinning, a large reserve labor force could be called upon to do the necessary tasks.

The farm and garden worked closely together. The farmers would supply the cow, horse, pig, and chicken manure, which the chief gardener and expert compost maker, Manfred Stauffer, would biodynamically prepare with herbal essences and render into the finest substance possible. This composted manure provided the basis for a steadily increasing fertility of the land under cultivation. Originally, the land had not been so productive; the soil is composed of the gravelly moraine of an old Rhône glacier, and the area enjoys the least amount of annual rainfall in Switzerland. Prior to the establishment of the village, one family had failed to make a living on this land trying to raise pigs. The canton of Geneva acquired the land with tentative plans to make it part of an agricultural experiment station or school, but soil tests showed it to be unsuitable. Consequently, it was leased for a nominal sum to the Camphill people. Over the next fifteen years, the population of the new community rose from twelve to nearly one hundred people, all of whom were fed from the amount of land where before one family had not been able to survive—it must be mentioned that a high investment of starting capital was necessary to get this efficient system going, some of which was derived from donations by parents of the disabled citizens, or by insurance payments. Of this population, only about 10 percent were actively and directly involved in agriculture, while the rest were able to perform other tasks.

The households ordered their daily vegetable and fruit needs each morning and disabled villagers delivered the freshly harvested produce. The records kept of this and sales outside the village show that production nearly doubled each year for a period of five years, before leveling off to a steady peak. During that time, the expert handling of biodynamic practices had increased the humus content in the soil to a noticeable extent. Before, the soil had been compacted, with few earthworms evident; now the soil had become darker, fluffier, and more alive with a small fauna. Much of this was due to bringing in organic outside material, a practice that is generally avoided in biodynamics but was initially necessary to raise the humus level on this gravelly soil in order to keep the water from leaching it out. For a few francs, city workers, driving truckloads of algae dredged from Lake Geneva, leaves from the parks, and dirt from roadside ditches, were persuaded to dump their loads at Aigues-Vertes instead of at the city landfill. Nonetheless, the greatest aid in soil building were cover crops and manure from the livestock. Everything organic was composted, including organic garbage, old cloth, chicken feathers, and leather scraps. Once, a visitor accidentally left her coat on a pile of rags only to return and find that it had been composted! Another time, a bookstore gave the village a truckload of books, mostly cheap French novels that could have been sold in town for a franc a piece. We decided to compost them, too. After soaking them to loosen the bindings, it took two years to get a compost that was so full of earthworms—genuine "bookworms" in this case—that it looked like raw hamburger when disturbed, a fact that made it the favorite exhibit for the many international visitors to the garden. We decided not to use the compost on our vegetable beds, though, after second thoughts about the lead contained in the printer's ink.

Experiments were made in the garden house to ascertain the quality of the various composts by seeing how well cress seeds *(Lepidium sativum)* sprouted, how quickly they developed mass, measuring the distance between internodes, etc. Controls were run under identical conditions on various soils and composts. Other tests were done to check quality indications by placing plant saps into test-culture dishes (petri dishes) to see when and which kind of bacteria or fungus developed. The composts were applied in a directed way, depending on the preceding crops, the needs of the new crops, and the condition of the soil. Outside sales eventually brought enough money to afford the building of a greenhouse and a pond to collect rainwater from the roofs of the village buildings. Rainwater was considered better than well water.

Despite ethno-scientific training, I had, at first, an excruciatingly hard time understanding the motives, postulates, and the worldview of the community. The results these people were getting with their "treatment" of the mentally challenged, in their agriculture, and in nutrition and the general effectiveness of their lifestyle were impressive. But they did not proceed from the scientific methodology that I considered the only basis of reality. Since I was there as an anthropologist doing research, I listened, observed, and made notes about invisible "etheric" and "astral" forces at work, planetary and lunar influences, "elemental beings" at work in the garden and village, etc. My notebook was filled with observations of the following sort: mountain crystals were pulverized and buried in a cow's horn in the ground for a year; a pinch the size of a pea was put into a barrel of lukewarm rainwater and stirred, using a birch-besom, rhythmi- cally clockwise alternating counterclockwise for one hour; the resultant "potentized" fluid was then sprayed over the fields and gardens. One time, noticing a leaking rain pipe on the roof, I fixed it. The next time it rained, it was leaking again and I fixed it again. A third time, the master gardener mumbled disconcertedly something about someone always fixing the rain gutter. I found out that it was intended to drip on a certain spot where a sheep's skull was buried with oak bark scrapings in it. It was supposed to rot there in a certain way for a reason that I did not comprehend at the time. Another time, aphids appeared on the beans and I was ready to counterat- tack with a brew of tobacco juice (I had even sacrificed my expensive British pipe tobacco to brew it), figuring that was the organic way of destroying pests; but the gardener just squatted down on his haunches and sat there looking and thinking. I wondered if he had lost his senses. "What is there to think about?" I demanded. "There is the problem and here is the solution." The gardener replied that it would be better to think about *why* the aphids were there in the first place.

"Well that's simple," I replied, drawing on my natural science studies, "they are most likely wind-borne or carried by another organism and we had better destroy them before they spread."

He then explained, "No, the reason they are here is more subtle than that; it has to do with how we fertilized the soil, what crop preceded it, and what weather patterns exist that weakened the plants so that they became susceptible."

Sometimes voles and gophers were a problem in the garden. Once in a while, the gardener's cat would catch one of the rodents. He would then take them, skin them, and hang the hides to dry while his wife fried the carcasses for the cats to eat. At a certain time, when Venus was in the sign of Scorpio, he would burn the pelts and sprinkle the ashes over the beds, causing, he claimed, the other gophers to reconsider where they had set- tled. It would hinder their reproductive vigor, since Venus has to do with reproduction, and Scorpio represents the region of the loins in the body of the cosmic human *(Meganthropus)* as shown in the zodiac.

I kept notes on all of this and had my own anthropological explanations.

By placing the phenomena into categories of "survivals of a primitive early European worldview" or into Sir James Frazer's "homeopathic and contagious magic," I was doing less for anthropology than for my own cognitive dissonance.

Other biodynamic farmers and gardeners that I met at this time engaged in similar strange practices, such as fetching water at the full moon or collecting and using herbs in unusual ways. One old white-haired farmer, named Arthur Hermes, boiled the shoots of the "red pine" (Norway spruce, *Picea abies*) for several hours and, diluting the brew with rainwater, poured it around his garden to keep slugs out. He reasoned that the spruce is a tree of Saturn, and the soft slimy slugs belong to the moon. The characteristics of Saturn are, among others, warmth and dryness, whereas those of the moon are wet and cold. The slugs will feel that they are leaving lunar territory and entering Saturnian territory, and will recoil at the prospect. This explanation, and others like it, seemed like the products of unbridled fantasy and it was hard for me to consider them to be real in the "real" world.[1]

Arthur Hermes, a man who reminded one of an old bear and who looked like a druid from the days of yore, became a friend and one of my teachers. I often visited him on his solitary farmstead in the middle of a forest in the Jura Mountains overlooking Lake Neuchatel. Next to the farm building was a knoll, covered by oaks, yews, holly, and ivy, in the midst of which a number of monumental stones (menhirs) dating back to Megalithic times were to be found. The thought crossed my mind that maybe Hermes was a reincarnated druid, or more correctly, a megalithic priest. At least he talked like one; not only was he in possession of down-to-earth practical knowledge, but also he was full of lore and wisdom, which he expressed using the vocabulary of Rudolf Steiner. He sowed the wheat and rye, which was to become his bread, on the day of Saint Michael in the fall. He plowed with a horse and seemed to be able to talk with it. He could call his cows to the barn by mentally connecting with them. Before sowing the beets or carrots into the garden beds or broadcasting the grain into the field, he held the seeds enclosed in his hand and concentrated on the sun, "as it shines in the heavens and in our heart." "It is the light of love," he explained, "one could call it the light of Christ."

It is from him that I learned how important it is to deal lovingly with the plants and animals in one's garden. He called the toads, birds, and ants "his fellow coworkers" and spoke with them as though they could understand. When he planted his cabbage, lettuce, or chard seedlings, he would water them and then pack them tenderly into the mulch. "They are like little children; when you put them to bed, you have to tuck them in real good." He taught me that this loving relation is more important than all theoretical knowledge.

Hermes said things that I had never heard of before, certainly not at the School of Agriculture, things that caused me to ponder: "Everything you do, whether it is sawing wood, sowing corn, or getting water from the well, must be accompanied by consciousness. This consciousness flows into the work and becomes part of it. This human consciousness is nourishment for the elemental beings, which will help you all along. They are etheric beings, they might be invisible to the outer eyes, but they are real nonetheless."

Despite my inability to understand the cognitive premises, Aigues-Vertes, the self sufficient mountain farmstead of Arthur Hermes, and other biodynamic places were shining examples of good husbandry, of healthy stock and plentiful produce. I stayed nearly three years in Aigues-Vertes instead of the one I had originally intended, and found the individuals working in biodynamics to be much more sophisticated than they had seemed at first. Rather than working with outmoded, hand-me-down superstitions, they were utilizing a metalanguage, a complicated system of symbols, to express and communicate fine and detailed observations about the workings of nature. I found out that many of the practitioners of this method were far from being uneducated; many had impressive academic and scientific credentials. In the meantime, my professor at the University of Berne with whom I was finishing my PhD dissertation and exam, became worried that I had lost my scientific objectivity. He suspected me of the greatest heresy of anthropology: identification with the subjects under study. Besides, I had made none of my research public. I began to feel, however, that I had found a level of cognition superior to the one on which I had been operating; in this book I try to formulate the new worldview.

Following the apprenticeship years at Aigues-Vertes, I tried my own hand at organizing a garden. A small home for the mentally challenged in Schwarzenegg, Switzerland, trying to achieve self-sufficiency, asked me to set up an organic vegetable garden. I set out to apply all of what I had learned. Old peasants would come by on their Sunday walks and look at the way things grew, nodding their approval. The weeds left in the garden deliberately for their companion plant effects, however, did not receive the appreciation of the immaculate Swiss peasant who stacks his manure piles and firewood in mosaic patterns.

Subsequently, I attended conferences for alternative agriculture. One conference was in Saas, Switzerland, where young people were using the biodynamic method to reclaim the abandoned mountain terraces of the Valais Valley. The peasants of this area had undergone modernization within the last fifty years, and the men were catering to the more profitable tourist business or working in a chemical factory in the valley after a highway had been built, while the women tried to carry on rudimentary agriculture at home. Before returning to the United States, I attended a month-long seminar on biodynamics at the Goetheanum in Dornach, Switzerland, and was duly impressed by the thoroughness of the research and the depth of understanding regarding nature. It is out of these experiences that the course at Rogue Community College and this book came about; after three years of organic gardening courses, my students asked me to write the notes into a book.

Chapter 1

Historical Sketch

No joy is so great in a life of seclusion as that of gardening. No matter what the soil may be, sandy or heavy clay, on a hill or a slope, it will serve well.

—Walafrid Strabo, *Hortulus*, ninth century

Agriculture started about ten thousand years ago, as archeological evidence from Asia Minor suggests. Ten thousand years is a long time for observations to accumulate and techniques to develop. Indeed, agri*culture* and *culture* are intimately linked, as anthropologists have shown many times in relating the connection of quality and form of lifestyle with various subsistence patterns. It might be claimed that a healthy agriculture is the basis of a healthy culture and healthy culture implies a healthy agriculture.

Early forms of agriculture include the *irrigation* practices of Mesopotamia, Egypt, the American Southwest, and other parts of the world; and *swidden* (or slash-and-burn) systems developed in the forested areas of the world.[1]

Swidden entails cutting or girdling trees; burning brush, thus releasing nutrients in the ashes; and sowing or planting food plants in the spaces. The soil is usually exhausted after a few years, forcing the primitive agriculturists to move to another location, to return to the same plot for a new cycle of clearing, burning, and planting perhaps even after a number of decades. When the forest has regrown the swidden farmers often return to the same area for a new cycle of clearing, burning and planting. Some of the early American pioneers practiced swidden, as did the Native Americans, for instance the Iroquois, who subsisted on the "three sisters" of maize (corn), beans, and squash.

The early ancestors of the Europeans practiced slash-and-burn agriculture until the time that the population increased and a more stable way of life developed, when more permanent forms of agriculture were devised. The fusion of barbarian and Roman lifestyles brought about the feudalistic, medieval way of life. Most of the populations were peasants engaged in agriculture, while a small percentage of the population, the nobility, provided protection, ensuring the peaceful agricultural cycle would not be unduly interrupted. The clergy provided guidance in the moral and ideological sphere. Generally, land was held in common, with each family tilling what it needed to survive and to pay as tax to the nobility and the church. If the family grew larger or became smaller, the amount of tillage in tenure would vary correspondingly. The crops were grown in *a three-field system* of rotation. One field was planted with summer crops, one with winter crops, and one lay *fallow*.² The fallow field was permitted to grow over with weeds, which helped restore the fertility to a large extent. The fields were also manured from time to time. On the average, the yields were low, but the fertility of the soil remained fairly constant. The animals were grazed on the *common lands* beyond the confines of the village and the *common woodland* served as a source of firewood, herbs, berries, beechnuts, and acorns for swine in the fall, etc.

A whole way of life and a cosmology supported by centuries of observations and lifetimes of experience were linked with early agricultural systems. There was nothing resembling modern scientific research at the time. The closest to such research was the activity in cloister farms and cloister gardens. Here, medicinal herbs were grown; along with vegetables such as carrots, leeks, onions, cucumbers, cabbages, lettuce, peas, parsnips, rampion, and chards; as well as some that are nowadays considered weeds, such as mustard, purslane, and lamb's-quarters. Plants for dyeing cloth were there, such as madder (red), weld (yellow), or woad (blue), and teasel flowers, used for combing the fibers or raising the nap. Plants rich in symbolic meaning, such as the rose, the lily, and the violet, were tenderly cared for. New insights were gained through

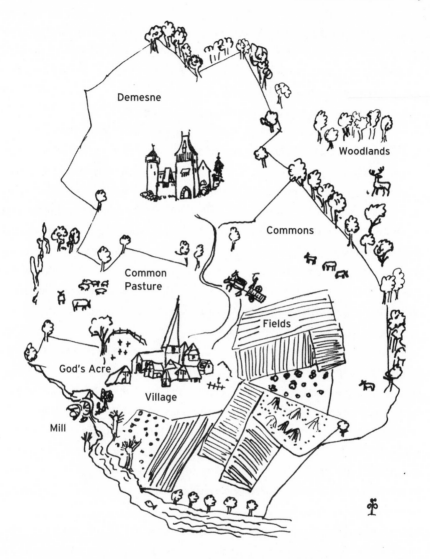

Figure 1.1. General outlay of the medieval system of land usage

meditation and observation, rather than by a method of controlled experiments. Old knowledge, the horticultural and agricultural writings of the old Greeks and Romans (Pliny the Elder, Cato, Theophrastus, Virgil) were kept by the monks and eventually filtered down to the illiterate country population in the form of oral folklore.[3]

The cosmology of the Middle Ages was suffused with the belief in numerous "supernatural" beings. Various elemental spirits were at work in nature: gnomes in rocks, nymphs in water, sylphs in the air, and fire spirits in fire and warmth. Each had certain tasks: the gnomes helped form the roots; the nymphs helped form the leaves; the sylphs wove the flowers; and the fire spirits helped the fruits ripen. There were other nature spirits, house spirits, and seasonal spirits that were taken account of by prayer, propitiation, or magic. Many of these, of pagan origin, had acquired a Christian veneer, reappearing as saints or angels. Each day of the year had a saint's name, rather than merely a number, and the nature of the day was associated with the nature of the saint. Thus, for example, it was noted that May 12, 13 and 14, bearing the respective names St. Pancras, St. Servatius, and St. Boniface, usually bring cold weather and the last frost. They were known as "The Ice Saints." Some saints had prophetic characteristics, such as St. Urbain (May 29): whatever the weather on St. Urbain, it would be the same later during the haying season.[4]

Certain saints' days were good for sowing this or planting that, harvesting this or reaping that. The saint himself was thought to be active in helping the plants sprout, grow, ripen, etc.— just as a person born on a certain day would have a special relation to the saint of that day and often would be named after the saint, as is still the custom in rural Latin America. The craft of gardening, especially vegetable gardening, was watched over by St. Fiacre (August 30), with an open book and a spade. The saints remind one of the functions of the revered powerful ancestors among the agricultural people of Africa and China.[5]

The old gods of the Romans and of the Slavic, Baltic, or Northern peoples did not disappear with the coming of Christianity—how could they, since they symbolized the forces that constitute the world? They continued to exist, metamorphosed into beings acceptable to Christian ideology (i.e., the thunder bearer Thor becomes identifiable as the archangel Michael; Mercury or Odin are metamorphosed into Gabriel, the messenger; the Celtic spring goddess Birgit becomes St. Bride; the ancient Mother Goddess reappears as Mary, etc.) or, in the later Middle Ages and Renaissance, the gods were associated with the spheres of the seven planets (Saturn,

Woodcut from 1511 by Albrecht Dürer: *Noli me tangere* from *Kleine Passion*

Figure 1.2. Christ appears as a gardener

Mars, Jupiter, the sun, Venus, Mercury, and the moon) as expressions of
the various heavenly spheres. These spheres did not just exist "out there"
but were active on earth as well, through mysterious *influences* (in-flowing)
and *correspondences*. The *signature* of the planets marked every creature, thing,
or state of being. For example, Jupiter's signature is found on earth in
the color yellow; in the liver and its functions; in the metal tin; in plants
such as dandelion, maple, liverwort, and others; and in the psychic characteristic of wisdom or the negative character trait of debauchery and
drunkenness. The signature of Mars, to give another example, is found in

the color red; the gall bladder; blood; iron; courage, fierceness, and anger; fiery steeds; and plants such as the solid oak, nettle, hops, plantain, etc.[6]

The fixed stars, which form the background against which the planets (Greek *planétés* = "wanderers") move and operate, were considered to belong to a higher realm, a more majestic sphere. This region, divided into twelve zones, constitutes the *zodiac*, twelve archetypal forces that influence the events here on Earth, modifying and influencing the planetary forces. Thus, a sun shining from Leo (in July) is a different sun than that shining from another background, such as from Pisces (in February). A full moon shining from Taurus, the cosmic bull, has very different qualities than a full moon, in Scorpio, for example. The sphere of the fixed stars, the zodiac, was experienced anthropomorphically as a giant man, a *Meganthropus*. Aries was considered to constitute the head of this macrocosmic man, Taurus, the neck, Gemini, the shoulders, and so on down to the feet, which were in Pisces. Each of these zodiacal signs was assigned to one of the four *elements* (earth, air, fire and water) and had great relevance as to when anything should or should not be done, when to plant, sow, till, cut nails, cut hair, cut timber, etc.[7]

Predictions and prescriptions based on saints' days, planetary and atmospheric conditions, and also on observations of animal behavior were stated as rules, often fitted into rhymes and couplets and passed on through the centuries by word of mouth. The rules are countless but we can give a few examples, such as the following weather oracles:

> St. Vincent's sunshine
> brings corn and wine.

This refers to the prediction that if the weather is clear on the twenty-second of January, St. Vincent's day, the harvest will be bountiful.

> When April blows his horn [thunders]
> it is good for hay and corn.
> All the months of the year
> curse a mildish Februeer.
> Green Christmas, White Easter,

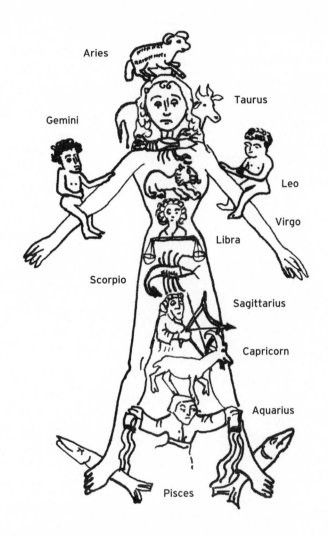

Figure 1.3. Meganthropus

That is to say, if Christmas is mild, it will surely snow around Easter.

> When clouds appear like rocks and towers,
> the earth's refreshed by frequent showers.
> In the waning of the moon
> a cloudy morn, a fair afternoon.

Other sayings concern the proper times to engage in this or that activity:

> Cut herbs just as the dew does dry
> Tie them loosely and hang them high
> If you plan to store away
> Stir the leaves a bit each day.
> Sow peas and beans in wane of the moon
> Who soweth sooner, he sows too soon,
> That they with the planet may rest and rise
> And flourish with bearing most plentiful and wise.
> The moon in September shortens the night
> The moon in October is the hunter's delight.
> Fruit gathered too timely will taste of wood
> will shrink and be bitter and seldom be good.
> At hallow tide [All Saint's Day, November 1] slaughter time
>   entereth in
> and then doeth the husbandman's feast begin.
> As January doeth lengthen
> winter cold doeth strengthen.
> The provident farmer on Candlemas Day [February 2]
> has half of his fires [wood] and half of his hay.
> When the likker's low
> or ceases to stew,
> The farmer doeth know
> the winter is through.
> Onion skin very thin
> mild winter coming.
> Onion skin thick and rough
> coming winter's cold and rough.

There are numerous sayings that regulate the right time to sow, plant, and reap and in which astrological sign to do so; and finally, there are some of definite humor, lest anyone become too serious, such as the following:

> A husbandman can surely know
> on the thirtieth of February there's never snow.

If rain falls on the rye,
the wheat and clover won't stay dry.
On Sylvester [December 31] snow, then clear
no more snow the rest of the year.

This, then, is what constituted the "science" of the old agriculturist. It was a science that was not yet divorced from religion, psychology, or everyday life; it was rather part of a holistic way of being. Their agriculture was a sacred way of life, as Jacob Burkhardt once remarked, not just a business to be carried on.

As the peasantry became more literate, these rules found their way into *Farmer's Almanacs*, or into publications such as Thomas Tusser's *Five Hundred Points of Good Husbandry* (1683), which was a standby for the New England pioneers.[8] It is surprising that despite education and scientific progress, the almanacs are still being used by a number of farmers and gardeners today; but the users are generally considered to be backward, quaint, and superstitious. These almanacs contain a calendar for the year with the daily corresponding astronomical data, a weather forecast, list of the holidays, tips on gardening, farming, fishing, horoscopes, recipes, weights and measures, and other items. Popular almanacs currently printed in the United States include *Old Moore's Almanac*, first published in 1697, *The Old Farmer's Almanac* (since 1792), *Grier's Almanac*, first published in 1807, and *Baer's Agricultural Almanac* of Lancaster, Pennsylvania since 1825.

The medieval way of life and cosmology did slowly come to an end due to a variety of demographic, socio-economic, and political factors, all of which are common history. By a series of enclosures, wealthier landowners saw to it that the common land disappeared from the manor. Country folk were forced off the land and absorbed as laborers in an industrial revolution that has not come to a halt since. Many peasants immigrated to the newly discovered continents and found themselves in new and unusual ecological and socio-economic situations. Other factors, also, helped destroy the old way, such as the calendric reforms of Pope Gregory XIII in the sixteenth century, whose replacement of the old Julian calendar brought about a shift of eleven days and fixed the beginning of the year in January—instead of March 25, as had been the case for centuries.[9] This very much confused such issues as the saints' days. Also, by this time, the gradual shifting of the relative positions of the planetary cycles to the zodiac (i.e., the spring equinox) had caused a discrepancy between the dates of the conventionally fixed signs and what could actually be observed in the nighttime sky. Finally, the new skepticism concerning old traditions and the empirical-logical scientism of the Enlightenment detracted greatly from the credibility of such folk rules. Many of the folk rules were applicable only in certain restricted ecological and geographical regions, and did not lend themselves to the formulation of general rules, as scientific standards demand.

Early settlers brought their rules and almanacs with them to America, but found them difficult to apply under such novel circumstances. Here and there they have managed to hold on to them, and even to found new local adaptions, as with the Amish of Pennsylvania and the mountaineers of Appalachia.

The Foxfire Book[10] lists a number of such beliefs among the Appalachians of Rabun-Gap Nacoochee in Georgia. Rules about Groundhog Day, on February 2 (if the groundhog sees his shadow, there will be six more weeks of winter) and about poison ivy (leaves of three, let them be) in the Midwest are of this nature.[11] In the Williams region, in southern Oregon, there is a rule about Grayback Mountain:

> Seven on Grayback, heavy with snow,
> all summer long, water will flow.[12]

This permits the farmer to plan management of his water resources for the coming summer since it refers to whether the springs will dry up or not. Though here and there these rules live on, a newer philosophy and commercial orientation have little use for such passed on traditions and homegrown observations that do not lend themselves readily to controlled experiments. And it is not to be denied that many such rules seem trite, redundant, or even nonsensical.

The Newer Agriculture

With the rise of the new experimental, scientific spirit, steady improvements in agriculture and horticulture can be registered.[13] Jethro Tull invented *drilling* grain instead of broadcasting it, which permitted "inter-drilling" or cultivating. At the same time in the 1730s, Lord Townshend of Norfolk developed a modern system of crop rotation: a four-year rotation of wheat, turnips, barley, and clover or beans with manure plowed in to boost production. New varieties of livestock and plants were bred. The yield per acre was significantly increased. In the 1810s, Albrecht Daniel Thaer discovered the significance of *humus*, and legumes were introduced as green manure.

The chemist Justus von Liebig inadvertently provided the impetus for chemical agriculture, which became the backbone of twentieth-century agribusiness. Von Liebig carried on convincing experiments in which he incinerated plants and analyzed the ashes for their content of elements and minerals. He reasoned that when a crop is harvested, a certain percentage of nitrogen, phosphorous, and potassium (NPK), as well as calcium, magnesium, and others are removed from the soil. In due time, the soil will deplete unless these elements are replaced in a chemical form or in an organic form (manures or composts) because nitrogen is nitrogen, phosphorus is phosphorus, and potash is potash, no matter in which form they are found. In 1842, a disciple of Liebig, J. B. Lawes, began to experiment with fertilizers on his estate of Rothamstead in Berkshire. He succeeded in producing and marketing superphosphates extracted by means of "vitriolization" from the bones from slaughterhouses and even old battlefields and from mineral calcium phosphate. In 1843, J. H. Gilbert, a chemist, joined him and helped wed chemistry to agriculture. Continuous experiments have been run in Rothamstead with basically three fields. One field has no fertilization, one is dressed with manure, and the other is given pure chemical fertilizer. The chemical fertilizer holds its own against the manure, while, of course, being a lot cheaper and easier to manufacture and handle. The experiments of Rothamstead seemed to show the way for a future of prosperity; the black horse of the apocalypse, famine, was forever banned; the old country folks' dream of the "land of cockaigne" ("Schlaraffenland," the land of milk and honey) seemed to come true. The flaws in the theory did not become evident until this century. For the time being, a completely materialistic worldview had it that the plant was considered a chemical factory needing a certain input of NPK, water, CO_2, and energy, which provide an output of sugars, starches, O_2, etc.

Phosphorus could be derived as a side product of the ever-expanding steel production—from the slag. Potassium was found in underground deposits, as those of Strassfurt, Germany. Nitrogen was derived from the sodium nitrate deposits of Chili, the famous Chile saltpeter, and from side products of coal-gas production. Farmers were, however, on the whole, slow to take the bait and before the 1890s, few actually used chemical fertilizers.

The First World War gave a big boost to chemical fertilizer usage. The Allied blockade had successfully cut the Central Powers off from imported food and from Chili saltpeter. Nitrogen is, of course, the basic ingredient of the ammunition that keeps the armies in the field. German scientists developed a method of fixing nitrogen from the air, which is composed of 79 percent N, as an inert gas. Thus, problem-solving in the arms industry and the fertilizer industry is a result of the war, with nitrogen salts becoming readily available and food production being subsumed under the war effort.

It is a similar story from the Second World War. Much research had been done in between the wars in chemical warfare materials, and poisons were stockpiled. When the second war broke out, both sides were afraid to use these stockpiles, so they became diverted toward the war against insects. DDT, used for the first time successfully by the Allies to save the liberated city of Naples from a lice and flea epidemic, was the first of a number of chlorinated hydrocarbons that would wage war against a healthy environment. The unfortunate and unforeseen effects are only now being realized.[14] The Vietnam War was not without its "spin-offs" for agriculture: complicated defoliants and herbicides were developed further and productive capacities expanded. Though that war is over, the stockpiled chemicals are marketed and passed off to the farmer and to county agencies that spray roadsides and irrigation canals, irrespective of the ecological damage incurred. It is not surprising; what other fruits can be borne out of war research, which is motivated by fear and hostility?

Chapter 2

Voices of Concern and Reform

When tillage begins, other arts follow. The farmers, therefore,
are the founders of human civilization.
—Daniel Webster, *Remarks on Agriculture*

Concern about the quality of the food and health of the people brought
about a number of reformers at the turn of the century, each with
some recommendations regarding special diets, baths, herbs, and nature
cures, among them names like Are Waerland; Father Sebastian Kneipp,
famous for his water cures and healing herbs; Sylvester Graham, known to
this day for his "Graham crackers"; and the Kellogg brothers, whose "corn
flakes" are still available.[1] Others were concerned with man's increasing
alienation from nature and the countryside, such as Dr. Daniel G. Schreber
of Leipzig, who instituted the practice of allotment gardens for city dwell-
ers so common now in Europe. The allotment guarantees every urbanite,
every working class family the right to a small piece of land on the edge
of the city, which can be gardened on weekends or in the evenings for
minimal rent.

There were other voices of concern that wanted to go back altogether to
a rustic life and turn their backs on the science and technology that seem
to have gotten mankind into such straits in the first place, while others,
representing the established interests, either held the opinion, "We never
had it so good," or "Sure there are problems, but more science and technology will eventually solve these problems." These issues remain the same
today, for the most part, though in an amplified form.

The organic gardening and farming movement, as pioneered independently by Dr. Rudolf Steiner and Sir Albert Howard, took a more moderate stand. Howard felt it was the misuse of science and a one-sided application of technology, in the interests of the profit-motive, which was at fault. Science should help man to live in a more harmonious way with nature, not alienate him from nature. For example, what could be more scientific than the construction of compost piles, knowing what goes on in each of the states of decomposition and humus formation, and understanding the action of the humus upon the soil? By contrast, applications of chemical fertilizers is not really scientific because it is harmful, in the long run, to soil fertility and detrimental to the health of mankind; it serves only the interests of a few to whom monetary profits are the major concern.

Rudolf Steiner also did not turn his back on science. He warned that an emotional, mystical reaction is as detrimental as a one-sided, coldly "objective" scientific approach. The scientific, rational, objective consciousness is a recent human achievement, whose development entailed increasing materialism and a dimming of the spiritual vision and soulful experience of the world that once was a part of man's heritage. In the times before the Enlightenment, people had visions, saw angels and elemental spirits, lived by a traditional wisdom rather than by the findings of empirical research, and peasants relied on their age-old experience and folk sayings rather than on the opinions of remote agricultural experts. These times have slowly faded, in the cities faster than in the country, in America faster than in the old world. Steiner sees this development as a positive necessity; only the time has now come, in the twentieth and twenty-first century, to pick up the older faculties, the soulful, intuitive, imaginative, and to recombine them with the currently one-sided rational, intellectualistic, scientific faculty to form a whole once again. It is not a matter of going backward and becoming serfs or savages again, but of picking up the baby that was thrown out with the bath water during the Enlightenment and the scientific development of the last two hundred years. Man is more than just an intellect, wisdom is more than what is garnered by reason; a feeling of sensitivity, creative imagination, and goodwill must be reintegrated into our way of dealing with our world, and with our farms and gardens.

Thus, going back to a Neolithic, medieval, a Native American, or an early American pioneer type of existence is not the point of the organic agriculture movement. Given the socio-economic and demographic situation of today, the attempt to do so would create unimaginable hardships, but even more so will the present course of big business, corporate and chemical agriculture, or the dehumanized, specialized collective farms as they existed in the former Soviet bloc. These are blind to the essence of nature and are just about to destroy the ecosphere itself. There is plenty of established scientific evidence and there are countless practical demonstrations in farms which show that organic gardening does work. The most striking example of this is, of course, East Asia, where, as F. H. King reports, farming and horticulture of the most intense sort has been carried on for over four thousand years without depletion of soil fertility. F. H. King, the founder of soil physics in the USA, spent nearly a year (1911) in rural China keenly observing agricultural practices.[2] In the early 1960s, Mao and the Chinese Communist Party ordered the "The Great Leap Forward" with emphasis on industrializing food production. This new policy was a disaster, leading to the starvation death of millions of people. A turnabout was made. In the 1990s "The Green Food Program" of sustainable, ecological organic agriculture was launched, making China to date the largest organic food producer in the world. Currently some food is imported, but for the most part this ecological agriculture is able to feed a population of over one billion people, nearly as many livestock, and nearly three times the number of hogs, on about the same amount of arable land as is available in the United States. Travelers to China report no starvation, poverty, or the like, and all of this not with huge doses of chemicals, insecticides and heavy petroleum-gobbling machines, but by careful composting of all organic stuff, time proven companion planting, rotation, and labor-intensive methods.[3]

Despite the claims of the U.S. Department of Agriculture that humanity would starve if we "went back" to organics, these facts do not indicate that organic agriculture is primitive. From my own experience, as explained in the introduction, the view cannot be shared that organic agriculture would lead to starvation; on the contrary, the more one works in harmony with nature, the better results one can expect. Organic agriculture is not a more primitive, but a more advanced form of agriculture based on a deeper and more thorough understanding of the ecological totality. The problems seem to be more those of social, political, and world-market economy factors. Organic agriculture is intensive and needs people to share the work; it lends itself better to the type of society that Thomas Jefferson envisioned, i.e., one of local independence, de-centralization, and self-sufficiency, and this is, of course, at variance with international corporative efforts, world markets, and centralized planning. Organic agriculture implies the shared work of several people, similar to the large family, the joint family of bygone days, or perhaps, in some newer social form such as the small community, or commune. Here the tasks can be meaningfully divided without the risk of alienating, one-sided specialization. Some people can care for the livestock, some can garden, some can bake bread or make cheese, etc. This kind of work sharing can lead to the satisfaction of social, psychological, and cultural needs much more effectively than the current truncated, isolated family. It is basically this social-political nature of organic agriculture that is threatening to the established interests, and not really the issue of whether it is scientifically sound or not.

History of the Modern Organic Movement

It was Rudolf Steiner who first formulated an organic approach to agriculture in the Western world. As stated before, there had been a series of health and nature movements in the latter half of the nineteenth century, but it was Steiner who saw the problems as related to each other: what one does to nature, to soil, one does essentially to other people and to oneself. An unhealthy agriculture and an unhealthy social and spiritual life have common roots, and his *anthroposophy*, intended to be a superlative of anthropology, tried to deal with all of these problems simultaneously. In 1924, the biodynamic movement of organic agriculture got underway and despite tension with Hitler's regime, suppression by the Communists, and the silent treatment by chemical agriculture, it has developed, over the years, into a strong movement. Its basic philosophy, as we shall see, is somewhat difficult, and an exclusive "in-group" attitude by some of the practitioners has made it, unfortunately, somewhat inaccessible to a lot of people.

Popular awareness about the deterioration of the environment and the possible link to mental and physical health did not reach a wider public until after the Depression and the Dust Bowl in North America. The concept of *conservation* and a number of important publications during this time indicate the concern.[4]

It was during this time that the work of Sir Albert Howard began to be known, and in 1940, his *Agricultural Testament* was published, followed by the important *Soil and Health* in 1947. It was at that time that the organic movement, as we know it today, was born. In America, J. I. Rodale picked up on Howard's work, entertaining contact with the biodynamic movement at the same time, and launched the movement in America with the *Organic Gardening and Farming magazine* and the book, *Pay Dirt* (1945). Rodale created an experimental farm at Emmaus, Pennsylvania, and was active in organizing garden clubs throughout the United States. Similar activity occurred in Britain and Continental Europe, albeit on a lesser scale.[5] It was at this time (1940) that the respected soil scientist William A. Albrecht, chairman of the Department of Soils at the University of Missouri, proclaimed: "NPK formulas (nitrogen, phosphorus, potassium), as legislated and enforced by State Departments of Agriculture, mean malnutrition, attack by insects, bacteria and fungi, weed takeover, crop loss in dry weather, and general loss of mental acuity in the population, leading to degenerative metabolic disease and early death."

After the activity in the 1940s and early 1950s, the organics movement slowed down, and its proponents were classed with the food faddists, the sunshine-and-health types, and all those other quacks and neurotics not to be taken seriously. Bumper crops and a booming unfolding of agribusiness had quieted the concern; it was hardly being noticed that traditional family farms were dying and that despite ever-heavier doses of insecticides, pests and diseases were on the increase, while major portions of friendly fauna, butterflies, birds, and wildlife were being depleted, some to the point of extinction.[6] In 1962, it was Rachel Carson's book *Silent Spring* that broke the spell and awakened people to the tragic and alarming state of affairs in agriculture.[7]

This was the start of the ecology movement, the beginning of the popular recognition of the interrelatedness of all life on this planet. It became increasingly difficult to scoff at the organic gardeners and farmers. Concern with organics included a wide spectrum of people at this point: from counter-culture rural hippies who dreamed of a loving relationship with Mother Earth and her children, to patriots who stressed independence, self-reliance, and survival; from leftist communards who included organic agriculture as a way of liberation from the "system," to practical, hard-headed realists and practical idealists such as those of the New Alchemy Institute or Alan Chadwick's gardeners at UC Santa Cruz, to those who would incorporate it in a new metaphysics, such as in Findhorn.

Chapter 3

The Pioneers of
Organic Agriculture

Nature, to be commanded, must be obeyed.
—Francis Bacon

Sir Albert Howard (1873–1948)

Sir Albert Howard, a British mycologist and agricultural lecturer, spent most of his life in tropical countries, mainly India. His astute empirical observations in agriculture led him ever further from the specialist, the "laboratory hermit," and into contact with the practicing peasant folk. He realized that an isolated laboratory, divorced from the multiple functional factors that make up the farm, would lead to erroneous conclusions. He formulated a holistic approach to farming and gardening, developed the successful *Indore compost-making process*, and stressed the need for taking account of and adapting to local situations rather than proceeding from laboratory generalizations.

As imperial botanist of the government of India (1905–1924), he proved in large scale practical farming that composting leads to soil health, and that a healthy soil provides for healthy plants that are wholesome and fit for human and animal consumption, and at the same time disease resistant. He drew attention to the importance of *mycorrhizae*, fungi found in good humus soils that enter into symbiosis with the rootlets of plants. These fungi coat the roots and grow into the root hairs themselves, supplying growth hormones and organically bound nutrients to the host plants while being provided carbohydrates in return. When the mycorrhizae die, the plant absorbs their protein bodies for further nutrition. These fungi, plentiful in humus soil and largely absent in chemically fertilized soil, are essential to disease resistance and quality in crops, according to Howard.

Figure 3.1. Mycorrhizae and root tubercles

He further proved that livestock fed on organically grown fodder was disease resistant, as were his oxen during an epidemic of hoof-and-mouth disease. In all cases he kept stressing the importance of healthy soil and the need to cycle organic products back into the soil in the "great wheel of nature." This, and not the constant breeding of new strains or the spraying of poisons, made for healthy plants, and, by extension, for healthy animals and healthy human beings. He drew attention to Darwin's last great contribution to knowledge, the work on the earthworm, that wonderful being that puts tremendous amounts of nutrients into the soil while working and aerating it at the same time.[1] He noted that the application of chemical fertilizer kills earthworms: the U.S. Department of Agriculture even recommends the use of ammonium sulfate for destroying earthworms on golf putting greens.[2]

Sir Albert Howard exposed the hundred-year-old experiments at Rothamstead comparing strips of land chemically fertilized with manured and unfertilized fields. As noted before, carefully kept statistics indicated that chemical fertilizer held its own against manure, while at the same time being cheaper and easier to handle and apply. Howard gave four reasons why these experiments were unsound.[3]

1. The experimental plots were too small and the conditions, that is, one hundred years of wheat, were too unnatural to be representative of anything in any farm or garden anywhere.

2. Nature was reacting to the continuous crop of wheat by plaguing the experiments with weeds. The weeds got worse and worse.

3. The plots were so narrow (and no steps were taken to isolate the plot from the surrounding land) that a lot of earthworms would migrate into the plot; though they were periodically destroyed by the application of chemical fertilizer, they themselves were a fertilizing agent.

4. The fourth point is perhaps the most important. New seeds, secured from outside sources, were used each time. Had the seeds from each preceding crop been used, the results would have been different. It would have shown, as other studies indicate, that the vigor, the germination ability, and the quality of the resultant plants would have decreased over a period of a few generations. The degeneration of seed stock is, after all, one of the major problems in agriculture today.

Sir Howard was fought by the specialists of the research station and by the fertilizer and chemical companies whose profits were at stake. Fortunately, his influence spread. In Britain, Lady Eve Balfour, sickly since childhood, found that her health improved and so did the health of her piglets after she had turned to the Indore method. Friend Sykes, a breeder of thoroughbred horses, found that organic fodder ensured easier foaling and sure winners. Together, they formed the influential Soil Association in Britain. In the United States, it was J. I. Rodale who understood what Sir Howard was saying:

> In the reading of *An Agricultural Testament* (Howard, 1940) I was affected so profoundly that I could not rest until I had purchased a farm in order to assure for ourselves a supply of food raised by the new method. The reading of this great book showed me how simple the practice of the organic method could be.[4]

The result was the popular monthly *Organic Gardening and Farming magazine* (1942), which reached a circulation of nearly a million copies per month in the 1970s and is still going strong, currently published as *Organic Gardening* with 275,000 subscribers (2010). Another result was the creation of organic gardening clubs all over the United States and Canada, as well as the circulation and publishing of information and the newest research results by the Rodale Press.

Rudolf Steiner (1860–1925)

Rudolf Steiner was an Austrian philosopher known for his contributions to child pedagogy (Waldorf Schools), curative education of the mentally disabled, contributions to medicine, and social science (the Three-fold Social Order).[5] In 1924, he was asked by farmers in Silesia to help provide insights into the problems that had begun to perplex their trade. The Silesian sugar beet growers were confronted with increasing crop disease and pests such as nematodes that were ruining their business. Other farmers had noticed a steady decline in plant vitality. For example, at one time, lucerne (alfalfa) could be grown up to thirty years on the same field while periodically cut for fodder, but it had turned into only nine years, then only seven years, and, at the time Dr. Steiner was confronted, only four to five years. Also, in former times, a farmer could use his rye, oats, wheat, and barley year after year for seed, but recently, it was only a few years before he was forced to buy a new variety. The seed quality just "degenerated." At the same time, animal health was getting problematic, with increased barrenness, difficult births, hoof-and-mouth disease, etc.[6] In June 1924, Dr. Steiner gave a course of eight lectures at Koberwitz, the country estate of Count von Keyserlingk. These lectures provided the basis for the *biodynamic movement* in agriculture.[7] Since the lectures a half a century ago, biodynamics has grown to a respectable form of organiculture. A number of scientists, as well as the farmers and gardeners who are directly involved in agriculture, have tested Steiner's indications empirically and have found them to be sound.

Steiner was trained in the natural science tradition, but in order to understand the thoughts that underlie biodynamics, one must realize that he also connects with the insights and terminology of the pre-Enlightenment scientific tradition in such a way that modern minds can follow and permeates them with intellectual clarity. In his work we feel that we suddenly have access again to ancient traditions, such as the Greek natural philosophers with their teaching of the four basic elements; with Aristotle's entelechy and *scala naturae*; and with the medieval cloister gardens and the alchemists with their concepts of transmutation of matter, correspondences of the microcosm and macrocosm, and planetary influences. He also delves into Christian mysticism, as represented by Jacob Boehme, whose world of nature was the cloak of divinity filled with spiritual forces; he discusses the natural science writings of the famous German poet Johann Wolfgang von Goethe, who believed in the primacy of the natural senses and refused to lose himself to abstract speculations and complicated instruments; and, finally, Steiner discusses the wisdom of folk traditions and of the obscure secretive lineage of European herbalists, such as the one he encountered as a student in the Vienna forest.[8]

Steiner felt it his mission to help recombine these ancient wisdoms and poetic insights with the findings of modern science, testing each for their soundness. Only such a holistic background can give the modern agriculturist the understanding he or she needs to deal with the complexity and depth of nature. This should be by no means a purely intellectual exercise; rather practical work is of major importance. We learn by doing and thinking; hand and heart are as important as the head. At agricultural conferences, at his headquarters in the Goetheanum in Dornach, Switzerland,

Steiner insisted that there should be as many practicing, down-to-earth farmers as scientists present.

Though one can practice biodynamics without specifically going into Steiner's philosophy, it will aid our purposes to list some of the concepts that make up the background of his agricultural lectures.

Biodynamic vs. Organic

Is there a difference between the biodynamic method and the organic method, or are they basically different names for the same thing? Although we have mentioned both concepts in the same breath so far, there are a number of differences:

The organic method is ecologically oriented. It tries to replace an overly complex, laboratory-oriented approach with a common sense approach, which the ordinary gardener and farmer can relate to. In many cases, the organic approach tries to understand how nature does things (for "nature knows best") and then tries to do gardening and farming in the most natural manner possible. Insects and diseases are combatted by the use of nature's own remedies (ladybugs, trichogramma wasps, lace wings, preying mantises, garlic and chili-pepper sprays, etc.). The aim is healthy soil for healthy plants for healthy human beings and animals.

Biodynamics is also ecologically oriented, but takes a much wider scope into account, including the sun, the moon, planets, and subterranean features, in its effort to understand the totality of all factors. The mental factor is also considered. Biodynamics, though not disparaging of common sense, is concerned essentially with consciousness-expansion in regard to plants, animals, and soil. The attempt is made to look into the deeper spirit of nature. Out of this deeper awareness, based on exquisite observation of nature, the approach calls for *not* necessarily letting things run their natural course, but for intensifying certain natural processes (creating optimal animal populations, making special compost preparations, planting selected companion plants in relation to certain cosmic constellations). The method concentrates on aiding nature where she is weak after so many centuries of abuse and shortcutting with destructive processes. The attempt is made to use human intelligence, kindness, and goodwill to foster positive developments (planting hedges for birds, planting bee pastures, creating ponds for amphibians, etc.).

Biodynamics is a human service to the earth and its creatures, not just a method for increasing production or for providing healthy food. The healthful and bountiful abundance is, so to speak, a natural result of the right view and treatment of nature. Healthy food is not enough to save humanity; the question is what are the energies provided by the good food going to be used for? Fighting bugs and disease prevention are not major concerns for biodynamics as they are for the chemical farming method, where tons of poisons are used to "solve" the problem, or for the organic method, where natural organic techniques are used for the war on bugs. Biodynamics can be summed up as putting one's energy into supporting the good instead of fighting the bad. Low productivity, insects, and disease are not the problem; they are the symptoms. Spraying bugs ground up in a blender, using trichogramma wasps, etc. is treating the symptom, whereas building the soil and one's relationship to the land is treating the problem.

Chapter 4

Basic Concepts

What is life? What is intelligence? What is force? These are the problems to the solution of which the ancients consecrated their temples of learning. Who shall say that they did not answer those questions? Who would recognize the answers if given? Is it possible that under the symbols of alchemy and astrology lies concealed a wisdom so abstruse that the mind of this race is not qualified to conceive its principles?
—Manly Palmer Hall

The Four Elements

The concept that everything in creation is composed of the elements, fire, air, water, and earth, is ancient indeed, forming a great part of pre-Socratic speculation about the nature of the universe, and continuing through our history until it was replaced by Mendeleev's periodic table of nearly one hundred elements. We feel that we have advanced a long way, and that the idea of four elements is rather simplistic. Yet, we should be cautious, for what the sages of old meant by an "element" is different from what we mean by an element of the periodic chart.

Aristotle, for example, sees primary matter as chaos that has only potential existence until it is impressed by the ordering formative forces derived from the cosmos. These forces have four manifestations in the four elements. Matter is made manifest to us in the continual interplay of fire, air, water, and earth.[1] In brief, Cornelius Agrippa of Nettesheim writes:

There are four elements and primordial basis of all formed things: they are Fire, Earth, Water and Air. All natural things of our world are formed of them not by mere aggregation, but by transformations and intimate combinations, which, when destroyed revert back to the original elements. None of the empirically sensible elements are in pure form, all are more or less mixed together . . . Plato is of the opinion that . . . the elements transmute into earth or into each other. Each element has two specific characteristics, one principle one and the other that serves as a connecting medium to the other elements. Whereas Fire is warm and dry, Earth is dry and cold, Water is cold and wet (moist) and Air is moist and warm. According to these characteristics, the elements form pairs of opposites, such as Fire and Water, Earth and Air. Other ways in which they form opposites are that Earth and Water are heavy while Air and Fire are light, for which reason the Stoics called the former passive and the latter active elements. Plato notes further distinctions, pointing out that Fire is sharp, rare and mobile, whereas Earth is dark, dense and at rest. In that Fire and Earth are opposites . . . etc.[2]

Figure 4.1. The four elements personified

Let us examine this a little more closely: Fire is the least dense element and, hence, the most spiritual. It has a purifying, transmuting character; it is anything hot, colorful, and quick, from a burning faggot to a choleric temper. Earth is most dense, and is manifested in anything in a solid, cold, and dark state, from a piece of lead to a solid thought. Water, flowing and sensitive, willing to assume all forms, is cold and dark, yet lets light travel through it.[3] Air is found in anything that is light, warm, and moving, be it the wind or in the soul.

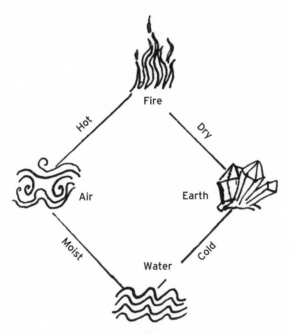

Figure 4.2. The four elements

In the manifest world, the elements are always mixed as, for example, in a wood fire: Fire is present in the heat and darting flame; Air in the light, smoke and fragrance of the burning logs; Water in the melting pitch; Earth in the ashes. Water, that is, our H_2O, can similarly be found in its earthy elemental state as solidly frozen ice, in its watery state as a liquid, in its airy state as vapor, and in its fiery state as a boiling substance.

The four elements are not just confined to the inorganic and mineral world, but bring into manifestation the other kingdoms of nature as well.

In the plant kingdom, the earth element predominates in the roots, the water element in the leaves and fluid system of the plant, the air in the lightness and fragrance of the flowers, and the fire in the ripening of fruit and seed. We can characterize some plants as having a special affinity to the heavy earth and water element, such as cabbages, potatoes, or beets, and others, such as cereal plants or aromatic herbs, as having affinity to the light and warmth element.

In the human and animal organisms, we can assign the earth element to bones and nerves, the water element to the lymph and fluid system, the air element to the respiratory system, and the fire element to the pulsating of the warm blood. Overall, one can imagine how the earth element predominates in the mineral kingdom, the water element in the plant kingdom, the mobile air element in the animal kingdom, and the fire element in the human kingdom.

Of what use is the concept of the four elements to us as farmers and gardeners? For one thing, the manifestations of the four elements are directly available to our senses, while the one hundred and some elements that the chemist talks about are not there for us to experience directly. Mendeleev's elements are available primarily to our intellect, but not to our senses. This is not to discount the careful work of diligent scientific specialists, rather it is to point out a way that the ordinary farmer and gardener can sharpen his or her own observation and trust his or her own judgment once again. In the four elements, we have a conceptual system that can be applied to everyday work with nature; it worked well in a time of direct unmediated experience and observation, not so much as a theory, but as an ideational description of what is already there. As we shall see later, it is a valuable way of describing and experiencing the seasons, the growing habits of plants, the quality of manure, the processes occurring in composts, etc. In farming, one can speak of cold, wet soil such as clay, which is too much earth, or of sandy soil, which is too light and heats up too quickly, as too much air and fire. Compost can be diagnosed as too watery, too earthy, too airy, and too hot; and how such compost will affect the vegetables can also be studied in these terms.

It is a good exercise to practice detecting the four elements and try to describe all observable phenomena in these terms. Many secrets of nature reveal themselves to the observer, and do so without the aid of complicated instruments (microscopes, spectroscopes, soil-test kits) or the technical literature that abounds with abstract jargon. If practiced correctly, one has at one's disposal a means of finding the keys to successful gardening without the aid of a distant specialist. This is one way of overcoming the alienation from immediate experience that ails so many modern people. I have seen traditional farmers look at the sky and know what the weather will be like in the next forty-eight to seventy-two hours on the basis of just such repeated observations, while the neighbor who had lost self-confidence in his or her own judgment and observation abilities will listen to the weather report on the radio to know whether or not to make hay. Since the weather patterns are much influenced by local idiosyncrasies, especially in the mountains, it is little wonder that the traditionalist's judgments were often more accurate than those who relied on experts who were far away in some city office where the predictions were made.[4]

Figure 4.3. After Barthelemy de Glanville's "Le Proprietarie des Choses," 1487

The four elements are not obvious and easy to discern at first, but a meditation on water will help, watching it change from ice to water, boil and evaporate, condense and freeze. Then compare dry ice to this. Where is the difference? Cooking, especially on a wood fire, if done correctly, is one of the finest contemplations of the transformations and interplay of the four elements (TV dinners do more than give an upset stomach; they also impoverish inner life by depriving one of the chance to experience these elemental transformations). It is in meditations like these that the alchemists experienced their work not only as externally changing, transmuting one substance into another (lead into gold, "muck" into humus), but of changing a base mentality into a heart of gold and a mind of crystal.

In the days of yore, the four elements found imaginative personifications as the workings of the gnomes and dwarves (Earth) who worked in crystal mines and on plant roots, nixes and undines (Water) found in all water interfaces, sylphs and fairies (Air), and fire spirits and salamanders (Fire). Nature can correctly and effectively be described in terms of the interaction of such elemental spirits.

When dealing with the four elements, biodynamic researchers tend to talk of formative forces, or *etheric formative forces:*

- the life, or earth, ether;
- the chemical, sound or water ether;
- the light ether,
- the warmth ether.

The ethers are the formative forces whose effects can be read in the forms and appearances in the physical world. In themselves, they are supersensory, or discernable to inner perception if this is trained. By looking carefully at the gesture a plant makes during its growth, one can read what forces were working on the plant to give it the shape and characteristics it has.

Etheric formative forces sculpt our visible world. As a cursory example, let us look at the physiognomy of leaves. Hemp leaves, for example, are formed by forces of light and warmth that gradually melt away the substance and leave only lacy, pointed lances as leaves that are filled with resin

Forces balanced | Inner forces stronger (earth-water/life-chemical) | Outer forces stronger (air-light)

Examples: oak, cabbage

Example: hemp

Figure 4.4. Etheric formative forces

and aroma. By contrast, the fleshy, succulent leaves of cabbage are predominated by the forces of water and earth that swell them with substance. The two plants are, by the way, good companion plants, complementing each other through positive allelopathy, such as to keep hungry insects at bay. In the stomach, too, heavy foods such as cabbage and potatoes are best complemented when seasoned with caraway seeds, for example, a plant that is formed by light and air ether.

The gardener can see to it that plants with an affinity for the earth and water ether (cool weather lovers) get the moister, cooler spots in the garden, for if the air and light ether become too strong, they will bolt. Those plants that have affinity to light and air ether should be aided to keep them from getting "stuck." In his *Agricultural Course*, Steiner gives hints on how to aid the flow of these etheric forces by the use of *silica* preparations which aid the light absorption capacity of plants; to strengthen the life and chemical (earth and water) etheric formative forces, he prescribes the use of calcium and cow manure preparations. These preparations will be discussed in the second part of the book.

A number of researchers have developed methods for making these etheric formative forces visible. The formation of floral and foliar ice crystal patterns on window panes in the winter, and the vibrations from musical instruments that can arrange fine dust on paper into various organic-looking, symmetric figures (Chladni's patterns) are examples of visible indications of these formative forces.[5]

The method of *capillary dynamolysis* developed by Lili Kolisko, using plant saps to be tested in a solution of silver nitrate, and then studying the characteristic patterns that are created by the capillary movement of this solution up a role of filter paper, provides picture images of the effect of these etheric forces that are working in substances.[6] Characteristic differences between biodynamically grown food and chemically grown food, between plants germinated during different lunar phases, can be shown by this capillary method.

Another method is the *sensitive crystallization* procedure developed by Ehrenfried Pfeiffer. Here, substances drawn from plant, animal, or human tissue are tested by crystallizing them in a solution of copper chloride. The patterns of crystal formation are characteristic. For example, roots will yield more compact crystals than flower extracts. The method is being used in anthroposophic medicine to diagnose various disorders by crystallizing blood,[7] as well as in biodynamic research to test the quality of wine.

Photographing the characteristic movements of water streams and drops through a viscous fluid, such as glycerin, is a method developed by Theodor Schwenk to make visible the formative forces of the water element.[8] Formative forces of sound, such as the spoken word and of musical instruments can be made visible by a sound-sensitive flame.[9]

In a discussion of the basic four elements, the fifth element, or *quinta essentia*, must be included. This fifth element can be interpreted as referring to the human element, human consciousness, as vital an essence as the others, but of a different nature. Thus for compost, for example, one must have enough solid matter, there must be enough moisture for the metabolism of the small organisms, there must be air spaces for gas exchange, and a heated metabolism must come about. But for all of this to happen properly, it takes the quintessence, the gardener, who arranges the compost heap. All four elements are present everywhere on any piece of ground, but by themselves, they do not form a garden: it takes the ordering principle, the quintessence, to arrange the four so that the garden can flourish in harmony. What the gardener is in a microcosmic sense, Christ as the master of the elements is in the larger sense, as shown in the previous illustration of Barthelemy de Glanville. Considerations like these might provide a key to humankind's place in nature.

Processes: Sal, Mercurius, Sulphur

Besides the four elements and their mutual interactions, the alchemists also talked about basic *processes*, which tie in with them. What goes on in the universe as movements, functions, and states of being can be under-stood as essentially three processes: that of *sal* (salt), referring to precipitation, crystallization; *sulfur* process, referring to dissipation, dissolution, going into sub-limation; *mercury* (quicksilver) process, which mediates the exchanges between the opposite poles, the contracting, cen-tripetal salt process, and the centrifugal sulfur process.

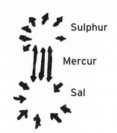

As an example, in the plant, the con-centrated nature of the root, drawing water and minerals, shows that the salt or *sal* process is stronger here than in other parts of the plant. The *mercury* pro-cess is evident in the breathing, assimilat-ing leaves and in the stems (xylem and phloem) with their transport functions; and the *sulfur* process is evident in the deli-cate flower and fruit, which dissipates itself in fragrance, pollen, and seed. This can be illustrated by an annual weed, noting the difference between the coarser lower leaves and the leaves as they move upward toward the flower; one can observe the leaves becoming lacy, more delicate and pointed, less substantial, as though the plant is dissipating itself.

In the annual seasons, we see these processes at work also: winter with its

Figure 4.5. Sulphur, mercur, and sal in a plant

freezing, crystallizing character, drawing all things tightly together, is a salt process; spring and early summer with winds, rains, and the rapid growth of vegetation indicate a mercury process; while late summer and fall with the heat and the dissolving of the lush vegetation into myriad color and fragrance show a sulfur process. This, in turn, gives way to a salt process in late fall when the birds gather into tight flocks to fly south and plants retreat into seed, into the roots and bark, or into the ground, hugging it tightly as a rosette formation.

In plants, animals, composts, and soils one can detect imbalances in the processes, or abnormal and one-sided expressions of the processes: as for example, fruits and vegetables that are too hard and woody, or stems that have hard knots on them, indicate an excessive *sal* process. On the other hand, the plant might rot, develop odors and mucus in the stem, leaf, or even root area: here we can say that the *sulfur* process is taking place too early, or is in the plant at the wrong place and at the wrong time. According to Paracelsus, *sal, mercur,* and *sulfur* have to be kept in balance by the *Archeus* (ether body). If this Archeus does not function, the process will split up and the organism will fall apart. Depending on where the imbalance lies, the organism will burn up, dry up, rot, or grow rank.

All of this can be carefully observed in nature. The observations can be diligently practiced at any time without the need for special equipment or instruments. One can see sulfur, mercury, and salt in a burning log: in the darting, dancing flames, the smell and odors of the smoke, and the remnant of the ashes. Just as with the four elements, we can meditate on this trinity in cooking, baking, pottery making and, of course, gardening. We can see plants such as the carrot, which bring sulfuric color and fragrance all the way down into the taproot. Pines bring the salt process all the way to their flowers (cones), which are dense and woody, while at the same time the sulfur penetrates leaf, stem, and root in the fragrant pitch. Composts in which the sulfur process is too strong dissipate their nutrients as foul-smelling methane or ammonia gases. Earthworms, by carrying decaying organic substance into the ground and mineral substance upward, carry on a mercurial function in the soil; initiating a sal process by applying ammonium sulfate will drive them off. The examples are endless.

The alchemists found these processes not just on the physical, material plane but as processes of the mind and spirit, as well. Here, *sal* is present as clear crystallizing thought; *mercur* as the ever-moving feeling and sensing; and *sulfur* as the will. A good gardener has to know these inner aspects of the processes, also, for they are to be found in he or she who is the quintessence of the garden. Proper thinking, feeling, and willing are as important ingredients to a garden as are water, fertilizer, and seeds. There is an *inner gardening* that accompanies the outer gardening; it is perhaps the key to the often talked about "green thumb," the "good vibes," that turn wastelands into gardens of Eden. They might account for the phenomenon of the so-called Backster effect (the fluctuating electric potential in plants in response to human presence, measurable by a galvanometer).

Microcosm-Macrocosm

Elements and processes work within the world of nature and the world of man. This takes us to another important universal concept found in ancient and primitive man alike, but difficult for the twentieth-century thinker: that of the macrocosm and microcosm. Man is a "little world" that contains all of the elements of the "greater world."[10] Both worlds contain an inner and an outer aspect. Man lives within the outer world of nature that reaches from the stars of the heavens to the sand grains of the seashore, and includes minerals, plants, and animals; through thoughts, feelings, instincts, through dreams, memories, imaginations, and intuitions he or she perceives the inner side of the macrocosm. Because the microcosm is of the same nature as the macrocosm, man can understand and has affinity with all that exists macrocosmically. As Goethe expresses it: "Thou art like the spirit thou doest comprehend." (Faust I)[11]

Certain Renaissance scholars, such as Giordano Bruno, Agrippa of Nettesheim, Marsilio Ficino, et al, drawing upon the hermetic-cabbalistic and Neo-Platonist traditions, postulated a spiritual origin of the universe, both macrocosm and microcosm, in which the creator, through his word, created the universe in a series of pulsations.[12] From the pure spirit emanated the world of soul (world soul), out of which the ocean of life forces (world ether) emanated, which then crystallized into the physical world. Other thinkers have the microcosm evolve out of the macrocosm, symbolized by an animal recreating itself by laying eggs (the Easter Bunny with his eggs might be a remnant of this lofty concept). The same forces that created the universe at large with its kingdoms of nature, created the human being with all of its faculties. Thus, there are *correspondences* and *sympathies* between the world of nature and the world of man all along the line. The one is the mirror image of the other: "As above, so below," proclaims the meditation formula of Hermes Trismegistos.

What is concentrated in man, the salt *(sal)* of the earth, is spread out in nature as millions of separate entities. What is laid out before him, as the animal kingdom in the macrocosm is found in man's soul as the many passions, desires, and feelings seated deep in his blood, respiration, and muscle tissues. What is called the plant kingdom in the macrocosm is the endlessly sprouting, growing, wilting, and decaying life of the imagination in human being with its base in the lymph and vegetative system. What is the solid mineral kingdom of the macrocosm, obeying rigid physical and chemical laws involving causality and exclusiveness, is in man the faculty for clear, logical thinking that has its physical locus in the bone and nerve tissue, which is most mineralized and least alive of the body tissues. This is one of the reasons why the logical, abstracting mind can deal so effectively with the physical, material world— because that world can be treated as a mechanism and its laws can be abstractly formulated. However, this faculty is not enough to understand the world of plants and animals, which engage the gardener, because these are more than mechanisms; they are living, etheric organisms, which can only be understood by making the proper imaginations (*imago* = picture) come to life in the mind.

Nature can be seen as man exteriorized, and man is nature internalized. Because everything found in external nature is found somewhere in man and everything found in man is found in some transformation in the realm of nature, the Renaissance Neo-Platonists postulated that in order to study the human being, one must study nature and in order to study nature one must study the human being.

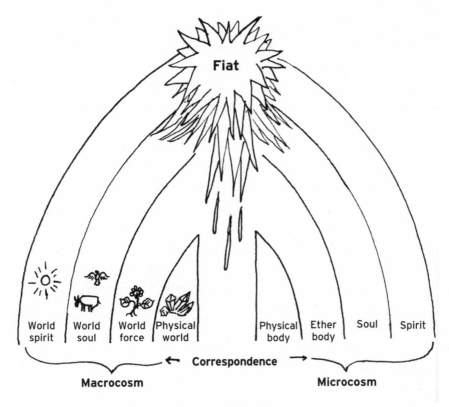

Figure 4.6. The fiat

The correspondences are found on all levels (physical, etheric, astral, spiritual), which we can only indicate within our context here. Again, it takes a lot of practice and imagination to get the feel of what is meant by them. Where, for instance, are the eagles and sparrows found in the microcosm? Are they not like high, soaring, lofty ideas or daily little fluttering thoughts? Where are snails or slugs to be found in man? Is it not in the tongue, for instance? Do snails not taste their way through the world and in a deeper sense are they not found in the character of slushy indulgence? And thunder and lightening . . . are they not like flashes of anger or flashes of insight whose manifestation—both externally and internally—was personified by the ancients as Thor, Jupiter, Perkunas, Indra, Thunderbird, or Michael?

Very archetypal imaginations of correspondences are those of the seven visible planets. Each planet has a *signature* working by means of etheric formative forces in order to manifest in nature and in man. Thus, Venus is not just a tiny speck of dead light in the starry sky, but has a macrocosmic signature in the color green, in the metal copper, in sexual attraction and reproduction, in plants such as mallows and birches, in animals such as cats and doves. And it is present in the microcosm as love, sensual or aesthetic, negatively in the livid green of jealousy, in the physical body as kidneys and their function. Jupiter's signature is in the color yellow and royal purple, the metal tin, in stately creatures such as stags and eagles, in chestnut trees and maples, in the microcosm in wisdom and the sense of justice, negatively in gluttony and drunkenness, in the body in the liver, etc. Mars is found in red, iron, nettles, and oaks, in the gall formation on oaks and in animals, in warlike fierceness and courage and, negatively, as cruelty. The sun's signature is found in gold, uprightness, and goodness, and has the heart as its organ. The moon has silver, growing and decaying, snails, worms, dogs, etc.; in the microcosm it shows its presence as dreaminess and "lunacy." Mercury has quicksilver, any movement, speed, message bearing, commerce, healing, vines and creepers, snakes, etc. among its signatures. Lead, dark colors, pines and beech forests, time, old age, etc. are among the signatures of Saturn. The list is endless because the world of phenomena is endless. Neither is it as simple as some astrologers have us believe, because the spheres of the planets interpenetrate each other and the influences are mixed so that seldom does the signature come out clear and unequivocal. Alchemists have always indicated that it is a difficult task to perceive these signatures and correspondences that exist in nature correctly; it takes keen external observation and perception of the senses matched the inner perception of the appropriate imagination.

Alchemists agreed that just as it takes clear senses to perceive the external world, so it takes a clear mind, not clouded by wishful thinking, lusts, and bad will, to perceive the supersensible qualities of the object under study. For, to the alchemists, the mind does not primarily think, but is a mirror that reflects what exists in the universe into the conscious part of the soul (that is why, for example, the brain was assigned to the lunar sphere which reflects the light of the sun). If the mirror is distorted by virtueless living, the images perceived will also be distorted.

The discussion of *imaginative perception* and of *goetheanistic* science will aid the methodology of our endeavor to understand these images.

Imaginative Perception

Just as there can be logical, clear thoughts that correctly apprehend the phenomena of the physical world, as opposed to illogical, obscure or erroneous thoughts, so there can be living imaginations that apprehend something of the life, soul, and spirit of the world. These imaginations must be distinguished from wild and idle fantasies that only confuse and do not explain or point out anything. Logical, discursive thought and imagination are not mutually exclusive; both account for different aspects of the same phenomena.

As an example: Walk through the orchard in late fall or early spring, just before sunrise. Delicate frost crystals growing on the bare, black branches sparkle in the light of pre-dawn. Quickly, the first beams ray over the hill and strike the branches. The crystals disappear at the touch of the sun-rays, filling the still grove with a rustling, sounding like footsteps or squirrels scurrying about as they fall onto the dry leave mulch. This lasts for a moment until the sun is up higher and then it is still again. The hoarfrost is gone.

This is a phenomenological vignette of what one might experience. Given the same phenomena, one can explain it in the fashion of logical, discursive thought that remains on a materialistic level, or one can explain it imaginatively. Both approaches are correct and one is not exclusive of the other.

A materialistic, mechanistic explanation would have the hoarfrost grow due to the special bonding nature of H_2O when the relative humidity has reached 100 percent (dew point) while the temperature is on or below zero degrees Celsius. As the position of the planet Earth shifts relative to the sun, the solar radiations warm, first of all, the black twigs (black absorbs the entire spectrum, converting the light into thermal units). As the branches heat above four degrees Celsius, the portion of the crystals attached to them liquefies, subjecting the remaining crystal structures to gravitational pull. The impact of the crystals on the mulch causes acoustically audible waves. In a matter of a few minutes, the air temperature, generally, has been warmed to such a degree that the fallen crystals liquefy, drip off the mulch, and are absorbed by the ground.

An imaginative explanation draws not so much from the abstractly formulated laws of physics and chemistry, but uses the metalanguage of age-old cultural tradition based on visions and images that have been passed on through the generations. The explanation of the phenomena might go like this: Helios, the sun king, is approaching; heralds in pink and tender blue vestments announce his approach. Gnomes and dwarves, who work with the crystallizing forces of nature, with ores and precious stones in the dark recesses of the universe, do not like to see the sun god directly. They prefer to hear about the sun through what the growing plant roots tell them during the summer. And they certainly are not on speaking terms with dumb sylphs who dance on sunbeams. So they scramble back into the earth, causing rustling sounds as they snatch up their precious crystals, losing most of them to the undines, the water spirits, who turn the crystals into liquid.

Sometimes, imaginative explanations serve the purpose of obtaining a holistic concept, a gestalt, of what is going on, better than a materialistic abstraction does.[13]

In gardening, we are dealing with such innumerable factors—the minerals, insects, birds, plants, weather, and cosmic influences—that often imaginative pictures comprehend the essence better than a materialistic, discursive form of thinking. Imaginations comprehend *gestalts*, that is, they grasp multifaceted totalities. They can deal with aspects that necessarily lie outside the parameters of our limited thinking. The gardener who thinks only materialistically is tempted to treat the soil, the plant, the animal like a machine or mechanism, which they are not; he or she is tempted to use abstract concepts of chemistry (NPK), fuel-energy input-output ratio models for the organisms, formulas, etc. in an analysis of a garden or farm organism. This is inevitably harmful, for it does not understand their true nature. Living processes must be understood by living thoughts. For bio-dynamic gardening, living picture imaginations are necessary, but they must be correct and fit the phenomena. They must give a clearer concept of reality.

Unfortunately, there is currently much occultist, one-sided, spiritual-istic nonsense written about gardening; fantastic accounts of talking with plants, drug-induced dreams of beings and forces that do not connect with the phenomena, but are idle, fluttering fantasies and illusions that will not help in a realistic way to create beautiful, productive gardens.

The Spheres, or Planes

To help us understand what plants, animals, man, and minerals are in relation to each other and to the universe, there lingers in the background of biodynamic epistemology the concept that the universe is arranged in a series of interacting, interpenetrating planes that are presided over or occupied by a hierarchy of beings, souls, essences, and spirits. Earliest cos-mologies, similar to those still maintained by shamanistic tribes of Siberia, illustrate it as a Cosmic Tree, at whose roots the primordial dragon dwells, where all beings live on some level along the branches, while eagles live at the top.[14] Such cosmologies are again imaginative expressions of content of inner and outer experience.

Starting with the empirical world, one can experience solid rock forma-tions always on the bottom, followed by a layer of water (lakes, seas), then a level of air (atmosphere) above which light and warmth (sun, moon) originate. This is how one experiences the physical world, not the other way around, though there are many intermediate realms and mixed states. This can be referred to as the *hierarchy of the elements*.

Some creatures are more at home in one element than in the other: worms and moles in the ground, fish in the water, fowl and butterflies in the air and light. Though these creatures live in the elements, they are different from them. As living creatures, they express the working of a life force, which can get a hold of and utilize the elements in its own con-struction. This life, or etheric, force creates a level of organization beyond

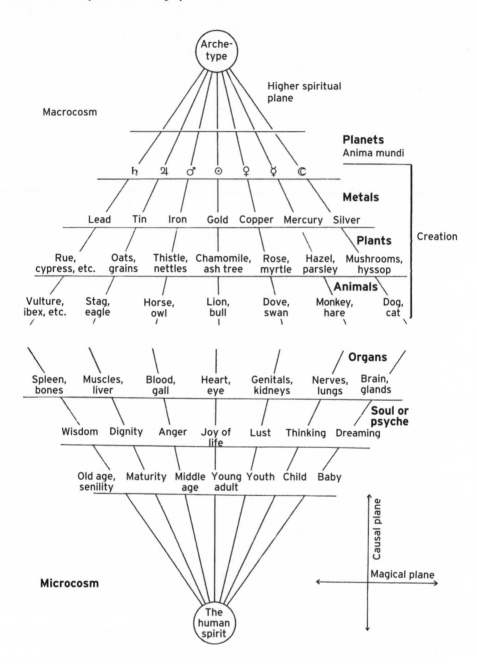

Figure 4.7. The seven planets with their signatures and correspondences

the elements, a level than can be called that of the *formative* or *etheric forces*. It is characterized by vitality, endless repetition of itself (i.e., plant growing from node to node, mitosis), symmetry and levity (as opposed to gravity). Phenomenologically, the living organisms referred to collectively as the vegetable kingdom can be explained in terms of elements (physical body) and life forces (ether body).

Other organisms have something in their makeup that goes beyond the purely etheric forces, something that turns ever growing life forces into another direction, that stops the endless replication of the formative forces and changes them into sensitivity, feeling, drives, and consciousness. These organisms are the animals, where the purely vegetative, unconscious growth has been turned into organs of sensing, nerves, and inner organs, which do not have the regenerative powers of purely vegetative cells. In that animals are sensing, feeling, and increasingly conscious beings, they represent a higher state of being, that of the incarnate *soul*; they are truly animated (L. *anima* = soul). Whereas plants incarnate physically and etherically, animals develop instincts, feeling and to an extent thinking, which helps them meet the exigencies of life. In other words, their soul or *astral body* incarnates into the physical world.

In the human being, however, a new level is reached, characterized by symbolic and abstract thinking, impulses of a moral nature and self-consciousness, which go beyond the sympathies and antipathies of the soul life.[15] We are here at the state of ego-hood or self-conscious *spirit*, where the question posed, "Who is it that is thinking, feeling and willing?" is answered by "I am!" Thus, man has a physical body, an ether body, a soul, and a spirit.

This, which has just been discussed, makes up the *natural world*, the place that in Germanic mythology was called *Midgard* (Middle Earth; the garden in the middle), which was regarded as the proper dwelling place of mankind.

Below the natural world are levels or spheres, which were in former times imaginatively called the abodes of demons and devils. These are the realms of sub-material forces that are no longer concrete matter, which the modern scientist perceives using powerful laboratory instruments and advanced mathematics. These forces—gravity, electricity, magnetism, and nuclear energy—might themselves be reflections of the formative forces, for they are known to have effects on vegetation (i.e., electro-culture).[16] These lower levels might be called the *sub-natural world*.

There is also a *supernatural world*. The wisest of humanity have never doubted the possibility that beings can exist in nonphysical manifestation. The possibility opens that elemental spirits, angels, and other non-incarnate beings who might have etheric bodies, astral bodies, or spirit bodies but not physical bodies, exist behind phenomena, and that with our materialistic thinking and physical perception we do not perceive them. (If we think we perceive them with our physical eyes, then we are probably hallucinating). Already through imaginative thinking one has images of beings that have their effects in the physical world, but are themselves not present in it as incarnate entities. How else does one explain the universality in human culture, attested to in ethnographic literature, of dragons, flying witches, dwarves, nature spirits, unicorns, etc.? Cultural traditions of myth, art, and poetry are clothing these nonmaterial beings (essences, forces) in forms that make sense to us. With developed inner vision, true imagination, one can perceive pictures on the *astral* or *elemental plane*. A higher faculty than the imaginative one is the *inspirational faculty* that perceives what lies beyond the picture images. Real inspiration is said to come from "heaven," a plane beyond the elemental and astral world, which is referred to as the *Harmony of the Spheres*, or the *lower spiritual plane*. Real inspiration is the rare experience of a few gifted people like Shakespeare, Dante, and Beethoven. An even higher level of perception than inspiration is that of *true intuition*, which realizes the archetypes by merging with the higher spiritual plane. Such intuitions, when available to an age through a great human being, are characterized as a great religious-sacred insight, bringing blessing and boons to mankind, such as the intuition of Zarathustra (or in Chinese culture, Emperor Shennong, the "divine farmer") who, according to legends, first taught humanity how to do agriculture.[17]

The various planes have been located imaginatively in external space, as well as in the inner space in the microcosm. Ancient philosophers have identified the various levels of the astral world existing in the macrocosm as the planetary spheres of Saturn, Jupiter, Mars, the sun, Venus, Mercury, and the moon. It is because of this association with the visible moving heavenly bodies that this realm is called the astral plane (Gk. *Aster* = star). In the microcosm the astral plane, and the true imaginations that derive therefrom, are associated with the corresponding seven main inner organs (spleen, liver, heart, etc).

The world of true inspiration has its locus in the fixed stars, the zodiac. The world of intuition is born in the realms beyond the fixed stars, in the so-called Crystal Heaven. In Christian mythology, as formulated by Dionysius the Areopagite, all these regions are populated by the angelic host, the three major choirs of angels. (See chart in figure 4.8.)

It is on the lower level of the super-sensible world, the astral plane, that the animals' guiding spirits or their *group egos* reside. From the realms stretching from Saturn to the moon, the spirit-beings that so wisely guide the animals are to be found. The migration of flocks, the building of nests, the running of salmon upstream, rutting seasons, the spinning of pupae, paper-making by the paper wasps, etc. are usually referred to as "instinct" or "innate behavior mechanisms" for lack of better understanding. When one looks only at the animal's nervous system and cerebral development, or their chromosomes, for that matter, one really cannot explain these complex behaviors. To do so is like looking at the hands of a clock, postulating an intrinsic reason for their movement without taking the background mechanism (the cogs and wheels) into account. In earlier times one tried to come to a closer understanding of the guiding forces of the animals by seeing their behavior in light of the rhythms of the sun, moon, and the other planets as they move against the background of the zodiacal constellations (Gk. *zoion* = animal; *kyklos* = circle; *Zoidiakos* = animal circle). Thus it was said that the I-Am, or the guiding spirits or egos of the animals, are not incarnated on the physical plane, as are the egos of individual human beings with their ego-bound self-consciousness. For animals, only the physical bodies, etheric bodies, and souls (*anima,* or astral bodies) are incarnated. One can say that there is an ego, or group-spirit, for each group or species of animal. This explains why in native tribes, almost without exception, medicine people or shamans claim in all seriousness to be conversing with animals that appear to them in (culturally modified) humanoid form.

	Spheres	Minerals	Plants	Animals	Man	Mode of perception	Hierarchies
Super-sensible world or super-natural world	Higher spirit plane	Ego or spirit of the mineral	Ego or spirit of plants			Intuition	Higher hierarchies, crystal heaven, logos
	Harmony of the spheres	Soul of the mineral	Soul of plant	Ego or group souls of animals		Inspiration	Twelve regions of the Zodiac, cherubim, seraphim
	Astral or elemental plane	Ether body of the mineral				Imagination	Thrones Kyriotetes Dynamis Exusai Archai Archangels Angels
		Gnomes	Undines	Sylphs	Fire spirits		
Sensible world (incarnate)	Earth plane (midgard)	Physical mineral (inorganic nature)	Physical and etheric bodies of plants	Physical and etheric bodies and souls of animals	Physical and etheric body, soul, and ego or spirit of humans (MICROCOSM)	Physical senses, reason	Earth
Sub-sensible or sub-natural world	Sub-terrestrial	Gravity	Electricity	Magnetism	Nuclear energy	Special instruments mathematics	Lower hierarchies

Figure 4.8. Correspondences in the super-sensible world and super-natural world

Native Americans, for example, would catapult themselves onto the imaginative plane of consciousness ("the world of the spirits") by ritually regulated fasting, isolation, monotonous drumming, dancing, or the use of psychotropic herbs. This allowed them to communicate with the "grandfather," "grandmother," or "boss" of the animals and ask for protection, guidance, or special favors, such as asking the grandfathers to release some of their children to be hunted and promising in return to respect certain taboos. Young Indians seeking guidance and a life's mission try to contact the animal spirits on the super-sensible plane. The mind that is incapable of imaginative consciousness considers this to be "superstition" and locates the causes of such behaviors in some intrinsic "socio-psychological behavior mechanism" or in the function of cerebral chemistry.

Whereas we have our ego-consciousness (or I-Am) on the physical plane and animals have it on the astral plane, the plants have their egos or group spirits on the plane of the Harmony of the Spheres. This plane is accessible to the form of consciousness referred to by Steiner and the early Rosicrucians as "inspiration" and was located by them in the realm of the fixed stars, which includes the twelve regions of the zodiac. It is from here that the plant-archetypes (sometimes called *Devas*) direct their children, who are their physical and etheric bodies on earth. This is expressed poetically and somewhat sentimentally in the case of violets:

> When God cuts holes in Heaven
> The holes the stars look through,
> He lets the little scraps fall down to earth—
> The little scraps are you.[18]

These heavens are filled with Pythagoras' "music of the spheres". This "music" gives the world its geometry and order and arranges with its euphonic, rhythmical influences everything from the dance of the atoms to the harmonious symmetries of flowers. It shows itself in the correlation of the numerical ratios between the movement of the heavenly bodies, music, and plant forms. Perhaps this gives a reason why, as a number of studies have shown, plants are influenced by the vibrations of music.[19] It is also interesting to note that this region is often seen as the "heaven" where the departed ancestral spirits dwell, who then work on plant growth, on vegetation on the earth below.[20]

The seven planets modify with their movement and vibrations the influences radiating steadily from the plant spirit archetypes in the fixed stars. The planets, especially the sun and the moon, are responsible for daily and seasonal rhythms of the vegetation. They are the movers; they constitute the "emotions" (Lat. *ex movere* = "to move out, excite") of the plant world. Thus, the ancient philosophers concluded, it is in the spheres of the seven planets that the *souls* of the plants reside. As Paracelsus states in his *De Caducis*:

> Where is the workman that cuts out the forms of the lilies and roses that grow in the fields? And where are his workshop and tools? The characters of lilies and roses exist in the astral (star) light, and in the workshop of Nature they are made into forms. A blooming flower cannot be made out of mud, nor a man out of material clay; and he who denies the formative power of the astral light, and believes that something can be taken out of a body in which it does not does not exist.[21]

The minerals have their physical bodies on earth, while their life force is found on the higher plane, where the animals have their egos and plants have their souls. The soul of the mineral is found in the fixed stars, while their archetypal spirits, or egos, are found in the highest heavens beyond the fixed stars. We can easily follow this in our thoughts, but to "realize" this we must have intuition, the so-called "stone of the wise." This is the sphere that the ancients referred to as the Crystal Heaven, and Australian aborigines express this when they claim that crystals found on earth must have broken off the seat of the highest god and fallen to earth, and that the greatest and wisest shaman carry such heavenly crystals in their bodies.[22]

Although this discussion of levels and spheres might seem complicated, it is nonetheless greatly simplified, for it involves complex cosmologies. We permitted ourselves to peek at these immense worlds because, as holistic gardeners, we do not want to limit our view of plants, bugs, and birds to a narrow and isolating fashion, but we want to explore their proper place in the universe in relation to each other and to human beings. The chart provided is a crudely simplified approximation to help interpret the interrelationships. The study of the works of Rudolf Steiner and careful investigation of alchemy, ethnographic records, and folklore can help to clear up our fogged vision. Steiner's works contain unusual and interesting philosophical perceptions, which he does not ask us to believe as pontifical pronouncements, but as working hypotheses to be tested against our practical work and logical thinking.[23]

If there is truth hidden in these cosmologies, could it be possible to really have contact with and "talk" with one's plants and animals? Could one tell the deer's "grandfather" to leave the garden alone, or tell the caterpillar's spirit to go easy on the cabbage, or invite the songbirds to live in the garden? There are gardeners who claim something to that effect. There seems to be an explanation in this for the unusual garden of Findhorn, where gardeners claim to have contacted friendly nature spirits and are "seeing" them and "talking" to them with the result of growing large, healthy vegetables in cold, inhospitable northern Scotland.[24] And perhaps the Amish are not just stubborn traditionalists when they link the powers of tractors and electricity with a demonic world; certainly the Amish have been able to maintain excellent farms without excessive destruction of the ecology.

In its more esoteric aspects, biodynamics works with considerations like these mentioned in this chapter, though a careful attempt is made not to take over unclear, atavistic, outmoded systems from the Middle Ages, Renaissance, or traditional native cultures, but to bring such ideas into accord with what is acceptable to modern rationality.

Chapter 5

Transmutation, Destruction, and Creation of Matter

In nature, there is less death and destruction than death and
transmutation.
—Edwin Way Teale, American naturalist

Alchemy, that ancient science clothed in obscure symbols and surrounded by strange allegories, was practiced in China, India, the
Mid-East, and medieval Europe. It concerned itself with the changing of
substance (in its visible, as well as its etheric and spiritual form) into other
substances, transmuting it into higher forms, composing and decomposing
(*solva et coagula*) it. The aim was to permeate matter with the form-giving
spirit, and to provide the spirit with substance. The alchemists studied
such natural processes as the metamorphosis of vegetation, the rotting of
composts, burning candles, and other instances where change of substance
could be observed. Chains of transformation were carefully studied, such
as when a candle is lit: the ponderable wax, cold, solid, becomes soft and
malleable, then it becomes liquid, mobile, creates a reflecting surface, and
then it vaporizes, becomes bright flame and, finally, dissipates itself into
warmth. In steeple bells, the heavier bells give off the lowest tones, the
lightest bells the highest tones. Countless observations like these led to
concepts concerning matter, rules such that there is a continuity in matter
ranging from ponderable, heavy, solid, earthy, crystallized substances to the
light, warm imponderables that link into the supersensible, that dissipate
themselves into cosmic regions. Candle wax and boiling water are examples

of such disappearing matter, whereas substances like milk, dew, or falling rain can be thought of as newly created matter, which, by a series of steps, can be crystallized into solid forms such as cheese and ice.

In its solid form, matter is dense and nonreceptive, subject only to the influences of the earth (i.e., gravity, magnetism). As a liquid, matter is receptive and reflective. It can receive influences issuing from the stars and planets, so that new impressions can be fixed into it.[1] In its imponderable, fiery and airy state, it is, given that the other factors are right, greatly transmutable. Thus, man and stars can work into and influence substances when they are liquid or volatile. Therefore, the alchemists, when carrying out their operations, studied the planets, their positions and aspects carefully. By understanding these processes, the alchemists hoped to aid nature to complete its foreordained development of matter uniting with the spirit in a "chemical wedding" that would lead to health, wholesomeness and perfection of creation.[2] The search was blessed by the finding of medicine *(arcanum)* and the ability to transmute what is base into what is noble, such as heavy, dark lead into gold, the sun in its mineral form. They were convinced they were pleasing mother nature by their efforts. *(Operis processio multum naturae placet).*

In this work the alchemists, having subjected themselves to various purifications (for according to their thinking, like affects like), proceeded to subject matter to all sorts of operations in order to induce transmutations. The operations included calcination, congelation, fixation, solution, digestion, distillation, sublimation, separation, creation, fermentation, multiplication, projection, blackening, vitriolizing (the bath in sulfuric acid), and so on. If gold has been transmuted, then with the right tincture, it could be multiplied. (Though there here are reputable testaments to the effect that this had actually been achieved, I have my doubts that it happened in the "real" material world. But who knows?)

This view of the nature of the material universe, especially the idea of the transmutation of elements, the concept of the four elements and the making of gold, was scathingly ridiculed by Robert Boyle (1627–1691); and with the newer, enlightened scientists a new concept of matter started making its appearance. The great chemist Antoine Laurent Lavoisier (1743–1794) formulated *the law of the conservation of matter*: "Nothing is created, nothing is destroyed, everything is transformed." By the nineteenth century, the concept of matter was well defined and posed little problem. Studied carefully by brilliant researchers operating with a modern, scientific methodology and charted into the periodic table by D. I. Mendeleev, matter is seen as composed of atoms which combine into molecules, has mass and weight, occupies space, and is subject to gravity, inertia, and the law of entropy (the second law of thermodynamics). After the original "big bang" (Kant-Laplace hypothesis), the law of entropy took over and now everything is seen as really in the process of winding down, like dust settling or a clock running down, until the energy is spent, the sun has burned out, and life is gone. Life and spirit are seen as "epiphenomena" of this inevitable process. In agriculture, this meant teaching the farmers that plant processes are chemical reactions, animals are really machines, and that Liebig's theories could deal with inevitable soil depletion.

At this time alchemy was interpreted as the crude, superstition-ridden beginnings of chemistry, or as the confidence operations of gold-hungry swindlers. On the other hand, scholars such as Franz Hartmann and C. G. Jung saw only symbolism in alchemy that was projected into the world and really referred to spiritual striving or psychological processes.

Ideas, like immortals, do not die but emerge transformed. Alchemical concepts were developed further despite rejection and ridicule on part of the new science. Samuel Hahnemann (1755–1843) founded homeopathic medicine, which makes use of a number of alchemical concepts. Utilizing the principle that like works on like *(similia similibus)*, Hahnemann took minute proportions of those substances, mainly plant derivatives, that when given in larger doses would produce certain symptoms of illness, and placed them in a liquid medium (water or alcohol) diluted 10:1, shaking them rhythmically for a long period of time. The solution, or tincture, would then be diluted again 10:1, again rhythmically shaken (D2), part of this would be diluted again 10:1 and shaken (D3) and so on until a very, very dilute potion would be achieved. By shaking the liquid it would be potentized or made receptive to the forces working in the substance. At a certain point of dilution, the original substance is not even molecularly present (using the Lodschmidt formula)—only the potentized water is left. This water contains the information of the substance, but not the substance itself. Hahnemann was scolded as a quack, but the proof was in the pudding: healing was achieved in many cases where official allopathic and chemopathic medicine did not help.

The nineteenth-century researcher Baron von Herzeele published the results of some 500 experiments between 1876 and 1883 that indicated the transmutation of elements within organic substances. He showed that the ash content of certain minerals increases within seeds sprouted in distilled water. He asserted that plant organisms could transmute CO_2 into Mg, Mg into Ca, Ca into P, P into S, and N into K. Herzeele comes to the conclusion that "it is not the soil that produces the plant, but the plant that produces the soil," and "wherever calcium or magnesium is found in the soil, a living organism must have preceded it."[3] These ideas run counter to everything that modern chemistry believes, such as the law of immutability of the elements, and, consequently, the publications were ignored until rediscovery by the mid-twentieth century.

When Rudolf Steiner was asked to hold his agricultural lectures in 1924 in response to the crisis in agriculture at the time, his recommendations and indications for preparations to aid the soil and compost smacked suspiciously of revitalized alchemy. He gave formulas for making preparations out of cow manure, quartz, and a number of herbs that were to be treated in various ways and then, greatly diluted, rhythmically stirred (potentized) to open them up to a number of instreaming forces from the cosmos. With this arcanum the vegetation was to be sprayed, the soil, composts, and manures treated. If homeopathic medicine works for the microcosm, then it should work in the macrocosm, to heal the ailing earth organism. Steiner treaded on thin ice when he proposed in the agricultural course that the distant planets work through the silica in the Earth to produce quality and form in plants, while the close planets (Venus, Mercury, the moon) create substance, mass, and quantity in plants and animals by working through the Earth's calcium. He speaks of transmutations that are occurring in the organic realm:

I know quite well, those who have studied academic agriculture from a modern point of view will say: "You have still not told us how to improve the nitrogen content of manure." On the contrary, I have been speaking of it all the time, namely in speaking of yarrow, chamomile, and stinging nettle. For there is a hidden alchemy in the organic process. This hidden alchemy really transmuted the potash, for example, into nitrogen, provided only that the potash is working properly in the organic process. Nay more, it even transforms into nitrogen the limestone, the chalky nature, if it is working rightly.[4]

He states that "silicon, too, is transmuted in the living organism— transmuted into a substance of great importance, which, however, is not yet included among the elements at all."[5] In another place he makes the statement that the human organism would, if within a closed room where the air consistency is somewhat low in nitrogen, create its own nitrogen.[6] In earlier lectures (Dornach 1923), he makes distinctions between earth substance that is being spiritualized and spiritual substance that is materializing.[7] The former are finely-wrought substances that have been thoroughly worked on by formative forces, such as the delicate plumage of birds, the dust on butterfly wings, the delicacy of flowers, and the physiognomy of a person who has spent his life in virtue and thought. The latter are new substances that are fresh in the earth-sphere, such as mother's milk, egg yolks, snow, and cow manure, which bring "spirit substance" to the earth. Elsewhere he talks of digestion as a process of the transformation of matter from the solid state by chewing it with the teeth to the liquid state in the stomach, to the gaseous state in the intestine, and the sublimation of matter and creation of warmth beyond the intestinal walls. The feces themselves are a waste product of this process, its ashes so to say. The process is analogous to what happens when the plant grows from the solid root or seed through the elemental phases and sublimates itself in flowering. On the other hand, the impressions of light and warmth that enter our senses condense in the body into form-building substance. Regarding the law of entropy, Steiner declares that it works in the purely mineral, physical world. But in the world of living matter, the opposite is true; forces streaming from the sun are constantly replenishing energy. We see that this philosopher is at home with concepts of the appearance and disappearance of substances, the transmutation of substances, the use of rhythm to create and dissolve forces in substances, the use of homeopathic entities, and other alchemical concepts.[8]

What are we to make of these concepts and of what value are they? A Jungian psychologist might say that they are psychic projections onto nature, and, as such, they have value for the farmer and gardener, for as he stirs and sprays his biodynamic preparations over the land, he connects his psyche with the realm of his activity, creating a personal relationship to the land. It is, nonetheless, merely a subjective phenomenon.

Or one might realize that this approach makes sense phenomenologically. Just as the geocentric model of the universe makes sense in explaining the immediate phenomena of observable astronomic data, though actually the heliocentric model is the "correct" one, one can say that Steiner's system of concepts makes sense on the phenomenological level in that it can adequately describe what one sees, such as the sprouting and blooming annual cycle of vegetation, the sudden appearance and disappearance of bugs, the production of milk and manure, the stages of composting, and so forth. But the question is: "Does it provide useful knowledge and does it make scientific sense?" The success of biodynamic farms speaks for itself, and the concepts involved even make a lot more sense now in the beginning of the twenty-first century than they did back in 1924.

The concept of transmutation of elements started coming back with the discovery of the unstable trans-uranic elements, which transmute into lead and other elements, while giving off rays and heat. The concept of the finality of solid matter has been shaken since Einstein's theorem $E = MC^2$ has been tested to show that matter can change into energy and vice versa. The discovery of trace elements, or micronutrients, in plant nutrition gives some credibility to the effectiveness of minute homeopathic dosages (i.e., molybdenum is needed at a rate of only 10 oz. per acre). The severe calcium loss experienced by astronauts in outer space raises questions about the appearance and disappearance of matter. For physics this is no longer a problem with the discovery of antimatter (positrons, anti-protons, anti-neutrons), black holes, and so forth. The collision of a positron and its counterpart, the electron, results in simultaneous disappearance, their masses reduced to zero. This annihilation of matter can be reversed in that gamma rays can turn into electrons and positrons. Fred Hoyle of Cambridge dispenses with the law of conservation of matter altogether, assuming that matter is being constantly created in space out of nothing "in response to the influence of other matter."[9] With the discovery of about two hundred subatomic particles, modern physicists can no longer say what matter is. It has been de-materialized; it almost looks like the Hindu's *maya*.

In a more immediate sense, Steiner's indications are finding confirmation by a number of researches conducted by scientists such as Rudolf Hauschka, Eugen and Lili Kolisko, Ehrenfried Pfeiffer, Louis Kervran, Henri Spindler, Pierre Baranger and others.

Kolisko and Kolisko carried out sixteen years of far-ranging research on the effect of the biodynamic preparations, on cosmic influences on plant growth, and on the effect of the use of homeopathic entities. The results verify Steiner's indications to a large extent.[10]

Rudolf Hauschka, longtime director of the research laboratory of the Clinical Therapeutic Institute in Arlesheim, Switzerland and director of the WALA pharmaceutical company, became know primarily for his book *The Nature of Substances*.[11] He took up some of Herzeele's findings, tested and verified them in the Arlesheim laboratory. Experimenting with cress seeds, he placed them in measured amounts of distilled water into hermetically sealed ampules. In weighing the ampules carefully three times a day, he found that the weight increased and decreased, fluctuating with the rhythm of lunar phases, with increases during the full moon and decreases during the new moon periods. The results were difficult for Hauschka to repeat. He found, however, that with organically grown seeds the results were somewhat more satisfactory. Perhaps the difficulty in repeating the experiment has to do with the nature of the subject under investigation, where often events occur together, but not causally (Law of Seriality described by Paul Kammerer)[12]; or, as Hauschka supposed, there are unknown factors involved.

The biologist Henri Spindler[13] discovered changes in the iodine level in the algae *Laminaria saccharina*. Within periods of twenty-four to forty-eight hours, he found that the iodine content varied up to 100 percent, even though the algae had been kept in hermitically sealed containers. He also noted an increase of up to 15 percent potassium content in the algae. He concluded that organic matter might *not* be derived from inorganic matter, rather that the mineral substances have been excreted from organic processes like the bark from a living tree. Spindler's research stimulated Professor Pierre Baranger of the organic chemistry laboratory of the *Ecole Polytechnique* of Paris to check out Herzeele's work with the aid of modern equipment and procedures. After thousands of carefully run tests, he reports that there is indisputable evidence that plants are capable of the transmutation of elements.[14] After ten years of research with legume seed, Baranger verified that during germination manganese had disappeared while an equal amount of iron had appeared.[15] He concludes that there must be unknown energies in living organisms that can carry out these transmutations.

Louis Kervran, in his book *Biological Transmutations*, notes the numerous discrepancies found in the chemistry of living organisms. He notes the countless instances where matter seems to be created anew or transmuted from another substance. For example, herbivorous animals whose nourishment contains small amounts of nitrogenous substances excrete more N that they take in; the opposite happens in carnivores. He notes the modification of the chemical composition of the soil due to earthworms; the increase in S, P, Mg, and Ca in dried fruit. His experiments show decrease in phosphorous in germinating lentils, increases in Ca in sprouting plants when calcium is lacking in the growing medium, and that hatched chicks have four times the calcium originally found in the egg. Hens kept on a calcium-free diet are capable of transmuting the potassium from mica flakes into the Ca needed for their shells. He notes that organic silica (as found in horsetail, for example) aids broken fingernails and helps mend broken bones by transmuting into calcium. He concludes that organic life cannot be explained in terms of inorganic chemistry; that the law of entropy does not work for living organisms; that experiments performed on dead tissue or in nonrepresentative, sterile laboratory situations are not conclusive for living substances; he cautions against generalizations: "the transmutations are operations requiring a specific production of enzymes and a medium allowing the physiological development of cells, or microorganisms. One kind of plant will thus make a transmutation that another cannot make."[16]

The findings of these scientists help us understand how, at the agricultural research station in Rothamstead, England, an experimental plot could be cropped for over one hundred years and still come up with a steady, although low, harvest of wheat without fertilizer. Rain and wind-blown nutriments could not cover the loss of elements incurred with each harvest. Also at Rothamstead, a clover field was cropped two to three times a year for seventeen years without fertilizer added:

> This piece of land gave cuttings so abundant that it was estimated that if one had to add what had been removed . . . (during the 17-year period) . . . it would not have been necessary to dump on the field over 5,700 pounds of lime, 2,700 pounds of magnesia, 4,700 pounds of potash, 2,700 pounds of phosphoric acid, and 5,600 pounds of nitrogen or more than ten tons of the products combined. Where had all of these minerals come from?[17]

This research also explains some of the phenomena observed by E. Pfeiffer,[18] who noted that there is accumulation of copper in some legumes and grasses although the soils are devoid of it; that tobacco is rich in potassium when it grows in soil poor in potassium and vice versa; that oaks rich in calcium (60 percent of the bark) grow in sandy, calcium-poor soil; that Spanish moss growing on wires accumulates numerous elements for its life functions, which would be difficult to get out of the air or rainwater. Pfeiffer assumes that plants have a remarkable ability to accumulate these elements and concentrate them. Another assumption one can make is that plants are capable of creating these elements.

Theodor Schwenk carried out a study of the dynamics of fluids, of the sensitivity of water. He shows convincingly that stirring and rhythmic shaking of water creates countless moving interfaces as the molecules move past each other at varying speeds. This "magnetizes" and sensitizes the water to substances dissolved in it and even to cosmic occurrences, such as eclipses and constellations.[19] His "drop method" of studying the characteristic forms of different kinds of water by letting it drop into glycerin indicates that the characteristic drops are affected by cosmic phenomena. Similar studies by Giorgio Piccardi, of the Institute of Physical Chemistry of Florence, confirm that water is affected by cosmic phenomena such as the outbreak of solar eruptions, and proposes that these influences working through the water continue to work in living organisms.[20]

In conclusion, we can see that Steiner's holistic concepts take on ever more credence. Gardening involves the incredibly complicated alchemy of life, involving not just plants and animals, but the entire cosmos and the microcosm. The agriculture of today is not capable of taking all of the facts into account, not even with the most sophisticated computer simulations. Modern agriculture should begin by reexamining its philosophical foundations.

Chapter 6

Goetheanistic Science

As for what I have done as a poet, I take no pride in whatever.
Excellent poets have lived at the same time with me, poets more
excellent lived before me, and others will come after me. But that
in my country I am the only person who knows the truth in the
difficult science of colors—of that, I say, I am not a little proud, and
here have a consciousness of superiority to many.

—Johann Wolfgang von Goethe, 1829, in a conversation
with Johann Peter Eckermann

It is a calamity that the use of experiment has severed nature from
man, so that he is content to understand nature merely through
what artificial instruments reveal and by so doing even restricts her
achievements . . . Microscopes and telescopes, in actual fact, confuse
man's innate clarity of mind.

—Johann Wolfgang von Goethe, *Sayings in Prose*

One of the first modern thinkers who combined the newer empirical science with the holistic viewpoint of the ancients was Johann
Wolfgang von Goethe, who is primarily known as the greatest German
poet and author of the epic *Faust*. Yet Goethe considered himself equally
a scientist and he actually added a number of discoveries to the annals
of science, such as the discovery of the human *os intermaxillare*, a theory
of color that differed from Newton's (which pleased artists more than
physicists), a concept of space, thoughts on the methodology of science

in general, and studies on the metamorphosis of plants and animals, geology and meteorology.[1] Rudolf Steiner became well acquainted with the scientific works of Goethe as an editor of the natural science writings of the scientist-poet and revived Goethe's basic methodology under the name of *goetheanistic science*.[2]

Goethean Methodology and Epistemology

Goethe's ways of approaching and looking at nature is an important consideration for us because many of the insights of biodynamics are based upon it. I came into contact with this approach when, as mentioned in the introduction, the beans were covered with aphids. Rather than rushing to spray with some organic insecticide, the head gardener beckoned patience as he squatted down by the beans scratching his head, rubbing his chin, and mumbling to himself. He explained to his puzzled apprentice that he was looking for the correct concepts, the proper mental image, for what was happening to the beans and, after a while, stated that he would not do anything, for within a week, the aphids would be gone by themselves. Later he explained that he had been trying to remember what previous crops had been there, what kind of fertilizer had been applied, what the weather patterns had been; in short, what conditions had existed earlier that could cause this infestation to come about.

The head gardener was solving the problem in a goetheanistic way. Goethean science relies on careful empirical observation and adds to it the concepts that fit the phenomena. Goethe rejects simplistic empiricism, which gives only an aggregate of isolated facts. He also rejects a facile rationalism that jumps to quick conclusions based on speculations and hypotheses. As he states *(Sayings in Prose)*: "It is a bad thing that many observers immediately follow an observation with a conclusion and consider both of equal value." Or, "Theories are usually the impetuousness of an impatient intellect, which would like to rid itself of the phenomena and replace them with images, concepts, or just words." He rejects a science that can only garner isolated entities and tries to connect them by a series of hypotheses, plausible explanations, or rationalizations. Instead, one must let the facts, the contents of the careful empirical observation, speak for themselves and let them draw out of the observer's mind the appropriate idea. For it happens to be that every empirical object is incomplete; it is only half there, and it must be completed by its other half, the *idea* proper to it. The scientist, thus, in observing, does not just observe an external world available to his senses, but must at the same time observe the internal world of ideas streaming into his mind in order to apprehend the totality of the phenomenon. Every empirical thing has its ideational aspect, which is perceived only by the human mind as the inner form of the phenomenon. Whereas external perception gives individual entities, the internal perception gives wider connections, underlying ideas and principles. Perception gives us individual dogs, the internal perception gives us the class, or species, or "dogness." This approach differs from our ordinary scientific approach, which tends to divide the world into the external world, which is considered real (objective), and the internal world of concepts, thoughts, and symbols, which is arbitrary (subjective). The Goethean scientist considers only quickly drawn hypotheses subjective and, indeed, of little value, and the proper idea *(imaginatio vera)* belonging to the phenomenon as objective, as is the phenomenon itself.

How does one arrive at the correct idea that belongs to the phenomenon? Not by hypothesizing or postulating something that does not exist (such as metaphysical explanations), but by staying with the phenomenon, seeing it in one light and then another, observing the coincidental aspects ("Erscheinungszusammenhänge," synchronicities) that make up the whole, the gestalt. Then the mind can make the proper connections without straying into the fantastic, speculative, and ungrounded, and concepts will arise that satisfy the mind's need for explanation.

In pursuing this holistic, phenomenological approach, the goetheanistic scientist tries not to distort the phenomena as they occur in nature by complex apparatuses and instruments, or by clever experimental methods that consider some factors "relevant" and others "irrelevant." All factors are relevant, and each manifestation is, on the phenomenal level, a unique one.[3]

Perhaps, as Goethe suggested, it takes a poet and an artist to understand this. The scientist needs an artistic, creative mind to understand the forms and creations of nature, to understand the ideas that properly belong to the phenomena. This by no means implies that an artistic science is less exact than experimental science.

For Goethe, nature is ordered and guided by divine reason[4] and man is to note the order, the basic ideas in nature, not project his theories and hypotheses into nature. This calls for a quiet, alert, meditative approach, rather than only an experimental approach that limits and tests segments of reality, but cannot fit the parts into an organic whole. Goethe expresses this in his *Faust I* (trans. Sir Theodore Martin):

> He that would study and portray
> a living creature thinks it fit
> to start with finding out the ways
> to drive the spirit out of it.
> This done, he holds within his hand
> the pieces to be named and stated
> But, ah! The spirit-tie that spann'd
> and knit them, has evaporated.

The "spirit-tie" is found not by dissecting the phenomenon, but by developing the appropriate ideas. Neither can instruments and devices replace the proper ideas:

> Ye instruments, at me ye surely mock
> with cog and wheel and coil and cylinder!
> I at the door of knowledge stood, ye were
> the key which should that door for me unlock.
> Your wards, I ween, have many a cunning maze
> but yet the bolts ye cannot, cannot raise.
> Inscrutable in noon-day's blaze,
> Nature lets no one tear the veil away
> and what herself she does not choose
> unask'd before your soul to lay,
> you shall not wrest from her by levers or by screws.

A training seminar in the goetheanistic method is held in Dornach,

Switzerland for young farmers and gardeners each year. It tries, among other things, to help the students to develop a sense of how nature forces artfully create their forms. This is done by painting natural forms, following them out with eurythmic body movements, and by continuous study of natural objects in their context. A very important part of the seminar is to experience the changing flow of natural phenomena by taking daily walks along the same path. The participants are not asked to identify or name anything, but to primarily observe the "same" natural phenomena under the different circumstances of a rainy or a clear day, in the light of dawn, at noon, at dusk.

A project assigned during one session was a tall oak tree whose three main trunks, which were covered by numerous sucker branches, tilted noticeably toward the north. South of the oak young spruces grew to the height of a man. The question posed was: Why had the trees grown in such a peculiar shape? Rather than come up quickly with a hypothesis to be tested, the students were asked first of all to observe carefully and let one phenomenon lead to the next until the answer became clear. All the contexts were carefully noted. The soil was decomposed limestone, conducive to beech/oak climax vegetation. Noting the direction of sunlight influx, it was an enigma why the top of the trunks grew slanted toward the north. The numerous suckers in the trunks were counted to have about ten yearly growth segments. A count of their internodes showed that the spruce trees were about twelve years old. Soon the idea dawned that the forest had been felled ten years ago, and only this oak by the path was left standing. Pines, not native to the area, had been planted in the clear-cut. The oak had been shaded on its south side before the forest was cut, and thus had grown northwards. Sunlight had drawn the suckers out of the trunk now that the other hardwoods no longer shaded it. Similar deductions showed that the oak itself had been felled much earlier, causing three axial branches to make up its trunks. In this way, a mental image was created of how the peculiar shape of the oak had come about and how the landscape had looked a decade ago. A true idea had arisen by letting the phenomena speak, an idea that is true and, at the same time, goes beyond the immediate phenomena.

Figure 6.1. Bent oak and pines

The faculty for this kind of thinking can be exercised and developed by anyone. One can, for example, look at a sunflower seed and let it grow in the mind's eye and then take it back to the seed again, going carefully step by step. One can trace in the mind's eye the path that the food on one's plate took to get where it is. Meditational exercises such as these help us develop an inner perception of the phenomena without letting the mind drift into fantasies or abstractions. The gardener does this anyway each time he puts in a garden and sees it grow before his mind's eye, foreseeing how it will look in midsummer, or in the fall. She does this when she sows the tiny seeds far enough apart because she can imagine how much room the plants need. (Beginners always sow and plant everything much too close together.)

The Primal Plant, or Ur-Plant

On a journey through the Swiss Alps and into Italy, Goethe noticed that plants of the same species, which grew in his home country, looked so different that one could be deceived into thinking one had a different species before one's eyes. (We can follow up the same observation if we take a plant such as plantain or dandelion, observe it growing with thin, pointed leaves on the dry hillsides, and compare it to when it grows succulently and fleshy in the moist lowlands.) These observations led Goethe to develop the concept of a primal plant, or *Ur-plant,* as a basic theme that is played in a number of variations according to the circumstances. These circumstances, the various formative forces in nature, radically modify the plant's expression. This Ur-plant is not a phylogenetic or prehistoric prototype but is present in all living plants. It is the appropriate idea that

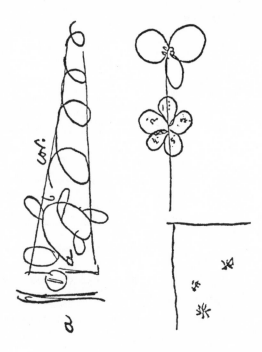

Figure 6.2. Goethe's Ur-plant (after original drawing by Goethe)

underlies the phenomena of all plants in their ever-changing variation. Whereas the various manifestations are apprehended by the external senses, the Ur-plant is perceived by the mind. Both the empirical plant and the Ur-plant belong together to give us the whole plant.

Various elemental forces modify the manifestation of the Ur-plant. The physiognomy of the empirical plant as it grows shows us what elemental and formative forces are at work, on one hand, but shows us the idea of the plant ever-anew on the other hand. As the plant moves from seed to leaf to flower and fruit and back to seed, it is always changing, always in the process of "becoming," of expressing its being, which is only comprehended by the inner senses. In characterizing the Ur-plant, Goethe sees the *leaf* as its basic organ, which goes through its various stages of metamorphosis from contraction to expansion, ever-changing and ever the same.

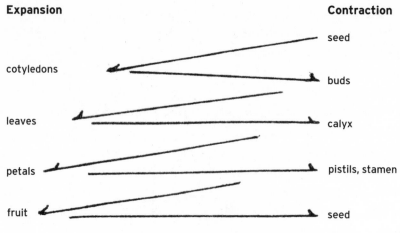

Figure 6.3. Expansion and contraction

Thoughts like these lead the biodynamic gardener to the conclusion that if crops are not doing well, growing stunted and subject to disease, the fault lies not so much within the plants themselves. It is the effect of various forces that work upon the plant, the combination of formative forces and vectors such as the mineral substratum, water, light, and warmth that give the idea of the plant its concrete manifestation.

It is through understanding the idea of the archetypal plant, the Ur-plant, which unfolds into various manifestations, that Goethe could assert that the laws of mechanics are all right for the inorganic world, but for the world of living organisms, other laws are at work. He delineated three laws that characterize living organisms, plants in particular. They are the laws of *dynamic polarity*, *metamorphosis*, and *intensification*.

1. *The law of polarity* shows that one of the major characteristics of plants is their dualistic nature. From the seed the plant grows geocentrically into the soil and heliocentrically into the air. Nowhere is something similar to be found in inorganic nature. The plant responds to the polarities of the day and night, winter and summer, waxing and waning moon. Polarity is found in the "male" and "female" flowers, in the round, "cosmic" bud and the extended "terrestrial" leaf. Wherever one looks into the realm of organic nature, the archetypal polarities manifest themselves, such as in the green chlorophyll molecules and the red hemoglobin molecules,

which are perfect mirror images of each other except that the hemoglobin has an iron radical where the chlorophyll has a magnesium radical attached. A fascinating polarity exists between the plant and the butterfly. Do the eggs not correspond to the seeds; the quick growing, segmented caterpillar to the quick-growing shoot that is segmented from node to node; then just as the plant folds itself into a flower bud, so does the caterpillar spin itself into a pupa to emerge in radiant color as a butterfly as the flower bud blooms into a flower. The butterfly's proboscis fits perfectly the flower chalice; and just as the one dies to lay eggs, the other fades to make seeds. Each step is thus exquisitely matched, as though one were watching a beautiful dance.[5]

In a meditative approach to gardening, the biodynamic gardener will look for such harmonies and symmetries, think of the roots when looking at leaf and flower, think of the opposites that make up the complete picture.

2. *The law of metamorphosis:* Living organisms do not grow by processes of mechanical addition or construction like erector sets. They grow in pulsating rhythms, at certain points reaching a crescendo and continuing at a qualitatively different pace. Consider an ordinary weed. Who can predict, upon seeing the mere little seed, what kind of plant it will become? The seed does not just turn into a bigger and bigger seed, but it radically changes, metamorphoses; it breaks open, sends out a rootlet and two cotyledons. Again, the appearance of regular leaves could not have been predicted from studying the cotyledons. As new leaves form at the internodes, they remain pretty much similar, only being broader and rounder at the base and finer, more laced and pointed the higher the plant grows. Then, suddenly, another unpredictable change occurs: the leaves totally metamorphose, turning into a corona of petals and sepals. Finally, yet another metamorphosis occurs in the fruiting and the creation of a new set of seeds. These metamorphoses occur rhythmically and in relation to terrestrial and cosmic factors. None of the states are deductible from the previous level of organization. Each time a completely new set of phenomena appears, yet they are all part of the same plant organism passing into ever new manifestation.

The biodynamic gardener can watch if the metamorphoses are occurring in a normal fashion in his or her plants, or whether these processes occur too fast as in the shooting into seed of some plants, or too slowly as in delayed ripening. It becomes a heuristic exercise to study different plants in their characteristic development. Comparing the different *brassica*-varieties, we see that kohlrabi is really an exaggerated stem, broccoli and cauliflower are in the floral stage, and collards and kales are fixated in the leaf stage, head cabbages are really overgrown terminal buds, etc. Each manifests a stage within the whole metamorphic range of the *Brassica oleraceae*. Onions like to hover in the bud stage. Oak galls are a "fruit" induced by the sting of a wasp. The examples can go on forever.

3. *The law of increment or of enhancing intensification* is another characteristic of organic life discussed by Goethe. In the mechanical, inorganic world systems wear down. The more energy is taken out, the less there is; parts wear out and depletion results. In the inorganic, physical world the second law of thermodynamics holds true. This is at the base of so much thinking in agriculture today: regarding weeds as competitors with the crops, insects as leaks in the energy system, fearing that the NPK continuously depletes and must be replaced as one would do with a mechanism. Goethe saw nature in a different light. Life is not just wearing down and depleting, but it is building itself up and creating energy at the same time. The more life there is, the more life it can support. On a farm, for example, the more varied the number and kind of organisms are, the better the ecosystem will sustain itself. Maintaining a complex ecosystem is part of the reason for companion planting, for controlled use of weeds, for not getting hysterical about a few bugs, and for circulating animal manures within the system. There is a mazeway of subtle interaction and mutual support among all the organisms in such a farm, such that insets and weeds will not be a problem and overall vitality and quality will be enhanced.[6] Contrary to the thought of some radical vegetarians, livestock, in the right number, are not competitors with man for a limited amount of vegetation; instead they are valuable symbionts enhancing growth and health of the vegetation. By comparison, farms and gardens that practice monoculture create imbalances that will deplete the regenerative and enhancing potentials,

will wear out the soil, and will experience weeds and bugs as competitors and incur heavy damage from them. We see here the mechanistic attitude turn into a self-fulfilling prophecy.

Chapter 7

Evolution

"I think Darwinism is too big to be confined to the narrow
context of the gene."
—Richard Dawkins in *The Selfish Gene*

In order to get a better idea of the plant and animal organisms in relation
to man and the cosmos, we will presently turn our attention to the idea
of evolution. Striving for a more complete picture, we will consider not
only the scientific inquiry of paleontologists, paleogeologists, embryolo-
gists, and pre-historians but we will also look at the ancient documents of
the wisdom and insights of philosophy. The scientist sees an evolution of
matter; the Bible talks of a creation by the Divine Spirit; alchemical philosophers see both: matter is formed and worked on by the spirit to create
a succession of forms, first in the macrocosm and then in the microcosm.[1]

We will examine this in detail by first looking at the animal world, comparing it to the plant world, and then relating it to the human being. Using
a goetheanistic approach, we will try to let the data speak for itself, rather
than merely imposing an abstract scheme upon the data. Though nature
does not "think" per se, it is ordered so that our thought can make sense of
it. As we examine the data, we find that it suggests a guided development,
which we might call the evolution of the human microcosm out of the
mineral, plant, and animal macrocosm. It is the flow of evolution itself that
suggests the possibility of entelechy or, perhaps, teleology.

Older cosmologies operated with rigid, static hierarchies. The idea of
progressive evolution is the great discovery of the nineteenth century,

the century of Lamarck and Darwin, which was a materialistic and biologistic age. Matter was considered primary; out of its molecular complexity life had evolved as an epiphenomenon, and consciousness was a tertiary product of matter, like so much froth upon a wave: "The brain secretes thoughts like the kidneys urine" (a *bon mot* from Ludwig Büchner, proponent of nineteenth-century scientific materialism).[2] Shadows of these sentiments are cast into the twentieth century as one can easily surmise when one opens up a botany text or a book on horticulture or agriculture. In this chapter we will examine the materialistic bias and try to show how the same phenomena can be explained satisfactorily in another manner.

The so-called occult evolutionists, such as Steiner and H. P. Blavatsky,[3] did not agree with the *a priori* assumption of the evolution of life and consciousness from dead matter. They turned evolutionary thinking around and saw matter as an end product of life, which itself was a creation of the Spirit. They envisioned an evolution from the highest hierarchies in a series of steps, of which only the last one, our present earth stage, consists of a material phase. The evolution passes from the spirit archetype, to the soul world, to life, which finally crystallizes into matter. Most of Steiner's elaborate work concerns itself with such an evolutionary process involving plants, animals, and man in relation to the cosmos.[4]

Steiner is less concerned with the picture of evolution presented by fossilized bone fragments and teeth, as with the evolution of states of consciousness. As four main stages of universal world development, he identifies the "Old Saturn" state where consciousness can be likened to the cataleptic deep sleep as is found in the mineral world today; followed after immense spans of time by the "Old Sun" state with a consciousness equivalent to deep sleep like that of our plants; this was followed in the immensity of cosmic time by the "Old Moon" state with a consciousness like that possessed by animals today; and, finally, in the "Earth" state of evolution wakefulness, the ability to think things and rational self-awareness[5]—after much preparation—came about. This evolution is not at an end, and higher states of consciousness are going to be achieved in further development. One can say that, in a sense, the minerals still live in the "Old Saturn," the plants are still on the "Old Sun," the animals are still on the "Old Moon," and man-kind has evolved "Earth" consciousness. The first three states of evolution occurred in the super-sensible realm, accessible only to the inspired seer, or to "spiritual science," which we have no way of counting or discounting. It is only the "Earth" period in its later phases that brings about physical manifestation, and is thus capable of being studied by the scientific method using the five senses and logic. Our paleontologists and geologists can only study this fourth state; only the latter part is visible in the fossil record. What happened before that time is in the realm of cosmology, spiritual science, and the origin-myths of all the tribes and nations. It would take us too far afield to pursue these interesting topics, so we will proceed from where the fossil record begins.

Prior to the Cambrian, the fossil record becomes sketchy and science becomes highly speculative. There are, however, pre-Cambrian indications of primitive "plant-animal" organisms found in the "stromatolites" near the Great Slave Lake, Canada, and in the Gunflint Cherts of Minnesota and Ontario. Symmetrical, harmonious forms of organisms are also found in the late pre-Cambrian Ediacara formations of Australia. Scientists in the 1920–30s (J. B. S. Haldane and A. I. Oparin) hypothesize a "dilute organic soup" composed of macromolecules of amino acids that were created when energy in the form of cosmic rays or lightning flashed through an early atmosphere of hydrogen, helium, methane, and ammonia and penetrated the water of the primordial sea. The now classic experiment by Stanley L. Miller (1953) of synthesizing amino acids by reconstructing in minia-ture such an atmosphere, water, and energy charges, lends support to the "dilute organic soup" concept. Today, scientists have modified the "organic soup" concept. It seems that with the constant influx of photons from the sun, carbon dioxide molecules fused readily with water molecules to cre-ate glucose packets, and release oxygen as a "waste product." This would constitute the beginning of the assimilation process basic to life. Whatever the case, from our perspective, we can say that we see here the *beginning of etheric forces taking hold of primal matter*: entelechy starts working as an inner formative principle upon physical substance, which by itself is subject to deterministic causality.[6]

The pre-Cambrian with its soft-bodied filter sediment and deposit feeding organisms, which are like bits of intestine floating or sliding around through a nutrient medium, gives way to the Cambrian, during which all but one phylum of invertebrate animals with preservable hard parts first appears. Animals and plants (algae) are now becoming clearly separated. Astrality begins to manifest itself slowly and cautiously as the phyla start developing hollow inner spaces, as they evolve not just tissue that is turned outward toward the macrocosm but inner tissues, endoderms, and mesoderms, which are separated from the immediate exposure to outside macrocosmic influences. In embryology this stage is marked when the little ball of cells, the *blastula*, starts to indent, to involute, to form the *gastrula* that creates inner spaces where the inner organs are predisposed and can eventually form. This is a step that plants never take! They stay at the state of a blastula, a complicated one for sure, constantly budding, branching and growing, but never really forming an inner space, comparable to lungs or the alimentary tract. Plants remain oriented toward the macrocosm.

The sponges, jellyfish, corals, and graptolites inhabiting the seas are still very macrocosmic but they are at the verge of forming cell colonies analogous to embryonic gastrulas. Like most of the lower organisms, their life is not centralized; even if strained through a sieve they will regroup or regrow into a new organism. Specialized organs of blood, respiration, excretion, and reproduction are absent, their function being performed macrocosmically. Their blood is the salt water of the ocean, their rhythms those of the tidal currents. Even though some of these early organisms develop hard shells by taking in calcium carbonate, silica, or calcium phosphate, in their larval stage they retain the free-floating, soft-bodied modus of earlier phases of evolution. They begin to recapitulate their phylogeny, as the great biologist Ernst Haeckel would say. Reproduction is mostly asexual, by budding, parthenogenic, or hermaphroditic processes, indicating that the astral principle has only weakly manifested itself in these organisms.

By the time we trace the unfolding entelechy to the shells (brachiopods), snails (mollusks), annelid worms, starfish (echinoderms), and crustaceans like crabs and trilobites, (arthropods), we find much clearer organ development and the beginnings of nerve ganglia as astrality starts

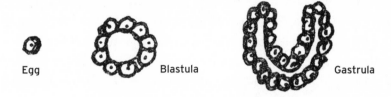

Egg   Blastula   Gastrula

Figure 7.1. Egg, blastula, and gastrula

to incarnate more strongly. Radial symmetry gives way to bilateral symmetry, so that orientation in space (up/down, front/back) becomes possible. The sexes start to separate and with this mode of reproduction rather than budding, mortality becomes reality. It marks life's entrance into the earthly dimensions of space and time. The arthropods are the first pioneers to venture out of the watery element into the light and warmth of the littoral. Many of the descendants of these organisms remain little changed in the ocean for millions of years as reminiscences of earlier eras.

During the Silurian period, the creative entelechy takes hold of the phylum of chordates, specifically the fish, which at first appear as cold-blooded jawless *(Agnatha)* bottom and suspension feeders without a solid inner skeleton but with bony armor like plates. In the Devonian period the limy substance of the bony armor starts to internalize to form partially calcified vertebrae and the incipient inner skeletons. During the upper Devonian the complex transition from a marine environment to a fresh-water environment is made. The rudimentary beginnings of kidneys, a two-chambered heart circulating blood, which contains about the same amounts and kinds of salts as sea water, is seen as an adaptation for an extra-marine environment. Of these fresh-water fish, it is the lobe-finned, air gulping fish *(crossopterygians)*, rather than the ray-finned fish, that slowly give rise to the carboniferous amphibians. The lobes are an extension of muscle tissue into the fins. We are now at the evolutionary juncture, where the internalized macrocosmic forces begin to work from within toward the outside.

The amphibians mark the transition of the chordates from the watery environment to the land. They now breathe with lungs, have a three-chambered heart, and walk or hop on four legs. However, to get to this point, they are forced to recapitulate all the stages of their development: they must return to the water to reproduce; the pond, lake or watery body functions as an external womb; the male may grab hold of the female and deposits sperm as she sheds her eggs. (The single-celled sperm and eggs floating in the water remind one of the protozoa at the beginning of life.) The resultant larva retraces all of its past evolution: blastula formation, gastrulation, bottom feeding, and breathing through gills, until it can finally crawl to land in its adult stage. Frogs, salamanders, and toads have remained at this stage; most rhythms are still determined by solar, lunar, and planetary cycles. The etheric forces work strongly in the amphibian, as seen in the rapid rate of reproduction; their greenish, plant-like coloration; and that like fish, many amphibians continue to grow their entire lifetime.

During the Permian the involution of the macrocosm continues in the evolution of reptiles. Reptiles no longer need to go back to the water to reproduce, for they have developed the amniotic egg, a miniature ocean with "nutritive organic soup" in which the larva, or embryo, can develop. Now the male and female are not just in proximity for reproduction, but real coitus occurs with the development of organs of internal insemination. Reptiles can now radiate onto dry land where they find Permian vegetation, gymnosperms such as conifers, cycads, and gingko, which are also capable of existing on dry land. The age of dinosaurs is the Mesozoic, during which the most varied forms are experimented with, including the giant brontosaurs, the ravenous tyrannosaurus, flying pterodactyls, and a host of other reptiles.

In the shadow of these mighty beings, the entelechy is working in the direction of birds and mammals. Birds, for the most part, leave the lower elements altogether and inhabit the lighter element, air. They liberate themselves further from the caprices of the macrocosm by beginning to develop warm blood. Unlike amphibians and reptiles, which depend upon the macrocosmic source of warmth, the sun, they internalize part of the sun's power in the form of a four-chambered heart and warm blood. Fertilization is internal, and the eggs are not abandoned as those of the reptile, but a nest (an external form of what would be a womb) is built by cooperation of both parents. The young are warmed externally by the parents as they brood and not left to the sun to hatch.[7] All of this indicates that soul-forces are ever more taking a hold of life and molding it to its purposes. Communication by song, the magnificent color of plumage, the attentive care for the young, and a constant warm body temperature are evidence of the progressive incarnation of a higher form of astrality in birds.

The development taken by birds is carried further with mammals. By the time placental mammals appear, the placenta replaces the macrocosmic environment of ocean, pond, and littoral habitat in which the young of the lower vertebrates are spawned; it replaces the eggs and nest of the birds; the placenta is a womb where the embryos are fed, warmed, and protected. After birth, the mammal offspring are fed further by the mother's milk, a microcosmic recreation of the dilute organic soup of earlier evolution.

Organically and physiologically the involution of the macrocosm is complete with the advanced mammals. Sophisticated, specialized inner organs have taken over from the diffuse, generalized functions that clumps of cells perform in the hydras, sponges, and starfish. An inner limb system that gives structural support has evolved out of the limy seas by way of an external skeleton with bony plates and shells. A complex inner metabolism has evolved out of a loosely organized system of cells that floated within its nutrient substance. Reproduction has gone from unprotected gametes deposited into the womb of the ocean to the inner micro-ocean of the womb. The solar and lunar tides that determined the ripening and depositing of the gametes became estrus cycles and, finally, in the anthropoids, menstrual cycles that have separated and emancipated themselves from direct lunar rhythms. An internalized rhythmic system of lungs and blood circulation has replaced the tides of the ocean. The external cosmic rhythms, though they still have their effects, do not so much determine the inner rhythms of the higher animals: sun, moon, and planets have entered the microcosm, transformed into the major inner organs of the body. Whereas the outer sun had to warm the amphibian and reptile, with mammals it is the inner sun, the heart that does the warming and keeps the blood circulation going. The body is kept at a constant temperature of 37°C, a state in which water is chemically the most active. Theodor Schwenk points out the connection between ocean streams and the sun, and their correlation to the heart and the streaming circulation of blood.[8] We can sense how the amoeba-like white and red corpuscles in the blood are kin to the protozoa of the oceans. Just as the planets move like a whirlpool around the sun, so are the organs of the microcosm connected to the heart by the circulating flow of the blood. The cosmic connection of the breathing-blood-circulatory system of the human organism with the sun is hinted at by the fact that, at the normal rate of eighteen breaths per minute, we breathe 25,920 times each day, which equals one platonic year (the number of years required for the sun to go through the zodiac and return to its spring point). 25,920 days would equal about seventy years, an average human lifetime.

In advanced animals, impulses are received and given ever more by a centralized nervous system, rather than by the automatism of macrocosmic influences working on notochords and ganglia via cilia and antennae. With the increasing concentration of nerve function in the head (encephalization) of mammals, the entelechy is preparing organic life for its next major metamorphosis, the microcosmic manifestation of the Spirit itself.

Late in geological time, at the end of the Cenozoic, in the course of the Ice Ages (Pleistocene), the new impulse is given. Having worked its way from the formless *Prima Materia* through its manifestation of etheric forces in the primal seas, through its manifestation of astrality in the development from fish to mammal, now the Spirit itself works its way into the microcosm after the groundwork has been laid.[9]

With *Homo sapiens* the outstanding characteristic is not so much an advancement of specialized physical organs, but the development of an inner world anchored in an increasingly larger cerebrum. Enclosed in the highly metamorphosed first segment of the spinal column, the brain undergoes explosive development. In lower Paleolithic tool use and manufacture, this inner, spiritual principle becomes manifest for the first time. In the use of fire by mid-Pleistocene *Homo erecti* we have the external picture of an internal process in man: the beginning of the indwelling of the Spirit, the "inner light." In the Magdalenian cave paintings showing numerous animals, we see the inner universe, lit up by the in-dwelling sun, step ever more into outward manifestation (just as with the muscles in the fins of the crossopterygians where the life force steps from inner to outer manifestation). The human spirit is leaving the "Atlantis" of the macrocosm.

The human being rapidly goes through all the stages of its evolutionary development (it recapitulates its phylogeny) as embryo, nursling, child, and adolescent. Then its body is organically complete. The etheric forces that have brought the body into an upright stance and have given it energy to learn to walk and talk are now freed for the use of the conscious life of the spirit. The spirit expresses itself in creativity, in speech and song: a long path from the silent fish to the chirping insect that resounds by mechanically rubbing its legs; to the vocal sac of the frog; to the mammals and birds who develop inner vocal chords; and, finally, to man, who not only produces sounds that have signal functions or are expressive of astrality, but whose sound can relate complex meaning, can conjure up the past as well as the future, can bless and curse, and can express worlds that do not exist anywhere in macrocosmic manifestation. With the human being, we have beings who can objectify the universe in thought, word, and deed; who can serve moral purposes beyond the immediate organic needs of eating, sleeping, reproducing, or self-preservation; and who can will and, to a large degree, determine their own future. Helen Keller, blind and deaf, was a great benefactor of humanity, a writer and humanitarian, whose indwelling spirit overcame severe organic handicaps. Beethoven was completely deaf when he composed perhaps the most beautiful piece of music that human-ity possesses. For an animal, on the contrary, that is sick, old, deaf, or blind, there is little inner light. It abandons life and returns to the macrocosm where its spirit dwells. Evolution is the chronology of the development of the microcosm out of the macrocosm—or from another perspective, the journey of the spirit into physical incarnation. Every organism we meet is a reminiscence of a step taken. Our animal brethren have accompanied us many steps along the way, but have preferred (temporarily) to remain at one place or another faithful to the macrocosm, to the mother earth and heavenly father.

Plant Evolution

Having scanned the panorama of animal phylogeny, we must now ask: What is our relationship to plants? Plants, too, have progressed out of the primal "slime," from the early "plant-animals" (the flagellates, bacteria, blue-green algae); to the humble, spore-bearing seedless vascular plants growing in the wet niches of the Devonian; followed in the late Carboniferous by primitive gymnosperms that could, by means of wind-pollination, colonize the dry land; and finally, to the flowering plants of the Mesozoic. Very early the sun laid claim to the germinal organisms that were to become the plant world, inducing the formation of chlorophyll and making them receptive of its form-giving forces.[10] Indeed, the plants in their growth and rhythm cannot be understood without taking the sun into consideration. The etheric world finds full expression in plants: ever growing, replicating segment after segment, silent, symmetric, and harmonious. As plants evolve further, their "organs" become more distinct and less generalized. In the vascular plants *(tracheophyta)*, true stems with fluid transporting vessels evolve and, with the flowering plants (angiosperms), distinct root, stem and leaf, flower and fruit formations appear, each with a specific relation to one of the four elements: earth, water, air, and light-warmth (fire). Except for plants such as algae, liverworts, and sporophytes of the bryophytes, which are dominated by the formative forces of the water element, the leaves and stems of mosses, ferns, horsetails, gymnosperms (pines, ginkgoes), and grasses are parallel-veined or radial, as though they directly radiate the etheric sun energy back into space. With dicots there are rounded leaves with netted veins so that the raying does not appear as direct, yet nowhere is the energy turned inward upon itself to form inner organs as in even the most primitive animals. Nowhere does gastrulation occur. Plants never internalize astrality like animals do.

The astral realm only touches the outer extremity of the plant in the form of insects that pollinate the flowers and worms that busy themselves at the root sphere. If insects eat up one's vegetables one can say that the astral sphere, represented by these animals, is pressing itself too heavily onto the plant. Something similar can be said when wasps, midges, or gall flies sting into plant tissue (like oak or rose leaves) causing fruit-like red, yellow, green, or black swellings, knobs or balls, called galls. But even here the astral component impresses itself on the plant from the outside. In the calyx formation of the flowers and in the ripening fruit, the plant makes a feeble, albeit beautiful attempt at forming inner organs. But in so doing, it loses vitality and growth, dissipates itself in nectar and pollen, color and fragrance, and contracts itself into tiny seeds in order to later resume its vegetative growth, its proper habitus. Only in some poisonous plants and insectivorous plants can one say, by their animal-like signature, that astrality has entered into the plant to a certain degree.

Let us look at the relationship of plants to astrality more closely. In his agricultural lectures, Rudolf Steiner, looking at the wider significance of the elements that make up most of organic chemistry, C, O, H, N, S, Ca, etc., identified nitrogen (N) as the element that represents movement and sensitivity, and as the anchor of the world soul, or astrality. Protein-rich animal tissue characterizes, in its constant movement and sensitivity, this ensouled state, the astral body.[11] As Rudolf Hauschka states,[12] the chemistry of plants is mainly a chemistry of C, O, H (carbohydrates, sugars, starches) except in flower and seed, which encroach on the astral sphere, whereas the chemistry of animals is that of C, O, H, N (proteins). This is true very generally speaking, for there are many important nitrogen processes going on in all plant cells. We must make finer distinctions. The plant's nitrogen is derived from animal excretions and bacterial metabolism in the soil. The roots absorb nitrogen as nitrate or ammonium ions; the plant combines these with organic acids to form amino acids, which might then be synthesized into true vegetable protein. These proteins are found mainly in fast-growing tissue. They are, of course, part of the DNA/RNA. The perfume and colors of the flowers are results of further protein metamorphosis, as are the albumen-rich seeds. As the plant blooms into flower and forms seeds, it starts engaging the lower levels of the astral sphere, the insect world.

Generally speaking, though, the protein of plants is not the structural protein as found in animals. These nitrogen substances are mainly incomplete proteins in a flowing transit through the plant organism. Often they are short-lived, functioning as enzymes, working as catalysts. This makes sense since amino acids are water soluble and hence readily mobile. The plant, surrounded by the air element (79 percent N_2) and the animal world (manures, insects) thus has nitrogen working on it mainly from the outside, or transiting it.

What happens when the plant, for one reason or another, holds up the flow of nitrogen through it, when it becomes, so to say, "possessive" of it? Then it becomes animal-like, in one way or another; it attains a distorted astrality; it becomes poisonous and it creates products of protein break-down ranging from uric acid to cyanide. Since these plants do not have renal organs, these products often do not leave but accumulate in the tissue of the plants. Most such products of protein breakdown in plants are called alkaloids; their connection with astrality is obvious in that nearly all influence the nerves, the soul life of man and animals, causing hallucinations, perceptual distortions, anesthetization, nerve paralysis, and the like. Commonly known alkaloids are morphine from poppies, nicotine from tobacco plants, caffeine and strychnine from several species, atropine from poisonous black nightshade, mescaline from a cactus, ephedrine from Mormon tea plant, and coniine from poison hemlock, which killed Socrates.

Most of such pharmacologically active plants have striking *signatures,* such as startlingly bright scarlet, purple, or black berries, strong smells that are often unpleasant, hairlike surfaces, and unusual growing habits. Poison hemlock has a pungent odor (smelling like the urine of mice) and purplish blotches on its stalks that look like symptoms of blood poisoning. Many of these poisonous plants fall out of step with the normal solar rhythms and withdraw from the sun's light into the recesses of the earth. In that they are similar to mushrooms, which also exhibit unusual nitrogen processes. Mandrake *(Mandragora officinarum),* whose narcotic roots take on humanoid shapes; the meadow saffron *(Colchicum autumnale);* and death camas *(Zigadenus venenosus)* hide away most of the year in the earth. Insect-trapping carnivorous plants are another group of plants that has an unusual relationship to nitrogen. Here, too, we have the signature of internalized astrality. The sundew's *(Drosera rotundiflora)* secretory hairs have such an astonishing sensitivity that they can distinguish between the stimuli of an insect victim and a piece of gelatin. When the former lands on the sticky hairs, the tendrils move at 8mm per minute. The Venus flytrap *(Diocea muscipula)* is much faster; it closes its trap in 0.01 to 0.02 seconds and then engages in protein digestion. The pitcher plant *(Darlingtonia)* has a strong animal signature: it is crustacean red, and a fishtail-like appendage hangs from its cobra-like head that makes up the funnel into which the hapless insect falls.

The legumes are another plant group that has internalized nitrogen processes. It, too, has corresponding signatures in its butterfly-shaped flowers, its lively tendril movements, its habit of flowering while at the same time still vigorously growing, and its fixing of atmospheric nitrogen with the aid of captive bacteria. Some of its members, such as the locoweed, are poisonous. Pythagoras taught that the enjoyment of legumes as foods weighs the soul down and interferes with advanced thinking; and of course Esau lost his birthright because of a meal of lentils. In the vein of this discussion it can be added that too heavy nitrogen fertilization of crops does pull the astral sphere into the plant region too strongly with the result of having aphids and insect damage.

Though we can say that the plant has evolved, we must say that it has done so within the realm of the macrocosm. It has no inner life with inner organs, senses, feelings, or voluntary movement. Even in the exceptions we have cited above, these qualities are highly rudimentary in the plant. The world of vegetation is entirely turned outward toward the cosmos. The philosopher Max Scheler defines plants as "ecstatic" (Gk. *ekstatikós* = "standing outside of one's self").[13] The sun, moon, and planets are their organs, not an inner heart, brain, liver, or kidneys. That is why it is correct for the gardener to plant by the "signs" if he knows what he is doing.

In a more immediate, down-to-earth sense, the animal world represents the astrality of the earth planet. In this way, animals function also as part of the immediate external astrality of the vegetable kingdom.

In the course of earth history we see plant evolution accompanied step by step by its animal "doppelgangers": marine invertebrates and algae in the early Paleozoic, amphibians and the giant horsetails and club mosses during the Carboniferous, gymnosperms and dinosaurs in the Mesozoic, flowering plants and birds, mammals, and butterflies in today's nature. One finds these parallels again and again: one need only look at the tomato hookworm and the tomato; the mutual dependence of the yucca moth and the yucca agave; or of the fig and the fig wasp; moth-pollinated flowers that open only at night; fly pollinated flowers that smell of rotten meat and even trap flies for a day before releasing them, like the wild arum; dead nettle which can only be fertilized by bumblebees; bird-pollinated flowers that lack scent but attract the pollinators with bright, contrasting colors; and there are even "bat-pollinated" flowers like those of the banana, which have dull-colored flowers that open at dusk and have mouse like smells.[14] Since plants cannot move, many of these animals carry on vital functions for the plants, distributing nitrogen compounds, enzymes, and other substances. One can say the hormonal or endocrine system of the plant is found outside in the animals. Pheromones, excretions, urine, and dung stimulate and affect plant growth and function.

In the animal and human being, there are internal organs of digestion. The food is ground by the teeth and broken down by enzymes and acids and the energies liberated are absorbed by the little hair-like *villi* of the duo-denum of the small intestine. Where does this process occur in the plant? We must look into the macrocosm: Organic substance is broken down first by chewing insects, the teeth of the planet; then, it is worked on further by acids and enzymes given off by micro-organisms in the soil rendering humus whose essence enters the plants through hairlike capillary roots. The soil is the intestinal content of the plant and the capillary rootlets are inside-out duodenal villi! The biodynamic idea of using the same herbs (chamomile, yarrow, dandelion, etc.) that cure upset stomachs and bad digestion as "medicinal remedies" on soils of afflicted plants begins to make sense. When the crop plants seem to be sick, the trouble lies with the soil, not with the specific plant itself.

Where do we find the rhythmic system of the plant, the heart, the blood circulation, the rhythm of breathing lungs? Again we must look into the macrocosm. The plant depends on the day and night cycle of the sun for its rhythm; transpiration is directly linked to the sun. The yearly solar rhythm affects weather, precipitation, and thus, the annual rhythm of plant growth. Its warmth is that of the sun. Its "blood," the green plant sap, is a mirror image of red blood, even to its chemical formula. The molecule for chlorophyll is the exact mirror image of hemoglobin, except that the chlorophyll has a magnesium ion were the hemoglobin has an iron ion.[15] No chlorophyll can be formed, however, without iron being present, just as no blood can be formed without magnesium being present. Red and green are complementary colors, for if one stares at one too long, the retina compensates by producing its opposite. In the respiration of animals and photosynthesis of plants, we have a mirror image again, where oxygen as a "waste" product of the plant becomes the life element for animals, and carbon dioxide, the "waste" product of animals, becomes the structure-building element for plants. Plants take in CO_2 and release O_2; animals take in O_2 and release CO_2.

Where is the calcium-phosphate endoskeleton of the plant? It is found outside of its body in the macrocosm in form of limestone and mineral deposits rock and the bones of decomposing animals. Where are the songs, the cries, and all the varied sounds of the animal world in the plant? They too are found in the macrocosm as the sound of wind, thunder, the chirping of birds and insects. Where are the reproductive organs of the plant? Botanists are quick to point to the stamen and ovary of the flower, but already Goethe was uncomfortable with this interpretation. The father of the plant is found in the formative forces streaming from the cosmos into the flower and seed; the womb of the fertile earth, the soil, provides the mother for the plant.

We can see in the plant a macrocosmic inverse image of the human being. Man experiences himself as the center of being in the universe, as an "I am." The plant experiences the universe as it's being. Its "I am" streams in from the periphery of the cosmos and at the same time from the depth of the earth. This is a significant distinction. Plato expresses this when he declares that the human being is a plant turned upside down with the roots reaching to the heavens and the branches to the ground.[16] We can interpret this concept of Plato's in the following manner: Man has involuted; he has, in comparison to plants, inverted his relationship to the macrocosm, by this, man has evolved his own inner world, his relative freedom

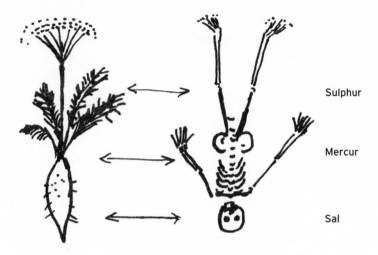

Sulphur

Mercur

Sal

Figure 7.2. "We can see in the plant a macrocosmic inverse image of the human being."

from the macrocosm. Animals stand halfway in between man and plants in this inverting process; even architecturally there is a link between the plant with its upward growing segmented stem, the animal, prone with its backbone in horizontal position, and the human being with its vertically upright backbone.

The plant is completely tied into the macrocosm: in its roots, the densest part, the *sal* processes dominate; in the leaves, the *mercury* functions rule; and in the flowers, the *sulfur processes*, related to reproduction, to dissipation and sublimation of matter, dominate. In the human being, the *sal* functions dominate in the head, the most concentrated part of the body; the lungs and heart carry out the rhythmical, mercurial functions of circulation and respiration, which mediate between the head and the lower body parts; the bowels and sex organs express the dissipation and sublimation of the *sulfur* process, in the form of metabolism, menses, sperm production, and the removal of urine and wastes. The odors of the lower body have their correspondence in the fragrance of flowers—both are the results of similar metabolic processes. Based on this three-fold model, some forms of naturopathic medicine prescribe roots (e.g., horseradish) for ailments of nerves and head, leaves for lungs and heart

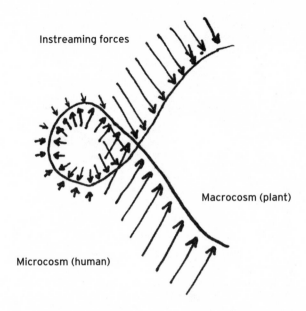

Instreaming forces

Macrocosm (plant)

Microcosm (human)

Figure 7.3. Instreaming forces, the macrocosm, and the microcosm

conditions (e.g., greens for blood circulation) and flowers for digestive problems (e.g., chamomile).[17]

In all of this, we perceive in the plant not so much an individuated being as in a higher animal, or a human being, but as part of a larger macrocosmic process. We can see the plant world as an organ of the earth, having evolved with the earth organism as a whole. Gerbert Grohmann calls the plant world the "light-sensitive organ of the earth."[18] Like the retina of our eyes, the plants' leaves, that 5 mm–thin layer of foliage covering the planet, are composed of photosensitive tissue that take in the light forces streaming in from the cosmos and transmit them to the earth. Whereas we humans create mental images of what we perceive, the plants form their bodies, leaf, and flower symmetries, out of the light ether they perceive.

Folklore tells that the dwarves who work in the dark recesses of the earth do not see the sunlight directly, but mediated by the plant through the roots, it is made available to them in form of sugar (glucose). (As R. Steiner says, sugar can be seen as mineralized sunlight!) Plants are part of the rhythmic system, the diaphragm of the earth organism. In the summer,

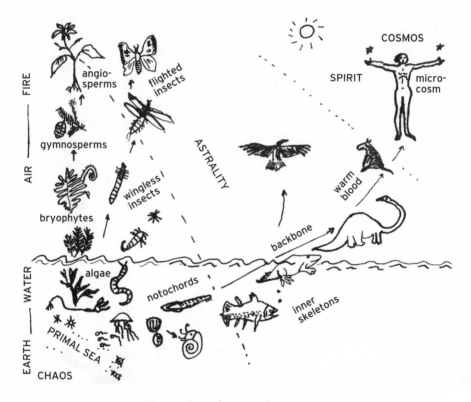

Figure 7.4. Chaos and cosmos

the earth "breathes out" its green plant forms and in the winter they return into the earth, retreating into root and seed. In the winter, the earth perceives the information that the leaves and flowers have gathered during the summer.[19] Or as Steiner said on another occasion, in the summer the earth sleeps, her soul flies into the cosmos and the vegetation is her dream; in the winter she wakes up again.

In another way, one can look at the plant as the mercury function of the earth. As a mercurial being, the plant connects the physical plane with the astral plane. In her flowering state she meets the astral plane by enmeshing with the insect world, and, as root, she grows making contact with the purely physical, mineral realm. She is the light-bringer to the dark mineral world and is food provider for the animal (astral) world. The plant mediates between the two realms. She mediates between light and dark, between life and death. It is this ability of balancing out one-sidedness that makes plants healers; they bridge what is separated, they heal what is broken. Since time immemorial the have been the best sources of medicine.

In conclusion, we can reemphasize that man is a microcosm: he has internalized the physical world in his body, the plant world in his etheric makeup, the animal world in his soul, and the spirit light in his "I am." The plant is present only as a physical body and ether body—its soul and spirit work on it from the outside. In its essence the plant is macrocosmic.

Chapter 8

Heredity

Oh sweet spontaneous earth . . .
How often has the naughty thumb of science prodded thy beauty?
  —e. e. cummings

Anything will give up its secrets if you love it enough.
 . . . I found that when I talk to a little flower or a little peanut they
will give up their secrets.
  —George Washington Carver

Worried farmers called upon Rudolf Steiner to talk to them at the Koberwitz estate because the continuing degeneration of seed varieties, the need to buy new strains of seeds every few years where previously the same strain had been kept for generations, and the mounting incidence of disease in livestock were ever-increasing sources of concern. The suggestion Steiner gave in response was to provide optimal conditions for the characteristic development of food crops and of animals. Good humus soil, made receptive to in-raying cosmic forces by the use of biodynamic preparations, would provide the living matrix in which the seeds of plants would retain their viability, quality, and other desirable traits. Similarly, animals fed on plants raised like this and kept in a way as befitted their species would not have problems such as sterility, loss of vigor, or hoof-and-mouth disease. Given an optimal environment, the archetype of the species would be able to express itself in a healthy, vigorous fashion.

Plants and animals that are raised in a manner contrary to their basic constitution and needs will evidence devitalization of genetic substance in the course of several generations. In the same manner, increasing vitality due to corrective biodynamic measures is not immediately evidenced, but shows in subsequent generations, a factor making short-term study difficult:

> In the sphere of vitality . . . there is always the law of inertia. That is to say, it might not appear in the present generation or in the next, but it will in the third. The vitalizing influence goes on beyond the first few generations. If you restrict your investigations to the present and do not extend them over several generations, you get a completely false picture. Then, when you observe the next generation but (only that) one, you turn your attention to quite other causes than the real ones, namely the feeding of the grandparent beasts. Vitality cannot be broken down at once. It is surely broken, but only in succeeding generations.[1]

Sir Albert Howard similarly notes the effect of unnatural habitat on the seed vitality of the plants:

> A new set of facts suddenly fell into place: the running out of varieties, a marked phenomenon of modern agriculture, to answer which new varieties of the important crops have constantly to be bred—hence the modern plant-breeding station—could without hesitation be attributed to the continued impoverishment of modern soils owing to the prolonged negligence of the Western farmer to feed his fields with humus. By contrast, the maintenance of century-old varieties in the East, so old that in India they bear ancient Sanskrit names, was proof of the unimpaired capacity of the plant to breed in those countries where humus was abundantly applied.[2]

Sir Howard pointedly criticizes the Broadbalk experiments at Rothamstead, noting that wheat grown year after year for nearly a hundred years on the same plot would probably had given out if no new seeds were procured from the best outside sources to grow each season's crop.

> Had the harvest of each plot been used for re-sowing, in a very few years an important result would have been obtained. The effect of artificial manures, which we know is cumulative, would soon have begun to influence the stability of the variety itself and cause it to run out. In some period between twenty-five and fifty years the wheat would have collapsed.[3]

He goes on to note that in nature there is "no running out of the variety and no necessity to supply new and improved strains, one generation follows another century after century . . . there is very little plant disease."[4] He states that a simple method for estimating the success of any method of farming is by seeing how disease-resistant crops are, and how normally and healthily livestock breed and reproduce.

Missouri soil scientist William A. Albrecht has reservations about plant and animal breeding. If the soil is alive and rich in humus, the plant will be able to express its genetic potential; if the soil is not in good heart, then no genetic tricks will be able to bring about good plants:

> But in spite of the belief by some folks that we can select or breed legume plants, for example, to tolerate soil acidity, and wheat to resist smut, such beliefs rest on fallacious logic. It will not stand the common test of *reducto ad absurdum*. If that reasoning is carried to its final conclusion, then we should be able to breed plants to tolerate starvation.[5]

Hybridization seems to contradict the above, but Albrecht points out that before hybridization corn contained 10.30 percent crude protein (1911), and by 1956 the protein content had decreased to 5.15 percent. The same holds true for other crops. Hybridization increased the yield measured in bulk, but the loss of protein and other qualities, and the increase in diseases and pests, show us that good soil husbandry is more important.[6]

Relying on long years of experience, the farmer Carsten Jens Pank feels that genetic vitality, the organism's life-carrying capacity, decreases when plants and animals are placed in unnatural environments (feedlots, battery cages, hydroponics), leading to loss of vigor, health, and good reproduction rates. The immediate external characteristics of form and color might not change, but the vitality does. Despite hybridization of plants, the overall vitality is decreasing. "We have a moral obligation to at least maintain for those who come after us that which has been handed down by our forebears: the genetic continuity of our domestic animals and cultural plants."[7]

Other farmers express similar views. One old-timer showed me his potatoes. They consisted of a variety that had been taken off the market nearly thirty years ago, for it had lost vitality and was subject to mildew and scabs. He surprised a government official with his healthy example of an "extinct" potato variety, which he had grown for so many years in good soils and treated biodynamically.[8]

What is implied in the above is that our current methods of fertilizing heavily with NPK artificial fertilizer, using insecticides, herbicides, fungicides, hydroponics, hybridization, breeding experiments, and other such methods that are hailed as the "Green Revolution" are a Trojan horse. The long run effect will be a devitalizing of the organisms we depend on for our foodstuffs.[9]

Is this correct or not? The scientific establishment and agribusiness, relying on neo-Darwinian or "synthetic" theories of genetics, vehemently disagree. It is out of the question, according to this point of view, that the extensive chemicalization of farming, the separation of food crops from animal manures, the use of feedlots and batteries, monocropping, spraying, and dusting have any effect whatsoever on the genetic structure of the species involved. The idea that the environment can, in any directional way, influence genetic inheritance is labeled Lamarckism (the inheritance of characteristics acquired by interaction with the environment), a thoroughly disproven heresy.

ESTABLISHMENT GENETICS

The modern, neo-Darwinistic geneticist and plant breeder would say that the quasi-Lamarckian concerns of a Steiner or Howard and the common-sense pronouncements of ordinary gardeners and farmers are unfounded. Even though Darwin himself supposed that the environment might account for inheritable changes in species, ever since the pea breeding experiments of Mendel were discovered, it is known that there is no way in which the environment can influence the genes. If changes occur in the somatic cells, brought about by diet, accident, debilitation, or exercise, the effects have no bearing on the reproductive cells and on the offspring. Mendel made the distinction between *genotype*, the genetic potential of the organism, and *phenotype*, the outward expression of the genes. Genetic characteristics, he showed, are not lost or gained due to environmental influence, but due to random combinations of parental gene plasma. These traits are not blended together in fertilization, but are retained as segregated units that are sometimes dominant, or sometimes masked in the form of recessive traits, which can reappear in homozygous combinations. The discovery of chromosomes as the location of the genes by Thomas Hunt Morgan elucidates the physical basis of heredity and adds more weight to the theory.

When August Weissmann cut off twenty generations of rats' tails to show that what happens in the environment to the phenotype has no effect on the genotype, the Lamarckian ghost was laid to rest. The twenty-first rat generation had just as long a tail as the first generation!

The unraveling of the DNA code gives further support to this theory of the "splendid isolation" of the genes. The DNA, the macromolecules in the chromosomes of the cell nuclei, have the remarkable ability to duplicate themselves. They are the key to the ontogeny of the new organism. They code the RNA, which in turn will key out the enzymes that build up specific amino acids and countless protein structures. The chain of causality is always from the DNA to the RNA to the protein, and never in the opposite direction. Thus, the outside environment has no effect on the DNA. One can reason that if the environment had direct effect, then the species would prove very unstable, in continuous flux, helplessly adrift in capricious external circumstances. The isolation of the genes guarantees the continuity of the species and accounts for some of them, like cockroach or ginkgo, not having changed for millions of years.

If the environment has no effect on the genotype, then how does evolution or change at all come about? The basic cause for change is mutation, which constitutes an accidental, random, non-directional alteration in the chromosomes themselves, brought about by radiation, cosmic and ultraviolet rays, high temperatures, chemicals, by a "mistake" in the DNA replication in the sex cells, or by "crossovers" and "deletions" in the random recombination of haploid gametes as they join to form the zygote.

These are changes in genotype, but they are purely accidental and indicate no purpose on the part of the plant or animal to try to change itself to fit better into the environment. Most such random mutations are disadvantageous, even lethal to the organism, so that the resulting phenotype will not be able to survive. Natural selection will weed out the unfit; they will not add the innovation to the gene pool. Only rarely, by chance, will there be an advantageous mutation that will spread itself throughout the population.

The mechanism is blind chance. There is no teleology and no entelechy. There is no volition on the part of the species. We do not have to worry about the sensibility of species when we breed them by selection, culling, hybridization, inbreeding, cloning, and by trying to induce mutations by the use of cobalt radiation. We are merely taking over the blind workings of nature of inducing mutations where we decide which effect will survive in the gene pool for our advantage. As the well-known modern geneticist Theodosius Dobzhansky points out, there is no archetypal or ideal species as Plato, Aristotle, or fundamentalist Christians assume. According to Dobzhansky, the "populational" thinking of neo-Darwinism has replaced such "typological" thinking.[10] Therefore, it is useless and meaningless to talk about degeneration, or of violating the plant or animal basic type. We are free to experiment in any way possible to produce new species or varieties. At the same time we need not worry about the impressions of the environment because these do not directionally affect the genes. We can breed super cows and super vegetables, keep them in feedlots and plant them in chemically fertilized monocultures.

Breeding experiments, the production of hybrid corn, square tomatoes that ship well and can be machine harvested, strawberries at Christmas, and other such modern marvels show that the theory is correct.

The fascinating advances of the Green Revolution have come out of the application of this theory. The production increases of western agribusiness brought about a reconsideration by the Russians of the Lamarckism furthered by the Soviet biologist T. D. Lysenko after Khrushchev. Lysenko intended to improve the genes of crop plants by raising them repeatedly in specific environments and by grafting, so that the acquired characteristics could eventually be inherited. Lysenko, also stigmatized by Stalinism, was not totally effective in showing that this could be done. He certainly did not get fast results.

Our modern biologists and geneticists are emphatic that the course outlined on the basis of neo-Darwinistic theory must be pursued to the point of genetic engineering if we are to "feed the starving millions." Genetic engineering is now commonplace . . .

WHO IS RIGHT?

Is there any validity in the statements by Steiner, Howard, and others that there is degeneration or a loss of vitality due to modern agricultural practices? There is cause for concern:

> Since the advent of "miracle" hybrid seeds, the older seeds have, in many cases, been lost through neglect—ending a genetic continuity of many millennia. Agricultural researchers are experiencing great difficulty in acquiring stocks of native seeds for preservation programs. According to a recent United Nations report on genetic resources "the older diverse (crop) varieties . . . are sown no more; many of the wild relatives with which they maintained genetic interchange have been swept away."[11]

Seed banks set up are usually not able to, or do not have the means to, stem this genetic erosion. "The consequences of the loss of native seed germ plasma are staggering, when one thinks that within one short generation, human beings could throw away key evolutionary links in the food system—all in the name of progress."[12] Germ plasma has been lost that took generations of careful and loving selection by farmers and gardeners to develop. They were lost because they were unsuited to machine production; they were susceptible to newly appearing blights, insects, or diseases that came in the wake of radically new farming practices. For example, about 75 percent of alfalfa and 90 percent of the clover breeding material has been lost since the turn of the century.[13] The result of the uniformization brought about by agribusiness, where hybrids have been selected for only one or two characteristics, is that our food plants are put on a very narrow genetic basis. The "miracle" wheat and rice of the Green Revolution, which makes locally adapted native varieties extinct, is completely dependent on high energy input in the form of chemical fertilizer, insecticides, irrigation, and machinery.

The yields farmers and commercial gardeners have getting with the new methods had been fantastic at this point. (That is if one does not calculate the energy input and collateral damage to the environment.) The dysfunctional aspects of these developments, however, include the need for consolidation of land and capital: forcing peasants and small family farmers off the land and, in the developing countries, the consequent crowded cities full of unemployed masses—not to mention the ecological abuse and the genetic erosion of crop varieties. The problems will multiply if the cheap oil runs out. Further complications are that the new "miracle" seeds are degenerating, losing vitality, viability, and have to be replaced by plant-breeding stations each season. Which farmer or gardener of today still raises his or her own seeds, adapted to the local climate, soil, or growing conditions and local taste choice?

The danger of a narrow genetic base was brought home in 1970 when the high-yield hybrid corn crop was hit by a blight that knocked out 15 percent of the U.S. production. Frantic breeding of new seed in Hawaii throughout the winter stayed the catastrophe that time.

With animals, which are selected for one or two traits, it is a similar story. Cows that are bred for fast-growing meat and dairy cattle for huge volumes of milk production become susceptible to all kinds of disease and sterility. One cannot breed cows for bigger udders, inject them with bovine growth hormones (rBGH), and artificially inseminate them, and expect—despite such intrusions into the sexual cycle—good fertility and easy birth.[14] Will the manure of such mistreated, protein-overfed cattle still have the healing, vitality-restoring effect on the soil, or is this link of fertility also weakened?

The next question that needs to be asked is whether the gene plasma is totally isolated, not subject to the environment other than occasional haphazard mutations that might occur, or whether there might be a grain of truth in the inheritance of characteristics acquired from the environment. Maybe genetic potentials are switched on and off by environmental impulses? If so, environmental care takes on new importance.

There are cracks in the armor of neo-Darwinistic genetic theory. Lamarckism had been refuted with the demise of Paul Kammerer's credibility and the fall of Lysenko. But no sooner had the Lamarckian hydra lost these two heads, than another one reared up under the name *teminism*. Howard Temin of the University of Wisconsin, as well as researchers at MIT and Columbia, found experimental proof that cancer-causing viruses in animals, once they invade the host cells, produce their own hereditary DNA. Frederick Griffith, working with pneumococci strains, found hereditary changes caused by the transfer of nucleic acids from one strain to another, a process referred to as *transformation*. This seems to indicate that the DNA does not live in as splendid an isolation as was supposed by orthodox theorists, and that the chain of effect from the DNA to the RNA to amino acid is not necessarily a one-way street.[15] It cannot be completely counted out that changes in body cells could (eventually working their way past all the filters and barriers by means of enzyme and hormone transmission) cause changes in the reproductive cells. There is also evidence of cytoplasmic inheritance separate from the DNA, such as the mitochondria that reproduce independently. When one considers the great number of known mutagens in existence today, the idea of the totally insulated germ plasma becomes less tenable. Numerous chemicals, rays, and other hazards have been identified.[16] The more primitive organisms seem to be able to cope and adapt "intelligently" to debased environments by genetic changes, as with resistant germs, viruses, and even insects. In plants and lower animals the strict distinction between reproductive cells and somatic cells breaks down anyway; all the somatic cells can function by budding to create new organisms. Arthur Koestler suggests that the "Weissmann barrier" against environmental effects is basically correct, but perhaps it is not an impenetrable wall as much as a filter, which lets select influences work on the germ plasma but otherwise maintains stability and functions much like the mind, which lets in only relevant stimuli from among all the potential stimuli.[17] The excess of mutagenic chemicals thoughtlessly released into the environment might swamp this filter. Koestler proposes that some of these changes are deliberately kept, others quickly eliminated. He quotes Waddington that "it may be unsafe to consider that the occurrence of directed (non-random) mutation related to the environment can be ruled out of court *a priori*."[18] There might, after all, be a guiding principle that gives intelligent direction to the development of a species. It is certainly hard to imagine that the complex plant and animal species that populate the earth have arisen out of aimless, nondirected mutations. How could such diversified, intricate features as the eye, the egg, the seed, have come about? So many isolated factors must have mutated at once to make up the new organ or species, or the mutations must have been kept until there were enough to form the new structure (Ernst Mayr's "pre-adaptation"). Even if the necessary mutations were present at the same time, they would not have constructed a complex organism, or as Waddington aptly states: "To suppose that the evolution of the wonderfully adapted biological mechanisms has depended only on a selection out of a haphazard set of variations, each produced by blind chance, is like suggesting that if we went on throwing bricks together into heaps, we should eventually be able to choose ourselves the most desirable house."[19]

If there were no entelechy or at least direction, why are we not comfortably adapted, rapidly multiplying one-celled organisms? Why bother becoming a multi-cellular complex? There is much validity is assuming as Lamarck, Bergson, and Nietzsche had thought, that "living things willfully seek their own ascending genetic change in obedience to a destiny that, once glimpsed, prescribes meaning of life on earth."[20] As Paul Kammerer has it, evolution "is not the merciless selection that shapes and perfects the machinery of life; it is not the desperate struggle for survival alone which governs the world, but rather out of its own strength, everything that has been created strives upward toward light and the joy of life, burying only that which is useless in the graveyard of selection."[21]

Kammerer, an eminent Austrian biologist, went as far as showing, in breeding experiments with a number of amphibians and the sea squirt Ciona, that the inheritance of acquired characteristics is possible. As Koestler brilliantly documents,[22] Kammerer's experiments in the beginning of the century were fought in the most unsavory and unfair way by the neo-Darwinian establishment, which could not allow the Lamarckian heresy to flourish. Kammerer eventually committed suicide when his experimental species had been tampered with to give the appearance of forgery.

One problem with these well-documented experiments is that no one up to now has been able to repeat them, to get the amphibians to breed in unusual laboratory conditions, to produce the desired inheritable effects. Why can't they be repeated? Here we are confronted again by that unknown factor which vexed Hauschka when he tried to repeat the experiments of the appearance and disappearance of matter. Perhaps the key to Kammerer is that he loved his experimental animals so much that he had a hard time bringing himself to kill any of them. One time, during a visit to a Moravian castle, he picked up a rare variety of toad in the garden and kissed it tenderly on the head.[23] Henceforth, he was known as the "Krötenküsser," the toad kisser. He even named his only child, his daughter, Lacerta, after the genus of pretty lizards, the *lacertidae*. It is perhaps this factor, this love for his experimental animals, that led to the remarkable, but as yet unrepeated, success with breeding for acquired characteristics. In a similar manner, Luther Burbank, George Washington Carver, and the Russian J. W. Mitchurin, who loved their plants, were able to achieve outstanding breeding results that have not been equaled. The inheritance of acquired characteristics has not been conclusively disproven, and the human factor of love and care, the personal relationship that Steiner advocated, has not even been considered. Both Burbank and Carver, when asked for their success, claimed that they communicated with the plants, and could not elaborate further on their methodology.

Are there archetypal patterns, or *leitmotifs*, for each species, akin to Plato's ideas, Aristotle's entelechies, or Steiner's etheric forms, which are plastic and adaptable within a certain range, but could be violated by being constrained in unnatural environments? Is there a "spirit" or *deva* of the plant or animal that, when violated too often by excessive breeding experiments, by deprivations, artificial inseminations, or dead soils, loses its joy of existence and slowly withdraws from manifestation, loses vitality and becomes "degenerate" or extinct? Is it possible that Burbank's flowers and fruit trees, Carver's peanuts, and Kammerer's salamanders responded to the warmth and love of these researchers?

Speciation has never been observed; it remains a theory. The countless fruit flies that have been subjected to doses of mutagenic X-radiation in the laboratories of H. J. Muller and Y. H. Morgan did not produce new varieties, but only trivial and deleterious changes, indicating more the destruction of genetic potential than the creation of anything new. Neither were the mutations random, but specific kinds of changes (blindness, wing stunting, bristle change) occurred at definite rates. Purebred (homozygous) blind flies suddenly had offspring with functional eyes again, as though there is a blueprint, an etheric model that re-manifests itself after a time. Such blueprints, or ether bodies, are evidenced in the regeneration of lizard tails, the root and flower development from leaf cuttings, wound healing, the regeneration of cut-up worms, a phenomenon that led H. Drietsch to the formulation of *Vitalism* as a principle opposed to pure physico-chemical causality. Even if we say that chromosomes with all the genetic material are found in each and every cell, how do these genes and chromosomes know when it is time to regenerate, and what part they should play?

Conclusion

We have voiced doubts about the practices resulting from modern genetic theory. What in Mendelian neo-Darwinism is based on sound logic and observation cannot be disputed; however, there are too many unexplained factors to permit raising the theory to the level of law. These are shaky grounds upon which to base our food sources.

The environment has a greater effect on the genetic vitality than is accounted for by the theory. Good husbandry and nurture require that an environment proper to the species be established and maintained if degeneration and loss of vitality are to be avoided. The archetype of the organism must find an environment conducive to its specific nature in order to thrive and reproduce well. To deny the existence of the archetype and to change species by hyperbreeding and induced mutation will only accelerate genetic disaster. We can understand genes better if we think of them as the anchors of supersensible beings in the physical world that constitute the essence of the plant or animal. By manipulation of the genes or by diminishing the environment of the genes, these nonmaterial essences will have an increasingly difficult time manifesting themselves.

The essences, or supersensible archetypal forms, for our plants and animals, are, of course, not available to the objective study by the scientific method because this method, limiting itself to external sensory data and mathematical, logical formulation, precludes such study. A meditative approach, a loving sympathy, a knowledge of the supersensible world as was part of all cultural traditions at one time, or a "spiritual science" as proposed by Rudolf Steiner, have an easier time understanding these things. A natural environment, good care, and a loving, personal relationship to the creatures of farm and garden, will, in the long run, provide better results than cold, mercenary practices hatched out in distant laboratories.

To those who operate by the assumption that we live in a dead and meaningless universe given up to chance, we will let Goethe reply:

> The world of the spirit is not closed;
> It is that your senses are shut off,
> It is that your heart is dead.

Things have changed since Steiner's Koberwitz lectures or Sir Albert Howard's agricultural observations, however the basic conflict of vision remains. On one side are those to whom life has an inner spiritual core and intrinsic worth, demanding the proper and respectful treatment of one's fellow creatures. On the other side are those who hold the reductionist view, that there is no inner core, that everything can be reduced to chemical and mechanical constituents, and that there is absolutely nothing that speaks against transforming and manipulating nature in the way we see fit.

The later position prevailed so far. Industrial farming has replaced the family farm, where animals were generally individually cared for and where the croplands were husbanded carefully. Today, giant agribusiness corporations operate endless monocultures of genetically modified corn, soya, or potatoes. Fields with genetically manipulated corn are sprayed with total herbicides, such as Roundup. The seeds produced cannot be saved, for they cannot germinate and give rise to new life; they are "terminator seeds," programmed to commit "suicide." This "genetic use restriction technology" (GURT) forces the farmer to buy new seeds each year from the corporation. This is one step up from the hybrid plants, whose seeds do not produce plants of the same quality. GMO (gene modified organisms) released into the environment can contaminate the non-modified relatives. This has happened with corn, for example. Once released, they cannot be cleaned up. Often they are toxic to other organisms. For example, when the larvae of the beautiful Monarch butterfly eat the pollen of trans-genetic Bt-Corn, they die.

Cattle, pigs, chickens, and other animals are subjected equally to such manipulation. Crammed by the tens of thousands in "concentrated animal feeding operations" (CAFOs), they are deprived of their inherent dignity. They are kept alive by massive application of antibiotics, which in turn are responsible for the creation of ever more antibiotic resistant supergerms. The urine and feces of these masses of tortured creatures becomes an environmental problem, creating stench and polluting ground water. For traditional farmers and gardeners, manure and slurry were never a problem, but a blessing; they provided fertility in field and garden.

Not only does the massive application of potent herbicides and chemicals necessary for GMO-crops have a devastating effect on the environment, but the food thus produced is also problematic. Food consists not just of calories and chemical building blocks, but is primarily information for our organism. What "information" are we receiving? What is the ultimate effect on our health? "Frankenfoods" and GMOs constitute a gigantic uncontrolled experiment, a kind of Russian roulette involving hundreds of millions of people.

Genetic manipulation was sold to the public as a humanitarian undertaking. We were told that this would be the only way to feed the millions of hungry mouths in the world. This is not true. In the third world, millions of peasants were driven off the land and are worse off than before. In India some 250,000 peasant farmers have committed suicide after taking loans out to plant genetically modified crops. When the promise of an insect free, bountiful harvest did not come about, they were left with debt, which they could not repay.[24] Not the people, but the agribusiness corporations, have been the beneficiaries of the "Green Revolution" and the "Genetic Revolution."

In the States there are ever more voices worried about the consequences of terminator seeds and GMOs as the basis of food supply. There is talk about "food collapse"—with the skyrocketing cost of hydrocarbons as the basis of fertilizer, pesticides, and agricultural machinery, and the loss of basic agricultural know-how, this is definitely a possibility. People are thinking about "survival gardening," of turning lawns into vegetable gardens. Terminator seeds and GMOs will not be part of these. Besides good seeds and natural fertilizers, discussed in the second half of this book, a more enlightened frame of mind that sees the divine archetypes in all creatures, is needed to find the way back to "middle earth."

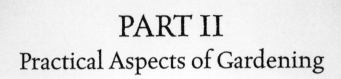

PART II
Practical Aspects of Gardening

Introduction to Part II

Whereas the first part of the book deals with modern ideas of organic and biodynamic gardening and delves into ancient cosmological concepts that have fallen into ill repute with the changing of the times, finding gold underneath their corroded surfaces, the second part is more concerned with practical applications. Though we are talking about micro-organisms and cat-ion exchanges, the focus remains holistic, comprehensive, and macrocosmic.

We begin with the great polarity, the **terrestrial factors**, mother earth, and **cosmic factors**, father sky, the sun-moon planets. Leaving the sphere of the elements, our attention is turned to the sphere of life, starting with **composting**, where life and death processes hold each other in balance, and how to prepare composts that will capture life forces and make them available to our plants. Then we attempt to make natural plant sociology work for us in correct **companion planting** and proper **crop rotation**. The major **plant families** that we meet in the garden are identified and the function of **weeds** is explored. Negative astral influences in the form of **pests**, insects, and fungi are discussed next, and natural biodynamic **medicines** and **preparations** are studied. Information on harvest, storage, seeds and seed production, garden tools, herbs, hints on cooking, and on social aspects make up the concluding chapters.

Chapter 9

Terrestrial Factors: Soil

> Soil is the "creative material" of most of the basic needs of life.
> Creation starts with a handful of dust.
> —William A. Albrecht (1888–1974), eminent soil scientist

Until recently, materialistic science thought of the soil as merely a substance to hold plants up and to provide chemical building blocks for their growth. Recent experiments with *hydroponics*, growing plants in a watery medium without soil, seem to verify this theory. However, studies show that, besides the need for constant flushing and oxygenating of the liquid medium, the hydroponically grown plants steadily lose vitality and germination ability after a number of years. These hypertrophying plants absorb the chemicals in an unbalanced manner. For the city dweller in crowded quarters, windowsill, balcony, or rooftop hydroponics might give pleasure and an occasional snack, but for larger scale gardening it is not to be recommended.

Before modern science came to view soil in terms of chemical constituents and mechanical processes, the soil was literally sacred. It was the mother earth from which all living creatures sprang and to whom they all returned, eternally virgin, ever fertile and receptive. Appearing in many forms and called by many names, she was worshipped in India as Prithivi, in Greece as Gaea, in Rome as Terra Mater, by the Celts as Dana, by the Slavic people as Siva, and by the heathen Anglo Saxons as Erce, the *eorthan modor* (earth mother); she is Izanami of the Japanese, Pachamama of the Incas, and so forth. We can appreciate how differently the peasant, his soul bound up with the soil for generations, related to the earth by a hymn from the Russian "Old Believers:"

> The first mother is the holy Mother of God,
> The second, the moist mother Earth,
> The third, the mother who gives birth in pain.[1]

We understand the immigrating Sicilian peasant who brings with him a handful of his native soil. For the alchemists the soil was an expression of the amorphous *prima materia*, the ever-receptive chaos, capable of reflecting the forms projected upon it by the microcosmic and macrocosmic spirit. In primitive cosmologies the Earth Goddess is usually paired with the Sky God, the carrier of the fecund thunderbolt, in a divine hierogamy. She is the *mater* (matter, matrix, mother) that receives the seed and gives birth to the Father's offspring. Thus, agri*culture* becomes a sacred *cultus* (L. cultus = to tend, care); plowing is the divine act of opening up the sacred womb.

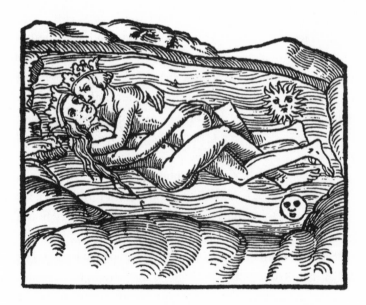

Figure 9.1. Earth and Cosmos as sun and moon from the Rosary of the Philosophers or Rosarium philosophorum, 1550

THE PHENOMENOLOGY OF SOIL

In keeping with the goetheanistic approach, we should first let the soil impress itself onto our senses before we project our metaphysical and theoretical considerations. What does the soil look like? Is it light or dark? How does it feel? Is it crumbly, gritty, or greasy; does it have a fine or a course texture? How does it smell? Does it have the good, plowed-earth smell? How much life is there in the soil and are there earthworms? Do the weeds look healthy and which weeds grow there?

Usually, when we dig a trench, we notice a profile of soil layers called *soil horizons*. Generally, the top layer is simply loose debris, covering darkly colored crumbly matter. The dark coloration is most often due to carbonaceous, organic matter. This layer is referred to as the *A-horizon*. This zone is most alive with microorganisms and is also referred to as the *edaphon*. The next layer, the *B-horizon*, is lighter in color and contains many suspended and dissolved organic silicate, clay, or iron particles. This is referred to as the zone of eluviation. Below this is usually weathered parent material called the *C-horizon*. It is important to familiarize oneself with the parent material, the bedrock, for this will tell a lot about the soil's needs.

The climate, temperature, rainfall, and topography are as important as the parent bedrock in the formation of the soil, so that only the general, overall characteristics can be given here. Sandstone bedrock will give light,

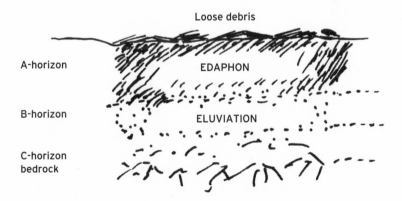

Figure 9.2. Soil horizons

sandy soils that will heat and also cool quickly, have poor water-holding capacity, and poor nutrient-holding capacity. They are well aerated, drain well, and easily worked. These soils readily transmit light and warmth etheric forces, so that carrots, potato tubers, and asparagus will do well in them. They provide a good basis for wine and herb cultures since light and warmth ether are related to quality and aroma. Granite bedrock,[2] a metamorphic-igneous rock, has a differential weathering rate, such that its quartz component weathers slowest, its mica component at a middle rate, and its feldspar component (orthoclase or plagioclase) is weathered the most quickly. The result is that the soluble minerals (Ca, Mg, Na, K) are soon washed out, while Si, Fe, and Al accumulate. This leads to a sandy soil that is acidic and poor in nutrients, especially phosphorus. Limestone bedrock will produce soils rich in Ca, whose structure is usually good and where life and chemical etheric forces (earth and water ether) work to produce good, quantitative yields. Legumes do well on these slightly alkaline soils.

If the parent material is clay, or shale, the derivative soils are heavy, compact, heat and cool slowly, hold much water, and drain badly. Though they are hard to work and slow to get warmed in the spring, they have great potential for fertility, especially if supplied lime and organic matter, for their colloidal structure has a large surface area that can hold nutrient ions. When Steiner indicates that clay is a good transmitter of etheric forces, this should not be confused with poor draining and warming ability; rather it refers to the potential of these soils for good quantitative and qualitative yields. Blue-gray clay indicates poor drainage (iron reduction), red clay indicates better aeration (iron oxidation), and yellow indicates hydration and oxidation of iron.

Humus refers to the organically derived compounds that give the soil a dark to black color due to the carbon contents.

A simple overview of the soil types is provided by the soil quadrant for classifying soils according to their humus, sand, lime, and clay contents:

The closer the soil is to loam, the more each of the four types are represented in the soil, the more ideal it is for good growing conditions.

The *texture* of the soil refers to the coarseness ranging from gravel, to sand (1/50" particles), to silt (1/500–12,000"), to clay (1/12,000" +).

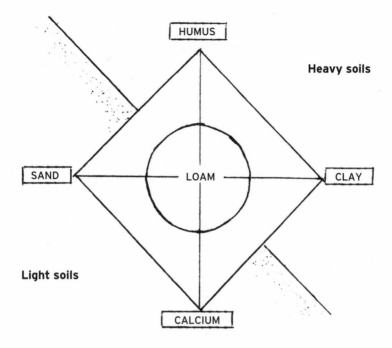

Figure 9.3. Light soils and heavy soils

Structure refers to the friability, crumbliness, tilth, or good heart of the soil. Its opposite is *compaction* and hard-pan. Good structure is indicated when a handful of soil can be molded into a ball and holds its shape until flicked by a finger, causing it to crumble readily. Good structure is due mainly to mycelial growth (the mass of interwoven hyphae of fungi) and the gummy excretions of microorganisms found in humus.

This humus in combination with inorganic colloids (clay-silicate colloids) forms the important *clay-humus complexes* that characterize rich, ripe garden soils. These clay-humus complexes, besides improving the tilth (friability), have the ability to hold on to six times their weight in water, to hold the positively charged *cations* (e.g., Ca, Mg, K, NH_3, Na, etc.)[3] and to buffer the soil against too much acidity or alkalinity. Whereas soil bacteria, humus, calcium, phosphorus, and clay help create this desired structure, or friability, the acid residues of artificial fertilizers in chemical salt form break down soil structure and clay-humus complexes.

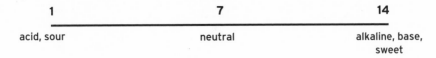

Figure 9.4. pH scale

Deep plowing and heavy machinery have a similar effect in increasing compaction.

Acidity or *alkalinity* or the sweetness or sourness of the soil, is indicated by the pH scale (Percentage Base Saturation), which ranges from 1 to 14.

Soils range from very acid soils of about a pH of 4, which is about the acidity of tomato juice, beer, or grass silage, to a pH of 8, which is about as alkaline as seawater or eggs. Most plants prefer to grow in earth that has a pH of 6 to 7. Humus buffers the soil between 6 and 7. Wet soils are usually sour; they have low base saturation because the bases (Ca, Mg, Na, K, etc.) usually leach out in the rain, leaving an excess number of hydrogen ions that are the indicator of acidity. Sandy soils, peat-moss formations, and the *podsols* of northern, wet climates furnish examples of this happening. In dry climates, as in southern California or Central Asia, for example, where the evaporation rate exceeds precipitation, the opposite happens; alkalinity increases and salts are deposited (as a white sheen) on the surface of the soil. Before indicator tests for pH came about, farmers could tell by looking at the weeds whether a soil was sweet or sour. The presence of sorrel, sour dock, buttercups, tussocks, hawkweeds, horsetails, knotweeds, cinquefoil, and daisies usually indicate acidic soil, whereas alfalfa, sweet clover, bur-dock, colt's foot, chamomile, and others indicate sweet soil.

The application of chemical fertilizer tends to acidify the soils so that the addition of large quantities of lime is concomitant with their use. Humus derived from careful composting, on the other hand, has such a buffering effect so that the organic gardener does not have to worry about the pH at all. Humus and microorganisms buffer the soil by letting excess H ions go when the soil is too acidic and letting Ca ions go when the soil is too base. If, for the sake of a special culture, the gardener wishes to increase the pH, he can sweeten the soil by the addition of ground limestone or dolomite;

or she can make the soil more acidic by adding pine needle mulch, coffee grounds, oak leaf mulch, cottonseed meal, etc.

HOW IS SOIL CREATED?

Soils are created out of the mother substance by the influence of cosmic forces working through fluctuations in climatic rhythms, temperature, rainfall, splitting, and erosion. These forces are usually labeled *mechanical forces*. Secondly, there are chemical forces working in the life and chemical ether such as *hydrolysis*, when water works on feldspar forming clay; *hydration*, where the water combines chemically with other molecules; *oxidation*, where the oxygen combines with such minerals as Fe, Mg, Ti, Cu, etc.; and *carbonation*, where water combines with carbon dioxide to form carbonic acid in which lime, soda, and potash become soluble. Most soil formation is, however, the direct result of *living* organisms working to create the proper living conditions for themselves. Roots and small soil organisms use a number of chemical forces (oxidation, reduction, carbonation) in order to modify the soil, and large roots and burrowing animals often act as mechanical forces.

We are essentially correct in following Rudolf Hauschka and Baron von Herzeele in concluding that wherever there is soil, living organisms have preceded it. When we consider, for example, rocks freshly exposed in a rock quarry: before long, lichens will appear on the bare rock, where they will thrive and spread. How are these plants able to survive these exposed, adverse conditions? From where do they get their nutrients? If we examine the lichen closely, we find two organisms, a fungus and an alga, living in a mutually beneficial association or symbiosis. The alga, containing green chlorophyll, can photosynthesize and create necessary sugars and starches for feeding itself and its partner. The fungus, in turn, provides a leathery covering for the alga that keeps it from drying out; it supplies the necessary minerals and transmits water to it. Where do these minerals come from? The fungus splits them out of the tightly held molecular bonds of the rock structure, dissolves and transfers them from the lithosphere into the biosphere. The lichens are capable of *chelation* (Gr. *chela* = claw, pincher), or of pinching the minerals off from the bare rock. The rock residues and older lichens, as they die off, become debris. The spores of mosses may fall into this proto soil. Mossy pads will form on the rock, assaulting it further with carbonic acids and other excretions. Older generations of mosses will form the substrata for next generations, creating a spongy mass that is able to hold water successfully. Soon, spores of more advanced plants, such as ferns, will find footholds. Gymnosperms and flowering plants will eventually find enough substance to gain a hold, developing strong roots that can crack the rock further. Small animals will now be added, who will supply nutrients to the plants at the same time that they feed on them. Here we have a picture of how soil is formed and can appreciate a miniature recapitulation of plant evolution therein.

A key factor is the chelating ability of plants, especially of the fungi. About 90 percent of the plant species live in a symbiotic relationship with a fungus that is associated with their root network. These root fungi, or *mycorrhizae*, make it possible for the great stands of conifers to find adequate nourishment in very poor soils.[4] Similar to this is the symbiosis between legumes and *rhizobia* that helps bring nitrogen into nitrogen-deficient soils. If artificial nitrogen is supplied to the soil, the rhizobia will not work. We see how plants actively work at creating for themselves the soil they need. Some plants function as accumulators and change the soil in one direction or another, e.g., daisies collect calcium in acid soils, horsetail collects silicon even in silicon-poor soils, orache (genus *Atriplex*) collects salt, etc.[5] When these plants die they will enrich the soil with these elements and change it correspondingly. Through their life activity, by fixing CO_2 and taking in sunlight, the plants penetrate the ground with their root masses and build light and warmth etheric forces into it. They modify the soil by retaining some elements and excreting others. They can do this *against* the diffusion gradient. (A diffusion gradient is defined as the passive transport of particles or molecules across a membrane from regions of higher concentrations to regions of lower concentrations.) The root masses are continuously growing and dying off, constantly adding new organic substance to the soil. However, the roots are not alone in this soil-building process; animal manures with their complex enzymes are constantly modifying the plant growth, and an astronomical number of microorganisms in the edaphon support these living processes.

THE SOIL AS A LIVING ORGAN OF THE EARTH ORGANISM

When we look at the microbial populations that inhabit the soil, we can in no way think of it as just a physical substance that obeys only the laws of inorganic chemistry and mechanical laws. In a teaspoon of good soil, there are literally billions of microorganisms carrying on life functions of continuous metabolism, respiration, reproduction, dying, excreting hormones and enzymes, exchanging cations and anions, responding to cosmic influences such as lunar phases and the daily and yearly solar cycles, and so on. The complexity is so great, the factors are so multifold, that no scientist can hope to completely understand what is going on, no laboratory can study all the interactions simultaneously, and no computer model can simulate them. We see beyond the physical elements into the world of etheric forces when we look into the world of the soil.

Soil organisms have the job of recycling the nutrients, regulating pH, aerating the soil, chelating minerals, and eventually creating the crumbly, good-smelling earth that can support vegetation. Furthermore, they decompose litter by reducing proteins and related substances to NH_4 and NO_3 that can be taken up by growing plants. Some produce sulfates, the only important form of sulfur utilized by higher plants. Some of the autotrophic organisms oxidize iron and magnesium, avoiding toxic buildups in the soil, while still others can fix atmospheric nitrogen.

Soil organisms are somewhat arbitrarily divided into soil flora and soil fauna. We must look at them more closely in order to get a concept of how alive and active the soil is. There are approximately one billion (1,000,000,000) bacteria in a gram of garden soil. A bacterial cell has the ability to produce seventeen million offspring in a day's time, and could produce, theoretically, a mass of protoplasm equal to the weight of the earth in a week's time. *Aerobic bacteria* need free 0_2 for their respiration and are important in rotting and composting processes. *Anaerobic bacteria* can survive in the absence of free oxygen, as in liquid manures, and are important in fermentation. Some bacteria are *autotrophic*, deriving their energy from the oxidation of ammonium, sulfur, iron, and other inorganic minerals, whereas *heterotrophic* bacteria derive their energy from metabolizing organic material by oxidizing carbohydrates, sugars, starches, cellulose, etc.

With the bacteria we are at the bottom of what Sir Howard calls the Wheel of Life; here is the place where destruction, decay, and dissolution of organic substances can come to a halt before they reach total mineralization, and are reintegrated instead once again into the life cycle. Whereas some ammonifiers of the bacterial population break down the proteins into amino acids and ammonia, others (nitrosomonas bacteria) start the buildup cycle by oxidizing ammonia into nitrite (NO_2), which, in turn, is oxidized further by nitrobacter into nitrate (NO_3) at which point the nitrogen is readily assimilated by young seedlings for the eventual rebuilding of protein substances. This fascinating locus, where death and life forces verge on each other, will be studied more closely in chapter 13, "Composts and Liquid Manures."

Soil bacteria work best when there is enough calcium (pH 6–8) available for cation exchange, so that calcium may pull the etheric forces into the ground. Organic matter is needed by heterotrophic populations for food. Soil bacteria are most active on warm, balmy days when the temperature ranges from 70° to 100° F. Their need for water is similar to that of higher plants, i.e., the soil is not soppy wet, but is moist to the touch. Aerobic bacteria need free oxygen, found in pore spaces of the soil, to be effective; in adverse conditions of cold, heat, or drought they will form spores and rest until favorable conditions are restored.

The half-bacteria, half-fungi-like slime molds, or *actinomycetes,* are almost as numerous as bacteria. These microorganisms are involved in later stages of decay, in the humification of organic residues, breaking down complex compounds such as cellulose, chitin, and phospholipids. They are drought tolerant, but need a somewhat high pH (6–7.5), being absent below pH 5. Because one species of actinomycete is involved with the potato scab, potatoes are usually not limed. Their presence is indicated by the good "earth" smell of a freshly plowed field or a freshly dug garden bed. Studies (conducted by soil bacteriologist Selman Waksman) show that they produce antibiotic substances, cleaning the soil of many diseases.

Fungi (mushrooms, molds, yeasts) are very important in the decomposing of organic material and fixing NH_3 and other volatiles into their tissues by ingesting the products of bacterial decomposition. By chelating minerals, the fungi are instrumental in making nutrients available to higher plants. The various *mycorrhizae* (fungi living in symbiosis with root-hairs) extend the rooting system of most plants up to a hundredfold, supplying growth hormones (auxins), aiding phosphorus uptake, and making moisture available. Like actinomycetes, fungi are capable of producing antibiotic substances, such as well-known penicillin and streptomycin, and thus performing the soil's neutralizing function of diseased and putrefied substances. The immense network of fine hairlike mycelia in some species gather together at times to make fruiting bodies that are recognized as mushrooms and toadstools.

When mildews, rusts, molds, and other parasitic fungi become problematic in the fall, especially in the cool, rainy weather when the overall life forces are waning, fine sprays of silicon solution made from waterglass or from horsetail *(Equisetum)* can be of help in the garden. In the spring, these same siliceous substances counter the "dampening off" or root rot of seedlings. Gardeners speak of "dampening off" when the stems of freshly sprouted seedlings die off at the soil line and fall over as a result of lesions caused by a number of fungi.

Various species of one celled, blue-green and yellow *algae* that have the ability to fix sunlight are also present in healthy organic soils. In temperate climates they are, however, of minor importance in comparison to the other soil microorganisms. In the tropics, especially in rice fields, blue-green algae play a more important role since they have the ability to fix N_2.

Roots should be included in the discussion of soil flora, for the rhizosphere (the zone where plants root) is not radically separate from the other life forms in the soil. The rhizosphere harbors most of these organisms. A constant exchange of substances is occurring between the roots and their surroundings. The roots and root hairs, continuously growing and dying, add food to the microorganisms. This is not an inconsiderable amount, either, for studies of rye and oat cover crops show that a single plant can grow three miles of root hairs per day, and up to five thousand miles per season.

The *soil fauna*, ranging from protozoa to arthropods, are less numerous than soil flora, but they are important in the subtle network of chemical exchanges, in allelochemics (the chemical interaction between species), in that they fertilize the soil upon death, and that they churn and aerate the soil. Microbes, amoeba, ciliates, flagellates, and other *protozoa* live in wet films surrounding the soil particles. They are held in check by antibodies produced by the soil flora.

Of the worms, the *nematodes* (threadworms or eelworms) are important in helping to decompose matter and mix the soil as they feed on decaying materials. A few species such as cutworms are predatory on soil fauna. Some species of eelworms are parasitic on higher plants causing "root knot" or "stunt" might be a problem. Root knot occurs when there is not enough organic matter in the soil and the plants are weakened because of it. Rotation of crops, companion planting of French marigolds *(Tagetes),* and compost applications will solve the problem better than fumigation, which is sometimes recommended but which harms other beneficial soil organisms.

Arthropods, such as mites, ants, chafers, and insect larva, and *annelid worms*, such as the earthworms, comprise the larger soil fauna that help aerate the soil and break down decaying vegetation. The earthworm is so important that its name should be spelled in capital letters.

EARTHWORMS

Darwin's last work, in which, as has been facetiously suggested, he tries to make up for the mischief of his evolutionary theory, deals with the earthworm. His research, showing the overwhelming beneficial effects of this unassuming creature, countered unfounded speculation in the nineteenth century about their harmful effects. Gardeners in those days actually gathered the earthworms and night crawlers from the garden beds and fed them to the chickens to get rid of them. Darwin could show that earthworms keep the soil in motion, mixing it vertically and horizontally, creating aeration and drainage. During digestion, they humify organic matter combining it with ingested clay colloids to form worm castings that are composed of clay-humus molecules, or stable humus. Stable humus is characterized by polymerized macromolecules, whose nutrient ions are not washed or leached out by rain, while at the same time possessing an increased water holding capacity. Researchers confirm that worm castings aid the soil-building bacteria and actinomycetes. These castings, produced under normal conditions to the order of twelve tons per acre per year, contain eleven times the potassium, seven times the phosphorus, five times the nitrogen, two and a half times the magnesium, and twice the calcium of the surrounding soil.[7] These nutrients are held in stable form, and they can be easily used by the plants as they need them.

Where does the increase in nutrients in the castings come from? Are they derived from soil and mulch and concentrated by the earthworm, or is there a secret alchemy of transmutation at work? How many sacks of fertilizer would the farmer or gardener have to haul to equal this achievement? Whereas invertebrates excrete calcium into hard exoskeletons, earthworms continuously excrete $CaCO_3$ as slime while they move through the earth, which helps the soil maintain a pH that is within the range preferred by the plants. By regulating the calcium processes, earthworms are instrumental in pulling life forces into the soil. They are able to combine—with the help of calcium—clay colloids with organic residues to form the basis for qualitative and quantitative plant growth.

Tending the earthworm population is as important as tending one's chickens and cows. Earthworms will starve in sterile soils. Organic matter derived from compost, manures, mulch, or tilled-in cover crops are needed to feed them. These helpful creatures appreciate an application of ground limestone or dolomite, but not quicklime that will burn them, and where clay is lacking in the soil, an application of powdered clay. The biodynamic preparation with valerian *(Valeriana officinalis)*, which is made from an infusion of the flowers, will aid earthworm activity when sprayed on the soil. Dandelions as "mother-weeds" or plantings of lettuce will also further them.

HOW TO CARE FOR THE SOIL

It cannot be stressed enough how important the soil organisms are for the organic garden. Animal manures, compost, crop rotations, companion planting, and mulching aid them. They are harmed by excessive plowing, monoculture, burning of fields, and soil sterilization, which reduce their overall number drastically and diminish the number of represented species. Pesticides, herbicides, fumigants, and fungicides are even more drastic in their effects. Chemical fertilizer harms them by changing the osmotic balances and the pH of the soil. Residues of sulfates and chlorides from chemical fertilizers are harmful to them. Reduction of these organisms involves a loss of humus, the collapse of soil structure, which negatively effects nutrition, aeration, temperature, pH, and water-holding capacity. Much of modern agriculture has been concerned with these problems. Soil acidity is dealt with by increased liming, which, if overdone, makes trace minerals (Fe, Mn, B, Zn, Cu) unavailable to the plants and can drive off nitrogen. Soil compaction is handled by building bigger machines for deeper plowing, chiseling the hardpan, or even by adding vermiculite or plastic chips to aerate the soil. Various watering devices deal with lack of water-holding capacity of the soil. A vicious cycle is set in motion by these practices.

For the home garden, establishing permanent *raised beds* that are not compressed by walking on them or running machinery on them helps the microorganisms. An expensive rototiller is not necessary in a home garden. Neither is it necessary to spade the garden bed in such a way that the soil is turned over, for the subsoil is then brought to the top and many microorganisms die due to the shuffling of their niches. The immediate effect is that the minute corpses of demised microorganisms will create a rush of fertilizing. In the long run, such a practice will wear the humus content down. If the soil is in excellent heart, then the *no-diggers* approach of some British gardeners or the mulching approach of Ruth Stout is recommendable. If the soil is not in good shape or one has enough energy and elbow grease, then the *double-dig method* is valuable.

Permanent beds are best four feet wide, for they can be readily reached from the foot-wide paths for easy planting and hoeing. Three-foot-wide beds can be straddled for weeding or planting, but when one considers the number of paths needed, one finds that this is an inefficient use of space—with three-feet wide beds one fourth of the garden space is taken up by paths.

Simply stated, for double digging,[8] the four-foot-wide beds are covered

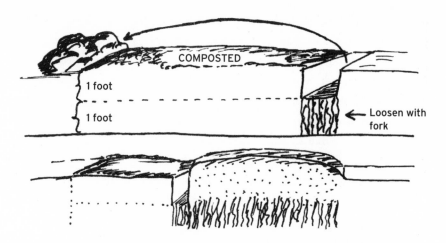

Figure 9.5. Half-finished double dug bed

with compost. Then a trench, one-foot deep, is dug at one end of the bed. The soil from the spade-deep trench is saved; then, with a digging fork, the bottom of the trench is loosened for another foot depth. After that, another spade's width is moved to fill the trench, creating a new trench. This is done without turning the soil, but by simply moving it over. Again, the digging fork will loosen the bottom twelve inches. This work continues until the end of the bed, where the soil from the first trench fills up the last hole. This is hard work, but needs to be done only once or twice in the garden's history because once the soil is aerated and composted, the microorganisms and worms will keep the bed in good heart. The effects of double digging are the enhancement of the activity of the soil organisms, better root respiration, and conservation of water by interrupting the capillary movement of water from one soil molecule to another toward the surface where evaporation occurs.

In the winter, the soil is protected by growing a *cover crop* or by mulching. All living organisms have skins and everywhere in nature the ground is covered by leaf litter in the winter. The gardener will do well if she does likewise, for this will protect the edaphon, and earthworm activity will continue right up to the mulch layer. Earthworms and microorganisms will be fed throughout the winter. In the spring when the mulch is raked away, a fine dark layer of humified mulch, of new humus, will be found on the soil. Cover crops can be sown into cleared beds in early fall. The best combination is a grain and a legume, such as rye or oats, with Austrian pea or vetch. The legume could be inoculated with the spores of rhizobia to increase its ability to fix nitrogen into the soil. The rye or oats, chosen as companion plants, grow an immense root mass, which will fiberize the soil and add much organic matter to it. The roots continue to grow all winter long, except on the coldest of days, for the soil below the surface does not drop radically in temperature. In the spring, when the lush, tender stems and leaves are about eight inches high, the green matter can be turned into the soil to feed the earthworms and to add fiber and organic matter.

Sometimes, however, the mass of green plants covering the soil in the spring can be annoying. For larger fields that are due to be plowed it might be okay. For my garden beds I prefer green manures that are killed off by frosts in the winter and form a natural mulch cover that can easily be raked off, so one can start gardening right away. Such winterkilled green manures include oilseed radish, which also discourages nematodes; buckwheat, which is a good bee pasture; certain vetches and peas, which enrich the soil with nitrogen; and mustard, which can be used also as a vegetable. My favorite is phacelia or scorpionweed, a fast growing delicate plant with beautiful bluish purple flowers loved by honeybees. Phacelia helps loosen the soil with its mass of fine roots, improving soil quality.

By double digging, composting, cover cropping, mulching, and other ecological forms of soil husbandry, the ideal soil composed of 45 percent mineral substance, 5 percent organic matter and 50 percent pore space (25 percent of which are filled with air, and 25 percent with water) will be achieved.

Soil air is important for the respiration of the roots and microorganisms. In compacted soils this air is diminished, the carbon dioxide from the respiration cannot escape, the plants become stunted, and the soil becomes sour (acidic). Soil water is found as *hygroscopic water*, which is held tightly by soil particles or is chemically bound and not available to plants; as *capillary water* or *cohesion water* which fills the pore spaces and makes up the main source of water for the plants; and as *gravitational* or *free water*, which occurs in a saturated soil and is usually drained off. Good humus content will increase the water-holding capacity of the soil by several hundred percent.

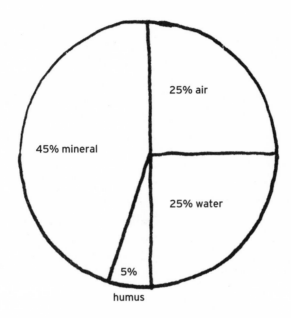

Figure 9.6. Composition of soil

In summary, we can appreciate the concept of the soil as a living organism, as the mother earth, the *prima materia*, ever receptive to the influences of the ordering cosmic forces expressed in the rhythm of seasons, atmospheric conditions and climate. We see that the soil contains a physical aspect in the mineral contents, obeying mechanical and chemical laws; an etheric aspect in the humus and flora, obeying laws of the etheric world; and an astral aspect in the fauna and the manures derived from the higher animals.

Chapter 10

Nutrients and Fertilizer

Fertilizer is no saint, but nonetheless it can work miracles.
—Old gardening proverb

So much emphasis is placed these days on mineral fertilizers that it is easy to forget that there are other important aspects to gardening. It is to the materialistic dogma emerging in the mid-nineteenth century that one must look to find the origin of this fascination with the basic nutrient building blocks. The search for these substances cast shadows on other advances in farming and gardening. Already in 1809, Albrecht Thaer discovered the significance of humus care and crop rotations.[1] It was the theory that nutrient depletion results from the harvesting of crops, as formulated by Justus von Liebig in 1850,[2] that set the ball rolling toward an understanding of the chemical nature of plant nutrition. Liebig's *Law of the Minimum* showed that crops often fail because they are limited by the deficiency of a single nutrient element. One could pour on as much lime, potash, phosphorous compounds, and other nutrients as one would like, but it would help the failing crops little if the deficiency was, for example, nitrogen. The analogy is that of a barrel whose staves are broken at different lengths; the barrel will hold only as much water as the shortest stave permits. In the illustration, the limiting factor would be the nitrogen. The water level of the barrel would be representative of the crop yield.

Following Liebig's theory, the ash contents were examined for percentage and weight of nutrient minerals present; and then the computations were made per acre, or per hectare, regarding how many pounds of

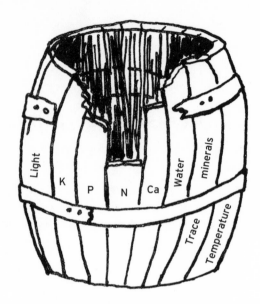

Figure 10.1. Barrel of elements

nutrients are removed from the soil with each harvest and from this, it was calculated how many nutrients would have to be replaced. It turned out to be a herculean task, leading to the fear that humanity would soon starve if the chemical artificials could not be found to replace these nutrients.[3] This gave impetus to the building of chemical fertilizer plants.

At this time, Julius Sachs and Wilhelm Knop pioneered methods of water culture, or hydroponics, in order to get a better understanding of nutrient requirements and enabling them to elicit at what point the deprivation of an element produced characteristic deficiency symptoms in a plant. Their research established that plants need a cluster of elements in the lower range of the periodic table, the so-called *macronutrients* (C, O, H, N, P, S, K, Ca, Mg). This research orientation continued into the twentieth century. Ever more elements were found to be necessary for plant growth, some in the minutest quantity—so minute, in fact, that due to impurities in the growing media, they had escaped the notice of earlier researchers. These *micronutrients*, or trace minerals, include Fe, Mn, Cu, Zn, B, Mo, Na, etc. The number of necessary elements keeps increasing. Recently, for example, it has been discovered that tomatoes need minute traces of silicon. So far, at least sixty elements of the ninety-two natural elements have been found in plants, but there is no indication as to how essential they are.[4] The picture is complicated by the fact that different plant species have different needs. The testing continues; one can imagine that eventually all the elements are going to be considered essential.[5]

Micronutrients are difficult to handle; they cannot be easily put into fertilizer because in excessive amounts they become toxic. Micronutrient availability has become more problematic because livestock have been removed from farms and homesteads, and the manures that contain and recycle these minerals in a biologically assimilable form are not there any more for the soils. Only in isolated instances has the deliberate application of micronutrients been of great value, as in Australia where many acres were made productive by the addition of molybdenum. In most cases, there is danger of overapplication. Deep-rooting hardwood trees will pull trace elements out of the substrata, and make them available in the leaves that are shed in the fall. A compost of deciduous foliage, manures, rinsed seaweed, and fish emulsion is all that is needed to restore all the trace minerals to the garden soil. Organic gardeners do not have to worry about trace minerals at all. Most of them, as Steiner suggests in his *Agricultural Course*, are a free gift of the heavens, supplied by wind and rain. The hydroponic method for

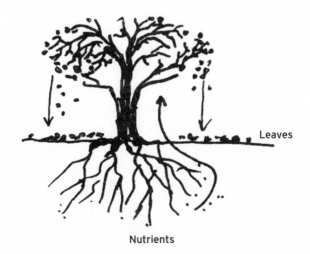

Figure 10.2. Nutrients and leaves

finding out the essentiality of trace minerals must be questioned also, for it is not representative of any garden bed or field.

The crude, materialistic outlook is more difficult to maintain as time goes on. The simple barrel analogy, the Law of the Minimum of Liebig, is not quite correct, for at times plants can substitute other elements for those that are lacking. At times there can be a partial replacement of K by Na, Ca by Sr, Mo by V, Cl, by Br, and probably also others.[6] When there is a good supply of N in the plant, it can take up phosphates and sulfates more easily.[7] The well-known plant physiologist Eilhard A. Mitscherlich (1909) pointed out that an increase in any one of NPK will increase growth, even if one of the macronutrients is deficient. That is, the deficiency symptoms are eased if all the other factors are in order. Aside from all these considerations, however, it is not a matter of simple test tube chemistry. Other factors play a major role: humus level, light intensity, temperatures, water availability, type of plant grown, type of fertilizer, and others. Liebig's experiments were done in exhausted soils where test tube equations work. He himself was one of the first to indicate that the soil is not the equivalent of the test tube or laboratory, and emphasized the need to build humus and use manure.[8] Though he is hailed as the "father" of chemical agriculture, in his later writings (which have been shelved), he warns against chemical fertilizers.

Much of modern agriculture consists of a complicated calculus of suitable fertilizer-combination formulas, soil tests, nutrient-requirement charts of plants, application-timing schedules, and charts on the mixability of fertilizers, distinguishing those which can be mixed and stored and those which must be used right away. Similar formula juggling occurs with pesticides, herbicides, and fungicides, which, as we have seen, follow of necessity in the footsteps of chemical fertilizers. Most gardeners are much impressed with this scientistic jargon. Impressive pseudo-cabbalistic numerology is passed between gardeners: "I've been using 16:16:16," an old neighbor told me. It sounds so scientific and smart.

Indeed, once the soil is lifeless to such a degree that it responds like a laboratory retort, one must resort to such magic. There are many possible mistakes that can be made. For example, most NPK-salts will leave the soil too acidic. Lime is copiously applied to bring up the pH, but this, in turn,

1	2	3	4	5	6	7	8	9	10	11	12	13	#	
	/		/			/	/	/					1	sodium nitrate
/		/	/	/	/	X	/	X	/	/	/	/	2	calcium nitrate
	/					X	X		X	/		/	3	ammonium sulfate
/	/					X	X	/	X	/	/	/	4	calcium ammonium nitrate
	/					X	X		X	/			5	potash ammonia nitrate
	/					/	X		X	/			6	ammonium sulfate
/	X	X	X	X	/			X				/	7	urea
/	/	X	X	X	X			X				/	8	calcium cyanamide
/	X		/			X	X		X	X			9	superphosphate
	/	X	X	X	X			X					10	Albert-slag
/	/	/	/	/				X					11	alkaline phosphate
	/		/										12	magnesium phosphate, potassium sulphate
/	/	/				/	/						13	kainite

☐ = mixable   ☐/ = half mixable   ☒ = not mixable

Figure 10.3. Pseudo cabbalism

makes the trace minerals (Fe, Mn, B, Cu, Zn) unavailable, and can drive N off. Chemical nitrogen fertilizers, when used excessively, cause poor root development (marble potatoes), poor flower and seed formation, ground-water contamination (as is the case in wide stretches of the Middle West, as in Decatur, IL, for example),[9] and accumulations of nitrites in leaf greens. Sulfate of ammonia is acidic; it is water-soluble so it leaches out, kills earthworms and microorganisms, and can damage germinating seeds. Urea can damage germinating seeds and is quickly volatilized. Calcium and sodium nitrate clump together and are hard to handle. Superphosphate ties up iron as insoluble ferric phosphate; it also binds calcium and aluminum. Potassium chloride raises the salt content of the soil. Mixing fertilizers presents a problem; when, for example, lime is mixed with ammonia fertilizers, it drives off the N. Superphosphates should not be mixed with nitrates and chlorides. Antagonisms exist between ammonium and K, Ca, Cu; between nitrate and P, between P and Mn, Zn, Cu; between Ca and P, Mg, etc.[10] The examples of complications can go on; no wonder one needs a college degree to know how to garden!

To study this is interesting, no doubt, but is not actually necessary for successful farming or gardening if the humus is maintained and the soil organisms are allowed to take over some of the workload. When the soil is made alive by the use of composts, manures, and green manures, slow-working mineral meals that can be chelated by soil flora, catch crops that keep nutrients from being leached out, mulching, and other biologically sound means, then there is no need for such chemical juggling. If mineral substances are to be used, they should work, as Steiner suggests, as they do in nature itself.

On the other hand, one cannot be dogmatic about avoiding the use of chemical fertilizer altogether. Even Sir Albert Howard recommended at times the use of "suitable artificials." One must just be very sure of what one is doing. A nitrogen fertilizer, i.e., synthetic urea, might be used in a compost of sawdust to bring the carbon-nitrogen ration closer, to speed up the rotting by supplying the bacteria with the nitrogen they need for their metabolism. Biodynamic researcher Elstrup Rasmussen writes about using limited amounts of superphosphate and potash salts in combination with manures on the sandy podsol (podzol) soils of his biodynamic farm in Denmark, in order to aid the development of legumes.[11] Similar methods were tried in Guatemala, in combination with the Clinico Bernhorst's efforts to achieve an adequate nutritional standard for the Indian population on their poor soils. These supplementary minerals are used in combination with legumes, especially in the warmer climates, and primarily with manures in the colder climates, or, preferably a combination of both. The criterion is always the livening-up of the soils, the improvement in plant quality and animal health. Especially the artificial nitrogen fertilizers are to be avoided.[12]

Just as one may, under special circumstances, use artificial fertilizer, depending on specific conditions, so also, are there times to be cautious about "natural" or "organic" fertilizers. Stockyard manure, created by unhappy, sick animals that are injected with antibiotics, chicken dung from chicken in mass holdings, and sewage sludge from big cities that has accumulations of heavy metals and medicines that people flush down their drains belong to this group.[13] Some natural rock meals that supply P or K might contain fluorides in larger amounts.[14]

In any case it is important to handle fertilizing intelligently, even organic fertilizing. The fertilizer should be tailored to the individual farm-garden organism and its specific needs in regard to climate, soil type, time of year, and kind of crops. The personal relationship to this farm-garden organism must prevail over abstract or generalized schemes of fertilization, be these chemical or natural. It is with correct composting that one cannot go wrong.

THE MAJOR ELEMENTS INVOLVED IN PLANT GROWTH

Most of the bulk of the vegetation is composed of carbon, oxygen, and hydrogen, which make up about 98 percent of plant substance. As important as NPK and other nutrients are, they make up relatively little of the plant. Carbon is derived from the carbon dioxide of the air; oxygen and hydrogen from the water and most, but not all, other nutrients are derived from the soil.

Jan Baptist Van Helmont (1577–1644) conducted the classical experiment of planting a five-pound willow sapling in a basin containing two hundred pounds of soil. For five years he gave it nothing but rainwater. After these five years, the tree weighed 169 pounds; and how much did the soil weigh? It was still nearly two hundred pounds, having lost only two ounces. This should make it clear that there is more to plant growth than juggling various chemicals and that there are important factors of water management and the influence of the formative forces coming from air, light, and warmth involved in the process.

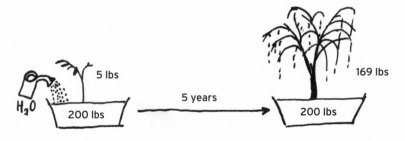

Figure 10.4. Van Helmont's experiment

As discussed elsewhere, the physical elements in the plant can be understood as the anchors for forces that are working upon the planet from various cosmic regions. We have discussed carbon as the anchor for the form-giving forces, oxygen as the anchor for the life-giving forces, nitrogen for the receptiveness of impressions, and hydrogen for the force that takes life forms out of manifestation. In the same light we can see all the rest of the elements as transmitters of forces of one kind or another.

Generally, in plants, the order of the amounts of elements present in a scale from the most prominent to the least goes from carbon to oxygen to hydrogen. At much smaller frequency are found nitrogen, then potassium, then calcium, magnesium, phosphorus, silicon, and so on to some sixty elements. This order of representation is not a passive mirror of the soils, which are composed of oxygen as the most frequent element, followed by silicon, aluminum, and so on.

In biodynamics, *silicon* (SiO2, quartz), which in orthodox agriculture is barely considered, is understood as a transmitter of forces of warmth and light.[15] Silicon helps plants ray into themselves these important formative forces, creating quality, aroma, and flavor. Because of this ability, it counteracts fungal diseases, which are related to cool, moist weather and to excessive nitrogen concentrations that increase the water contents in the leafy tissue.

Silicon is present in nearly all plants, but especially in the grains and grasses, found mainly in the sheaf and spelt. It makes straw stiffer, so that it does not lay down in a thunderstorm; it makes it more difficult for pests, aphids, and fungi to penetrate the tissues.[16] Silicon, which makes up 48 percent of the earth's crust, is not highly reactive in its inorganic state as quartz; Steiner calls this element "an aloof gentleman." It must find its way into organic compounds in the form of silicic acid (H_4SiO_4) to work organically. Silicon effectiveness can be increased by the biodynamic cow horn preparation (501), in which mountain quartz crystals are pulverized and buried in the ground over the summer in a cow's horn so that microbial activity works on the silicon. This, finely diluted, is sprayed on the foliage of maturing, flowering, fruiting, and seeding plants to increase the quality. Studies show that NPK fertilizers create an effect similar to that of plants grown under moist, shady conditions, whereas silica preparations increase the effectiveness of warmth and light.[17] Silica-rich water glass (sodium silicate) solutions (2 percent) and horsetail tea *(Equisetum arvense)*, sprayed on plants, are effective against mildew and aphids. Quartz sand sown with carrots and other members of the *umbelliferae* family increases the light-absorption of these plants, creating better quality.

Whereas silicon works with the imponderables of light and warmth, *calcium* works more with the ponderables. Contrary to silicon, it is highly biochemically reactive and involved in soil and plant metabolism. Lime furthers soil bacteria, especially nitrogen-fixing bacteria in legumes. It aids soil structure, opening up heavy, clay soils; it neutralizes excess acid, balances potassium and sodium in plant sap, thus decreasing viscosity. It also works as a mediator of cosmic forces originating in the sub solar planets. One can lime too much, driving off the nitrogen and locking up many trace minerals. For this reason, quicklime should be avoided; ground limestone and ground dolomite is preferable. Dolomite contains *magnesium*, which is essential in chlorophyll development and activates a number of enzymes. All plants need magnesium and fruit trees, tomatoes, and vegetables growing in sandy or peaty soils need a lot.

If sulfur is needed, *gypsum* (calcium sulfate) can be applied. Usually sulfur does not pose a deficiency problem, as in industrial areas the rainfall usually brings it in plenty of it. Traces of sulfur are needed for vitamin synthesis and in some amino acids. Of course sulfur causes an acid reaction, with the sulfur turning into sulfuric acid. That is one of the reasons to be careful with putting the sulfur containing ashes of anthracite coal into the compost or on the garden beds. On the other hand, on alkaline soils, as found in the arid Southwest, this effect is welcomed. In compost, gypsum favors the fungi but decreases the cellulose-digesting bacteria.

Any mineral substances that are needed in the garden are best worked sparingly into the compost instead of dumped directly onto the soil. In the compost the microorganisms can work on them and tie them into the structure of the humus molecules.

Biodynamic farmers and gardeners are more interested in processes and forces than in the substances themselves and have developed their herbal preparations as guidance for these processes. The yarrow preparation harmonizes sulfur metabolism, the oak bark and chamomile preparations guide calcium processes. (See chapter 17, "Teas, Preparations, and Biotic Substances"). These special preparations are also added to the composts.

THE MAGNIFICENT THREE: NPK

Our attention now turns to nitrogen, phosphorus, and potassium, the NPK of the commercial fertilizer formula. In the generalized plant, the *phosphorus* works mainly in the fruit and flower development; *nitrogen* works on leaf development, as seen in its effect on greens and spinach; and *potassium* works on the roots.

Nitrogen, as one of the major plant "foods," is always best applied in organic form from manures, composts, cover crops, and possibly feather-, horn- and hoof-meal, and fish scraps. Both liquid manure and solid manure of animals contain large amounts of nitrogen.[18] Liquid manure should be fermented in vats or storage tanks that are stirred once in a while to supply the liquid with oxygen and it should be treated with nettles, B-D preparations, old compost, or compost starter to stabilize it. (See Composts and

Figure 10.5. NPK in the plant

Liquid Manures.) Legumes, inoculated with the spores of nitrogen-fixing bacteria before sowing, and grown as cover crops or fallows, increase the nitrogen supply.[19] These nitrogen-fixing bacteria can accomplish this task at ordinary pressures and temperatures, compared to the one-thousand-pound pressure and the six thousand calories needed per kilo of nitrogen fixed by industrial processes.[20] Sewage sludge might work as a nitrogen source on individual farmsteads or in rural China, but in a mass consumer societies the sludge has too many toxic residues.

Plants that are tough, spindly, and have older leaves turning yellow and dropping off indicate a lack of nitrogen. Excessive nitrogen is shown by rank, lush, green growth of the foliage and stems, but poor root and flower/seed development. Aphids, insects, and fungi appear, as if wanting to soak up the excess nitrogen. Cows do not like fodder grown under these conditions.

Phosphorus, needed for good flower, seed, and fruit development and sugar metabolism, is best derived from powdered rock phosphate or colloidal phosphate, both of which are added to the compost where organic acids and chelates break it down into forms usable by plants. Chicken and other bird manures are good phosphorus sources. Lupine and vetch used as mulch or cover crops gather P. Bonemeal is a good source of P, and the bones chewed by one's dog or from the soup kettle can be burned in the fireplace, then pulverized and added to the compost. The biodynamic preparation 507, made from the juice of valerian flowers, helps soil and compost regulate the phosphorus metabolism.

Lack of phosphorus becomes evident when plants will not mature, show reddish-purple discoloration on leaf veins and stems, and have defective seeds. In corn, or maize, this is indicated by irregular rows of kernels. In tomatoes, the underside of the leaves turns purple.

A nice little vignette about the transfer of phosphorus in nature appeared a long time ago in a Hartford newspaper:

For the purpose of erecting a suitable monument in memory of Roger Williams, the founder of Rhode Island, people searched private burying ground for the graves of himself and his wife. Everything had passed into oblivion. The shape of the coffins could only be traced by a black line of carbonaceous matter. The rusted hinges and nails, and a round wooden knot alone remained in one grave, while a single lock of braided hair was found in the other. Near the graves stood an apple tree. This had sent down two main roots into the very presence of the coffined dead. The larger root, pushing its way to the precise spot occupied by the skull of Roger Williams, had made a turn as if passing around it, and followed the direction of the backbone to the hips. Here, it divided into two branches, sending one along each leg to the heel, when both turned upward to the toes. One of these roots formed a slight crook at the knee, which made the whole bear a striking resemblance to the human form. There were the graves, but their occupants had disappeared; the bones even had vanished. There stood the thief, the guilty apple tree, caught in the act of robbery. The spoliation was complete. The organic matter, the flesh, the bones, of Roger Williams, had passed into an apple tree. The elements had been absorbed by the roots, transmuted into woody fiber, bloomed into fragrant blossoms—and more than that had been converted into a luscious fruit, which from year to year had been gathered and eaten. How pertinent then is the question: Who ate Roger Williams?

Potash, or potassium, needed mainly for good root development, is found in greensand (glauconite), which also contains Fe, Si, Ca, P, and trace minerals; in granite dust; in wood ash, especially from hardwoods; in pig manure; in seaweed, bracken, fern, vetch, and alfalfa used as mulch or compost. The biodynamic dandelion preparation (number 504 as described on page 274) helps regulate the potassium processes in compost and soil.

Lack of sufficient potash is indicated by the edges and tips of leaves looking dried and scorched and by stunted plants. Nubbin corn, fruits that are soft and ripen unevenly, carrot leaves that curl, and beetroots that taper are examples of potassium lack. Sufficient K is needed to ward off root-infecting organisms.

In concluding this chapter on mineral fertilizing, we can say the main concern is to make the soil as alive as possible. It takes compost, animal manures, and legume cover crops to do this. To this are added minerals with low solubility: basalt flour, greensand, dolomite, rock-phosphate, and other "conditioners" and natural fertilizers, which can be made available by microorganisms. A careful study of one's soil and crops will indicate when, what, and where these should be applied. Each farm and garden, each crop, climate, and time of year has different requirements. For this reason a soil test from a soil test kit or the agricultural extension agent is only an indicator. In a gram of living soil there are thousands of simultaneous chemical reactions occurring in fractions of seconds. This is enough to indicate that no fixed statements can be made. The nitrogen content is lower in the spring than in the summer, and in the morning than later in the day. Phosphorous and other elements fluctuate during the course of the year in living soils. Soil tests are more important on lifeless soils than they are on soils with good structure. Simple tests can be made by growing cress seeds *(Lepidium sativum)* in pots containing the soils and composts to be tested and by observing germination speed, growth pattern, and general appearance of the plant on a comparative basis.

Chapter 11

Cosmic Influences

Nothing exists nor happens in the visible sky that is not sensed
in some hidden moment by the faculties of Earth and Nature.
—Johannes Kepler (1571–1630) *De Stella Nova*

To assume that what comes to pass in the wide expanses that surround
planet Earth has little or no effect on the life of the earth is the legacy
of the worldview that described planets solely as dead physical matter held
in orbit by purely mechanical forces and held that the stars, as infinitely
distant suns, could not possibly transmit anything across the vacuum of
space. This legacy is still a cornerstone in the thought of such laboratory
scientists as the majority of biologists who work on "biological clocks."
They claim that these clocks only appear to be affected by cosmic rhythms
but try to show in laboratory test cases that they are endogenous, adaptive
mechanisms intrinsic to the biochemistry of some species. The chemical
base or the mechanism of the clock itself has, as yet, not been isolated.
Apart from mechanical, photoenergetic influences derived from the sun
and moon, our planet appears to be a hermetically sealed space capsule
run by intrinsic machinery.

In contrast to this kind of thinking, the sages of all the peasant and
gardening societies have never doubted the influences of forces stemming
from the cosmos, which control the seasons and influence plant, animal,
and man alike. These influences were not seen as mere mechanical forces,
but experienced as powerful, personified beings that could be appealed to
and dealt with in various ways. All these peoples employed calendar makers

and specialists, who were able to interpret seasons and celestial events.[1] In this way, the ecologically appropriate action could be taken when the signs were right. The Tukano of Brazil, for example, know that when the Pleiades dip below the horizon in the evening after sunset, it is time to plant the crops just in time for the seasonal rains. When Sirius started to appear on the horizon just before sunrise, it was time for the fertile midsummer flood of the Nile Valley marking the start of ancient Egypt's agricultural year. The European peasant rules for sowing, planting, harvesting, animal husbandry, and herb gathering, many going back to ancient Babylonian, Chaldean, and Egyptian sources, are of the same order. The Romans Pliny the Elder (23 AD) and Virgil (70–19 BC) record agricultural rules relating to astronomical phenomena. The countless sky, moon, and sun deities of tribes and nations throughout the ages, each demanding certain taboos, rituals, feasts, and proscriptions, are considered by current anthropologists not so much superstitions, but as functional ways of adapting to specific environments.

In the West, with the change of calendar and the influence of the Enlightenment, the planetary gods were shorn of their powers and dethroned. Only the most backward peasants clung stubbornly to a tradition, which degenerated into superstition and eventually lost its empirical base. What was at one time a functional belief system came in time to be relegated to the velvety parlors of "official" occultists, esoteric mystics, and astrologers. It was safely relegated to those with a leaning toward mystery and the obscure, whose nerve had failed them in the "brave new world." As the crisis of modern culture deepens, more people are drawn to these topics, while at the same time, there lingers in the mind of some farmers and gardeners the feeling that there must be more to the plant and animal world than is taught in agricultural extension courses. Our current situation finds a revitalized interest in the beliefs of astrology and moon-sign planting.[2] One need not merely believe in astrology or intuitively follow archaic tradition to benefit, because clear evidence is accumulating quickly that the earth is not a sealed mechanism, a "spaceship" as Buckminster Fuller called it, running its course, but an organism that is open and responsive to the influences streaming in from the cosmos.

BASIC GEOCENTRIC ASTRONOMY

A distinction must be made at this point between *astrology* and *astronomy*. Astrology, as used by those who cast horoscopes, is a belief system that is based on the way the planetary motions and the equinox appeared about two thousand years ago. Most astrologers never look at the sky but consult ancient charts to work out their horoscopes.[3] Astronomy is concerned with what the sun, moon, and planets are doing at this point in time in relation to the constellations of the fixed stars. Whereas academic astronomy takes a *heliocentric* perspective, taking the sun as the center of its model with the earth and the planets orbiting about this glowing star, we prefer here to use a *geocentric* perspective. After all, we live on the earth and not on the sun. Whereas a heliocentric conception might be easy to think abstractly, the geocentric is available direct to our senses. Likewise, the plants in our gardens experience the cosmic forces from a geocentric perspective as they stream from above into the atmosphere. As they spread their light-sensitive organs, the leaves, like antenna to receive the luminous vibrations emanating from above, they certainly do not experience the sun heliocentrically.

Geocentrically, we have our feet firmly planted on the ground. Our garden becomes the center of the universe. When we look up into the sky, we perceive the overawing cosmic rhythms of day and night. The sun lights up the day, rising in the east and setting in the west. In the yearly cycle the sun has its lowest stand on the shortest day, at winter solstice when it finds itself in the constellation of Sagittarius ♐; it has its highest stand on the longest day, at summer solstice when it finds itself in the constellation of Gemini ♊. In between these points there are days when day and night are of equal length, the spring and fall equinox. These four points mark the *cardinal points* of the year, which are celebrated by feasts and rituals in nearly all societies.[4] The cycle of vegetation, animal migration, and rutting seasons, the seasons of sprouting, growing, flowering, fruiting, and dormancy are synchronized with this overall yearly cycle.

The nighttime sky contains the visible stars and planets. Following the Greek geocentric tradition, we include the sun ☉ and moon ☾ among the seven visible planets. The planets (Gr. *planetes* = wanderers) move fairly much along the same plane as the path of the sun, the *ecliptic*. Their

PLANETS

☿	Mercury
♂	Mars
♀	Venus
♃	Jupiter
♆	Neptune
♅	Uranus
♇	Pluto

Figure 11.1. Cosmic influences

movement along this plane can be clockwise (retrograde) or counterclock-wise (direct). The movement occurs against a background of *fixed stars*. This ribbon of fixed stars is divided into twelve regions, each 30° wide, which make up the "animal circle" or *zodiac*. The whole heavenly vault moves in clockwise motion, so that we can talk about the rising and setting of the stars as a whole.

A picture of this would be a clock and, indeed, the clock is an abstrac-tion of the basic movements of the sun (big hand) and the moon (little hand) through twelve hours (signs of the zodiac). The great cosmic clock includes not just two hands (sun and moon), but also Mercury ☿ and Venus ♀ that are always moving near the sun and thus appear as the morning or evening stars. The clock includes the distant planets, Mars ♂, Jupiter ♃, and Saturn ♄. Each of these is moving at its own speed relative to the zodiac. Sometimes the planets Mercury, Venus, Mars, Jupiter, and Saturn reverse their movement and move backwards (in retrograde). It takes the sun a year to go through the zodiac and return to the spring point at equinox, which is in Pisces ♓.[5] The moon is, of course, much faster and completes the journey around the zodiac in twenty-eight days (precisely in 27.32 days); Mercury swiftly runs its course in eighty-eight days. Venus needs 225 days. Mars has a sidereal period of nearly two years; Jupiter, approximately twelve years;[6] and the old man Saturn requires nearly thirty years to journey around the zodiac. If we imagine the clock with these seven hands, moving backward and forward against the zodiac positions, we must also imagine the entire clock itself revolving in a daily motion from east to west. (Medieval scholars called this the *Revolutionibus Orbitum Coelestrium.*)

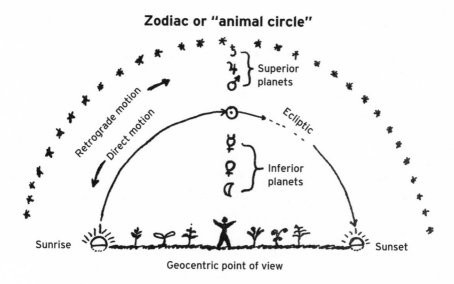

Figure 11.2. Geocentric point of view

This by no means exhausts the movements that occur in the visible sky. The moon has other rhythms than the *sidereal* or *sideric rhythm*, which marks the 27.32166-day cyclical (twenty-seven days, seven hours, forty-three minutes) journey to the same place (sign) in the zodiac. Most obvious to the sky-watcher are the four *lunar phases* or quarters of the moon, the *synodic month*, alternating between conjunctions with the sun (new moon) and opposition to the sun (full moon). The first quarter, the new moon, or waxing crescent moon, gives way to the second quarter, or gibbous waxing moon, which is followed by the third quarter or waning gibbous moon and, finally, by the fourth quarter, or waning crescent moon. This cycle lasts about 29.531 days (twenty-nine days, twelve hours, forty-four minutes). When looking at the moon, one can tell if it is waxing or waning in the

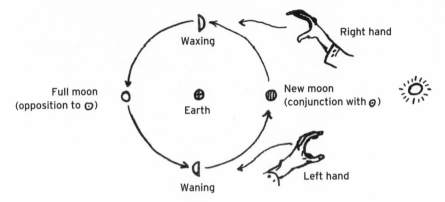

Figure 11.3. Curvature of the waxing and waning moon

following way: if the curvature looks like that of the right hand, it is a waxing moon and if it looks like the left hand, it is a waning moon.

Another lunar cycle is the *anomalistic month,* where the moon alternates between *perigee* ◑, closest to the earth, and *apogee* ◐, farthest from the earth. The elliptical orbit around the earth involving a distance variation of 40,000 km or 16,000 miles causes this cycle of 27.555 days.

The *draconic* or *nodular month,* or lunar nodes, caused by the moon's wobbling about 5° above and below the sun's path (ecliptic), is a cycle of 27.555 days. When the moon dips below the ecliptic one speaks of the moon's *descending node,* or *dragon's tail* ☋. When the moon rises above the sun's path, one has the *ascending node,* or *dragon's head* ☊. It is at these nodes that a sun or a moon eclipse is possible.

A fifth lunar rhythm is the *tropical month,* lasting about 27.32158 days. Just as the sun in its yearly cycle has a northern and a southern tropic, its lowest and its highest point on the horizon, so, also, does the moon, except that it does not take a year but only 27 days. In almanacs this is referred to as the moon's *descension* and *ascension* (please see illustrations of symbols). These points usually occur in the sign of Scorpio-Sagittarius and Taurus-Gemini.

As one can see, these varying lunar periodicities make for a complicated astronomy. The rhythms are close, but not synchronized. Just for two rhythms to get back in step, the synodic and the sidereal moon, for example, takes eighteen years and seven and one-half months. The rhythms that we reckoned for the moon can be described for the other planets also. For example, one of the Mayan calendars was based on the phases of Venus.

The complexity of these rhythms *in toto* has the result that the conditions of the heavens are never exactly the same. They are always somewhat different, although their orbits and cycles are orderly. We see then, that the analogy of a clock is not quite justified, for in the clock we have a finite system, where events are repeatable, whereas in cosmic conditions we have an infinite system. The heavens never go back to an exact original starting point, a fact that makes a perfectly accurate calendar impossible. This makes the analogy of an organism with its rhythmic life much more appropriate.

For scientists, research on lunar and planetary effects becomes a hot iron, since the factors are innumerable and no experiment is exactly repeatable. One cannot say to the moon: "Wait a minute, could you repeat this?" or say to the planets: "You are insignificant variables; we will not consider you in this experiment." It is safer for such a scientist to infer an endogenous system of biological clocks and intrinsic mechanisms to explain plant and animal life, while considering the whole cosmos an "irrelevant variable!" However, evidence points in other directions: to those that indicate cosmic influences. The farmer and the gardener can be assured that when he plants his crops in the right seasons and in the right signs and phases, that there is something to it.

DIMENSIONS OF TIME AND SPACE

All of life is rhythm and pulse. Death is the cessation of rhythm. The rhythms of living plant and animal organisms are in synchronicity with, or permutations of, cosmic rhythms. These living pulsations, be they circadian, monthly, annual, four-year, eight-year, nine-year, or other cycles, all have some cosmic counterpart. In plants and in lower animals these rhythms are in direct phase with the cosmic phenomena, whereas in the higher animals these rhythms are obscured by the fact that internalized rhythms and impulses are provided by the inner cosmos of the inner organs and endocrine system.

The rhythms of life (growth, petal movement, assimilation, etc.) are expressed as manifestations and de-manifestations in material space.

Organic forms, but also some inorganic forms such as crystals, are images of cosmic form giving forces sculpted into matter. Flowers and leaf nodes show spiral relations that are mathematically equivalent to the ratios of the movement of planets as seen from a geocentric point of view. Organic forms, such as spirals, vortices, radial symmetry, bilateral symmetry, and the combinations and allometric permutations thereof, are archetypal, hinting at sympathy with planetary orbits, galactic whorls, lunar phases, and other cosmic occurrences.

Given these analogies of rhythm (time) and form (space configurations), one can postulate a connection of some sort between organic life and cosmic influences. The connection could be one of causality, in which the cosmic force causes the organism's response. It is easy to imagine how organisms, in their life functions, can vibrate with the wide range of electromagnetic energy that constantly bombards this planet from outer space. Such energy reaches from the extremely short gamma and X-rays, through the ultraviolet, the visible spectrum, the infrared to the long radio waves. We see the effect of lunar gravity on water, causing the tidal behavior of seashore fauna; and the plants with their green tissue are photo-receptive like our retinas, monitoring the instreaming visible light from the cosmos.

On the other hand, the relation between the cosmic phenomena and the terrestrial counterpart might not be one of causality, but might be one of *synchronicity*, both of them the expression of a deeper-lying archetypal factor.[7] Time and space have been separated analytically in Western thought. In some other cultures, as for example as among the Hopis,[8] such distinctions are not made. For them, each time has its space and each space has its own time. Though time and space are principally connected manifestations, we will treat them separately in our discussion of cosmic influences.

TIME AND COSMIC RHYTHMS

The most common and simplest rhythm is the daily (*circadian*, after Franz Halberg, 1960) movement of the sun (solar day) or the revolution of the heavenly vault (sidereal day). This rhythm profoundly affects all life, including one-celled organisms. It includes the daily opening and closing of flower petals, and the movement of leaves in some plants, such as

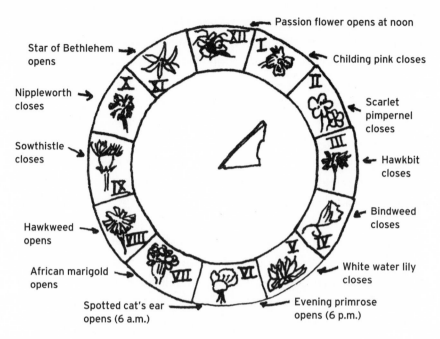

Figure 11.4. Flower clock.

the bean, into nightly vertical sleep positions and horizontal day positions. These daily rhythms are so accurate that, in the eighteenth and nineteenth centuries, flower clocks were planted in gardens where it was possible to tell time by the opening and closing of the petals.

Günther Wachsmuth describes the daily bipolar rhythm in plants. A period of concentration around 3:00 a.m., characterized by maximum cell division, auxin (plant hormone) production, starch accumulation in the roots below and a minimum of sap excretion, gives way in the morning to the opening of leaves into the daytime position with increases in assimilation, respiration, secretion and sap flow. In the afternoon at 3:00 p.m., there is maximum glucose production and cell elongation, which gives way in the evening to starch accumulation in the roots after the plants assume sleeping positions.[10]

A ten-year study by Frank A. Brown Jr. of Northwestern University shows a daily metabolic cycle in potatoes.[11] Brown shows that there is peak metabolic activity in potatoes at sunrise, at noon, and in the evening. This cycle follows yearly fluctuations: while in January the noon peak is the greatest, at mid-year it is less significant, and in the fall, the morning peak is the greatest. "The metabolic pattern varies systematically with the celestial longitude of the earth as it makes its annual journey around the sun."[12] He concludes that geomagnetic and electromagnetic forces seem to be at work, which are, of course, affected by the planets. Other studies show time awareness in cockroaches, which scavenge at night, and in fruit flies, which hatch only in the early morning hours when moisture (dew) exists. Even human beings show circadian rhythms, which are upset when a jet trip crosses time zones.[13]

Lunar rhythms, which work mainly through water, are effective in all organisms.[14] Most organisms are composed mainly of water, and all organisms go through an amorphous zygote stage, in which these forces can be especially influential. Instruments have been developed that are so sensitive that they can measure lunar tides in a teacup. Researchers find that it is harder to sterilize water during the full moon. Pliny the Elder writes in his *Natural History* that it is best to sell fruits picked before the full moon because they will be plumb full of water, but for one's own use, it is wise to pick around the new moon period for they will keep better. He states that it is best to castrate animals or prune trees during the new moon to avoid excessive bleeding. Modern scientists find this to be true also.

Frank Brown, in a study on fiddler crabs, finds that besides the diurnal cycle of color change, a lunar rhythm of 12.4 hours, timed exactly to the lunar tides. Oysters, which open their shells at high tide and close them at low tide, when transported from the East Coast to Evanston, Illinois, changed their rhythms to what the tides would be there, if the seashore were in Illinois.

Lunar rhythms are especially evident in the lower animals, particularly in the reproductive cycle. The timing of these animals is sometimes awesome. The grunion, or smelt, of California, ride the last flood tide wave onto shore to deposit eggs and sperm in the sand and ride the first ebb tide wave back out into the sea. Two weeks later, the next tide that is equally high, is the exact moment when, at the crest of the tide, the larvae hatch to be swept out into the sea. Similarly dramatically, the female palolo worms living in the coral reefs of the South Pacific rise to the ocean surface at an exact time at dawn when the moon reaches its last quarter in November, where their egg-laden tails break off and float. Immediately all the males rise to the surface where their sperm-containing hindquarters also break off.

In relation to fertility, Eugene Jonas of the Czech Republic found that in the human female the ability to conceive coincides with the lunar phase when she was born. From this insight, a non-chemical birth control method was developed, which is claimed to be 98 percent effective.[15] Weather, rainfall cycles, barometric pressure, changes in the magnetic field, and other phenomena have been correlated with the moon. Police officers, bartenders, and caretakers of mental patients also tell of the effects of the moon on the human psyche.

Planets are the source of powerful radio waves, and each planet leaves in its wake a tail of electromagnetic disturbances. We can easily assume that the planets, other than the moon and sun, have an effect on the earth. One such effect is the eleven-year sunspot cycle first observed by Sir William Herschel (1801). Sunspots occur when planets are in conjunction or opposition to the sun, that is, when they form one gravitational arc that has an uneven pull on the corona of the sun. The effects include more icebergs afloat off of Iceland, good vintage years for Bordeaux, drought patterns in India, the shift of flowering dates of some plants, earthquakes, and others. There are thirty-five and eighty-five-year rhythms superimposed on this eleven-year cycle.[16] An eight-year precipitation cycle has been related to Venus. In his laboratory at Dornach, Switzerland (1971), George Unger, using the drop-method investigation of fluids developed to indicate water quality, showed the effects of the constellations on water. Measured quantities of fluids to be tested are dropped into glycerin, creating characteristic drop patterns. The glycerin is so sensitive that the characteristic drop patterns are disturbed slightly when conjunctions and oppositions occur.[17]

Joachim Schulz made an interesting observation in his investigations of beechnut harvests. Beech trees bear heavily about every six to eight years, according to records kept since 1799. The irregular quantity of the harvests is not dependent only on the climate and weather, since the whole species in various locations bears well during good years despite climate variations. This seemed to be random behavior. In the years 1948 to 1951, Schulz was able to correlate the harvest patterns with Jupiter, Mars, and Saturn positions in various constellations. The trees bear fruit when these three planets are in a trigonal position (120°) to each other, as seen from the Earth perspective. He set up probable harvest predictions on this basis up to the year 1985. Gerhard Wolber and Susanne Vetter reinvestigated this in 1971 and found the predictions verified.[18] Other investigations on planetary influences by Lilli and Eugene Kolisko show that the crystallization of certain salts in the laboratory is affected by the positions of the planets.[19]

The growth rhythms of the various plant families correspond to the sidereal rhythms of the planets. The rapidly growing herbaceous annuals are linked with the fast moving sub-solar, or nearer, planets. This places most monocots under the influence of the moon and Mercury, and the dicot herbs with Venus and the sun. Biennials and shrubs are related to the two-year rhythm of Mars, perennial herbs and hardwoods to the twelve-year cycle of Jupiter, and most of the conifers to the long-enduring cycle of Saturn.[20]

Sidereal cycle	28 days	88 days	225 days	1 year	2 years	12 years	30 years
Planets	☾	☿	♀	☉	♂	♃	♄
Plants	Monocots	Annual	Dicots		Biennials		Perennials

Figure 11.5. Sidereal cycles and plants

The preceding might seem to be somewhat simplistic, analogical thinking, but, in keeping with the goetheanistic approach, we will make note of such analogies of simultaneously appearing phenomena before jumping to conclusions. Here we are perhaps not dealing with the law of causality, but with the law of synchronicity or significant coincidence. In the next section on plant forms, other factors will become evident, which show that the correlations indicated are perhaps not quite as arbitrary as they at first appear. We are only touching on the subject of rhythms and their correlation with cosmic phenomena here. There are undoubtedly other rhythms, ranging from cycles of glaciation (250,000 years) to very short-term rhythms occurring within organs or cells, which can be correlated in frequency curves with various short wave patterns derived from the cosmos.

It is the studying and understanding of such rhythms in their relation to the etheric formative forces that underlies the rhythmic preparation of homeopathic medicines, and of the stirring of liquid manures and biodynamic preparations.

FORMS AND SHAPES

All life is rhythm (energy) and matter is temporarily frozen energy. The archetypal patterns of organisms indicate rhythmic movements that have temporarily taken on physical form and substance. Formative forces are indicated by crystal formations in frost flowers, snow flakes, tension lines in cooling liquids, hexagonal honeycombs, and others which Steiner indicated as vector lines originating in the region of the earth-distant planets. Hard as it may be to prove by conventional means, it is certainly a probability that can be visualized by means of projective geometry.[21] These straight hard linear forces, originating in outer space and working through the earth into crystal formation, are akin to the "earth" etheric forces. The formative forces of "water" and "air" express themselves in flow patterns, spirals, and vortices. They are seen in whirling galaxies, cloud formations as photographed from space satellites, wind and ocean currents, whirlpools, snail shells, the hair whorl on the back of the head (cowlick), the calyx of flowers such as the morning glory, the spiral placement of leaf and bud around the stem, seed placement as in sunflowers, all the way to the double-helix spiral of the minute DNA molecule.

Water and air etheric forces reveal themselves in concentric rings found from the rings of Saturn, to tree rings, to water disturbed by a thrown pebble, and equally archetypal are reflections and bipolarities found in higher organisms and in magnetic fields. Another form of primal energy is seen in the raying, outpouring energy as that of the raying sun, the primitive radiolarians and other and other planktons, the radial symmetry of horsetails (*Equisetum*) and other primitive plants. Such archetypal forms and patterns are found in the whole range of nature, from the telescopic to the microscopic universes.[22]

Leaf arrangements (phyllotaxis) occur in opposites (one-half around the stem to the next leaf), in thirds (one third around the stem to the next leaf), or in spirals of two-fifths, as in blackberries where one has to go twice around the stem to arrive at the fifth leaf directly above the first one. Other species have ratios of 3/8, 5/13, 8/21, 13/34 and so on.

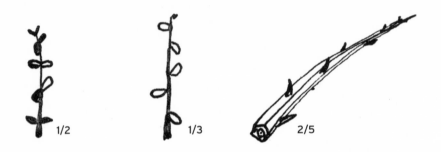

Figure 11.6. Examples of phyllotaxis (leaf arrangement)

Similarly, the flower petal arrangement and seed placement patterns of such plants as the composites (like the flower of the sunflower) reveal spirals that intersect clockwise and counter-clockwise, according to the above-mentioned ratios. These ratios are not random but form a mathematical progression that was discovered by the Renaissance mathematician Leonardo da Pisa, also know as Fibonacci, after whom this *Fibonacci sequence* is named.[23] A further point of interest is that the ratio between any two numbers in the series (after the third) approaches that of the *Golden Ratio*, or Golden Section (1:618).[24] The existence of the Fibonacci sequence in the arrangement of leaf and flower spirals indicates well enough how "God ever geometrizes" (Plato), but the astronomer Joachim Schulz has pointed out that this sequence is also found in the movement patterns of the visible planets as perceived geocentrically.[25]

The force of the sun pulls the vegetation upward (heliotropism), giving it the vertical tendency. Just as the planets move in and out of conjunction with the sun and cross the ecliptic above and below, so do the buds, leaves, and flowers move about the vertical stem of the plant, mirroring the mathematical relationships that hold sway in planetary movement. Schulz tries to show the opposition and twofold symmetry in plants relates to the moon, which alternates from full moon to new moon. The path of Mercury reveals three loops (retrogressions) and six yearly conjunctions with the sun, three above and three below the ecliptic. Moon and Mercury symmetries are found permeating the world of the monocots, the lilies and grasses.

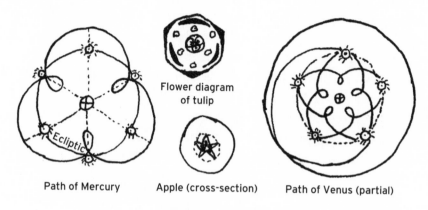

Flower diagram
of tulip

Path of Mercury   Apple (cross-section)   Path of Venus (partial)

Figure 11.7. Paths of planets in plant structures

Venus forms five loops (retrogressions) below the ecliptic in eight years, dividing its path into five parts; much like the bud and leaf placement of the five-sided blackberry stem, going around twice to get to the same place, creating the next ratio of the Fibonacci series, 2:5. A picture of the geocentric perspective of Venus's path looks like the core of an apple and characterizes the geometry of such plants as the rose family *(Rosaceae)*. The spiral configuration of Mars approaches a 3:8 ratio, as found in the leaf placement of the mustard or cabbage family *(Cruciferae)*. Most dicots prefer either the Venus ratio of 2:5 or the Mars ration of 3:8 for their leaf or flower placement. The Jupiter ration of 5:13 is found in many composites and in the figworts *(Scrophulariaceae)*. The Saturn ration of 13:34 is approached by some conifers and can be counted in the placement of scales in the pinecones. The even higher ratios in the sequence are extremely rare, found only in fossil plants, or in primitive plants such as mosses and club mosses. For the higher planets, the ratios only approximate those of the plant geometry because these patterns are never closed patterns, but show slight progressions.

A methodologically more sophisticated work, building upon Schulz, is a book by Ernst M. Kranich,[26] who analyzes a number of plants in morphological detail and relates their growth processes to similar structural relationships found in the movement of planets. He relates the rooting process to the moon and the vertical growth to the sun. The leaves and flower petals, as they diverge from the vertical stem tendency, are an image of the movement of Mercury and Venus bilaterally to the sun, as experienced from a geocentric position. Anther and pollen formation relate to Mars, fruit formation to Jupiter, and seed formation to Saturn.[27] He details the studies with careful botanical observations and flower diagrams.

It is not possible to go further into correlations between morphology, phyllotaxis, and geometry of plants within the limits of this exposition. These studies do establish the possibility of connections and partially

Figure 11.8. Planetary influences on different types of plants

vindicate some of the older planetary designations of plants, such as those of Culpeper and Renaissance scholars.

All plant species, from primitive algae to complex fruit trees, have characteristic patterns. A whole gestalt dominates each species, giving it its overall characteristic form. When, for example, leader branches are removed on trees, another branch takes over to maintain the characteristic gestalt. Scientists have succeeded in culturing the entire plant out of one cell; regardless of whether that cell has been taken from the root or from the leaves, it eventually took on the form characteristic of the species it belonged to. This indicates that there is a "blueprint." It is hypothesized that this blueprint is found in the cell as the DNA code of the chromosomes. We advance the contention that the DNA provides the physical substrata upon which the formative forces, deriving from etheric space, from the periphery of the earth, can find expression. Or as H. Poppelbaum expresses it:

The "blueprint" of an organism does not result from the chemistry of the various components of protein, etc.; it images an extra-spatial order that gives form and position to the organs and also determines the earthly-cosmic layout of the organism as a whole. The enzymes, hormones, etc. that move about in the organisms are not shaping causes; rather, they are mere indicators of the relationships in the form-field at a particular spot. The total structure of the living being proceeds from the super-spatial form that is developed in etheric space.[28]

Loss of the order-producing, rhythmic impulses of the formative forces leads to death. Interference with the flow of these forces produces a loss in geometry, or harmony, as in the so-called callus growths, plant tumors, and destruction by means of insects and disease.

George Adams, in an exposition of projective geometry, *Physical and Etheric Spaces*, talks about manifold streams and influences flowing together from the cosmos. "At the place where they interpenetrate, there arises by their interplay (it is a *qualitative* interplay, but its effect is at the same time spatial) the etheric organ as a whole. These currents from the universe are the cosmic parts, the etheric member of the organ. The organ as a whole is therefore smaller than its parts. This is an absolutely real process, perceptible to supersensible consciousness . . ."[29] We can clarify this by looking at a seed. The forces working on the seed from the cosmic periphery are as much a part of the plant as the visible members of the plant. In its manifestation within space and time, the plant is diminutive, whereas etherically the plant is greatly, though not visibly, expanded.

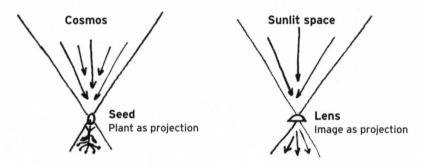

Figure 11.9. Plants as projections of cosmic forces

Practical Application

The illustration suggests that the plant is a projection of cosmic forces focused by the seed point, in analogy to the sunlit space that is focused by the lens of the eye to provide a retinal image as a projection. Steiner, and later Grohmann, conceive of the green vegetation as the eyes of the earth organism, open in the summer and shut in the winter.[30]

Having attempted to establish the possibility of cosmic influences upon plant life, it now becomes a question of practical concern about how to use these forces. If they are always present, how can one do anything about them? The gardener can amplify or tone down these forces in his or her work. He or she can create "relationships and dis-relationships of plants as they are governed by the *Revolutionibus* of the whole ordinance of the sun with the *primum mobile*, the *secundus mobilus*, the stars that we see and the ethereal world that we cannot see."[31] How can this be done? It is done by allowing the plants to become receptive to the cosmic rhythms through providing living compost and biodynamic preparations, and, just as important, through sowing one's seeds, working the soil, and planting the seedlings at the right times. We do the latter automatically with the solar cycle, which is the most obvious. The lunar cycles are less obvious, but just as important.

In order to plant by cosmic rhythms correctly, one must learn to identify the astral phenomena, such as the sign in which the sun, moon, and the other planets find themselves at the time, as well as the phases of the moon, the conjunctions and oppositions. A good astronomical calendar that indicates all the necessary data correctly and a good book on the constellations or a movable start chart will be of help in learning. Secondly, it is important to keep note of the sun's position, and the sign, phase, node, ascension and declension, and the apogee and perigee of the moon in one's garden diary day by day. In this way, a good scientific record can be kept indicating correlations over a number of years between nature phenomena (the appearance of certain bugs, the first and last frost dates, rain periods, etc.) and celestial phenomena. In the same entry, the garden work that is done each particular day should be noted. Such a record, if kept up diligently over a few decades, will be a valuable aid in understanding a number of cycles and patterns that have bearing on the farm and garden.

The solar cycle: Most of us have an idea when to plant in the spring and to harvest in the fall, although I had students from California who wanted to plant watermelons and other warm weather crops in November. One has to plant early enough in order to get a crop. Cold weather plants can be planted before the frost-free date, whereas warm-weather-loving plants must be planted after the frost-free date. (See chapter 16, "The Garden Calendar.") For biennial plants, which include many of our vegetables, such as beets, cabbages, kale, Brussels sprouts, carrots, celery, etc., the vegetative growth takes place during the first year, and a cold period *(vernalization)* must be passed through for the plant to bloom and make seed the following year. This is important for gardeners who want to make their own seed.

Photoperiodism, or the ability of plants to perceive and respond to differences in length of day and night, is related to solar cycles. *Long-day plants*, such as most garden plants (beets, lettuce, poppies, carrots, radishes, spinach, and others) flower when the days get longer and start to exceed twelve hours. These are plants that flower into the summer. This explains why radish and spinach go to seed in the summer. *Short-day plants*, originating mostly in the more southerly latitudes, need shorter days for flowering and will start to flower in late summer and fall as the sun's arc narrows; they include tobacco, corn, hemp, and cosmos. *Day-neutral plants*, such as shepherd's purse, chickweed, tomato, and sunflower, do not have any special preferences.

Lunar cycles: Lunar cycles are very handy in our attempt to create "relationships and dis-relationships" with the *Revolutionibus*. The moon works through the medium of water. Since most organisms consist of mainly water, it is little wonder that there is a noticeable effect. The most important lunar rhythm to work with is that of the moon phases (synodic or synodial moon). Anyone who has sprouted alfalfa seeds for salad, or closely watched the garden by comparing a new moon to a full moon, notices accelerated growth during the full moon period, especially if it has rained. It is best to sow or plant in the second quarter, or a few days before the full moon. Root crops can be planted in the third quarter. The fourth quarter is a rest period in the cycle during which weeding and pruning can be done. The first quarter is characterized by slow but steady growth.

Lilli Kolisko carried out fifteen years of experiments with wheat, barley, and oats in order to study the effect of the moon.[32] A large number of seeds were sown out during different lunar phases with other variables, such as soil type, water, and fertilizer, held constant. Exact measurements carried out on weight, length of roots, leaves, and internodes produced curves that showed maximum growth always occurring in the waxing second quarter moon. Another series of tests showed that germination is best

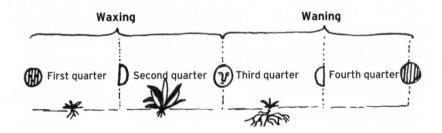

Figure 11.10. Waxing and waning moon effects on plant growth

two days before the full moon. Comparisons made between plants (carrots, tomatoes, peas) planted two days before the full moon, with controls planted two days before the new moon, showed that full moon sowings had significantly larger harvests and grew better than the controls. Plants sown in the advantageous phase surpassed those plants sown in the new moon, even when the latter were put into the ground two weeks earlier. Vegetables sown around the full moon were juicier, whereas those sown at the new moon periods were found to be drier and "woodier." Some plants are exceptions to the rule; potatoes and legumes can be planted during the new moon phase.

The lunar phases are not the only consideration for planting by the moon. The zodiac sign in which the moon finds itself (the sidereal moon) is also important. Older, quaint traditions give each sign of the zodiac a specific value regarding barrenness, fertility, moisture or dryness, and masculine or feminine traits.[33] Interesting as these assignments may be, they seem to have little empirical substantiality but belong, rather, to the way things were categorized in the medieval worldview.

Maria Thun, continuing investigations carried out in Europe by Franz Rulni and other anthroposophic researchers on the effects of the sidereal position of the moon on plants, found that differences occurred in test plots of radishes despite the weather, crop rotation, fertilizer, seed, lunar phases, and planetary conjunctions.[34] Taking a hint from Günther Wachsmuth about the formative forces and their relation to the zodiac, Maria Thun sowed equal amounts of radish seed daily into little experimental plots, while noting the sign in which the moon was to be found. After about four years, the typology became clear. Radishes sown in the "earth" signs showed good root development, those sown in the "water" signs showed abundant leaf development, those sown in "air" and "fire" signs tended to bolt and seed well. The typologies were amplified by always sowing "earth sign" radishes from seeds obtained from previous generations of earth sign radishes, and taking seeds from water sign radishes to sow on water sign days, etc. Even the working on the beds, the hoeing, weeding, and harvesting was done on the respective sign days. Other experiments with potatoes, cereals, and fodders were carried out along with the radish experiments for nearly three decades. Professor von Boguslawski, of the University of Giessen, Germany, investigated the claims of Maria Thun and found them scientifically sound; he sent his student Ulf Abele to do a PhD dissertation on the subject. As a result of this research, the old rules of astrological planting seemed to be vindicated. Thun also found that the typology comes out clearer and more typical on organically fertilized soil.

Other researchers, including master gardener Manfred Stauffer, with whom I worked in Village Aigues-Vertes (Geneva), were not so successful with planting by the zodiac signs; the results were by no means as unequivocal. Perhaps they were too skeptical to begin with, or it was the plant spirits themselves, which did Maria Thun a favor in growing the way she expected them to grow. As gardeners know, there is always an unknown factor, related to the mythical "green thumb": for some people, it seems, that plants grow well and for others they do not. Cheyenne medicine man Bill Tallbull told me that the plant spirits could read the thoughts of humans; sometimes plants adopt a favorite human, giving him inspirations or appearing in her dreams. Shamans of other tribes in close nature contact confirm this. Anthropological field reports are full of such stories. We can surmise—setting conventional scientific viewpoint for the moment aside—that perhaps it was the spirit, or deva, of the radishes, whose seeds Maria Thun sowed in her plots each day for over thirty years, which granted her the results she wished for.

Be it as it may, many biodynamic gardeners and farmers swear by Maria Thun's planting calendar. They are convinced that one aids root crops when they are sown in Taurus, Virgo, and Capricorn; flowers are best planted in the air signs of Gemini, Libra, and Aquarius; leaf crops are aided by the water signs of Pisces, Scorpio, and Cancer; and fruits do best in the fire signs of Aries, Sagittarius, and Leo.

As to the tropical month, when the moon travels up into the high signs (Taurus/Gemini) and back down to the low signs (Scorpio/Sagittarius), tradition has it that there is an increase in vitality when the moon is in *ascension*, which is good for grafting because the juices flow better in stem and leaves. When the moon is in *descension*, it is good for root development, sowing root crops, for transplanting, and for hedge trimming. In much of

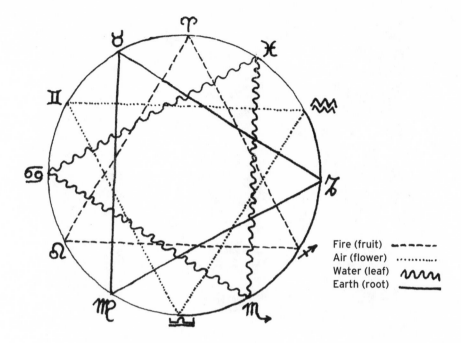

Figure 11.11. Trigons formed by the sidereal moon

Europe, especially among the Swiss peasants, this tropical moon is carefully observed.

Apogee (Ag), the moon at its greatest distance from Earth, tends to further bolting in plants sown on these days. This would be somewhat good for seed crops. Potatoes like to be planted at apogee. Plants planted in *perigee* (Pg), when the moon is closest to Earth, tend to be more subject to pests and mildew. In general, it is a good practice *not* to do major planting or sowings on either Ag or Pg. The same can be said of the *lunar nodes*, when the moon crosses the ecliptic. It is best not to do any major gardening work on these days.

As for the planetary influences, Maria Thun and others have found evidence that insects are affected in their habits by certain conjunctions and planetary positions in the zodiac. This has been little researched otherwise. Rudolf Steiner mentions of burning insects and pests in certain planetary constellations in his *Agricultural Course*.

Figure 11.12. The signs of the zodiac

In conclusion it may be said that planting at the right phase and sign can be one of the many factors that lead to successful gardening. The good soil must be there as a basis, for it is the soil with its teeming life that is mainly receptive to these influences. If all the other factors are handled well—crop rotation, companion planting, good soil husbandry, composting, and good watering practices—then the planting by the signs will be an extra plus. By itself astronomical gardening does not guarantee a great garden; by the same token, if a good planting day has to be missed because of weather or due to other commitments, it will not be, in itself, catastrophic.

Chapter 12

Atmospheric Factors

Sunshine is delicious, rain is refreshing, wind braces us up, snow is exhilarating; there is really no such thing as bad weather, only different kinds of good weather.
—John Ruskin

Moderating, transferring, and mediating between the great polarity of the terrestrial factors and the cosmic factors are the forces of wind and water, the climate, weather, sunshine, and rain that make up the atmospheric factors. Included are the following:

- *Moisture,* involving humidity, rain, hail, sleet, snow blankets, dew, and fog
- *Wind,* involving strength, direction, seasonal variation, and local breezes
- *Air pressure,* involving barometric changes
- *Light climate,* involving cloud covers, angle of sunlight, length of days, and shadows cast by buildings, trees, and hills
- *Temperature,* involving temperature averages, extremes of day and night, extremes of seasons, and frosts and chills

All of these factors are intimately involved with how the garden grows. The gardener must be very aware of these factors, for they will determine to a large extent when to plant and harvest, when to water or cultivate, when there is danger of aphid or mildew infection, and what the quantity and quality of the produce will be like. Entries should be made into the garden diary for each of these factors, providing a valuable record after a number of years that gives predictability for the local situation. Simple instruments can be used to aid in the observations, such as a *thermometer* for temperature measurements in sunny and shady locations; a *weather vane* for showing the wind direction; a *hygrometer* to measure humidity;[1] a simple *anemometer*, which is a whirligig that indicates the speed of the wind;[2] a *barometer* to give information on the air pressure, the highs and lows; and a *rain gauge*, which shows the amount of precipitation. The position of the sun in the zodiac, the place on the horizon where it rises and sets each day, a measure of the angles of the sun's rays, and a charting of the procession of shadows across the garden and other observations belong in the diary next to entries concerning composting, cultivating, planting, fertilizing, and rotations.

Nature observations, hints by old-timers, and local folk sayings provide a rich storehouse of information. Farmers tell that animals in the barn are nervous and cows hold back on their milk when there are impending changes of weather, and that aches and pains in the joints and old wounds mean the same thing. All animals, because of their more immediate contact with nature, give indications regarding atmospheric conditions, if one

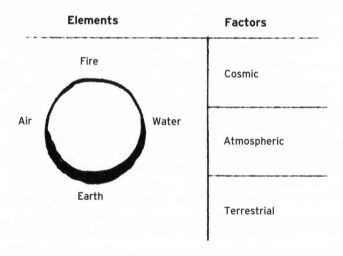

Figure 12.1. Four elements and three factors

can read them. Especially insects, which are still very closely tied into the macrocosmic processes, reflect the weather and even predict it. When gnats and mosquitoes dance high in the air, the weather will stay fair, but when they fly low and bite, the weather will change. Bees are nervous when the weather changes; they are more likely to sting when it is humid and windy; they strip the pollen off their legs to fly home faster when there is a storm on the horizon. Yearly forecasts can be made by observing bee larvae; when the brood is large there will be a sunny year, good for fruits and flowers; when there are few larvae, the year will be rainy and cool. Ants are interesting to watch in similar respects. Wooly bear caterpillars, which are often seen crossing roads in the fall, indicate the kind of winter that will follow. If the brown band around the caterpillar is broad, the winter will be mild; if it is narrow, the winter will be harsh. Crickets are regular thermometers; they chirp faster when it is warmer and proportionately slower the cooler it gets. Some observant old-timers can actually tell the degrees Fahrenheit by counting the chirps in a certain way. Similarly, spiders, besides being useful bug catchers, are good weather forecasters. When the little spiders hatch in the spring, it is a sure sign that warm weather is coming; when spiders weave fine nets, there will be a spell of good weather; when they build nests, it is a sign of coming cold; and when they weave thick strands, it will be cloudy or rainy.[3]

Mindful observation of the plant world gives good hints to the gardener regarding seasons and weather. Each step of the season is marked by its particular phenomenon in the flowering world. In southern Oregon, it is a sure sign of spring when the hazelnut blooms, the miner's lettuce, slender toothwort, plums, and others start flowering. Shooting stars, ragged starflowers, camas, grass widows, and others follow this early flowering. Successive flowering continues until midsummer is graced by the sun-like St. John's wort to be followed in the fall by asters, chicories, and others. Watching the natural flowering patterns is a surer way of knowing at which point the season stands than relying on abstract numerical dates. For predictions of the coming year, the greening oak and ash are compared in early spring. If the oak greens before the ash, the summer will be wet; if the ash greens before the oak, the summer will be dry.

Other natural phenomena can be helpful, too. In the Grants Pass area of Oregon, for example, the weather starts to get milder in February, making it possible to put out peas and spinach, but the last frost can be as late as the beginning of June. Newcomers to the area are usually fooled into putting their summer gardens out way too soon, only to find that a succession of unexpected frosts kills them off. The seasoned gardeners know that only when the mountaintops are free of snow is it safe to put out corn and tomatoes. A planting rule going back to the Iroquois in the Midwest that says not to plant corn until the leaves of the white oak are about the size of a squirrel's ears. Such lore holds only conditionally true for other regions. For each local area, the gardener should observe cloud formations, the intensity of colors at sunrise and sunset, wind directions, rising and descending fog, and other natural phenomena—at best over a span of a number of years.

Magical Weather Control

Since weather is an important factor to all people, especially agricultural and horticultural societies, propitiation of weather deities and spirits, and magical weather control, was (and is) universally practiced. In Western culture, notwithstanding, there is a long tradition of lore regarding weather. Germanic tribes propitiated Thunar (Thor) to ward off giant elemental beings of frost and ice with his thunderbolt, and to send fertile rain for the boor's swidden. Woden (Odin), the god associated with winds and storms, was seen with his wild spirit warriors sweeping through the winter storms on his gray steed. Zeus was the thunderer, cloud gatherer, and rainmaker for the Greeks. Iris brought the rainbow and Poseidon brought sea storms. Zephir brought moist, mild west wind; Boreas the cold north wind; Notos the hot desiccating south wind; and Apelides the cool east wind. Helios was the sun god and Apollo the god of light. In North America the winds are different: for the Ojibwa, Mudjekeewis, the grizzly bear, is the guardian of the west, bringing dry air; Shawnodese, the trickster coyote, brings the warm, rain bearing winds from the south; Wabun, the wise eagle and guardian of the east, brings the eastern rains; and Waboose, the spirit of the buffalo, brings the icy arctic winds from the north. These and other gods, lesser spirits, and elementals were accountable for the changing phenomena in the macrocosm, as well as the changing moods and passions within the microcosm. Because of this macrocosmic-microcosmic kinship, the human being, in the form of a priest, sorcerer, or magician, could approach the spirits and deities that operated behind the phenomena. He or she could talk to them, beseech them as a priest or priestess, and pray for rain, the cessation of rain, for warm weather, or the cessation of a heat wave; or work as a theurgist, as a magician, and compel the weather deities to act according to his or her wishes.[4] He or she could work for the welfare of the suffering community or, like Shakespeare's witches in *Macbeth*, create harmful winds and storms. We still speak of a spell of weather, a cold spell, a rain spell, or a spell of sunshine. Spells were originally woven by chanting, singing magic songs, making smoke with special herbs, or by casting runes, or bones and sticks engraved with sacred symbols.

Ethnographic research shows that public rainmakers are universal. As the anthropologist James Frazer has amply documented, making rain by the "sympathetic" magic of sprinkling water to imitate clouds, drumming to imitate thunder, dressing in dark colors to look like rain-laden clouds, pouring water into a fire, and other practices, while the community sings and dances for rain.[5] Men cut their arms or bleed animals for sacrifice and in imitation of the rain. Often weather rituals are carried out in stark nakedness, or in garments of foliage. If these rituals are of no avail, the recourse is often taken by threatening or abusing the saints or gods associated with weather control. To stop rain, its elemental opposite, fire, is used. Torches are thrown in the air or at the clouds. Wind is controlled by the imitative magic or blowing, or summoned by the clapping of hands. English sailors tied three knots into their handkerchiefs and hoped to release the wind by untying the knots. Christian hymnals contain prayers and songs beseeching God to send rain and protect from ill weather.

A modern scientist cannot but help consider these practices superstition born out of ignorance, as attempts at control based on faulty pre-scientific premises (James Frazer), or as rituals that function psychologically to relieve anxiety (Bronislaw Malinowski). For the scientist who counts as real only the objective world of empirical sensory data and logical think-ing, this must be the right conclusion: weather is something we can't do anything about. Maybe scientific weather control projects, such as HAARP, could possibly influence the weather, but certainly not wishful thinking and magic rituals.

If, on the other hand, one considers moods and states of mind as real and effective as physical things, then one can appreciate the possibility of sympathy or resonance between people's hopes, desires, and frame of mind and the external state of nature. Perhaps what were once effective means of channeling energies through rituals have at this time in our evolution become empty superstitions, in a time when the intellect overshadows our other human faculties. Many gardeners are almost intuitively aware that there is more to weather than just mechanistic processes. Remembering our discussion of the plant as a macrocosmic being, we can think of the climate with its changing moods of weather as part of the plant's wider nature, as vectors of formative forces working on the visible expression of the plant, just as the storms of passion, the hot and cold temperaments, the moods of joy and gloom reveal themselves in the physiognomy of the human microcosm. Could there be a subtle sympathy between the temperaments of people and weather phenomena? In light of the recent weather irregularities and calamities, perhaps these standpoints should be reconsidered.

Working with the Microclimate: Practical Aspects

Even if we are not able to significantly affect the macroclimate, the overall weather patterns, there is a lot we can do to create *microclimatic* conditions that are conducive to good plant growth. We shall deal with practical con-siderations for warmth, light, watering, frosts, and wind protection.

LIGHT AND WARMTH
It is best to choose a sunny location for the garden. Light and warmth, in interaction with carbon dioxide and the plant's water, produce sugars, starches, oils, essential oils, and fragrances that account for flavor, good

keeping quality, and resistance to disease.[6] In planning the garden space and layout, one should watch the sun over its year's path to see how the shadows of houses, trees, and hills are cast. Warm weather crops should be put into the sunniest part of the garden.

If the terrain is hilly, it is important to know the warming pattern and the angle of the sun on the hill. At a 90° angle, the sun is much more intense than at a 45° angle. The southwest of the hill is the hottest and driest, while the northeast side is moister and cooler. The east slope is cooler because the dew has to dry in the mornings before it can warm up. Hillsides are usually slightly warmer than valleys because at night cool air moves downslope. Because frosts are more severe in valleys, and light radiation is not quite as intense, it is a good idea to put fruit trees on slightly higher grounds, on southern slopes. As for the ground itself, dark humus absorbs warmth faster and keeps it longer, whereas light soil (sand) reflects the light and absorbs less heat. A light background for reflection of light is made use of in trellises for fruit grown next to house walls.

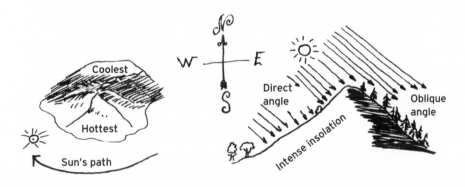

Figure 12.2. Microclimates according to the sun's path

FROSTS

Old Jack Frost is usually a problem in the spring, just when the plants are still small and tender. In the early spring, the ground is still cold and only its surface warms up during the day. At night the little amount of stored up warmth is given off, radiating into space, while cooler air rushes in to replace the warmer air. This is especially a problem in drier climates where the daytime temperatures might be fairly high (seventies), and because there is little water to hold the moisture, the nighttime temperatures become cold (twenties).[7] In southern Oregon, where heavy logging has reduced the ameliorative effect of forest vegetation, the daytime-nighttime temperature difference in the spring months amounts to over 40° F. Moister soils, although they heat slower, will keep the warmth longer than dry soils, and they take much more cold before the frost point is reached. For this reason, one cultivates a little later in the spring, so that the soil does not dry out so much. Shrubbery, groves and hedges, or a nearby pond or river raise the humidity and give some frost protection. A clouded sky reflects back the heat given off by the ground, so that on overcast days no frost can be expected.

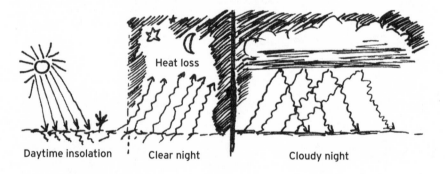

Figure 12.3. Heat at different times of the day

Since cold air flows like a river, following the path of least resistance, it is a good idea to study the flow patterns and the low areas where the frost settles. This flow of cold air at night will continue as long as there is snow in the mountains. At dawn, one can literally see the advance of white patches, the footsteps of frost giants, as old Nordics would say, as the cold moves down into the valley. One can deal with the cold flow by not putting the garden in a very low area but on slightly higher ground. One can either block the flow with a wall or a hedge, or one can make sure that the frost is not impeded as it moves past. The main thing is to prevent it from settling. One can create the equivalent of a protective cloud cover by setting up plastic tunnels over one's beds in the spring. These are opened during the day simply by pushing the plastic up on both sides and closed at night. In orchards smudge pots are used for similar purposes, or ventilators are set up to keep the air moving. Turning on the sprinklers during the coldest hours at night will keep the frost from harming the plants, because as long as there is fresh water to be turned to ice the temperature of the leaves will not dip below the freezing point. It is also a good idea not to mulch until the frost danger is past, so that the ground can sufficiently warm up.

In other words, what one has to watch for, especially after a cold front has passed, is a clear sky, dry wind, still air, and dry, cool ground. Given these factors in early spring, one can expect frost.

In the fall, the first frost will kill most of the warm weather plants such as tomatoes, eggplants, peppers, beans, squash, etc. One can extend the season somewhat by the use of plastic tunnels and spraying the plants with biodynamic preparation made from valerian (see Preparations, Teas, and Biotic Substances).

AIR AND WIND

The gardener should be familiar with local wind directions and velocities and know what kind of weather the major winds bring. Does the southwest wind bring warmth and rain, while the northeast wind brings cold and clear skies? Are there cool evening breezes from the hills or from bodies of water?

If wind sweeps too swiftly across the garden plot, several problems result. Wind cools, dehydrates, and removes the carbon dioxide that is needed by the plant for sugar production. Carbon dioxide, which is slightly heavier than normal air, hovers above the ground among the foliage layers (having been given off by the respiration of soil organisms, from whence it is absorbed by the pore openings (stomata) on the underside of the leaves). With adequate wind protection the crops will be a week ahead of time, and production will increase by about 10 percent. Wind protection is best provided by hedges, shrubbery, or lattice fences. Hedges are not havens for vermin, but provide shelter for useful animals such as toads, garter snakes, birds, and weasels, which eat mice and gophers. A hedge can shelter beehives, and provide nuts, berries, healing herbs, or beanpoles or tomato stakes. To make a hedge denser, one should trim it. Trimming the shoots, or having animals graze or nibble on them, encourages the side branches to grow. Gooseberries, red and black currants, and other berry bushes can function as a windbreak as well. In a new garden where there has not been time for a hedge to grow, the tall crops on the border of the garden can give some wind shelter (for example, Jerusalem artichokes, runner beans, corn, and peas).

Hedges and fences should have about 40 percent permeability, just slowing the wind but not stopping it. An impermeable barrier, such as a wall, creates turbulence farther on that can be destructive.

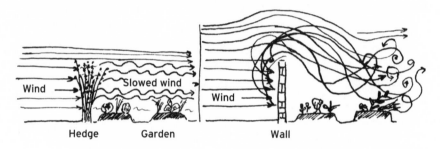

Figure 12.4. Effects of wind on a garden

WATER

The gardener must know the rainfall patterns of the region and the water-holding capacity of the soil. In southern Oregon, the year divides itself into dry summers and wet winters. One can have problems of waterlogging during part of the season, and dryness during the other part. If waterlogging becomes a problem, it is good to set up a drainage system by laying tile pipes or open trenches that empty into a lower area. If there is no lower area to empty into, it is profitable to dig a pond. A pond will keep a more steady humidity level, which moderates temperature extremes; one can raise fish and ducks in it, and use it as a water source for one's plants. Raised beds are also beneficial where the soil is soggy in the spring planting season. Roots need air pockets as they can drown in waterlogged soil.

One might have collecting tanks or barrels to catch rainwater from the roof. Rainwater collected during a thunderstorm is rich in nitrates and that collected during a full moon period is rich in the formative growth forces that are connected with the moon. Water of this nature is preferred over tap water or city water for watering the garden. Chlorinated water should be avoided, for it harms the valuable soil microorganisms and the delicate root hairs of the plants.

DRY WEATHER GARDENING

During dry weather, or drought conditions, one can improve the water utilization of the crops in a number of ways:

1. *Double digging* is a means of enlarging the rooting zone so that cultivated plants can more easily grow into the deeper, moister levels of the ground. The loosened soil interrupts the capillary action of water molecules as they move upward in the soil, where they eventually evaporate on the surface.

2. *Compost* is used to increase the soil's clay-humus complexes. A clay-humus molecule holds six times its weight in water and retains up to 900 percent of the moisture compared to sand. Its electrostatic charge holds on to four molecular layers of water, which are not given up to gravity or the sun's evaporative pull, but are made available to the plants when their transpiration rate makes it necessary. It is shown experimentally that plants lacking in nutrients need more water; they have to transpire more water to get the equivalent amount of nutrients that plants rich in humus soil would be getting. It is for this reason that during droughts organic gardens stay green while those relying on artificial fertilizer instead of compost wither and even die.

3. *Mulching* is the equivalent of bringing an overcast day to the level of the ground; the evaporation is greatly reduced. Ordinary mulch can reduce evaporation about 50 percent, whereas straw, which reflects light, can reduce evaporation by 70 percent.

4. Create *wind shelters*, such as hedges or fences, which will decrease the amount of evaporation caused by the wind.

5. *Correct watering* means watering less often, but more thoroughly. In the spring, it is important to keep the seedlings from drying out and more frequent watering is recommended, but after midsummer the watering

should occur less frequently. Many people spoil their plants by turning on the sprinklers every day. The plants respond by making a shallow root system and as soon as the top layer of the soil dries, they begin to look wilted, waiting for a new shower. It is better to train the plants to root more deeply by watering less, but then to soak the ground thoroughly so that the deeper zones become moistened also. After such a soaking, the garden should be mulched to keep the evaporation rate down. If no mulch is available, it is advisable to "dry mulch" by hoeing after each sprinkling or irrigation in order to interrupt the evaporative pull by interrupting the capillary movement of the water molecules. This is how the Pueblo Indians are able to grow gardens in the desert. After each rain, the whole village races to the fields to start hoeing.

Watering should never be done in the noonday sun, but at night or in the mornings, for the sudden shower of cold water on the warm leaves creates a shock for the plant. It traumatizes the leaves of the plant, which are physiologically set for the hot sunny day. As a result, the plant hesitates in its growing and this blockage of energy flow becomes a signal to insects and slugs to start eating.

Some people become worried when the leaves of beans, squash, and other plants droop in the late afternoon, thinking it is time to water. Actually, the plant organisms are just adjusting to the hottest part of the day, protecting themselves from excessive transpiration. If done right, one need not water more than once, twice, or three times during a month, depending on soil and location. One of the best times to water is just before the full moon so that the lunar forces can work on the vegetation through the water. Cool-weather-loving plants—the potatoes, cabbage family, beet family, and carrot family—do not mind overhead sprinkling, but the warm-weather-loving plants, especially the tomatoes and beans, are sensitive to having their leaves wet. For the latter, soaker hoses and drip irrigation are recommended.

The soil should have the wrung-out sponge feeling all the way down to the root tips. One must make sure to water deeply enough. For experimental purposes, one could dig a hole to get an idea of the watering depth and assess the amount that is right for the soil. Faulty watering is one of the greatest causes for garden failure. In the Midwest, where the land is blessed with weekly thundershowers, this is no problem.

6. The *close spacing* of plants as recommended in the French intensive method of gardening helps shade the ground and reduces evaporation. The plants are grown or planted so that as they grow the leaves touch each other; the plants (lettuces, cabbages, chard, etc.) are individually selected and harvested, giving the others a chance to grow and cover the gap with their leaves. In this way the bed remains covered by a green canopy.8 This method might be of merit in arid climates, where the soils easily dry out. It is a method that works well in home gardens, where one harvests the vegetable fresh for each meal, but less so for commercial gardens, where the plants are harvested in bulk. One has to be careful not to crowd the plants too much, preventing the archetypal form of each plant from coming into expression.

7. Choosing *drought-resistant varieties*, as advertised in some catalogues, might be helpful in dry climates.

A final consideration for maximizing the microclimate of one's garden ecotope is to mulch between the rows. Each kind of mulch has a different effect:

- *Straw mulch* is light in color, reflects the sun, and therefore cools the ground; this makes it good for members of the cabbage family and other cold-weather-loving plants.
- *Hay mulch* feeds the soil organisms, as does straw to a lesser extent.
- *Paper mulch,* such as shredded newspaper, will do in a bind, but is messy because it blows away easily.
- *Plastic sheets* warm the ground and might be good for giving strawberries, tomatoes, eggplants, and peppers a head start, but they inhibit air circulation, causing anaerobic soil reactions. Black plastic keeps longer than clear plastic and warms more efficiently, but all plastic is difficult to get rid of. Burning it causes air pollution, as the fumes are toxic: some types of polyvinyl might even release traces of dioxin, and others release endocrine disruptors.

- *Pine needle mulch* is very acidic and is not recommended except for strawberries and azaleas.
- *Oak leaf mulch* discourages slugs, but like most leaves, it is slightly acidic.
- *Fresh sawdust* will rob the soil of nitrogen until it is finally broken down after a couple of years.

Mulching and Ground Covers

Mulching primarily saves water, but it also prevents weeds by depriving them of light. A six-inch mulch cover practically eliminates weeding and hoeing, while feeding and protecting the soil. Mulch buffers the soil, so that the hiatus between the atmosphere (air and light) and the soil (earth and water) is not so abrupt, making it possible for earthworms and microorganisms to work to the very top layer of soil. Mulch feeds the earthworms. Mulch keeps the soil from crusting over after a rain, which lets the soil breath and keeps the lettuce and strawberries from being splattered with dirt.

One problem with mulch is that it might shelter slugs, but with proper watering practices, such as not sprinkling every day, this should not be a major problem. Slugs can be a worst problem in gardens with clean cultivation (where weeds are destroyed and no mulch is given), where living plants are attacked. Since slugs prefer wilted greens, the right kind of mulch might even lure them away from the crop plants.

For further ideas about mulching, the best-selling *Gaia's Garden* by Toby Hemenway and the classic but now out-of-print *The Ruth Stout No-Work Garden Book* make for interesting reading.[9]

In this chapter we have touched upon the so-called atmospheric factors and indicated how we can modify and meliorate some of the extremes of temperature, water, and wind, by creating beneficial microclimates that make the garden into an oasis.

Chapter 13

Composts and Liquid Manures

Behold this compost! Behold it well!
— Walt Whitman, "This Compost"

Composting (L. *compositum* = something put together) is the deliberate putting together of any number of organic substances for the sake of rotting them in such a way that a high-quality natural fertilizing agent, a medium of microorganismic life, can develop. We must distinguish between 1) the *ingredients* and 2) the *processes* of composting itself; both must be carefully attended to if the end product is to be good, stable, permanent humus.

In nature's Wheel of Life, composting occurs on the bottom of a cycle, where death processes are turned back into life processes. The cycle starts in the spring, when seeds lying dormant in the soil are awakened to life by moisture and increasing warmth. Quickened vegetative growth characterizes the vegetable kingdom from spring until midsummer, when the rapid buildup of carbonaceous substance (biomass) comes to a halt and increasingly the impulse toward flowering and subsequent seed formation is given. Older leaves start yellowing and dying off; they are chewed and shredded by insect populations, as the overall annual *breakdown cycle* picks up speed. Finally, in late autumn, fallen leaves and stems litter the ground as mulch, and the *breakdown cycle* continues as bacteria and fungi metabolize the carbohydrate substances. By spring this mulch and detritus is broken down and metamorphosed into humus as the *buildup cycle* of vegetation commences anew.

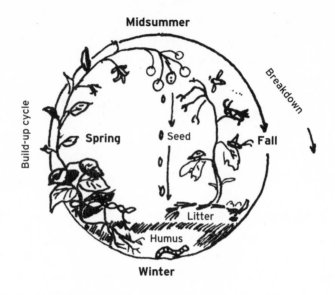

Figure 13.1. The Wheel of Life

We get a grand picture of the rhythm of life and the interconnected-ness of soil and plants when we contemplate how the plant during half of the cycle grows as lush vegetation, and during the other half of the cycle separates into a tiny viable germ (the seed or bud) on one hand and litter and debris on the other hand, to be finally reunited in the spring when the seed grows once again out of the humus. Animal substances, manures, urine, secretions, and corpses work into this cycle of life and death, bringing nitrogen and enzymes into it.

In biologically sound organic farming and gardening, soil building by composting is the key. In nature we observe composting processes at work all the time as decaying leaves, litter, dead animals, tree stumps, and other remnants of life whose etheric forces have left them or been weakened, and are being putrefied, rotted, decayed, or fermented. Some gardeners feel that it is important to imitate these processes on their garden beds. Mulching continually or letting the mulch rot on the ground as time goes by is the way they try to do this. This kind of "composting" is very much like nature does it. There is nothing to be said against this practice, however, building a compost pile and conducting a guided decomposition process is lending nature a helping hand. Composting is biodynamics *par excellence*, for here, one is neither letting nature take its course, nor is one violating nature's principles, but one is aiding nature, speeding her up a bit, and guiding the changes in such a way that it is beneficial for the garden organism.

The art of composting is very ancient. Pliny the Elder (Plinius), the renowned Roman naturalist, wrote about it; the eleventh-century Arab scholar Ibn al Awam discussed it; alchemists practiced it to find the secrets of transmutation; and peasants and yeomen have practiced some form of composting for quite some time. In the West this tended to be the dung heap, where manure, carcasses, scraps, and stall bedding was thrown and left to rot. These were reeking piles that lost much nitrogen to the atmosphere due to denitrifying bacteria and anaerobic putrefaction. In East Asia, more careful management of compost had been practiced for centuries, making it possible for large families to survive on two to five acres. Here, everything organic, weeds, human excrement, animal manures, pond dredgings, and sod were composted in special composting sheds that formed part of the cluster of buildings that made up the farmstead.[1] Roofed over manure piles were also found on Swiss farmsteads.

Compost science and care was neglected in the decades following the advent of chemical farming and the displacement of animals from the farms: of horses by tractors; of cows, chickens, and hogs into feedlots. This development has a serious ecological impact and puts the permanent fertility of the land into jeopardy. The organic agriculture movement has reemphasized the importance of composting (for example, Sir Howard's Indore method) and biodynamics in particular has added valuable scientific data to the art of compost making by analyzing ingredients, composting stages, and kinds of special compost for specific crop needs, and by providing preparations made from herbs to guide the decomposition in the most favorable way. (See chapter 17, "Teas, Preparations, and Biotic Substances.")

Compost Ingredients

Any organic substance can be composted. There are different types of composts that can be made from different materials for different purposes.

Common garden compost can be made from organic garbage, weeds, manures of domestic animals, leaves, paper, and sod. The ingredients should be mixed as well as possible; this is even better than layering the ingredients. Chopping the materials as finely as possible with a silage chopper or *shredder* can be of great advantage, especially when dealing with such ingredients as sunflower stems, cabbage or corn stalks, and other tough haulms. A neighborhood or a garden club could share the cost of a compost shredder.

The *carbon-nitrogen ratio* (C-N ratio), the relative amount of carbon to nitrogen in the compost materials, is of major importance in correctly setting up a compost. Sawdust, which has 500 parts carbon to 1 part nitrogen, is said to have a wide ratio, whereas sludge, which has a ratio of 6 parts carbon to 1 part nitrogen, is said to be close. An ideal C-N ratio at the start of the composting process is about 30:1 or 25:1. After the compost starts working, it will lose volume due to the escape of carbon dioxide and water vapor, which brings the end product close to an ideal of a 15:1 to 20:1 ratio.

Compost Ingredients

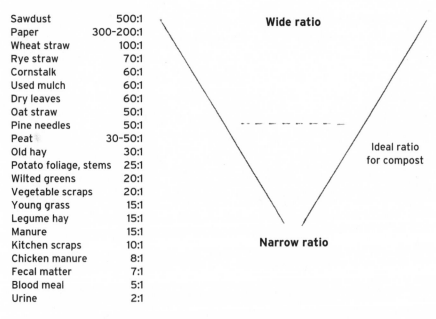

Sawdust	500:1
Paper	300-200:1
Wheat straw	100:1
Rye straw	70:1
Cornstalk	60:1
Used mulch	60:1
Dry leaves	60:1
Oat straw	50:1
Pine needles	50:1
Peat	30-50:1
Old hay	30:1
Potato foliage, stems	25:1
Wilted greens	20:1
Vegetable scraps	20:1
Young grass	15:1
Legume hay	15:1
Manure	15:1
Kitchen scraps	10:1
Chicken manure	8:1
Fecal matter	7:1
Blood meal	5:1
Urine	2:1

Wide ratio

Ideal ratio for compost

Narrow ratio

Figure 13.2. Carbon-nitrogen ratios in compost materials

If one has substances such as sawdust, paper, straw, or leaves that have a wide C-N ratio, then one must balance this out with substances having a narrow ratio in order to approach the ideal 25–30:1 C-N ratio. This is done by adding manures, guano, blood meal, bone and horn meal, wool, feathers, urines, chicken manure, pig bristles, slurry, and even hair sweepings from a barber shop.

Fresh sawdust might even be treated at first with artificial nitrogen (i.e., urea, ammonia sulfate) to narrow the C-N gap and help bacteria break it down. After such a predigesting, the sawdust pile can be reworked into a regular compost pile. This is one of the few exceptions where artificial substances might be cautiously used.

Too close of a C-N ratio at the beginning of composting leads to nitrogen losses, which can be detected by the foul smell of ammonia. This also attracts flies. Properly prepared composts should not have strong odors.

Too wide of a C-N ratio slows the composting considerably. If lack of sufficient nitrogen is coupled with low temperatures and too much moisture, an acidic, peat-like end product, resembling the peat in northern climates, will be the result.

Besides the ingredients that furnish the C-N ratio, other substances are added to the compost:

- *Earth,* or regular garden soil, at the most 5 to10 percent, can be mixed in to aid the earthworms (red wrigglers) and the humus formation.
- *Clay* that has been dried and pulverized can be sprinkled among the layers of compost materials. When examining a clay-treated compost, one finds that most of the earthworm eggs and young earthworms are active near the clay particles.
- *Lime,* or *calcium,* preferably in the form of dolomite or ground limestone, should be dusted among the layers of the compost, as though one were dusting a cake with powdered sugar. This is done when the compost is set up or every time it is turned. This is a better way of adding lime to the soil than broadcasting it directly onto the soil; in the compost it becomes tied into the per-

manent humus molecules and facilitates the cation exchange. The right amount of lime keeps the compost from souring and discourages flies. Too much lime must be avoided for it will drive off the ammonia and, because of its alkaline reaction, discourage the ammonia-absorbing compost fungi. Cellulose-digesting bacteria, on the other hand, need the presence of some calcium.

- *Wood ash,* which supplies potassium and minerals, should also be finely laced throughout the compost. Like lime and clay powder, it should not be put into the compost in large clumps, for then it forms caustic lye (potassium hydroxide) when moistened. Only the ash of a wood fire should be used, not from a coal fire or from burned trash. Ashes from black coal contain too much sulfur to be of good use. Ashes from plastics, colored, glossy paper, and chemical stuff should definitely be avoided.

- *Granite flour,* basalt flour, green sand, rock phosphate, colloidal phosphate, and other amendments are put into the compost in the same way.

There are a number of *compost starters,* or compost-activators, on the market. J. I. Rodale was of the opinion that they are not really needed, for the bacteria and spores of microorganisms are everywhere in the ground, air, and water so that the pile, given the correct C-N ratio, will take off by itself.[3] I basically agree and do not use compost starters. Many biodynamic gardeners are convinced that one is more successful with Pfeiffer's biodynamic compost starter, containing bacteria isolated from the biodynamic preparations made from herbs, for this brings the right kind of bacteria into play, so that the rotting will proceed favorably.[4] Pfeiffer himself compared his compost starter to yeast added to bread. One can mix the flour and water and then leave it exposed to the air to catch wild yeast spores that will ferment and raise the dough, but, what an awful taste! Yeast must come from a select strain to make good bread.[5]

Permaculture advocates are enthused about the use of the so-called *Effective Microorganisms* (EM) developed by Teruo Higa, professor of horticulture at the University of the Ryukyus (Okinawa), as an aid in creating compost materials. The EMs consist of about eighty microbial species, mostly yeasts, lactic acid bacteria, and other anaerobic strains that one finds also in beer mash, sauerkraut, and silage. These "friendly" microorganisms are indeed effective in fermenting slurries, sludge, compost teas, *bokashi*-compost (anaerobic composting in sealed buckets), and "*humanure*" (recycled human night soil and urine); they have been effective in reviving eutrophicated (polluted, biologically dead) lakes and aquatic ecosystems or soils that have been damaged by pesticides and agro-chemicals. But as far as standard composting, which relies mainly on aerobic bacteria, I don't think one needs EMs.

Old mature compost is, in my estimation, a most excellent starter when sprinkled into the new heap. A few handfuls suffice. "*Russian tea*," or a fermentation of cow dung in ten parts water; "*Chairman Mao's compost starter*," made from a four to one dilution of urine; *nettle tea* or *nettle ferment*, made by brewing nettles or fermenting them in rainwater; or a ferment of *comfrey* leaves *(Symphytum officinale)* help to get the proper rotting processes started when added to the compost.

When, Where, and How to Set Up the Compost

It is best to have a permanent composting area, centrally located in the garden for easy transport of materials. The compost should be placed on the bare ground and not on wooden or cement platforms so that bacteria from previous piles can infect it and earthworms can travel into the subsoil and back into the compost. The compost should not be put into a pit, and certainly not be trampled down, for that would result in anaerobic decomposition, in putrefaction and fermentation, with the result of an inferior end product. Nitrate-producing bacteria need plenty of oxygen, since they are aerobic. Therefore, the composts should be somewhat loosely piled on top of the ground, where the pile can be kept moist, but not waterlogged. The materials are shredded as finely as possible to increase the surface areas for the bacteria to work on.

The composting site should be either shady or roofed over in warmer, drier localities. Elderberry, hazelnut, birch, and alder make ideal compost

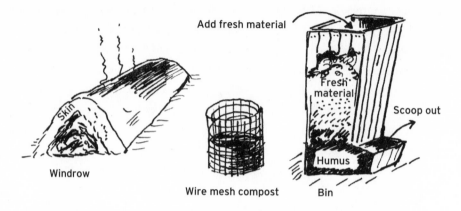

Add fresh material

Fresh material

Scoop out

Skin

Windrow

Humus

Wire mesh compost

Bin

Figure 13.3. Compost heaps

shade trees, for their leaf and root exudates aid in the decomposition processes. However, some trees and shrubs, such as willows, will send their roots into the compost pile and leach all of its nutrients. It is a good idea to cap these roots with a sharp spade once in a while. In cooler climates, composts should be put into wind-sheltered, sunny areas. It is well worth protecting the compost with a layer of black plastic or old carpets, which keeps the compost from drying out during a dry spell, and, on the other hand, keeps the nutrients from leaching out during a rainy season. Evaporating moisture will condense underneath the plastic and percolate and circulate through the pile. A roofed-over compost place also protects from drying or leaching.

Windrows about four-feet high, six feet wide, and as long as necessary are the best shape for the composts. In this way, a "critical mass" is achieved, for the biochemical reactions to take place. If the compost pile is too small, it will not heat and decompose properly; if the pile is too large, the inner core will still be raw, besides being deprived of air, while the outside mantle will have already broken down.

Like any living organism, the compost must have a skin to keep the gases, such as ammonia and methane, and other products of metabolism from being dissipated. A mantle of peat, old sawdust, straw, or other nitrogen-poor substance keeps the odors, which are really fertility in volatile form, from passing into the atmosphere. Underneath, the compost might be bedded upon straw, hay, peat, or a similar absorbent substance if there is a chance of run-off of liquids.

For smaller gardens, a wooden composting bin or a roll of wire mesh make good composting devices. Fresh material is pitched into the top, while finished compost can be scooped out of the bottom.

Special Composts and Manures

There are a number of composts other than the ordinary garden compost that is made from available weeds, leaves, and kitchen scraps. Special composts for legumes *(Fabaceae)* can be made from clover sod or some other legume sod that is composted together with manure for a year with some lime added. This method, developed by N. Remer, can be used to fertilize legume fields and pastures. It produces a special virulence among the rhizobia and will stimulate nitrogen fixation.[6] Compost can be made from old tomato plants, together with soil and manure. This is good fertilizer for tomatoes, which have a narcissistic predilection for growing on their own rotted remains. Special earthworm compost can be made from shredded paper, straw, and manure with clay powder added.

Special composts can be made for specific purposes from various animal droppings and manures. In general it can be said that the manure of a particular animal species best fertilizes the part of the plant upon which these animals characteristically feed. Here the characteristics of the different kinds of animal dung:

> *Pig manure* is rich in potash and when well humified is best applied to *root crops*, especially potassium-hungry leeks, celeriac, and potatoes. Pigs are primarily rooting animals and prefer to feed on roots they dig up with their snouts.[7]

> Composted *horse manure* is light and will lighten heavy, clay soils. Horses feed primarily on foliage and grass; consequently their manure aids leaf and foliage development. Horse manure, which is rich in ammonia, will heat steadily for a long time. This makes it ideal for use in hot beds for raising seedlings in the spring. For

a home garden, or even a larger garden where no greenhouse is available, this is a good way to start plants. (See chapter 16, "The Garden Calendar.")

Cow manure, when well rotted, fertilizes the entire plant, but especially leaf and foliage.

Rabbit manures, which are rich in nitrogen, are good for foliage, stem, and shrubbery development.

Chicken, pigeon, and other *bird manures* are good for seeds, flowers, and fruits, because their manure is rich in phosphorus and complicated indole compounds (auxins involved in flower and ovary formations). It is on the perimeter of the generalized plant, on the border of the macrocosmic etheric and astral planes, that the chickens feed as they peck for seeds and scratch for worms and grubs. In this they feed on the opposite end of the plant as the rooting hogs; they are far enough apart on the food chain that hungry hogs are not averse to devouring chicken droppings. Chicken manure, which is sticky, wet, and odorous, is hard to compost. It is best made into liquid compost by mixing it into ten parts water and letting it ferment in a barrel. This potent brew should be stirred briefly every day. It is ready in about six to eight weeks and makes an excellent liquid fertilizer for the heavy feeders that are to flower, fruit, or seed, such as tomatoes, corn, okra, squash, or cauliflower. It turns out that pigeon manure is also excellent for asparagus.

Sheep and *goat manure* are excellent for increasing the quality and aroma of fruits, the essential oil (i.e., terpineol, phenols, ketones, aldehydes) content of herbs, and the fatty oil content of seed crops such as rape, mustard, hemp, and flax. Sheep manure helps the mint family members *(Laminaceae,* or *Labiatiae),* so that it is a good idea to graze sheep in large mint fields where they clean out the weeds and, because of their manure, increase the essential oils of the mint.[8] One can appreciate how sheep and goats fit into the ecology of the drier Mediterranean region, such as Greece, southern Italy, or the Provence, where olives and world-renowned culinary herbs are grown.

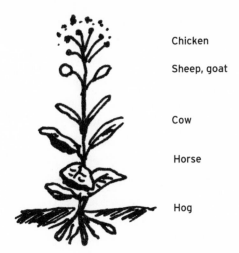

Chicken

Sheep, goat

Cow

Horse

Hog

Figure 13.4. Animal manures and plant growth

Manures are composted like other substances, with the addition of small amounts of earth, clay, lime, wood ash, and rock flours, as well as straw, hay, weeds, or other vegetable matter. For heavier manures, such as cow or hog manure, special care has to be taken to bring air into the compost pile. This can be done by mixing it with straw and other light materials, tossing it with manure forks into a pile so it does not clump as much, or, on farms, setting the manure spreader on "stationary" and running it through onto a heap.

Composted manures aid the garden crop by creating ideal conditions for the edaphon and feeding the soil life, not just by feeding the plant itself. Growing in such a living medium, the plant expresses itself truer to type; the stages of metamorphosis, the rooting, foliage unfolding, flowering, and fruiting are more clearly defined. The increased vitality of the plant helps ward off disease and insect troubles.

The Sacred Cow

It is worth looking closer at the cow and the manure she produces. The cow pie is the queen of fertilizers. This becomes obvious when we examine the

long, complicated digestive organism of this animal. Cud-chewing ruminants like the bison or buffalo made the humus-rich prairies possible, which
became the breadbasket of the world.[9] Were it not for sacred cows, India
would be in much worse shape than it is. These cows are not competitors
as some Western technocrats believe, but they live in symbiosis with human
beings, eating weeds and roughage that could not otherwise be utilized and
returning milk, draft power, and manure. This dung amounts to seven
hundred million tons annually, half of which serves as fertilizer and the
other half as fuel (the thermal equivalent of twenty-seven million tons
of kerosene, thirty-five million tons of coal, or sixty-eight million tons of
wood).[10] In countries of the cooler latitudes, cows are one of the mainstays
of fertility because high rainfall and low temperatures leach the soils and
they become acidic, leading to podzol soils and peat formations. Inside
their warm organisms cows carry a microbial flora and fauna that break
down, ferment, and digest cellulose, proteins, carbohydrates, and other
such substances that might be done externally in the soil in the warmer
latitudes, but here must be done inside the animal organism. The intestinal
microorganisms help to bind the nutrients into the manures so that the
acidic, starved northern soils and podzols can become fertile.

When one looks at the ruminants, one finds four-chambered stomachs.
In the first two chambers, the rumen and the reticulum, chewed plant
material is stored and fermented. Bacterial florae by the billions are involved
in this pre-digestion. Regurgitation of the food and a further chewing of
the cud serve to completely break down fiber and roughage. Bacteria and
protozoa secrete enzymes (cellulose), which digest the glucose-yielding
cellulose. Complex acid-base relationships permeate the digestion process. These microorganisms synthesize amino acids, vitamin B12, and fatty
acids for the cow. No other animal can make such good use of roughage.
Feeding grain, dried Peruvian sardines, and nitrogen-rich alfalfa to cattle
violates their basic nature and makes these animals sick (scuttles, milk
fevers, etc.). In a lecture (1923) in Dornach, Switzerland, Rudolf Steiner
stated that cows that were fed protein supplements derived from meat or
bonemeal would go mad. He, thus, basically foresaw the possibility of the
mad cow disease (BSE; Bovine spongiform encephalopathy) that ravaged

these gentile grass-eating herbivores at the turn of the century (around 2000) after having been fed processed wastes from slaughterhouses in order to increase their milk production.[11]

The alimentary tract of cattle is richly endowed with nervous tissue, monitoring the digestive process the whole long distance of the alimentary canal. It takes twelve days for this process to be completed. It is appropriate to compare the complexity of the cow's digestion to that of the human brain. Whereas in primate fashion, our senses are turned outward to the world at large, the seemingly dull cow has its senses turned inward, into its digestion, "meditating" on the forces and energies that are fixed into the vegetable kingdom and liberating these forces during digestion. No wonder the cow is sacred in India, for besides its utilitarian uses, it is the very image of a consciousness turned inward upon itself in deepest meditation. With this in mind, is it any wonder that cow dung, cow manure, has a special healing value for the soil and makes the best compost material imaginable?

It is one of the greatest sins of our time to have severed the cow from the land and placed them into concentrated livestock operations, to have deprived the human being of his/her association with this beatific beast, and to have chemical salts replace their valuable manure. An average feedlot of twenty-five thousand cattle produces 650 tons of manure daily; its removal is expensive and its storage causes runoff-pollution problems.

Natural cow manure compost is one of the best for the gardener to acquire. It is best to get the manure from cattle that are fed on local fodder, for the cow's digestive processes produce manure that is hormonally and enzymatically geared to the specific needs of the soils on which the fodder was grown.

Liquid Manures

Liquid manures, used in the watering of the heavy feeders during the growing season or as compost activators, can be made from a number of substances that are placed into a barrel with rainwater or pond water at a ratio of 10:1 and left to ferment for a number of weeks. *Stinging nettle liquid manure* is rich in iron, needed for the chlorophyll formation of green leaves, and helps in the humus buildup of the soil. *Cabbage leaf slurry* aids the sulfur metabolism of the soil. *Comfrey,* rich in various minerals (CA, K, P, Ma) and vitamins, makes effective liquid manure.[12] Chicken and pigeon dung, as well as cow pies, can be fermented in water and used for special feeding purposes: the bird slurry for flowers and fruits, the cow manure for aiding root development in general.

Liquid manures, which involve anaerobic fermentation, can produce unpleasant smells like rotten eggs (hydrogen sulfide), ammonia, and swamp gas (methane). To keep the odors at a minimum, it is advisable to stir it occasionally to bring air into the brew and to inoculate with old compost, compost starter, Effective Microorganisms (EMs), or shredded stinging nettle to help guide the fermentation processes in the right direction. Some gardeners put a floating layer of peat moss, chopped straw, or sawdust on the slurry to absorb the fumes. In the summer, the inch-long sluggish, fat rat-tailed maggots of hovering flies or drone flies (genus *Eristalis*), which feed upon decaying liquid substances, will develop in these potent brews as an indication that the liquid is biologically ready to be used.

The Composting Process

Just watching what one puts into the compost as ingredients is not enough to ensure its success. What happens to these ingredients is important. One can compare the composting process to the digestion occurring in animal intestines, which is a process similar to composting. The same kind of fodder, such as clover and grass, can be given to a goat, rabbit, horse, or cow. Though the input is the same, the output is different because of dissimilar digestive processes are involved. Each will come out with its characteristic manure. Responsible are the different lengths and shapes of the digestive apparatus, the different intestinal flora and enzymatic secretions, and the varied time needed for digestion (twelve days for cows, four days for horses, etc.). Cow manure is heavy with its distinct, aromatic smell; pig manure is heavy and sour smelling; horse manure is light and gives off ammonia vapors; sheep, goat, and rabbit manures are dry. Each kind of manure has its typical shape and other characteristics. In the same way, the compost can end up as a nitrogen-poor, peat-like substance, as a heavy, dark humus high in ulmic and fulvic acids, or any range in between, depending on how the decomposition has proceeded. In an extreme case, one can lose most of the substance of the compost into the air if the breakdown cycle is not accompanied by the buildup cycle, if the bacteria metabolize the carbon into carbon dioxide, the nitrogen into ammonia and N_2, and the hydrogen and oxygen are given off as vapor.

For achieving the aimed for *guided decomposition*, the four elements—earth, water, air, and fire—must be in a balanced relationship:

Earth is the solid matter, including the 5 percent of soil mixed into the compost and the mineral amendments. Too much earthy substance slows the composting processes down.

Water involves the critical moisture content that is needed by the bacteria in their metabolism. Especially in the earlier composting stages, enough water must be present. The right amount of water is indicated when the compost has the feel of a wrung sponge; when squeezed, it moistens the surface of the hand, but no drops come gushing out. The gardener must keep a check on maintaining this kind of moisture content.

Air is needed for oxidation. Handling the air element involves making sure that the compost is not packed too tightly (a shredder helps here) so that oxygen is available for the aerobic bacteria, and keeping one's nose alert to the possible loss of ammonia.

The *fire* element involves the initial heating process of the compost, which might reach temperatures of up to 140°–160° Fahrenheit.

When the composting activity deviates into the direction of the lighter elements, when the compost is too dry, too loose, or has lost moisture during the initial heating phase, it will develop a musty smell, white mildew, and an unusually large number of pill bugs or sow bugs *(Amadillidium vulgare)*. If the compost deviates into the direction of the heavier elements, it is too wet and too compacted, then it will putrefy, develop strong odors, turn black and slimy, and maggots (fly larvae) will appear as the characteristic animal. If the compost in centered and balanced among the elements, then the smell is pleasant, almost like perfume, the color is rich brown, and the characteristic animal is the manure worm, brandling worm, or compost worm, also known as the red wriggler *(Eisenia foetida)*, a very close relative of the night crawler earthworm. This earthworm species is much more efficient at humifying organic material than the pill bug, which works in a drier medium.

In biodynamic agriculture, the decomposing processes and the buildup of new substance is not left to circumstance. Special preparations made from common herbs (dandelion, oak bark, nettle, yarrow, chamomile, and valerian) are placed into the compost to guide the processes. This is discussed in detail in chapter 17, "Teas, Preparations, and Biotic Substances."

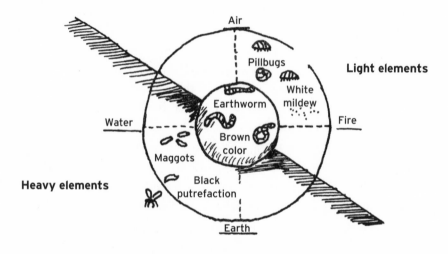

Figure 13.5. Light and heavy elements in compost

Compost carries out life functions and goes through distinct stages. In that sense, we can speak of the compost as a living organism: not the specialized organism of advanced animals, but a very generalized, amorphous organism like primitive sponges or algae in which the life functions are not centralized. Like all living organisms, it does best when given its characteristic shape, that of the windrow in this case, and a protective membrane, a skin of straw, peat moss, or plastic so that the vital odors do not escape.

Only composts whose processes have gone awry develop odors, just as only when animals are sick do they develop unpleasant smells.

There are three life stages to this generalized organism, somewhat in analogy to man's lively childhood, adolescence, and ripe old age. The first stage (Stage I) is the thermophile *bacteria-fungus stage*. This is still part of the overall breakdown cycle in the revolving Wheel of Life. Bacteria break proteins down into amino acids and finally ammonia. Carbohydrates are broken down into simple sugars, organic acids, and carbon dioxide. Other compounds are similarly broken down. If this bacterial breakdown were to continue, the organic compounds would be reduced to inorganic substances such as free carbon dioxide, atmospheric nitrogen, sulfur, oxygen, hydrogen, etc. This does not happen because the buildup cycle meshes right into the breakdown of the original organic substances. The buildup cycle proceeds with fungi, which eagerly ingest the free ammonia and rebuild the amino acids in their mycelia. Stage I is characterized by the generation of much heat given off by energy liberated during metabolism of thermophile organisms. When one sections a compost at this stage, one can see how the bacteria eat their way into the center of the pile and how they are followed immediately by the whitish mycelia of the fungi, which absorb the gases given off. During this stage, the moisture content is critical and must be monitored by the gardener.

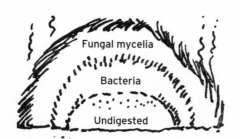

Figure 13.6. Profile of compost in Stage I

The second phase in the compost's life cycle is the *earthworm stage* (Stage II). During this, the adolescence of the compost, the heating has reduced, the heat-loving bacteria have formed spores, and the fungi have pre-digested the organic substances for the earthworms and *actinomycetes* to work on. Actinomycetes are bacteria resembling fungi in that they form webs of hyphae. One can see their presence at this stage as the whitish gray film in the compost, or one can smell them, for they are responsible for the typical pleasant "fresh earth" odor. These useful microorganisms degrade tough substances like chitin (the exoskeletons of insects), cellulose, and linin (wood), while at the same time producing a range of antibiotics that keep pathogens in check.

If Stage I has not gone completely satisfactorily, with undigested, putrid or dry sections remaining, then this would be the time to turn and remix the compost for a brief recapitulation of Stage I, causing a brief reheating. No further turning of the compost is necessary if Stage I has been completed successfully.

The earthworms now proceed to mix the organic substances that the fungi and actinomycetes have pre-digested with small amounts of clay in the presence of calcium, as they eat their way through the heap. In doing so, the polymerized carbon chains are reconstituted in the form of clay-humus complexes, which absorb cations such as calcium, ammonium, magnesium, potassium, sodium, and others.

The as yet little understood clay-humus molecule is more than a simple anion, but also coats itself with phosphates, sulfates, and nitrates. In other words, this macromolecule becomes a sponge for nutrients. Whereas Stage I compost would interfere with the growing process of plants, Stage II compost can be already used as mulch or as fertilizer for such heavy feeders as cabbages, corn, okra, pumpkins, squash, and melons. At this point of development a number of arthropods, such as centipedes, millipedes, and predatory metallic looking carabid beetles, start to settle the compost.

For young seedlings and for root crops such as carrots, beets, oyster plants or parsnips, it is better to wait for the compost to reach the *stage of ripeness*, or maturity (Stage III), the stage of the humus bacteria. It is during this stage that the compost turns into good, crumbly, fragrant humus earth. Nitrates and saltpeter, which are needed by root crops and young sprouting plants, are made available by organisms that further oxidize the nitrogen substances.[13]

The speed at which the compost goes through its three stages depends upon extraneous factors such as climate, temperature, the size of the heap, and the kind of ingredients. The quickest composts, such as Miss Bruce's Quick Return Method or the University of California Method, succeed in making compost in two weeks under ideal conditions.[14] Quick-rotting materials that are shredded to increase the surface area; a narrow C-N ratio supplied by fresh grass clippings, legumes, manures, and amendments such as bird manure, blood meal, fish meal, or cottonseed meal; and maintenance of the right quantum of moisture and air by frequent turning result in a usable fertilizer in the shortest time possible. The product basically only goes to Stage II before the earthworms enter. The clay-humus molecules that account for creating permanent fertility do not result from this speeded-up process. Quick composts seem to be symptomatic of our age of instant success and instant gratification. The quick composts make good top dressings and feeding for heavy feeders, but like sheet composting, they do not lead to permanent buildup of fertility. Ripened composts that have taken six months to a year are more stable. Some compost can even take up to four years and be fitted into four-year fertilizing cycles.

Human Wastes

Agricultural people in Asia, Central America, Africa, and elsewhere have used human excretion extensively. In rural China, every bit of night soil is collected and turned into fertilizer by fermenting it in pits or composting it. Contractors are paid for the privilege of collecting the night soil of the cities, which they in turn sell to the peasants; and privies along country roads are set up so that the traveller might benefit the famer with a bit of fertility.[15] Most of these wastes are fermented anaerobically and the slurry is eventually applied to the crops by long-handled dip buckets after a heavy rain. In dry, arid climates, night soil is dried and pulverized and then mixed into compost for turning into humus.[16]

In much of the Western world, such practices were not entirely unknown. The runoff wastes of barn and latrine were collected in large pits and utilized by the peasantry. They were spread as fertilizer with "honey wagons" and "honey buckets" onto fields and pastures in the late fall or early spring. American pioneers planted fruit trees over outhouse holes when these were full to supply nutrients to the growing tree. With the increased urbanization of the industrial age, disposal became ever more of a problem and the findings of L. Pasteur and R. Koch about the existence of pathogens in excrement (*Anthrax bacilli, tuberculosis bacilli*, salmonella, and viruses) led to the development of the sanitary flush toilet. Subsequently, the Western world flushes millions of tons of basic fertilizing nutrients into rivers and oceans, while relying increasingly on chemical fertilizers. King cites figures of 5,794,300 pounds of nitrogen, 775,600 pounds of phosphorus, and 1,825,000 pounds of potassium that are produced per annum per million population, which if not returned to the land are flushed into the ocean.[17]

What about the utilization of human feces and urine in smaller gardens? Generally, gardeners have not had the need to utilize human excrement because of the availability of manures and organic substances. Biodynamic practitioners have avoided the use of human excretion, except within the circulation of matter of the closed, self-sustaining farm organism. Most organisms avoid their own excretions. Cows and horses, for example, will not eat the grass that sprouts lusciously around their own droppings; but cows will eat where horse droppings have fertilized and horses cherish the grass benefitted by cow dung. Between the excrement and the consumption of food, a number of conversions and natural cycles must intrude. In the wake of the First World War, when biodynamics was pioneered, fertilizer was expensive and raw sewage had been used on fields surrounding larger cities, such as Berlin, to close the fertilizer gap. The resultant vegetables, especially the cabbages, had an awful taste. It was then realized that human wastes cannot be used immediately as they are; if, however, they are fully composted, and perhaps passed through other organisms, then they are perfectly good sources of nutrients. Biodynamic farms that I visited in Switzerland collected barn runoff and latrine runoff in large cement containers. These containers are treated with the biodynamic preparations and stinging nettle cuttings to help them ferment in the right way. The stench of such anaerobic decomposition is avoided by floating a six-inch layer of shredded straw, peat moss, or sawdust. When they are full, the tanks are then left to ferment for two to four years while another tank serves for collecting. The fully fermented slurry is distributed over the pastures, where it completes its cycle by being used by soil organisms and plants. The plants are fed to cattle that close the biological cycle by producing milk.

For smaller gardens, the cycle must be different. The Findhorn garden made use of human wastes in its early stages by emptying the night buckets together with straw onto the compost heaps and letting it go through regular decomposition. This seems to have been satisfactory, though it is not such a long cycle.[18] John Todd of the New Alchemy Institute reports of a longer cycle involving a number of organisms to purify sewage. A series of pools are set up through which the sewage circulates. Aquatic plants are grown in the first pool that are then fed to aquatic insect larvae, which feed fish; these are, in turn, fed to chickens, which, in turn, feed the humans again. The final runoff is used to irrigate tree crops and lawns.[19]

Composting toilets,[20] such as the Clivus System, the Van der Ryn System, or the Könemann closet[21] are worth investigating. In any case, a thorough composting process and a long biological cycle must be made use of in order to get the best and most sanitary results. The composting can be done either aerobically, as when dried sludge is composted with other ingredients and goes through a good heating process, or anaerobically, as when digesters are used to produce methane that can be utilized to fulfill other energy needs and result in a fertilizer of sorts.

Humus

The desired end product is, of course, *humus* that is composed of long-chained molecules that act as a sponge for nutrients and water. Four molecular layers of water held by excessive electrostatic charge cover good humus. It has 900 percent the water-holding capacity of sand. This water becomes available to the plant when it needs it. Humus creates good structure, or tilth, and keeps the soil from compacting. The clay-humus complex produces steady fertility. Since it binds the nutrient ions in its macromolecular structure, it is not subject to losing them by volatilization or leaching. Humus is the home of soil organisms, which are a fertilizing factor themselves because of chelation and by adding their bodies to the stock of nutrients when they die. Humus warms the ground more quickly in the spring. Studies show that humus stimulates the sugar production in plants[22] and leads to better oxygen utilization. It results in better seed germination. Vitamin, protein, gluten, and carotene contents increase in plants grown in humus as opposed to those grown in soils salted with synthetic NPK. Humus buffers the pH, maintaining the degree of acidity-alkalinity preferred by plants.

There can be no doubt about the central importance of proper humus management to the well-being of farm and garden and to man and beast. In view of the fact that in the short span of the last one hundred years, some 60 percent of the world's humus reserves have been lost, and that the cost of supplying chemical fertilizers will go up as energy shortages increase, humus management becomes ever more urgent: and composting is the right way to go about it.

Chapter 14

Companion Planting, Crop Rotation, and Weeds

Weeds are people's idea, not nature's.
—Author unknown

But while his men were sleeping, his enemy came and sowed tares (weeds) among the wheat, and went away.
—New American Standard Bible, 1955

It is a basic understanding of organic and biodynamic gardening that nature functions as an interacting whole. Every part has an effect on every other part. Why should plants growing next to each other in the garden bed not follow this principle? Many gardeners have observed such mutual influences. Scientists have been slow to study these effects because the current scientific methodology has great difficulty isolating and locating the exact interactions and the semiochemicals (pheromones, allomones, kairomones, repellents, and attractants) involved. As we have seen, a similar problem exists in the study of lunar and planetary influences on plants; it is nearly impossible to separate the significant from the insignificant variables and to repeat the exact conditions in experimental settings.

Nonetheless, few scientists deny such interrelationships among plants, and a fledgling field of synecology, plant sociology, and allelochemics (the study of the effects of plant excretions on one another) exists. Pfeiffer has mentioned research done in the 1930s.[1] Helen Philbrick and Richard B. Gregg undertook a pioneer effort on the subject in a book called *Companion*

Plants and How to Use Them.[2] It is admittedly a primer and not a scientific treatise, but it is useful for gardeners since it lists all the entries in alphabetical order. Louise Riotte wrote a similar book called *Carrots Love Tomatoes: Secrets of Companion Planting for Successful Gardening.*[3]

What are the reasons for companion plant effects? Different species are accumulators of different substances that are vital within the whole ecology. We all know how legumes function as accumulators of nitrogen, creating beneficial effects for plants growing beside them or following them in rotation. Other plants have other functions within the organic totality. For example, daisies, broom, buckwheat, dandelion, and chamomile accumulate calcium, even if growing in calcium-poor soil. Henbane, thorn apple, and valerian specialize in phosphoric acid. Foxglove collects Fe, Ca, Si, and Mg. German chamomile collects K and Ca; horsetail is an avid collector of Si; yarrow collects K, Ca, and Si. The list goes on indefinitely.[4] Measurements are hard to specify because some plants increase the percentage of elements with age as the plant grows, other decrease the percentage. Hauschka indicates rhythmical variation during the year and during the lunar cycles. Conditions of the soil substrate influence the chemistry of plants, so that, for example, tobacco is rich in K when it is grown in soil poor in K and vice versa. Furthermore, the study is complicated by suggestions of elemental transmutations as researched by Kervran, Hauschka, and Spindler.

Plants are not passively at the mercy of their environment, but actively engaged in selecting and rejecting nutrients, sending root hairs throughout the soil and then dying back, altering the soil in the process and providing specific conditions for the myriad of microorganisms, which in turn alter the chemistry of the soil. These biological processes make use of mechanical laws such as diffusion, osmosis, and so forth, but much of it occurs contrary to purely mechanistic laws, just as plant growth itself counters the law of gravity. As the great Dutch botanist Hugo de Vries pointed out in 1905, the chemical combination of the plant does not conform to that of the soil or water in which it grows, and sometimes the variation in two adjacent plants is very great.

Not just the elements are accumulated and given off by specific plants, but also the complex compounds such as amino acids, hormones, enzymes, auxins, growth inhibitors, and others, not all of which have as yet been discovered. These biotic substances are given off into the surroundings of the plant as the perfume or pollen of the flowers, as essential oils by the leaves, by excretions of the roots, by the discarding of dying plant tissue, and they are carried in insect droppings or by insect go-betweens, as is the pollen by the bees. Sometimes the quantities given off are minute, occurring in homeopathic dosage or at the rate of trace minerals. A few years ago, such incredibly small quantities would have been scorned as ineffective, but now it is known that some elements, even when removed to a distance, have an effect on the living organism of a plant.[5] Plants, especially herbs, as they give off minute substances that alter soil flora and other plants, work within the ecology of the soil much like the endocrine glands within the microcosm of the animal organism, by regulating metabolism, reproduction, and other life functions by minute chemical programmers. Since we are dealing with a macrocosmic process, the effects are not as compact as they would be in a more specialized organism. The companion effect can be created by purposeful planting of certain species next to each other, or sometimes by the administration of herb teas and ferments to the soil. Companion plant effects are probably more widespread than we realize. One need only look at fields, meadows, and forests to realize that some species prefer to grow with specific others, fitting together like the pieces of a jigsaw puzzle. Up until the dawn of ecological studies, our biological science labored under the assumption that the first law in nature is the struggle for survival and the survival of the fittest. We have seen that this dog-eat-dog idea is more a projection of the conditions created by industrialization and class struggle than a true understanding of biology. Why should plants not have evolved for mutual benefit? As the conservationist Joseph Cocannouer shows so effectively, even weeds, having evolved right along with horticultural practices, often have beneficial companion effects; they are not just mean competitors for nutrients.[6]

Flowers make good companion plants, also, besides adding beauty to the vegetable garden. The suggestion has been made that flower saps keep predators alive when pests are in low supply. The predators of sugar-sap-secreting aphids are kept around the garden by having flower nectars available.[7] Borders of aromatic herbs keep hungry insects away from crop plants, possibly because the fragrance masks the odor of the other plants. Other companion plants distract the insects from the crops.

As Alan Chadwick points out, concerning the effects and influences of plants upon one another, here, too, it is the craft of the gardener to create "relationships and dis-relationships" by planting some plants together and avoiding others.

Many native horticulturists have been aware of companion planting and have incorporated it into their agricultural lore. King reports examples of "multiple crops" in the Far East, such as wheat, Windsor beans, and cotton, or alternating rows of beans and millet.[8] Other examples are cited in ethnographic accounts, but much more research could be done in this area. Famous are the combinations of the American Indian companion cropping of corn, beans, squash, often with amaranth and a number of weeds that served as soup greens. The anthropologist Clifford Geertz tells of the almost "uncanny imitation" of the natural ecosystem of many slash-and-burn horticulturalists: "The swidden plot is not a field at all in the proper sense, but a miniaturized tropical forest composed mainly of food producing and other cultivates."[9] Anthropologist Roy Rappaport writes about the Tsembaga of New Guinea. He reports that the use of companion and successive planting results in maximum utilization of the sun's energy by the leaves, protection of soil against washing out even on hillsides, discouragement of insects, and the availability of alternative food supply if one crop does not yield. The jungle-like atmosphere is recreated when he writes: "A mat of sweet potato leaves covers the soil at ground level. The taro leaves project over this mat; the hibiscus, sugarcane and pitpit stand higher still, and the fronds of the banana spread out above the rest."[10]

As a final example of interplanted gardens, we read the description of a typical Guatemalan garden as seen by a botanist:

> The garden I charted was a small affair about the size of a small city lot in the United States. It was covered with a riotous growth so luxuriant and so apparently planless that any ordinary American or European visitor accustomed to the puritanical primness of

north European gardens, would have supposed (if he even chanced to realize that it was indeed a garden) that it must be a deserted one. Yet when I went through it carefully I could find no plants, which were not useful to the owner in one way or another. There were no noxious weeds; the return per man-hour of effort was apparently high. . . .[11]

He goes on to describe the great variety of plants complete with fruit trees, shrubs, flowers, vegetables, and beehives, stating that though it was on a slope, there was no problem of erosion because of the intertangled root systems; pests and diseases were checked because individuals of the same plant species were separated by other plants; and there was high efficiency in terms of production per pound of vegetables and fruits per man-hour per square foot. "In terms of American or European equivalents the garden was a vegetable garden, a medical garden, a dump heap, a compost heap, and a bee yard."[12]

The biodynamic, French intensive method of gardening as taught by Alan Chadwick has reintroduced such high energy gardening into the temperate latitudes.[13]

Since other books have been written on the subject, only a partial listing of companions is made here. These were gathered by observant gardeners and gleaned from tradition.

A Few Good Companion Plant Combinations

- *Beans* grow well with almost everything, especially cucumbers, strawberries, early potatoes, cabbage, and celery.
- *Cabbage* grows well with bush beans, is aided by border plant-ings of dill and chamomile, and when interplanted with hemp (*Cannabis sativa*), it has less problems with the cabbage moth. Fall cabbage will do well when preceded by early potatoes.
- *Celery* and any member of the umbellifer family, such as carrots, parsnips, Hamburg parsley, and celeriac, will grow well with any member of the lily family, such as onion, shallots, garlic, and leeks.

- *Carrots* and leeks grown together will discourage carrot fly and onion fly. Carrots are good to grow after flax, which loosens the soil. A combination of onion, lettuce, and carrot makes an excellent early bed.
- *Corn* combines well with beans, squash, and cucumbers.
- *Cucumbers* grow well with corn and lettuce.
- *Herbs* make good companions for all vegetables. Stinging nettle increases the volatile oils of mints.
- *Kohlrabi* grows well with beets and onions.
- *Leek* grows best with celeriac or celery because both like potash fertilizer and require the same amount of care. Wood ashes, composted pig manure, or a mulch of bracken fern provide K.
- *Lettuce* does well when interplanted with carrots, radishes, strawberries, or cucumbers.
- *Onions* are good with beets, lettuce, beans, and any member of the carrot family.
- *Peas* grow well with radishes, carrots, cucumbers, spinach, and turnips.
- *Potatoes* benefit from beans, cabbage, and peas. A border of horseradish and hemp is beneficial for them.
- *Radish* likes nasturtium, chervil, and peas.
- *Spinach* grows well with strawberries.
- *Swiss chard* can be interplanted with cabbage and endives.
- *Tomatoes* like New Zealand spinach, parsley, and basil as a ground cover. They also grow well near a row of asparagus.
- *Turnips* grow well with peas.

Some plants do *not* make good companions. The vegetable *Florence fennel* is unsocial and likes to have the bed all for itself, although I have grown good carrots among the fennel. Carrots do not like dill. Onions do not go well with peas and beans. Potatoes become stunted when sunflowers or Jerusalem artichokes are grown with them, and they do not like cucumbers.

Surprisingly enough, often what tastes good together when cooked into a meal also makes for good companion planting. For example, good food or planting combinations are beans and savory; beets and onions; cabbage and dill; carrots and leeks; corn and beans (succotash) or peas; tomatoes and parsley or basil; lettuce with carrots, onions, and radishes; horseradish and potatoes. Of course, this rule, like so many other rules in gardening, cannot be absolutized.

Intercropping

Intercropping is similar to companion planting in that several species are planted into the same bed, but the purpose is less that of mutual symbiotic effects than that of maximum utilization of garden space. A main crop, such as cabbage, bush beans, squash, etc. that takes a long time to mature is interplanted with quick-growing, quick-maturing crops, such as loose-leaf lettuce, kohlrabi, radishes, garden cress, or spinach. The secondary crop will be harvested before the main crops spread out to fill the space, or they are hoed into the ground as green manure. Another kind of intercropping is practiced when a tall growing crop is grown with a low, crawling plant that will provide ground cover, or living mulch. For example, cucumbers can be grown among corn, New Zealand spinach or nasturtiums under tomatoes, or squash under pole beans.

The *staggering* of crops refers to sowing or planting the same species at different times of the year, such as lettuce, peas, or radishes, which can be sown out every month before it gets too hot. This can be worked into a system of intercropping and companion planting.

The gardener must keep good records in his or her diary of each of these sowings, in order to work out the best combinations and rotations for one's particular situation.

Crop Rotation

Just as companion planting is in keeping with the natural plant associations, so crop rotation makes use of the principle of natural *plant succession*.

A landslide or a freshly bulldozed plot will quickly be settled by fleabane, nightshade, docks, mulleins, Queen Anne's lace, and other annual and biennial pioneer plants. They are first-aid plants, holding the soil and keeping it from being washed or blown away, working much like scar tissue on a body. Next in the succession are the tightly matted thorns and brambles guarding the ground, warning us, "Sorry, you can not go through here now, but, here, don't be angry, have some berries!" Amidst the shade and protection of the brambles, trees make a start, quick-growers like willows and cottonwoods, or, in drier areas, Manzanita and sugar pine. Many decades later the climax forest reestablishes itself if nature is left to itself. Such is a natural succession as one might find in Oregon.

In the garden the induced succession is not as elaborate but it, too, follows its own natural laws involving crops and weeds. Abundance of nasty weeds, or of a singular species of weed, tells us that the soil has been treated one-sidedly. Weeds are a sign that the earth wants a change to redress whatever imbalance there is in the soil.[14] Lamb's quarters will take over land that is tired of potatoes, for instance. A season of weeds makes a good fallow to restore balance, a practice made use of in the three-field system of the Middle Ages.

There are several rotational plans that may be followed by the gardener. One is to identify the *heavy feeders*, consisting mainly of leaf crops (i.e., cabbage, lettuce, Swiss chard, spinach, celery, leeks, corn, cucumbers, squash, and nightshades such as tomatoes, eggplant, peppers); the *soil improvers*, consisting of nitrogen-fixing legumes (peas, beans, broad, or fava beans); and the *light feeders*, consisting mainly of root crops (carrots, beets, parsnips, Hamburg parsley, rutabaga, turnips, onions, Jerusalem artichokes). The rotational cycle starts with heavy feeders planted in freshly fertilized soil (compost in Stage II or III). After they are harvested the soil is given a rest with a leguminous crop, which fiberizes the soil and restores some of the nitrogen. Then the light feeders may be sown in, with a dressing of very ripe compost (Stage III), to complete the cycle. A weed fallow, or a crop of completely unrelated plants such as a bee pasture of scorpion weed (phacelia), flax, or buckwheat, which are not ordinarily in the rotation, may follow; or the cycle can be started again immediately.

Another plan of rotation is similar but starts from different considerations. In order that the entire four-fold plant finds expression in the garden so that the four ethers are harmoniously balanced, one should plant root, leaf, flower, and frit-seed crops. A bed starts out in the first season with *leaf crops* which are mainly heavy feeders, followed by *flowers,* which are beautiful and easy on the soil, followed by *seed and fruit crops,* including legumes, and, finally, in the fourth season, followed by *root crops,* which include most of the light feeders. In essence this method is not much different from the first one mentioned, though it may be easier to remember.

One more consideration enters the planning of functional rotations. One must know the plant families to which the crops belong, so that members of the same family are not planted on top of one another. Family members tend to have the same nutritional needs and would wear the soil one-sidedly if planted in succession. It is surprising that out of the many thousands of plant families, only a mere dozen or so have chosen to let themselves be cultivated. The following is a list of some of the common vegetables and the family affiliation.

Families of Cultivated Vegetable Plants

MONOCOTS[14]

1. **Grasses** *(Gramineae)* include the staples upon which the civilizations of the world are built such as wheat, barley, oats, rye, millet, and rice. Of importance for the gardener are Indian corn *(Zea mais)* and oats and rye that are grown with vetch or peas as a winter cover crop.

2. **The lily family** *(Liliaceae)* includes onions *(Alliium cepa),* garlic *(A. sativum),* leeks *(A. porrum),* chives *(A. schoenprasum),* and asparagus *(Asparagus officinalis).* Plants of this family are considered to be pure and sacred in folklore. Their innocence is shown by the white of the flowers, so that Gabriel is shown holding a lily at the Annunciation. Liliaceae do not make wooden parts, indicating that they have not descended into matter to the degree that the red, thorny rose has, which was thought of as their opposite

during the Middle Ages. These plants can take cold weather. Leeks and asparagus are heavy feeders.

DICOTS

1. **Crossbearers, or mustard family** *(Cruciferae),* named after the flower petals that arrange themselves in a cross, are cold weather plants, heavy feeders, which like plenty of moisture, and include the following members: The cabbages *(Brassica),* spring from a Mediterranean sea shore weed *(Brassica maritima),* hence their ability to tolerate an environment of "salty" soil, fairly fresh manure, and lots of moisture. Thanks to their content in mustard oils and sulfury essences, the brassica do well in northwestern Europe, a region with so little sunshine that the indigenous people have evolved light skin, blue eyes, and fair hair in response. All through this region various cabbage plants are eaten: kale, sauerkraut cabbage, head cabbage, red cabbage, savoy cabbage, collards, cauliflower, broccoli, Brussels sprouts, kohlrabi, turnips *(B. rapa),* and rutabagas, or swedes *(B. napobrassica).* From the Far East are added such delicacies as pe-tsai and pak-choi (bok choy, *B. chinensis*), daikon radish *(Raphanus sativus* var. *longipinnatus),* mizuna greens *(B. rapa* var. *nipposinica),* and for stir-frying, komatsuna leaves *(B. rapa* var. *komatsuna).* Other crucifers include horseradish *(Cochlearia amoracia)* with its pungent root; scurvy grass *(Cochlearia officinalis),* which is an excellent spring tonic; garden radish *(Raphanus sativus);* garden cress *(Lepidium sativum),* used as a soil and compost tester; water cress *(Nasturtium officinale)* and mustard *(Sinapis alba)* that is used for its seeds or grown for greens. One is amazed at the plasticity of this family, from root through stem, leaves, bud, flower, to seed, every part has a use for man. Common garden weeds of the crossbearers include shepherd's purse, charlock, penny grass, bitter cress, wild radish, and others.

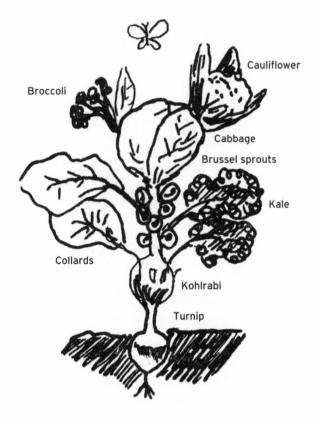

Figure 14.1. The archetypal brassica

2. **The pea, bean, or butterfly-flower family** *(Leguminosae,* or *Pa-*
   pilionoidae) includes beans *(Phaseolus),* many of which, such as lima
   beans, kidney beans, navy beans, pinto beans, black eyed peas,
   wax beans, French beans, and scarlet runner beans originated in
   the gardens of Native Americans; broad, fava, or horse beans *(Vi-*
   cia faba) which, like vineyards, were brought along wherever the
   Roman Army went; and soybeans *(Glycine max)* from China. The
   leguminosae include peas *(Pisum sativum)* found already in Neolithic lake dwellings of Switzerland; snow peas; lentils, peanuts,
   garbanzos, or chickpeas *(Cicer arietinum);*[16] vetch *(Vicia),* which
   makes a good winter cover crop; and alfalfa and clover, which
   feed our livestock and bees.

Legumes are characterized by astrality that penetrates the plant all the way down into the roots where the nitrogen-fixing rhizobia inhabit the root nodules. Unlike most other plants that reach the culmination of their growth when flowers indicate contact into the astral realm, the legumes continue growing while below, at the same time, they keep on flowering and making seeds. Most plants—nightshades for example—that allow astral forces penetrating so deeply into their physical bodies would respond by becoming poisonous, but legumes turn this astral impulse into usable protein. Pythagoras warns, however, that the enjoyment of legumes will create insensitivity to subtler forms of spirituality,[17] and in the Bible dull-witted Esau sells his birthright for a pot of lentils, indicating that the enjoyment of legumes affects the human psyche (astrality) also.

3. **The carrot family** *(Umbelliferae,* or *Apiaceae),* a family that gives us some of our important root crops, herbs, and medicines, is characterized by its openness to the etheric forces of light. They possess slender, hollow stems that radiate symmetrically into numerous branches, which in turn radiate into myriads of tiny, usually white flowers (umbels) that are accompanied by lacy, feathery leaves whose substance seems to have melted away in the sunlight. Light seems to shoot through the plant, creating bright, fragrant roots that are rich in vitamins and sugars. Such is the characteristic of the carrot *(Daucus carota),* the parsnip *(Pastinaca sativa),* Hamburg, or root, parsley *(Petroselinum crispum),* celeriac, or root celery *(Apium graveolens),* the fragrant stems and foliage of Florence fennel *(Foeniculum sativum),* celery stalks *(Apium rapaceum),* dill *(Anethum graveolens),* chervil *(Anthriscus cerefolium),* parsley *(Petroselinum sativum),* herb fennel *(Foeniculum vulgare),* and lovage *(Levisticum officinale).* Numerous seed herbs, containing essential oils, include coriander *(Coriandrum sativum),* anise *(Pimpinella anisum),* caraway *(Carum carvil),* and others. The root of angelica *(Angelica archangelica),* or angelwort, has such vitalizing medicinal properties that the folklore of many nations considers this plant

to be sacred and a protector from many evil spirits. Most of these plants are light feeders and can take cool weather.

A totally forgotten root vegetable belonging to this family and well worth reconsidering is the turnip-rooted, or parsnip-rooted chervil *(Chaerophyllum bulbosum)*. The plant grows wild from Siberia to Central Europe and has been cultivated since the seventeenth century. The roots resemble the French round carrot and have the taste of chestnuts.

Umbellifers also include some strongly poisonous plants, such as poison hemlock, or hellock *(Conium maculatum)*, whose infusion was the death drink of Socrates, water hemlock *(Cicuta maculate)*, fool's parsley *(Aethuas cynapium)*, and others that the gardener should easily recognize as they can occur as weeds in the garden.[18] Some common weeds belong to this illustrious family, such as the wild carrot, or Queen Anne's lace, cow parsnip, or gout weed, which have medical qualities.

4. **The goosefoot family** *(Chenopodiacea)*, providing leaf and root vegetables, is involved in *sal* processes as indicated by the fact that these plants collect salts and sugars. The chenopod family includes red beets *(Beta vulgaris esculenta)*; Swiss chard *(Beta vulgaris cicla)*; sugar beets *(B. vulgaris altissima)*; mangles *(B. vulgaris)*; spinach *(Spinacia oleracea)*; orach *(Atriplex hortensis)*, which has a salty taste; and Good King Henry *(Chenopodium bonus henricus)*. Lamb's quarters and saltwort as well as the tumbleweed are weeds belonging to this family.

Malabar spinach or Malabar nightshade *(Basella rubra; B. alba)* is a succulent herbaceous plant that does well in warmer regions. It is a delicious spinach that does not bolt in hot weather. Formerly considered a member of the goosefoot family, it is now classified as belonging to its own family, the *Basellaceae*.

5. **The nightshade family** *(Solanaceae)*, which includes potatoes *(Solanum tuberosum)*; tomatoes *(S. lycopersicum)*; eggplant *(S. melongena)*; chili peppers; paprika *(Capsicum)*; ground cherries, or husk tomatoes *(Physalis)*; and tomatillos *(Lycium pallidum)*, used

to make green taco sauce, have derived, for the most part, from the warmer regions of the Americas. These often rank-growing plants with their colorful fruits indicate that this plant family is eager to absorb astral forces. This is also evidenced by the fact that some of our strongest psychotropic poisons and alkaloids are derived from the nightshade family, such as tobacco *(Nicotiana tabacum)*, and the inevitable ingredients in the witches' brew, thorn apple *(Datura stramonium)*, belladonna *(Atropa belladonna)*, and black henbane *(Hyoscyamus niger)*. Because of their own heavy astral nature, these psychotropic plants can affect our astral bodies (soul life). Bittersweet nightshade *(S. dulcamra)*, horse nettle *(S. carolinense)*, and black nightshade *(Solanum nigrum)* are common weeds in some fields and are poisonous. The black berries of the black nightshade are sweet and edible, but only when they are fully ripe; otherwise they contain the glycoalkaloid solanine, which causes when ingested severe gastrointestinal and neurological disorders. Even potato tubers contain solanine when their skin is green. Petunia, a flower of this family, is not considered poisonous and has been used as a companion plant for potatoes.

The first potatoes were grown in Europe in 1589 by the botanist and medical doctor Carolus Clusius. In a sense, the spread of the potato marks the beginning of the age of materialism in Europe, at which time the gentry forced the peasants to grow potatoes because the new field crop seemed so much larger and more nourishing than traditional grains. Potatoes were destined to feed the industrial masses and the large conscription armies. The Irish were forced to grow potatoes to feed the burgeoning industrial cities of England. Failures of the potato monoculture in Europe, especially in Ireland, caused millions of peasants to settle the New World. Except for potatoes, which originate in the cool, foggy slopes of the Andes, most of the nightshades prefer warm weather and are heavy feeders.

6. **The gourd family** *(Cucurbitaceae)* is at home in the warm, moist climate of tropical regions and in rich soils. It includes many gourds, melons *(Cucumis melo)*, and cucumbers *(Cucumis sativa)* originally from India; pumpkins *(Cucurbita pepo)* and squash *(Cucurbita specis)*, from the New World; watermelons *(Citrullus vulgaris)*, originating in Africa; and the prolific zucchini *(C. pepo)* developed by the craft of Italian horticulturists.

7. **The composite family** or **sunflower family** *(Compositae;* syn. *Asteraceae)* blesses humanity with numerous flowers, medicines, and foods. The composites represent the culmination of the evolution in dicots with their complex flower heads, which are composed of many individual flowers finely arranged into a head. Each little flower is complete, yet it is part of a greater whole, so that it could well symbolize to humanity a harmonious society. The vegetables of this family include all the lettuces *(Lactuca sativa)*; summer endive *(L. sativa longifolia)*; winter endive *(Cichorium endivia)*; sugarloaf *(Cichorium intybus* var. *foliosum)*, Belgian endive or witlof *(C. intybus)*; sunflower *(Helianthus annuus)*; Jerusalem artichoke *(H. tuberosus)*; artichoke *(Cynara scolymus)*; cardoon *(C. cardunulus)*, an edible thistle; oyster plant, or salsify *(Tragopogon porrifolius)*; Spanish oyster plant *(Scolymus hispanicus)*; and black salsify *(Scorzonera hispanica)*.

   One unusual vegetable coming from this family is the beautiful garland chrysanthemum *(Chrysanthemum coronarium)*, also know as chop suey green or by its Japanese name *shungiku*. The leaves are eaten in salad or soup. And if one does not harvest all the greens, the plants will turn into an attractive row of golden flowers. Speaking of flowers, few gardeners realize that the beautiful dahlias *(Dahlia* spp.), known for their showy blossoms, have edible tubers. Indeed, natives of southern Mexico have grown them as food for centuries. There are many kinds of dahlias; some members of the genus are rather unpalatable, others bland, and some outright delicious.

The sunflower family includes dandelion, chamomile, and yarrow, which are medicinal herbs and are used in the biodynamic preparations. It includes such medical plants as arnica *(Arnica montana)*, a tincture for wounds; mugwort and wormwood *(Artemisia vulgaris* and *A. absinthium)*; chicory *(Cichorium intybus)*; sagebrush *(Artemisia tridentate)*; tarragon *(A. dracumculus)*; marigold *(Calendula officinalis)*; and many others. Common weeds of this family include the groundsel *(Senecio vulgaris)*, giant burdock *(Arctium lappa)*, and common burdock *(A. minus)*;[19] all thistles *(Cirsium* and *Carduus)* belong to this family, as does sowthistle *(Sonchus)*, hawkweed *(Hieracium)*, goldenrod *(Solidago)*, asters *(Aster)*, fleabane *(Erigeron)*, dog fennel, field chamomile and pineapple weed *(Anthemis* and *Matricaria)*, ragweed *(Ambrosia)*, French weed *(Galinsoga)*, wild lettuce (or compass plant, which sets its leaves in a north-south positions), and numerous others.

OTHER PLANT FAMILIES COMMONLY FOUND IN FOOD AND HERB GARDENS

Most of our fruits and berries, blackberries, raspberries, cherries, plums, apples, strawberries, quinces, and rose hips belong to the rose family *(Rosaceae)*, although goose berries and red and black currants that grace the borders of our gardens belong to the saxifrage family *(Saxifragaceae)*. Most of our herbs, which are important in the garden though they are not vegetables, belong to the mint family *(Labiatae* or *Lamiaceae)* and include mint, garden sage, oregano, marjoram, thyme, rosemary, basil, lemon balm, bergamot, savory, and others. One interesting root vegetable belonging to the latter family is the betony artichoke *(Stachys sieboldii)*. Discovered some hundred and fifty years ago in Japan, these delicate, fine tasting white roots are becoming ever more popular.

LESSER KNOWN VEGETABLES AND GARDEN CROPS

The preceding plants constitute most of our vegetable species. Most of us are creatures of habit so that we tend to sow or plant species that we know and are used to. It is good to consider other kinds of crop possibilities. If they belong to other families, it is all the better for the crop rotation plan. Other families that have made minor contributions to the food garden include the following:

- The buckwheat family *(Polygonaceae)* is a plant group that provides us with rhubarb, buckwheat, and sour dock. It includes the knotweeds, smartweeds, docks, and sorrels as common weeds. The tender spring shoots of the invasive Japanese Knotweed make a good seasonal vegetable in early spring.
- The morning glory family *(Convolulaceae)* supplies us with sweet potatoes, yams, beautiful heavenly blues and pearly gates, and as a nasty weed, the bindweed.
- The mallow family *(Malvaceae)* provides us with okra or gumbo (lady's fingers) as a vegetable, and flowers such as hollyhocks and mallows, whose young leaves and green seedpods make good potherbs. The marshmallows that we roast at campfires were once made from the mucilaginous roots of this plant; today however, they are mainly made from cornstarch and gelatin.
- The nettle family *(Urticaceae)* includes stinging nettle and hops, both of which make good vegetables. Nettle "spinach" and "hop asparagus" made from the young shoots are a delicacy. Hemp and mulberries are closely related to this family.
- The pokeweed family *(Phytolaccaceae)* provides poke greens, which Elvis sang about in "Poke Salad Annie." Though it can't be included in the crop rotation, pokeweed is a pretty shrub that can be grown on the border of the garden.
- The carpetweed family *(Aizoaceae)* provides New Zealand spinach *(Tetragonia tetragonioides)* as well as the ice plant *(Mesembryanthemum)*, which does well in warmer climates such as California and has tender leaves, good for salads.
- The amaranthus or pigweed family *(Amaranthaceae)* exists in endless varieties and is cultivated for its nutritious seeds or as a potherb and spinach (the young leaves) all over the world.

- The purslane family *(Portulacaceae)* consists of mostly succulent herbs, many of them ground covering pioneer plants. Gardeners have spent endless hours hoeing the "damn pursley" not knowing that in Asia and Greece it is considered a gourmet salad herb and nutritious leaf vegetable. In France one can even buy the seeds of a specially selected garden variety called *pourpier potager*. Another member of this family is miner's lettuce *(Claytonia perfoliata)* that once saved the gold miners in California from starvation. This also is grown as a gourmet green in Europe.

- The evening primrose family *(Onagraceae)* includes such pretty flowers as the fireweed, the fuchsia, and the evening primrose. The latter has an edible root, which was cultivated under the name of German rampion and enjoyed popularity as a garden vegetable in the nineteenth century.

- The daylily family *(Hemerocallidoideae)* is known for its beautiful mostly salmon-colored flowers. Few are aware that in China, the day lily is grown as a vegetable. The young leaves and shoots are harvested in early spring, the flower buds in the summer. Both shoots and buds can be eaten raw or cooked; they are stir-fried in the wok or used in soups.

- The poppy family *(Papaveraceae)*, a group of herbaceous plants often containing milky juice, include such beautiful cultivars such as the corn poppy, the California poppy, and medicinal plants such as the greater celandine (specific for liver and gall bladder afflictions) and the opium poppy. In many countries including the United States, it is unlawful to grow the latter because it is a source of opiates. Poppy seed cake, poppy seed oil, and poppy seed bagels are very popular. The seed is very nourishing and does not contain the opium alkaloids. What is not known is that the young plant in the spring makes a good salad green and can be used readily for mixed salads.

Weeds

Like the insects, weeds have caused a lot of thoughtless reactions—providing targets, for instance, for misplaced fixations about cleanliness. Some "gardeners" are fanatic about keeping weeds out of the garden, as though they were dread enemies and use strong herbicides that not only wreck the garden ecology, but prove to be adverse to human health as well. This paranoid attitude even finds its way into the literature where, for instance, it is written of the sheep sorrel *(Rumex acetosella):*

> Sheep sorrel is a communist. It waves the red flag wherever it moves in and it moves in wherever it finds the democratic grasses struggling against adverse conditions. Small though it is, its snakelike rootstalks crawl under and among the grass roots and send up new "reds" among the grass bunches.[20]

Often a xenophobic attitude is revealed, as when a naturalist writes of noxious weeds as aliens that have been naturalized.[21] These aliens must be dealt with in a drastic way, for they are suspected of harboring plant pests, lowering the economic value of the crops; "their rank growth and unsightliness" is a "perpetual nuisance in turf," they are a safety hazard, poisonous, and cause hay fever.[22] The latter was taken from a popular textbook on horticulture.

What are weeds when viewed objectively? They are the primary succession of plants where the soil has been disturbed. Usually they are followed by grasses or brambles. They are indicators of poor soil, showing the observant gardener that his or her soil is becoming too acidic, too poor, too compacted, or too alkaline.[23] Weeds do not, for instance, drive the grass out of a pasture; they merely come in and fill the gap when the soil will no longer support the grass. Thus, weeds are symptoms and not causes of our problems. Spraying for weeds is, again, putting the cart before the horse. Weeds will appear in abundance only if the conditions are right; the seeds lay dormant in the soil until such a time. For example, the fireweed and some fleabanes sprout only after a fire has gone over the ground, others germinate when the land has been ploughed, and some germinate only when there are specific planetary constellations.[24] "Analyses of soil in fields have shown that a square foot of soil down to the depth of plowing may contain 7,000 viable seeds representing a number of species."[25] These seeds are waiting for specific conditions before they will grow. By maintaining good soil husbandry, these weeds need not be a problem at all. If the soil does go out of kilter, it might even be a good idea to include a fallow of weeds to restore a balance of the soil organisms and soil nutrients.

Joseph Cocannouer, in *Weeds: Guardians of the Soil*, speaks of weeds as a blessing in disguise. Weeds are deep rooters; they explore the depths, breaking through the plow sole so that the weaker roots of the domesticated species may follow, providing them with a larger feeding zone. They fiberize the soil, countering compaction. During rainy or windy seasons they hold the soil against erosion. They help bring water to the topsoil by the capillary action of water molecules along their roots. They aid the organisms of the edaphon through exudations and chelates. When harvested, they enrich the compost with minerals and nutrients and in the pasture they provide sources of vitamins for livestock, resulting in fewer veterinarian bills. Following the lead of F. C. King, Cocannouer suggests letting select weeds grow in the garden to serve as "mother weeds" for domesticated crops. Mother weeds, such as sow thistle, lamb's-quarters, annual nightshade, ground cherry, or ragweed, will let the roots of the domesticates grow alongside into the deeper horizons, making water and nutrients available to them. Other weeds can be hoed and left on the soil as green manure, while still other weeds, such as purslane and chickweed, will provide living mulch for the taller crop plants.

According to Alan Chadwick, healthy weeds, properly managed, create an aura of vigor and health in the garden. He sows a mixture of fava, vetch, sonchus (or sow thistle), rye, senecio (or groundsel), anagallis (or scarlet pimpernel), veronica, plantain, and others mixed in with his cover crops.

According to Robert Rodale, there is experimental evidence that weeds act as insect controlling factors. In a South American study it was shown that weeds among corn reduce the leafhopper by 40 to 53 percent and the cutworms by 68 percent.[26] This, of course, involves the principle of companion plants.

Weeds also aid the soil fauna. Dying root and leaf parts feed the earthworms and the channels left by the deeper roots provide passage tunnels for the earthworms as they travel from the higher to the lower horizons of the soil.

Bargyla Rateaver and Gylver Rateaver list the following companion plant effects in their *Organic Method Primer*:[27]

- Weeds that are soil improvers because they either absorb excess salts and bind them organically or fiberize the soil include goldenrod, nightshade, ragweed, purslane, and shepherd's purse.
- Weeds that hold the soil against erosion include ragweed, pigweed, and clovers.
- Weeds that attract earthworms and aid the soil with root exudates include stinging nettle, plantain, dandelion, and thistles.
- Other weeds work directly as companion plants, such that bindweed helps corn; nettle and yarrow improve the volatile oils in herbs; jimson weed helps pumpkin; lamb's-quarters and sow thistle aid cucumbers and melons; mustard is good under grapes; dandelion helps strawberries; nettles aid the tomatoes; pigweed (amaranth) is good with all nightshades (potato, pepper, eggplant, and tomato); purslane is a good mulch for corn; and sow thistle, yarrow, dead nettle, and valerian are good for all vegetables in general.

Thus it makes good sense to know one's weeds and use them in a dynamic way. It is mainly during the spring sowing that the germinating weeds must be kept in check, so that they do not smother the crop plants. Working the soil about two weeks before planting, letting the weeds sprout, then cultivating again before sowing the vegetable seeds is the best way to accomplish this. Regular hoeing during the early growing season and hand picking within the rows will keep the weeds down between the rows. After the cultivated varieties are strong enough, one can mulch and the weeds should not be a problem. If they are a problem, then the soil is most likely one-sided in an unhealthy way. The few weeds that make it despite should be welcomed as mother weeds or possibly as edible greens. Grasses, which form a succession to the weeds, must be kept out of the garden, for they feed in the same rooting zone as the domesticated species and can be real competitors.

Instead of chemical warfare, flamethrowers, and hysterical reactions, one can enjoy the weeds and even eat many of them, as Ben Harris suggests in a book called *Eat the Weeds*.[28] Coconnauer writes that many Native Americans made no linguistic distinctions between weeds and "good" plants, so that the women cultivated the "weeds" as pot greens and medicines right along with the vegetable crops. The eating of weeds has a long tradition. The stomach and intestinal contents of the Tolland man who was preserved in a Danish bog after having been sacrificed to Odin some 2,000 years ago shows a last meal consisting of a gruel made from barley, linseed, wild flax *(Camelina sativa)*, knotweed, and many different weeds associated with cultivated land, including bristle grass, dock, black bindweed, and chamomile. The Grauballe man, another Iron Age sacrifice preserved in the peat muck, contained a springtime menu of clover, goosefoot, buttercup, lady's mantle, black nightshade, yarrow, wild chamomile, smooth hawksbeard, and nearly sixty others.[29]

Good, common, edible weeds that are found in most gardens include burdock *(Arcutium lappa)*; curly dock *(Rumex crispus)*; dandelion *(Taraxacum officinale)*; lamb's-quarters *(Chenopodium album)*; milkweed *(Asclepias syriaca)*; peppergrass *(Lepidium)*; purslane *(Portulaccea oleracea)*, which used to be grown as a vegetable in cloister gardens; sorrel *(Oxalis)*; sow thistle *(Sonchus oleraceus)*; pigweed *(Amaranthus)*; plantain *(Plantago)*; chickweed *(Stellaria media)*; wild mustard *(Brassica arvensis)*; ground ivy *(Glechoma hederacea)*; and many others. Some of these are eaten raw in salads, some must be cooked, and others have only some edible parts. It goes beyond the scope of this book to go into further detail. Care must also be taken to identify those weeds, such as the hemlock, that are poisonous.

Chapter 15

Insects and Other Beasties

Tell me, how can I get rid of the sparrows,—the gardener asked—
and the caterpillars, and the bugs,
the vole, the earth- flea, wasps and worms
and the rest of the devilish brood?
Just let them be, so that the one can eat the other!
—Wolfgang von Goethe

The use of (pesticide) sprays is an act of desperation in a dying
agriculture.
—William A. Albrecht, soil scientist

There is much paranoia these days about the multitudes of six-legged,
eight-legged, or thousand-legged fellow inhabitants of our earth. The
appearance of a few bugs in the garden often causes a hysterical reaction,
even to the point reported in a newspaper of a gardener who sprayed so
much that he was found dead among his cabbages from a self-inflicted
overdose of chemicals. Hysterical spraying is just another sign of people
alienated from the actual workings of nature. It amounts to a fear reaction
that leaves little room for calm observations.

This fear is fed by the chemical industry, which sells its poisons worldwide at a rate of over forty billion dollars annually. Pesticide sales rose by
169 percent from the years 1952 to 1968 in America,[1] and despite advances in
organic agriculture they have not stopped rising since. Vested interests fan
the hysteria through mass media by showing defoliated fields and forests, by

computing fantastic projections of the reproductive capabilities of insects,[2] and suggesting clever sayings such as "The only good bug is a dead bug," or "Raid kills 'em dead." Entomologists working with the chemical corporations write chilling reports in a clinical language that, covertly or overtly, gives way to the most life-negating, sadistic fantasies. Echoes of Cotton Mather and other puritanical fanatics are conjured up in such statements as, "It is either us or the insects!"

The attitudes toward the insect are those of total war; and it seems to be a war that mankind is losing, although he is winning some battles. Insects are, indeed, becoming more problematic. Species that have hitherto not been a problem, suddenly become pests and others are becoming immune to new poisons almost as fast as they are produced.

What are the facts? The cost of insect damage is not as great as it is made out to be. The millions of dollars assessed as insect damage are exaggerated because they include the cost of preventative spraying, research, equipment, advertising, and distribution, not the actual damage of the insects to the crops. Little has been done to realistically estimate the real impact of the insect. As we know, the spraying itself is a factor in increasing insect damage because the natural predators that keep pests in check are greatly reduced and the pest, which recuperates more rapidly, has a free go of it.

Mildews, rusts, molds, and adverse weather conditions do more extensive damage to crops than insects. The eminent biologist Vincent G. Dethier writes that the "black mount of the Third Horseman of the Apocalypse, Famine, rides in many guises, but he is not an arthropod."[3] Although insect pests are increasing due to monoculture, crops grown outside of their natural habitat, destruction of ecological balances, and increased transportation, "evidence that insects compete seriously with us for food in unconvincing. Weather, plant pathogens, and complex socioeconomic factors are the principle agents that threaten our food supply."[4]

A Glimpse at History

People's relationship to bugs has not always been as fearful as it is today. With the exception of locusts, there is little record of insect infestation in the past.[5] When locust swarms appeared, whether in the ancient Middle East or in medieval Europe, they were seen as punishment by God.[6] Many times they appeared in conjunction with other plagues such as flood, drought, pestilence, war, and famine. The recommendations for insect control in these cases were penance for the sins committed.

Some writers cite the prophet Joel as evidence that insects always have been a major problem to the grower:[7]

That which the palmerworm hath left hath the locust eaten; and that which the locust hath left hath the cankerworm eaten; and that which the cankerworm hath left hath the caterpillar eaten. (Joel 1:4)

However, we are dealing here with a prophet's warning, and he includes droughts, earthquakes, fires, war, the sun turned to darkness, and the moon turned to blood in subsequent verses, in order to bring the people back to the path of righteousness, at which time, the Lord promises to "restore to you the years that the locust hath eaten, the cankerworm, and the caterpillar, and the palmerworm, my great army which I sent among you." (Joel 2:25) then, "ye shall eat plenty" and swords will be beaten into plowshares and spears into pruning hooks. In pre-modern times, the relationship of man to the little beasties has been one ranging from delight, to awe, to reverence and respect. According to Nahuatl tradition, the red ant brought mankind corn, being commanded by the gods to find food for humanity. The Iroquois say that the locusts put their *orenda* (power) to work by chirping to control the summer heat for the ripening of the corn.[8] Italian and Swiss-German peasants made similar connections: "*In agosto quando canta la cigala dicono: è segno che il panico e il granturco maturane bene*" (When the locust sings in August that the millet and maize will ripen well); "Wenn die Grille im September singt, so wird das Korn billig" (When the crickets sing in September, the grain will be plentiful).[9]

Sir James Frazer cites examples of magical propitiations of the insects by peasants.[10] Estonian peasants will not let a child kill a weevil, admonishing: "The more we hurt him, the more he hurts us." Weevils are given a fine name and are buried or put under a stone with a corn offering. Transylvanian Saxons guard against leaf-flies by shutting the eyes and casting three handfuls of oats in different directions. To guard the field against bird, insect, or beast, the sower goes over the field imitating broadcasting with the empty hand, saying: "I sow this for everything that flies and creeps, that walks and stands, that sings and springs, in the name of God, the Father, etc." A garden is kept free of caterpillars by the German peasant woman by walking at night all around the garden dragging a broom, not looking behind, while saying: "Good evening, Mother Caterpillar, you shall come with your husband to church." All the while the garden gate is left open. Frazer tells that the Sea Dyaks of Sarawak catch vermin such as grasshoppers and put them on a tiny boat well-stocked with favorite food and then float them down a stream. If that does not work, a model crocodile is set in the fields and offered food, rice wine, and a chicken; it is then hoped the crocodile will devour the crop pests. In the Balkans and the Mideast, bugs such as locusts and beetles are buried and a funeral is held for them. In Syria, when caterpillars invaded field or vineyard, "the virgins were gathered and one of the caterpillars was taken and a girl made its mother. Then they buried it and bewailed it. Thereafter, they conducted the 'mother' to the place where the caterpillars were, consoling her, in order that all the caterpillars might leave the garden."[11]

In the Middle Ages, insect prevention was based on prayer, but once they became a problem, they could be taken to court. A set of regulations written by Burgundian tells us how legal procedures were carried out against grasshoppers:

> A court would be convened upon written request, a judge appointed, and a prosecuting and defense lawyer assigned. The prosecutor would present the case against the grasshopper and demand that they be found guilty and burned. The defense would argue that the demand was illegal because first the grasshopper had to be requested to leave the country within a specified period of time. If at the expiration of this period they had not left, the proper sentence was excommunication.[12]

Some jurists at that time argued for the rights of the birds who would suffer at the extradition of the grasshoppers. In Berne, Switzerland, caterpillars were excommunicated by the archbishop and banished in 1479 and in Lausanne, maybugs (common cockchafer) were banished for their misbehavior in 1493.

In many instances bugs were not considered in a negative sense at all, as children's rhymes and peasant sayings indicate.[13] Some bugs were sacred to humanity. For the Egyptians the scarab beetle, rolling a ball of dung, was a sacred symbol of the sun being moved across the heavens. The hornet was a war symbol, as was the fly, of which an amulet was given to brave warriors for their courage and impudence in battle. When the seven grasses bloom in the fall, the Japanese catch or buy crickets and other insects and place them in little cages. At a certain ceremonial moment, the little prisoners are freed and fly at the light of the many paper lanterns chirping to the delight of all the participants.

In most cultures insects are seen as omens sent by the gods. Some insects like the ladybird, or ladybug, are held in high esteem, called "*vaches à Dieu*" (God's cows) or "*Bete de la Vierge*" (the Virgin's beast) by the French, "*Marienkäfer*" (Mary's chafers, Mary's bug) by the Germans, and "*Himmelguegerli*" (heaven watchers) by some of the Swiss. Ladybugs should never be harmed.[14] Folklore sees in bees and ants symbols of wise industry, selflessness, and prudence.

Figure 15.1. Grasshopper

What Is an Insect?

For Darwinists, the insect, like man, is a parasite on vegetation, and is therefore, a competitor with man for limited food resources. A different picture reveals itself when we operate with the understanding of nature as a super organism, when we see that the insect has its definite place in the *scala naturae* and plays an important role in the Wheel of Life.

Insects and other invertebrates are part of the macrocosmic breakdown cycle, the cycle of de-manifestation in the Wheel of Life. This is evident when we see ants, carrion beetles, and maggots break down organic tissue where the life force (or etheric body), which provides structure and form, has left the organism at the mercy of the chaotisizing forces of dead matter. This is evident in the blow fly maggots, which eat gangrenous tissue, while at the same time secreting allantoin that helps wounds heal faster.[15] We see this in the appearance of wireworms in soils that have undecomposed organic substances in them, such as newly turned over sod. Even the beautiful bees and butterflies help dissipate the flowers by carrying off pollen and nectar before the flower dies back and returns to seed. Life would not be possible if it were not for the armies of insects breaking up dead or dying plant and animal tissue, so that bacteria and fungi can recycle them for new growth.

Plants that are eaten by insects, especially if the damage is heavy, are already weak or dying; their etheric forces are ebbing low. Any gardener will have observed that it is precisely the weak and sickly plants, probably at the end of the bed where the compost or irrigation did not reach, that are devoured by the bugs. In the same way, farmers will notice that it is the runty, weak animals that are most infested with lice, ticks, and other vermin. With unbending instinct and persistence, the insect world will attack and devour that which is not fit for life. This helps us realize that an insect infestation is not the cause of the problem, but the symptom. Plants that need to be protected by insecticides are unhealthy and unhealthful to begin with; they do not make good food, as their deficiency in life force is transmitted to the animal and humans who feed upon them. In order to avoid insect troubles, our work as gardeners must be to maintain the life force in plants. The gardener's main duty is to see that this vital flow of etheric forces goes on uninterrupted from seed and seedling, through the vegetative growth phase, through the flowering phase, and, finally, to the fruiting and seeding stage.

The insect "doppelganger" accompanies the metamorphic stages of the plant all along, from egg to its own vegetative larval growth, to the budlike pupa, and finally to the flowerlike adult. Like mirror images these two kingdoms of nature indicate their relationship, as is poetically expressed by the idea that the flower is an earthbound butterfly and the butterfly is a liberated flower.[16] Though some bugs are general feeders, many are associated with one characteristic plant of their own, such as the cabbage looper *(Trichoplusia)* with the brassica, the bean weevil with beans, the carrot caterpillar with carrots, the Colorado beetle with nightshades, or the pretty monarch butterfly with milkweed. The proboscis of the butterfly and the nectar-filled chalice of the flower form a symbiotic whole; this is the case with many plants and insects. Only abstract, alienated thinking can conceive of an insect-free garden, or fantasize about the "eradication" of insects. An insect species that gets out of control and seriously harms a crop is only an indication of an existing imbalance in nature. There is some evidence that insects are needed by the plants upon which they feed, their droppings containing trace minerals, hormones, and other substances synthesized in their bodies that are of benefit to the growth of the plants. Studies show that some plants can lose up to 30 percent of their leaf mass without much lessening of the yield.[17]

In a healthy situation, the insect larvae will feed upon older leaves that have been shaded out and are yellowing. Others feed upon mulch and litter. Only if the ground is bare will some insects (or slugs) consume the entire plant. Only if the whole plant is unhealthy, or weakened, will the whole plant be attacked. A healthy plant protects itself with numerous exudates that are becoming known to organic chemistry as alkaloids, glycosides, terpenes, tannins, alcohols, esters, acids, saponins, steroids, carotenoids, etc., as well as pheromones that will attract insect predators. Sickly or weak plants do not manufacture enough of these substances.

Another way of looking at the insect and invertebrate world is to see it as the lower level of the working of astral forces in nature. The border between the manifested etheric (the plant world) and the manifested astral (the animal world) is where the pollinating insect meets the blossom and the worm meets the root which has outlived its function. At these places the plant loses its true characteristic; it dies or dissipates itself. In the flower petals the etheric vitality of the green leaves and young shoots has been sacrificed; the plant falls apart into pollen, nectar, fragrance, and seed.

Bees, butterflies, moths, bumblebees, and others help to dissipate the plant into temporary non-manifestation by dispersing the pollen and nectar. Approximately 85 percent of our domesticated plants depend on insects for pollination. We would be in a sad state of affairs if these proverbially industrious beasties were not at work. This is something humanity should consider with all the dusting, spraying, and fumigating.

Even general feeders, such as locusts or gypsy moths, which appear in massive infestations, fall into the role of dematerializing organic substance that is low in life energy.[18] They appear at their worst during droughts, unseasonal weather, and other environmental disturbances, when the etheric energy of an entire region is at a low point. That this is so is shown by the fact that locust plagues are associated with other disasters, such as droughts, famines, bubonic plagues, pestilence, etc. as recorded in Asia, ancient Egypt, and medieval Europe.[19] Sometimes these disasters are related to cosmic rhythms that superimpose themselves on the etheric of the earth.[20]

Another way of looking at the insect is in terms of the old teaching of the four elements. The insect, when its metamorphosis is complete, goes through the four elements in its life cycle, starting from an earth-egg stage (often a saline solution concentrated in an egg, buried in the ground), to a water-larval stage (succulent, mobile larva, often living in a liquid medium), to an airy-pupa state (a cocoon exposed to air and light), and culminating in a fire-adult stage. The goal of the insect is to grow into elemental fire. Its affinity to the fire element is shown in the attraction that the flame and light have for the adults of many species; it is shown in the luminescence of some, and in the nuptial flights of bees and ant in the sunlit springtime air.

In the old elemental teachings, earth and water are connected with the coming into manifestation, whereas fire is connected with the going out of manifestation, with the sulfur process that involves the disappearance from the visible world. The insects, with their affinity for the fire element, work as an astral fire upon the etheric world of the vegetation. Just as physical fir takes wood and other combustible substances out of manifestation, so the insect, working on living or near-living substances, takes the plant or animal that has lost its life force out of existence. In peasant imaginations insects have been associated with the fire spirits or salamanders. The skaldic poets of the North tell of Loki, a fire god, being able to change himself into a fly.[21] Many cultures associate destructive insets with demonic forces that return cosmos (the orderly, structured world) back to chaos (the amorphous and unstructured world).[22] In Goethe's *Faust*, Mephistopheles reveals himself as the lord of insects and the son of Chaos. He is the doppelganger of man, just as the insect is of the plant. Perhaps one of the reasons for the irrational fear people have of insects, of the fire beings, is that they are often associated with death. Even butterflies have been linked to death, the adult slipping out of the chrysalis likened to the soul leaving the body. Also bees, associated by early Rosicrucians with selfless service and selfless death, must die when they sting in defense.

The fundamental idea of biodynamics is to channel energy into positive developments, and not to squander energy fighting what is deemed negative. Instead of poisoning insects, this positive direction calls for good composting practices, crop rotation, planting by the signs, companion planting, and good garden care in order to deal with the insects. The insects will still be there, but will pose no problem. On the other hand, investing energy into fighting the negative is severely frustrating. Ever since the advent of powerful insecticides and other sophisticated methods of fighting insect pests, the problems have gotten worse.

It seemed such a simple solution when—as a side product of war-related research—chlorinated hydrocarbons and organophosphates were discovered to poison pests. Instead, we have poisoned our environment, our fellow birds and mammals, and ourselves; our groundwater is contaminated and toxic residues remain in our foods. The bugs were able to mutate and adapt to every poison devised, becoming resistant to the point where some species even now thrive on the poison. Predators that keep the "pests" in check are wiped out instead, or greatly reduced, because, for one thing, being higher up on the food chain, they accumulate more toxins. After insecticidal application, it has been noted that other insect species, formerly harmless, become pests.[23] Agriculturists' profits have been shrinking because of the great cost of insecticides, and yet the crop losses due to insects increase despite (because of) ever-heavier doses.[24]

New pests, which have no historical record of being very detrimental in earlier times, have been cropping up in increasing numbers. In the United States in the last two centuries, the Colorado beetle, Hessian fly, cotton weevil, screwworms, grasshoppers, armyworms, gypsy moth, chinch bug, and others have become a problem. This is due to un-ecological cultivating practices, monocropping, insects transported with goods into new regions, crops grown outside their natural environment, the destruction of natural predators, as well as the synergistic effects of chemicals in the ecotope. Herbicides have been shown to trigger pest outbreaks; for example, the 2, 4, D sprayed on corn increased the corn borer larvae and made the moths more fertile.[25] Fertilizer imbalances brought about by the application of synthetic NPK fertilizer cause insect problems. This is tacitly admitted by the perpetrators of the Green Revolution, whose "miracle crops" only survive with the application of massive doses of poison. Nitrogen is especially problematic. As Steiner indicates in his *Agricultural Course*, nitrogen is the carrier of world-astrality. Healthy plant growth depends upon a proper balance between the etheric (in part manifested by sugars, starches, and other carbohydrates) and the astral (in part manifested by proteins and amino acids). Excessive nitrogen application draws aphids and mites, while too little draws other bugs to devour the sickly plants. Phosphorus deficiency increases white fly and spider mites.[26] Modern fertilizing techniques have decreased the amount of silicon content in plants, especially in cereals. Silicon in the tissue makes many plants insect-resistant and unappealing to insect mandibles.

The need (or wish) for large and quick profit has misled many a farmer and gardener to the use of strong poisons against these beings whose function merely indicates unhealthy processes already present. Instead of turning to the wisdom of a loving, organic agriculture, further black magic practices are being devised. These include bacteriological warfare; the breeding of radiation-exposed sterilized insects that will not be able to produce viable offspring when released to mate with fertile partners; the use of "juvenile hormones" that retard the larva and prevent it from ever reaching maturity; new and more insidious poisons; the use of lights and scents (pheromones) that lure, trap, and destroy multitudes; and others.

The newest stroke is to genetically modify crops so that they will poison the insects that feed on them. Genes of the *Bacillus thuringiensis* (Bt) were incorporated into corn, cotton, potatoes, peanuts, and other crops. In the United States, 85 percent of the corn is genetically modified with Bt in order to poison the corn borer, the cornear worm, and others. Collateral damage on non-target insects occurs, as evidenced by a 30 percent decrease in the monarch butterfly population (monarch caterpillars eat the pollen of Bt corn that dusts their food plants).[27] Even with these new methods, there are indications that the insects are mutating, adapting, and becoming resistant, and that there are most likely other unforeseen, harmful effects on the rest of nature. The entomologists and chemists involved remind one of the sorcerer's apprentices, whose every solution to the basic problem creates new problems.[28]

Perhaps the Bible is right when it considers insects (locusts) to be sent by supernatural agencies in consequence of having erred from the path of life. It is suggested that the insect pests are stopped by repentance (L. *re pensum* = to reconsider) concerning the way mankind has been carrying on its business.

Materialistic science cannot really understand insects. The tremendous adaptability to adverse conditions brought about by DDT, arsenic, and other poisons indicates a great biological "intelligence." Despite very costly efforts to eradicate pests, not one species has been eliminated successfully. Who has not been amazed at the rapidity with which aphids can suddenly populate a cabbage or bean patch? Already as it is born, parthenogenically and viviparously, the young aphid has embryos of several hundred more developing inside it.

Consider the marvelous architecture of the hexagonal honeycomb, the paper wasp nest, the air-conditioned termite hills in Africa; consider the uncanny camouflage of the walking stick, the tomato hook worm—which looks like a rolled up tomato leaf—or moths that look like old yellowed leaves; consider the tachinid fly larva that slowly eats its caterpillar host from the inside, making sure that no vital organs are damaged until it has completely hollowed it out and is ready to slip out. Some insects seem to have established their patterns hundreds of millions of years ago;

and some have found a niche for themselves only yesterday, such as the drugstore beetle, which can live in bottles of arsenic and other poisons for years as its favorite habitat. What overwhelming intelligence is there in the social insects, in ants, bees, and termites, as they divide into social bodies of egg-laying queens, armies of workers, fighters, nursemaids, and other functionaries! This remarkable adaptability of insects cannot be explained merely by microscopic or chemical analysis of individual bugs. We do our observations more justice when we consider once again the notion of an organizing genius for each species, that guides and directs each insect as part of a concerted whole, much like the cells and organs of our bodies are subject to an overall structural, functional gestalt. That this organizing intelligence exists beyond the makeup of the single individual insect is seen when a single ant is removed from its colony and errs haplessly about until it dies. A hive or a colony of social insects might be analogous to an organ for the "individual" that marks the genius of the species. At this point, we once again reconsider the idea of supersensible "group souls," "group-egos," "animal bosses," "grandmothers," or "grandfathers" that are spoken of in the lore of most native peoples. Shamans are specialists who natives claim can "talk" with these supersensible beings. With this in mind, perhaps we can find a better way of dealing with insect problems.

Insect species are still very macrocosmic beings. They have not condensed and centralized into a single body with centralized organs. Considerations of this nature show us that killing an insect is not of the significance that killing a bird or a mammal is. It is more like pruning plants or cutting hair or fingernails. It is not a deeply incarnated astrality, let alone a self-conscious ego that is killed, but a being with very diffuse macrocosmically rooted soul functions whose essence is found in supersensible realms.

Beneficial Insects

Estimates of the number of insect species vary. There are several hundred thousand species, of which 90 percent are considered beneficial. Of the remaining 10 percent, only a small portion qualifies as serious pests. Some so-called pests might cause slight scarring of the fruit rind, resulting in cosmetic damage that in no way diminishes the quantity of quality of the food.[29]

Pollination is one of the most important functions of insects. All of our fruits (citrus, apples, pears, strawberries, cranberries, etc.), most vegetables, grains, cotton, tobacco, and the clovers, which feed our livestock, depend on insect pollination. Some insects are specialized to pollinate only one or a few species, such as the fig wasp, the figs. The members of the rose family are pollinated by bees; the legumes by bees and bumblebees; night-flowering plants by moths; and the carrot family (umbellifers) by flies, bugs, and wasps.

We are dependent on insects for honey, beeswax, silk, shellac, and various dyes and medicines.

Many insects and other arthropods are important as predators and parasites that keep populations of potential pests in check. Entomophagous insects include the dragon and damsel flies that eat mosquitoes, ladybug beetles that eat aphids, and wasps *(Vespidae* and *Sphecidae)* that eat caterpillars and grasshoppers; lacewings (whole larvae are known as ant-lions) eat aphids; various shield bugs *(Hemiptera)* eat caterpillars; praying mantises eat grasshoppers and any other creeper or crawler they can get their *tarsi* on; tachinid flies parasitize other bugs by laying eggs in them; and so on.

Carrion beetles, dung beetles, dung flies, and others function as scavengers, removing diseased and obnoxious substances. Ants, termites, and beetles turn dead logs into humus for the forest. Soil insects are important in churning, aerating, and adding organic residues to the soil. Some species keep weeds in check. Most insects are food for the animals that delight our senses: fish, frogs and lizards, birds, skunks, moles, shrews, and hedgehogs. Finally the aesthetic delight of delicate butterflies and moths; the shiny, metallic glimmer of beetles; the humming of the bees; the songs of crickets, locusts, and katydids; and the dance of fireflies in warm summer nights must not be forgotten.

With this in mind we can appreciate the need for caution when it comes to indiscriminate spraying or poisoning. Even organic, biodegradable insecticides should be used with caution, if at all.

Practical Application

Most biodynamic gardeners are not much worried about insects, for seldom do they become a problem. Biodynamics works on a preventative, prophylactic basis. Once again, it is the practice of conscientious composting, companion planting, rotation, seeking to plant at the right cosmically determined moment, and the use of biodynamic preparations that maintains the balance. A healthy garden *must* have bugs in it, at least a thousand different species! One can even admire the squash bug and take delight in the cabbage butterfly without having to panic.

Pest damage is kept low by insuring smooth, steady growing from seed to harvest. This involves proper watering, avoiding droughts or sudden cold showers during the heat of the day, for this shocks the plant and interrupts the flow of vital energy. Planting in the proper season and sign implies making cosmic energies available to the plants. Composting guarantees the kind of nutrient release that will not be excessive or too slow, making for harmonious growth of insect-resistant plants. Companion planting consists of picking varieties that grow well together, as well as planting flowers and herbs that keep insect levels lower. Flowers and herbs on the border of the garden plot help mask odors attractive to insects, according to one theory, and flower nectar keeps predators alive when pests are in low supply.[30] Here are some examples:

- Garlic is such a companion for many crops; nasturtium is good with squash for protection against white fly and wooly aphids.
- Beans and potato rows alternated keep both bean beetles and Colorado beetles down.
- Carrots alternated with leeks or onions keep the carrot fly as well as the onion maggot in low frequency.
- Marigolds keep nematodes from infesting the soil (nematodes, or eelworms, are mainly a problem in soils with insufficient organic matter).
- Aromatic herbs reduce bug damage: savory aids beans; basil helps tomatoes.[31]

- Certain *catch crops*, such as soybeans, calendula, radish (for flea beetle), and tomatillo, attract hungry insects and will keep the other plants relatively bug free.

Besides companion plants which add color, fragrance, and beauty to the garden, one can create optimal conditions for other predators of insects, such as birds, amphibians, reptiles, and some mammals. It takes keen observation and becomes a lifelong study to see the intricate ecological connections that exist in the garden. In the chain of nature, the birds eat at the extreme periphery of the plant; they eat seeds or bugs from the crown of the plant and scratch grubs and worms from the foot of the plant. Some birds tend more to the side of the seeds, such as seed-eating sparrows, blackbirds, finches, and pigeons; others are mainly or purely insectivorous, such as swallows, whip-poor-wills, purple martins, warblers, vireos, wrens, robins, and woodpeckers; whereas most are omnivorous, varying their diet between seed, berry, and bug. Most of our beautiful songbirds are strongly insectivorous. To lure these creatures into the garden ecotope, trees and hedges, bird feeders, baths, and shelters must be provided.[32] Various seeds and suet (for woodpeckers, titmice, and chickadees) can be fed. Birdhouses are easily made.

Hedges not only keep chilling and desiccating winds from blowing across the garden, but make for ideal bird shelters. The wild fruits and berries found in a hedge can feed the gardener as well as the birds. Elderberries make good diaphoretic tea from the blossoms and wine and jam from the berries. Hawthorn, roan, rose, blackberry, mulberry, chokecherry, and other berry bushes provide teas or jams, or both. Hazelnut hedges bless the gardener with filberts. One can plant hedges of hackberry, dogwood, barberry, viburnum, and others that are of aesthetic appeal and keep the birds from some of the prized domesticated berries—though nets might become also necessary for the latter. Even wild patches of evergreens or blackberry thickets are useful for nesting areas for our feathered helpers, or as shelters for toads, garter snakes, turtles, and skunks, all of which are avid gobblers of bugs. Toads like to live in the moist atmosphere of the compost pile. From the magnitude of their droppings, consisting of hundreds of chitinous skeletons, one can ascertain how beneficial they are. If new toads are procured, it is a good practice to leave them in their cages in the garden for a few days, for they need some time to acclimate themselves; otherwise they will start hopping back to where they came from. Garter snakes like to patrol the garden, keeping insect populations at a minimum. Some gardeners let bantam hens, ducks, and geese range in the garden but might lose a lettuce or tomato or two in the process.

All these procedures and precautions, aided by some handpicking, should be enough to prevent any major insect problems in the garden. If for some reason, however, there is an infestation, the gardener ought to investigate thoroughly and study the problem closely before reacting with poisons. Even organic poisons kill beneficial predators and upset the biological balance. With the aid of one's garden diary, one should recall the weather conditions, type of fertilizer used, type of crop, stellar constellation of planting date or outbreak, preceding crop rotations, and other vital data that might indicate what led to the outbreak. One might also study the life habits of the pest to see how one can cope with it in the simplest way.

Ecological interconnection must be understood before any drastic action is taken. Sometimes people find holes in their cabbages or tomatoes with an earwig, pill bug, or even an earthworm in it, promptly declaring these hapless creatures guilty. Real observation would show that they merely sough shelter in these cavities, feeding on the droppings left behind by the slugs, which ate the holes in the first place.[33]

During adverse conditions, when plants are likely to be befallen by a bug, or in the early stages of an infestation, nonpoisonous teas and preparations can be given to strengthen the plants. Helen and John Philbrick, in *The Bug Book*, provide a number of such recipes.[34]

Compost water, manure teas, and comfrey or nettle ferments aid weakened plants in regaining their life forces. Stinging nettle ferment or tea slightly changes the makeup of the plant sap, so that the plant does not taste as good to the bug as before. Only as a final measure, if all else fails, might one resort to some organic, biodegradable poison. Most insecticides can be grown right in the garden. Plants from which insecticides can be made include beautiful flowers such as pansies, marigolds, asters, chrysanthemums, petunias, cosmos, nasturtium, coreopsis, tobacco, and herbs such as feverfew, wormwood, tansy, coriander, and garlic.[35] Most of these flowers or herbs can be dried, pulverized for dusting, or brewed into a tea. Tea mixed with old-fashioned soap, such as green soap, to make the poison stick to the leaves longer, will do the job. There is really no need to buy commercially sold insecticide sprays and dusts made from tropical plants such as derris (rotenone), pyrethrum, or ryania, which unfortunately also kill useful cold-blooded animals such as toads, frogs, and snakes. If used at all, they should be used selectively and not applied in a blank, indiscriminate fashion.

Importing predators, such as praying mantises, trichogramma wasps, or ladybugs is probably not necessary. Often they will not stay in the garden, and usually there should be enough natural predators in the area, unless mindless spraying has severely decimated the predator population.

It should not be necessary to use such radical interventions as viral (e.g., nuclear polyhedrosis) and bacteriological (e.g., *Bacillus thuringiensis*) means. Light traps and electrocuters, composed of fluorescent tubes and a high voltage grid, are to be avoided, for they lure insects from the surrounding countryside and often friendly or harmless bugs are destroyed *en masse* this way. The use of pheromones, hormonal control (juvenile hormones), and putting bugs through blenders and then spraying them seem unnecessarily cruel. Such practices probably work to shock the "genius" (group soul) of the species and will most likely have unforeseen repercussions. It goes without saying that the synthetic sprays that are carcinogenic or mutagenic—that kill friendly insects, birds, and mammals; contaminate soils, groundwater, and mother's milk—should be avoided altogether.

For more specific information, the reader is advised to consult the literature of the Organic Gardening Movement (Rodale Press) and of the Biodynamic Farming and Gardening Association.

Fungus, Virus, and Bacteria

Fungi (mildews, rusts, smuts, molds), bacteria (rots) and viruses (mosaic, leaf, curl, yellows) are signs of environmental disturbances that weaken the flow of vital energies in plants. Fungi and bacteria are saprophytes that take hold of tissues whole life is declining. The disturbances are often weather induced. Dry weather followed by wet, drizzly weather is ideal for fungus infections. At such times the ground is often still dry but the moist air induces the stomates, or pores, of the plants to open, so that fungus spores can easily grow into the weakened plant. Artificial fertilizer, such as sulfate of ammonia, which releases nitrogen too rapidly as opposed to steady-release compost, creates softer tissues, which rupture and dissolve more easily when atmospheric conditions favor fungi and bacteria. Low silicon content, correlated with artificial fertilizer, makes it easier for mildew infection.

Prophylactic measures include healthy soil that can deliver nutrients and water steadily, care in watering, and mulching to prevent soil moisture from fluctuating, as well as compost application, which aids the mycorrhizae, which as Waksman and other soil biologists have shown, give off antibodies that can be absorbed by the roots of the crops. Thinning plants to the proper distance so they have access to sunshine and air keeps many fungi in control.

On rainy, cool days it is a good idea to spray the plants with horsetail tea and a 2 percent water glass solution, whose silica content helps to transmit light to the plant tissues. Chamomile tea, milk, dilutions of sulfur, solutions of garlic juice, and a tea made of chives inhibit mildew on cucumbers and other plants. Spraying chamomile tea, horsetail tea, and mixing peat moss into the bedding soil can prevent dampening off of young seedlings in seedbeds. Fungi, bacteria, and viruses related to fluctuations in weather and other environmental factors are generally more detrimental to plants than are the insects.

Chapter 16

The Garden Calendar

> The gardener who imagines that his work can be reduced to a set
> of rules and formulae, followed and applied according to special
> days marked on the calendar, is but preparing himself for a double
> disappointment. Few things are so certain to be uncertain as the
> seasons and the weather; and these, rather than a set of dates, even
> for a single locality, form the signs, which the real gardener follows.
> That is the great trouble with much book and magazine gardening.
> —Frederick Frye Rockwell, *Around the Year in*
> *the Garden,* 1917

The seasons express themselves differently in the diverse locations and altitudes of the country. Most garden books and almanacs have general information that is fairly safe to follow. The monthly indications given in the *Organic Farming magazine,* the *Calendar of Organic Gardening,* and the voluminous *Encyclopedia of Organic Gardening* (all put out by the staff of Rodale Books) divide the United States into general climatic zones, giving hints for month by month gardening activity.

The gardening calendar discussed here is based on data collected locally in the Rogue River Valley Area. Other parts of the country will have similar, but not exactly the same seasonal distributions. The *frost free date* in spring, the first frost in the fall, the thaw out after a winter freeze, the length of the growing season, the average yearly temperatures, the relative amount of cloud cover and rainy days compared to sunny days, each of these factors will be different from location to location. It is best to ask the old-timers in areas where one is a newcomer.

In Southern Oregon the year divides into a dry, sunny, warm season that lasts from the end of May into October and a cool, rainy, cloudy season that starts with the protective fogs in November and lasts on and off until May. The sunny season is ushered in by frog concerts and a parade of the most beautiful spring flowers. As the summer proceeds, it gets progressively drier. As madrone (*Arbutus*) and manzanita shed their bark and previous year's leaves, the woods are alive with the metallic rustle of locusts and desiccated foliage. Thunderstorms are rare and do not bring the relieving moisture as in the Midwest, for example. The cold, rainy season, coinciding with the half of the year when the moon makes a higher arch in the heavens than the sun, brings an abundance of lunar vegetation, including many mushrooms that are a gourmet's delight (boletus, milky caps, russula, coral mushroom, puff balls, as well as hallucinogenic psilocybin mushrooms) and lichens and algae that coat the oaks in their winter garments. There is an echo of early spring when the rains start, with grasses, chickweed, miner's lettuce, and dandelions turning green and lush until frost nips them.

There is never the long, hard freeze and continuous blanket of snow that makes it impossible to dig in the ground in the winter as in other parts of the country. In February, as the days noticeably lengthen, it is already possible to put in the first crops (peas, snow peas, broad beans, arugula or garden rocket, spinach, onions). Yet the frost-free date is still a long way off. As long as the white shimmer of snow stays on the mountains, it is not safe to put out summer crops. Many a newcomer has been fooled by the mild weather interspersed with rain lasting from February to April and May, putting summer crops in, only to see the tomatoes, eggplants, peppers, beans, and squash limp and black after a frost has passed in the early morning. Frosts lasting to the end of May and into June make gardening tricky in this region, and the dry conditions of July, August, and September make it ever more difficult. It is no wonder that the native tribes, such as the Takelma or Klamath, preferred hunting and gathering to horticulture, for they could not make use of such techniques as irrigation, sprinkling, or setting up protective plastic tents. Native Americans in the more hospitable Midwest, East, and Southeast were, on the contrary, master horticulturists.

In the spring, *raised beds* help to warm and drain the soil more quickly. The winter cover crops (legume-grain combination) will have gotten high enough by February and March that they can be turned in and still have plenty of time to rot and feed the earthworms before the summer crops go in. After midsummer solstice, it is important to concentrate on watering and mulching to cut down water evaporation. Usually the fall weather is mild and lasts a long time, so that it is easy for the winter garden to get a good start. (See Appendix I: Winter Gardening in Oregon.)

The following is a month-by-month description of how the gardening year might proceed in the Rogue Valley area:

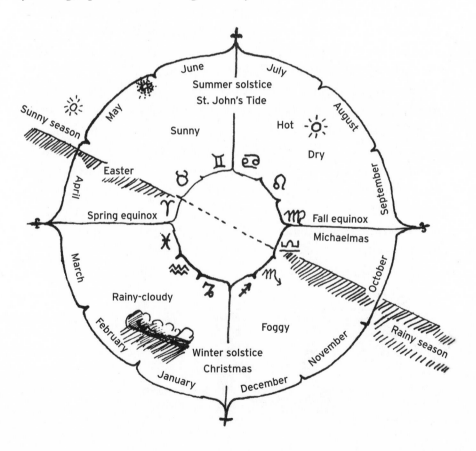

Figure 16.1. The gardening year

January: Prune fruit trees and berries in late January. Feed your bird friends with wild birdseed mixes and include suet for the hairy woodpeckers and chickadees. Build bird shelters.[1] It is a good time to visualize the garden in one's minds eye, to plan the year's garden crops and rotations, to read garden books and catalogues, and to order whatever seeds one might need.[2]

February: On drier days in February one can prepare the double-dug beds for sowing the first crops. Toward the end of the month, fava (or broad) beans, snow peas, pod peas, corn salad (or lamb's salad), onions, shallots, garden cress, and radishes should be already sown. Local gardeners pick George Washington's birthday (February 22) as the day to sow peas. Pea beds can be interplanted with early lettuce, spinach, and radishes, with the tall peas on the north or west side of the bed and the short peas on the south side of the bed for better light utilization. The peas and fava beans should be inoculated with nitrogen-fixing bacteria spores.

These new plantings can be protected from frost by stretching clear plastic tents over them. A frame of PVC pipe can support these tents, which is the cheapest material to use. Care must be taken to air the tents out regularly in order to prevent mildew, to uncover them when the sun is shining to prevent cooking the seedlings, and to cover them over on cold, clear nights. If it gets really cold, an extra layer of plastic, blankets, or even straw can be placed over the tent. Milk jugs filled with hot water can be put under the tent; water gives off its warmth slowly enough to prevent freezing.

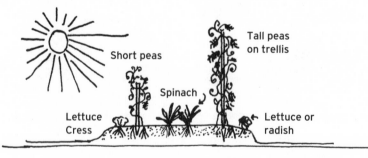

Figure 16.2. Early garden bed

The winter cover crops can be turned over and left to rot. Root crops that are still in the ground from the previous season (carrots, oyster plant, beets, Hamburg parsley, parsnips, celeriac) are imperceptibly getting ready for new sap flow in their biennial cycle, and can be removed to a cool root cellar to delay their growing and getting stringy and tough too soon.

March: In early and mid-March the following plants can be sown into carefully prepared soil of the cold frame: summer cabbage, broccoli, cauliflower, collards, and other members of the cabbage family; lettuce, Swiss chard, onions, leeks, celery, celeriac, and endive. The cold frame, composed of a sifted mixture of good soil (one part peat, one part sand, one part ripe Stage III compost, and two parts good garden loam) is framed with boards and has a lid made from storm windows or stretched plastic. Most gardening books give directions how to build such a frame.[3] Into this cold frame the seeds are sown into little patches of one or two square feet; later, when the seedlings are big enough they are transplanted. The seedlings need good care after they germinate. They must be watered, weeded, and thinned so that they do not crowd each other. A light shower with horsetail-chamomile tea once a week is recommended to keep the seedlings from dampening off. The cover should be closed at night and lifted slightly during the day, in order to let the air circulate and keep the leaves dry. Like all the umbelliferae, celery and celeriac take a long time to germinate (three weeks), so patient weeding and gentle watering of the soil are necessary. Celeriac seeds are so small that mixing the seed with fine sand is recommended before sowing so that the seeds will be spaced more evenly.

From mid-March toward the end of March, oyster plant, dandelion, garden orache, beets, carrots, kohlrabi, mustard, parsley, Hamburg parsley, parsnips, turnips, and rutabagas can be sown out directly into the garden. Slow-germinating carrots can have a few lettuce or radish seeds mixed in to mark the rows. The row distances vary; most seed packets and garden books give recommendations and directions. The rows should be spaced wide enough to be able to cultivate with a thrust-hoe or a draw-hoe (pendulum hoe). It is recommended that the bed is worked two weeks before sowing, so that weed seeds will have had ample time to sprout and can consequently be destroyed by hoeing and raking. After sowing the rows, the beds must be hoed between the rows to prevent the soil from crusting, to facilitate carbon-dioxide/oxygen exchange, to stop the capillary movement of water molecules upward to the soil surface where evaporation takes place, and to keep weeds from overtaking the crop plants. This is done regularly, but especially after rain or watering.

In March one can still put out more peas, corn salad, onions, and spinach and also sow asparagus for later transplanting. March is also the time during which potatoes can be put into the ground. St. Patrick's Day, in honor of the patron saint of the Irish whose fate is so tied up with this tuber, is a good time to plant the potato, providing the moon is in a good position. The potato, a very lunar plant, is best planted near apogee and in the earth sign of Taurus. Scorpio and Cancer do not make for good potatoes. Like legumes, they can be planted in the new moon.

Like most staples, such as rice and corn, the potato is surrounded by magic and ritual.[4] It seems that almost every gardener has his own procedure as to how best to grow potatoes. Some swear by mulch, some by hills, some by planting them in tires, but in any case, an old saying goes that "the dumbest farmer has the largest spuds," meaning that gut feeling is just as important as intellectual acuity. The method, which works for me, involves the following steps:

1. The soil is fertilized with well-rotted manure or old compost (Stage III) and a light dressing of wood ashes; ideally one could also add a spraying the biodynamic preparation 500, the horn dung preparation.
2. The seed potatoes are laid in a box onto the windowsill for a week to green out.
3. On the day of planting, they are cut into sections containing an eye each (each eye forms a new plant). These sections are dipped in pure hardwood ashes to cauterize the fresh cut and to provide them with the potassium they like.
4. The cuttings are then laid in rows two feet apart, at a distance of a foot and half within each row.

5. The soil is raked over the rows, forming a ridge. As soon as the first leaves appear, more soil is raked over the ridges, leaving just the top leaves exposed.
6. In the summer, the potatoes are heavily mulched.
7. As soon as the potato plants flower the first tubers can be dug up for eating (late June).
8. When the foliage finally dies back in September, the field can be cleared and the potatoes stored in the cellar.

At the end of March, toward the beginning of April, if there is no greenhouse available, a *hot bed* can be put in for growing the seedlings of tomatoes, tomatillos, peppers, eggplant, okra, New Zealand spinach, Malabar spinach, cucumbers, and squash. The hot bed is made by digging a bed three or four feet wide, to a depth of three feet. Two feet of fresh horse manure is packed in and soaked with liquid manure, animal urine, slurry, or sludge. A five-inch layer of peat moss covers the manure to absorb ammonia and methane, which might otherwise escape and injure the young seedlings. A foot of good garden loam, a mixture similar to that which is used for the cold frame, is put on top. Into this good soil the seeds for the warmth-loving summer crops are sown. The sides are boarded up and glass or a stretched plastic cover is put over the seedbed at an angle toward the south exposure to catch and collect the sun's warmth. In this way the seedbed will be heated from above and below. The horse manure mixture heats steadily and gently for about six weeks, a fact made use of by alchemists who "cooked" their concoctions in horse manure.[5] All the rules relating to the cold frame must be observed here, too: gentle watering with slightly warmed water, careful weeding, thinning to space the seedlings, airing the bed, and covering during cold nights. A system like this demands constant, daily attention, but it will be much cheaper than buying pony packs at a store or nursery, and it will give good, hardy seedlings, which can be set out after the frost free date has passed. The squash, zucchini, and cucumbers, if they are grown in the hot bed, should be placed into *peat pots*. Later each peat pot, with the young plant in it, is planted directly into the soil; this makes the transplanting less traumatic for these sensitive plants.

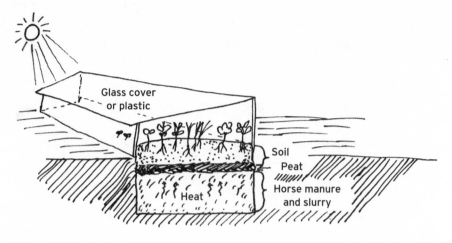

Figure 16.4. Hot bed (side view)

Also during the month of March, certain perennials such as asparagus, horseradish, pokeweed, rhubarb, Jerusalem artichoke, and comfrey can be planted in permanent beds along with hardy herbs such as nettle, chives, lavender, sage, hyssop, and others. Chamomile can be sown at this time in slightly alkaline soil, preferably into the garden paths. Chamomile, like its relative the pineapple weed, does not mind being trampled on.

April: In April much of the work started in March continues. More sowings of hardy plants can be made. The cold frame and hot bed need special care, as do the composts. Easter season, determined by the full moon after equinox, is known to be the most fertile time of the year, when the land is greening with astonishing vitality. Some old-timers put in special Good Friday gardens.

May: Very hardy plants such as cabbages, broccoli, cauliflower, endives, lettuce, Swiss chard, and leeks can be planted out a couple of weeks before the frost-free date. Toward the end of May, one should be eating some snow peas, pod peas, perhaps some fava beans, plus spinach, nettle, lettuce, green onions, cress, and radishes. After the frost-free date, the warm weather plants can be put in their beds.

June: By now, as midsummer, or St. John's tide, approaches, forces of light and warmth streaming in from the cosmos make it possible to put out more of the warmth-loving plants. Transplanted from the hot bed into the regular garden beds are tomatoes, okra, New Zealand spinach, Malabar spinach, eggplants, peppers, ground cherries, tomatillos, cucumbers, and squash. At first it might be a good idea not to mulch so that the ground can warm up some more, but later, mulching is essential. At this time the celeriac needs to be planted out; any earlier would not endanger its survival, but would adversely affect its tuber-forming ability. Tender herbs such as basil, savory, marjoram, rosemary, and nasturtium are sown out at this time.[6] Beans, corn, and summer lettuce can be sown directly into the ground. The early pea and spinach beds can be cleaned out now, making more room for the summer plantings. Strawberries should be thinned and mulched now, and the runners transplanted to a new bed. It is also high time to stop cutting rhubarb and asparagus so that they will have a chance to acquire strength for the next year.

July: Mulching and correct watering is the main concern now. Tomatoes should be trained up stakes so that the fruits will not rot on the ground. The suckers should be snapped off so that most of the energy of the tomato plant goes into the main shoot and the fruits. Similarly, cucumbers should be trained up chicken wire fences so that they do not sprawl all over the ground and can be picked without moving the vines when they get ripe; usually it is because the vines have been moved that the cucumbers become bitter.

The cold frame is needed again by the end of this month to sow out fall cabbage, cauliflower, kale, Brussels sprouts, broccoli, sugar hat, lettuce, and endives. These seedbeds must be kept moist and shaded by lattice, burlap, or cheesecloth.

For more winter vegetables, carrots, turnips, kohlrabi, rutabagas, Chinese cabbage, Hamburg parsley, and beets can be sown in any beds that are still unoccupied. A more shaded location, good humus, sufficient moisture, and special care might alleviate some of the problems of seed germination at this time of year. Often it is necessary to re-sow these rows because of poor germination.

Melons must be thinned to keep them from crowding each other. Zucchini and cucumbers must be harvested continuously in order for them to keep producing. Now is also the time to sow out Florence fennel, so that it will grow the big, bulbous leaf bases that make delicious fall and early winter eating.

August: The July work continues in August. By mid-August the seedlings in the cold frame can be planted out into the fields. These plants must receive a scoop of good compost and be watered and mulched immediately. This is the time to cut and dry many of the herbs, just before they bloom. (Except the ones from which the flowers are used, such as chamomile, mugwort, or calendula, for example.) The best plants can be marked for saving for seed. By now, an abundance of fresh food will bless the gardener.

September: There is still time to plant sugarloaf (witloof) salad, endives, corn salad, and spinach for fall and winter. Cover crops can be sown out wherever there is room. Putting them in at this time of year insures good, lush growth before the days get too cold and the birds, still having plenty of other food to eat, will not be so tempted to scratch up the seeds. Garlic cloves can be put in. Most of the other work consists of harvesting the summer crops, this being the time most traditional harvest festivals were celebrated.[7]

October, November: With the passing of fall equinox, or Michaelmas, the jungle-like profusion that characterized the summer garden is gone. Jack Frost and other such elemental beings might be appearing soon, so it is wise to get one's plastic tents ready to put up in case of a cold night. Sprays from valerian flowers or from the roots of the Japanese knotweed can be used on tomatoes and bell peppers to extend their frost hardiness. Jerusalem artichokes, having finished blooming, are now ready to harvest, but can be harvested throughout the winter right from the ground, unless the winter is exceptionally cold and there is a risk they will freeze. Toward the end of November, it is advisable to put leaf and straw mulch over the winter crops that stay in the garden soil to protect them from later frosts and light freezing. Strawberries, asparagus, and rhubarb rows are now mulched with old, rotted manure. As the beds are cleared and leaves raked up, composts are built that last through the winter. These composts are fed during the winter with kitchen wastes and various manures. They should be sufficiently humified for use by the time spring comes around.

December: This is a good time to relax, eat pumpkin pie, and count

Figure 16.5. Winter tree trimming

one's blessings. The compost should be watched so that the rains do not leach them out. The twelve days of Christmas, from Christmas to Epiphany, used to be taken as oracles for the coming year; each day represents the consecutive months of the year. How the weather and the moods are on each day is an oracle of what is to come.

This cursory description of the gardening year is by no means complete. Each landscape, each farm-garden organism, as well as each year has its own particular character. Some years this or that crop will do very well, and another year rather poorly. Each year has a distinct weather pattern and the kinds of bugs, birds, or weeds will be slightly altered. There can be no exact how-to-do-it manual, as in mechanical sciences.

In the winter months when the garden rests within the mind of the gardener, as well as within the form-giving forces of the cosmos, we can awaken the intuitive sense and pictures of imagination that are as important in gardening as the tools and the practical manuals are. We can let the coming year pass before the mind's eye and, while looking back on the store of experience of past years, plan the manifestation of the garden in its next season.

Chapter 17

Teas, Preparations, and Biotic Substances

The preparations we add to the manure vitalize it in such a way that it will then be able to transmit its vitality to the soil from which the plants are springing.
—Rudolf Steiner, *Agriculture*, Lecture [5]

Usually, when strangers ask, I do my best to explain these preparations in solid scientific terms; but between you and me, they are "food" for the gnomes and elemental beings.
—Master gardener Manfred Stauffer (with a twinkle in his eye)

We have seen how very alive the soil is with its billions of churning, breathing, metabolizing organisms. Like all living organisms, the soil is sensitive to a number of influences. Chemical fertilizer, insecticides, fungicides, herbicides, and even the exhaust fumes of farm machinery sprayed on the soil in very fine doses will have an effect on the soil organisms. If the soil is healthy, it can buffer the adverse influences and draw on eutrophic influences, buffer the pH, the moisture, mediate between cosmic and terrestrial factors, and thus provide a living, healthy medium for plants to grow in. Plants, as we have seen, do not end at the tip of their roots or leaves, but are intimately connected with all that goes on in the surrounding soil. Plants cannot be sick by themselves; rather sick plants are registering disturbances in the environment of the plants.

If the plants are ailing, then medicines can be used to lead the soil back into its life-supporting state and to strengthen the plants. Since similar biological, biochemical processes go on in the soil and plant macrocosmically as go on within the human or animal organism microcosmically, the use of such medicine makes sense. Such medicines are infusions, decoctions, macerations, and extractions made from herbs or manures, which having gone through living processes, work more gently on the soil than would chemical salts.

The biodynamic preparations help to restore abused soil over the years, and to maintain healthy soil. They can be used prophylactically for various problems. "Preparations create conditions under which plant and soil become sufficiently sensitive to react to and absorb the incoming stream of life from the cosmos."[1] The preparations are not "food" for the plants, but facilitate the work of etheric forces. They are not the usual compost starters, although they stimulate compost organisms, and Pfeiffer bases his compost starter *(PayBac)* on the soil bacteria that accumulate in the preparations as they are made. The preparations are the "dynamic" part of biodynamics.

How the Preparations Are Made

The preparations, arbitrarily labeled 500 though 508 by the same research group that provided the name "biodynamics," are based on indications given by Rudolf Steiner in his fifth agricultural lecture.

* **Preparation 500,** the **horn-dung preparation:** Fresh cow manure is packed into the horn of a healthy cow that has fallen to the butcher's knife. In the fall at equinox, the horn is buried in good soil two feet under the ground and left until spring. After spending the winter in the ground, the horn is taken out; the dung, by this time, is well rotted and gives off a pleasant smell. One uses a pinch of this horn dung, about as much as a pea's size, and puts it into a normal sized bucket of lukewarm rainwater. This is then stirred for one hour, preferably with the

hand. The stirring is done in one direction until a funnel is created in the water, reaching to the bottom of the pail; then the direction is abruptly changed. Again a funnel is created, the direction of the vortex is abruptly changed again, and so on. Preparation 500, which aids rooting processes and terrestrial forces, is then sprayed by a knapsack sprayer onto the ground that is to be planted, onto the prepared beds. A whiskbroom can be used if a sprayer is not available. The best time for spraying is in the late afternoon, when the earth once again "inhales" the etheric energies it expanded in the early morning hours.

- **Preparation 501,** the **horn-quartz preparation**: Quartz rocks, preferably quartz mountain crystals, are pulverized. The resultant powder is made into a paste by adding rainwater and then it is inserted into a cow horn. The horn is buried in good soil about two feet deep and left in the ground throughout the summer to be excavated in the fall. Again, a pea-sized portion is used for stirring rhythmically, creating alternating whorls, in a bucket of water for one hour. This preparation, which aids the light and warmth transmitting cosmic forces, is sprayed directly onto the leaves, flowers, and young fruits. It should not be sprayed on seedlings and seedbeds. The best time to spray the horn-quartz preparation is early in the morning, when the earth "exhales" its etheric energy.

    We see that the horn-dung preparation and the horn-quartz preparation form a pair of opposites, the one amplifying the terrestrial etheric forces, the other facilitating the cosmic etheric forces.

Preparations 502 to 507 are mainly used for preparing the compost to develop certain processes, break down quicker, and retain and amplify energies that might otherwise be lost:

- Preparation **502, yarrow blossoms**: Moistened yarrow (*Achillea millefolium*) blossoms, gathered in early summer, are packed into the bladder of a deer stag or hart. The bladder is hung into the

sun (i.e., in an airy, sunny spot on the edge of the roof) over
the summer and buried into good soil over the winter. The
contents, dug up in the spring, will aid the compost to regulate
potassium and sulfur processes.

- Preparation **503, chamomile blossoms** *(Matricaria chamomilla)*:
Chamomile blossoms are gathered in the summer. They are
moistened with chamomile tea shortly before they are stuffed
into the small intestine of a freshly butchered cow, made into
little links of sausage, and buried into good humus in the fall.
They spend the winter in the ground in an area where the melt
water of snow is accessible to them. The chamomile preparation
helps regulate the calcium processes in the composts.

- Preparation **504, stinging nettle** *(Urtica dioica)*: The nettle is
buried in the soil for the duration of a whole year, preferably
enclosed in a mantle of peat moss. It aids the humification of the
compost.

- Preparation **505, oak bark** *(Quercus robor)*: Scrapings from the
outer rind of the oak bark are placed into the skull cavity of a
domestic animal such as a goat, sheep, or cow. The skull is left
whole. The oak bark is put in through the foramen magnum.
The skull is buried in the fall into a ground that has water
percolating through it, for example under a leaking drainpipe.
The contents are usable in the spring. This preparation works on
the calcium processes and contributes to making plants disease-
resistant.

- Preparation **506, dandelion blossoms** *(Taraxacum officinale)*: In
the fall, moistened dandelion flowers that have been gathered in
the spring and dried are folded into the mesentery (the membrane that holds the intestines fast) of a cow. This is buried into
the soil until the spring. It helps to regulate the silica processes
in relation to the potassium processes.

- Preparation **507, valerian, or garden heliotrope, blossoms**
(Valeriana officinalis): This final one of the compost preparation is
made from freshly squeezed valerian flowers. The juice, diluted

with rainwater, will regulate the phosphorus processes when sprayed on the compost. The compost preparations, which are admittedly difficult to make, are used in very minute amounts. A teaspoon-sized amount of each (502 through 506) suffices for a normal garden compost of three cubic yards. Traditionally, the small amounts are placed into holes poked into the compost about a foot or two deep, in the following order, as one looks at the compost from the top.

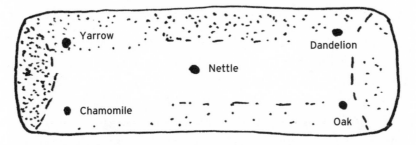

Figure 17.1. Compost preparation spray

Valerian preparation, made from a drop of valerian stirred rhythmically in a bucket of water for an hour, is sprayed with a whiskbroom over the entire compost. Once the preparations are made, the supply will serve to treat many compost heaps for many seasons. After they have been dug up in the spring, they can be kept in glass jars, packed in a box lined with peat. The valerian preparation is kept in a tinted, corked bottle in the same way.

• A preparation of a different order is preparation **508, horsetail** (*Equisetum arvense*): It is made by boiling the horsetail for twenty minutes. This decoction can be stored and later, when used, diluted with water. This is not one of the compost preparations, but is used as a prophylactic spray against mildews and other fungal disorders.

There are, of course, other possible preparations in addition to the biodynamic ones. Any *materia medica botanica*, if understood in its relation to the etheric forces, has potential for agricultural-horticultural use. Finding other preparations is even a necessity in those parts of the world where climate and ecology do not permit the growing of the standard preparation herbs. What is one to use in place of stinging nettle, yarrow, valerian, etc. in Africa, Australia, or South America? Much research needs to be done and the traditional "wortcunning" of our ancestors and of native medicine men and women, *curanderos* and shamans, needs to be investigated again.

How Can One Explain the Preparations?

For those trained in current scientific agriculture, it is easy to understand why biodynamics has been referred to as "muck and magic." I myself, when first introduced to the preparations, thought that if there was any virtue to them at all, it would be found in the psychological feeling of participation with the garden that one experiences while making and applying them:[2] for are not the feelings and thoughts of the gardener one of the factors that make up the totality of the farm or garden organism? However, to say that psychological projection is all there is to it would be incorrect. This has been shown by experimental evidence.[3] For a comprehension of the preparations (the same holds for comprehending Steiner's *Agricultural Course*) one must have a grasp of the whole picture before the parts make sense. One must be an observer of subtle interconnections and synchronicities in nature and share an understanding of Steiner's conception of the world, his anthroposophy, as is painstakingly spelled out in a number of his lectures and books, before one can realize that one is not dealing with a number of arbitrary and abstruse practices which one is asked to blindly believe.[4] Instead one is given something that is rooted in a wide conception as to the nature of the universe, and one is asked to constantly employ critical intelligence to come to terms with and grasp the scope of biodynamic practices.

We will try to look a little closer at the possible rationale of the preparations. Why, in the horn-dung and horn-quartz preparations, are the horns of a cow used? To answer, we must look once again at the nature of the cow, this animal with a four-chambered stomach that processes its food for twelve days, digesting and utilizing cellulose and roughage with the aid of the most varied intestinal microbial flora. The resultant cow dung is a highly astralized substance containing numerous animal secretions in the form of digestive juices. It is as though the cow, in its chewing of the cud and slow digestive process of taking the fodder apart, is meditating on the energies set free from the herbage. The being of the cow is thus experiencing inwardly the cosmic and terrestrial forces that had been bound into the plants. Perhaps that is why the cow is outwardly so dull, much like the proverbial guru in deep meditation. The horns and hooves at the cow's extremities keep the etheric forces from raying outward and dissipating themselves. The cow's horn is thus a device that concentrates and throws back the energies pressing into it, much like a condenser.[5]

At first glance this seems farfetched but when we look at the importance of shapes per se, it is certainly a probability. For example, spatial relations alone account for the smooth running of an automobile, as in the setting of the valves or the spark gap in the internal combustion engine. The tone quality of instruments, such as violins, trumpets, or drums, depends on the shape of the instrument. If the shape is off, the sound vibrations are disharmonious. Studies on the shape of pyramids indicate that the pyramidal containers made after the exact geometric of the great Cheops of Giza can naturally mummify carcasses, keep maggots out, and seem to collect alpha waves.[6] Czech engineer Karel Dbral took out a patent for sharpening dull razor blades inside a pyramidal box; and Czech brewers found that the quality of the beer lessened when they switched from the traditional round barrels to more functional rectangular containers.[7] The shape of the lens focuses light waves in optics. Suggestions have been made that bees could not make honey were it not for spending their larval stage in hexagonal cells, and humans would not be able to think were it not for a spherical cranium. Perhaps, then, it is possible that the architectural form of the cow's horn concentrates the earth's forces as they work on the dung or on the pulverized quartz.

Embryologist and pediatrician Dr. Karl Koenig, in his discussion of the compost preparations, makes the point that it is not so much the substances of the animal sheaths that surround the vegetable matter, but that it is the tectonics of the sheaths that concentrate and amplify formative forces, which are essential. These organs do so in the animal and continue this function in the soil when handled properly.[8]

Most of the preparations are buried into the ground: the horn-dung, dandelion, yarrow, chamomile, and oak bark are buried into the ground in the winter; the stinging nettle stays in the ground both winter and summer; and the horn-quartz preparation is buried during the summer. This is not an arbitrary arrangement, either, for different forces work in the ground in the summer than in the winter. In the winter, the earth becomes, contrary to casual thought, more alive. The plants retreat into the ground in the form of seeds, tubers, roots, and rosettes that closely hug the earth, leaves fall off, and the external picture of summer vegetation disappears. Animals such as frogs, insects, and mammals tend at this time to burrow into the soil to hibernate. During January and February, the cosmic crystallization forces are the strongest, even penetrating the earth in the form of frost and ice to a degree. It is this concentrating force that is captured by the horn-dung preparation, which will eventually aid root formation.

The horn-quartz, on the other hand, will aid the fruiting and flowering and is related to the forces of light and warmth. For this reason, a mountain quartz crystal is preferred, to obtain the silica. When it is put into the ground in the summer in its cow-horn sheath, it makes use of the expanding, centrifugal forces of nature when the vegetation is shooting upward and outward toward the sun.[9]

The horn preparations are used at the rate of a few pinches per acre, and the compost preparations at the rate of one teaspoon per compost.[10] Regarding these minute quantities, one might find it presumptuous that they should have an effect. Yet what has been discovered about the effects of trace minerals, micronutrients, catalysts, hormones, and enzymes should lend credibility to the possibility of such effects. In homeopathy, for example, dilutions so fine that they are not grasped by conventional physics and chemistry are known to have curative effects. Often these are substances that are very poisonous in larger doses, while in homeopathic dilution they are rendered harmless and stimulate the organism. Swiss cheesemakers know that just one milking from a cow that has had a penicillin injection will spoil vats of a thousand liters or more, making it no longer usable for their cheese. This is even after the small amount of substance has travelled through the cow's large organism. More than an ounce of molybdenum per acre will make the plants so toxic that the animals will not eat them. The phenoxy herbicide 2,4,5-T that is sprayed on roadsides and forests contains an impurity created as a manufacturing by-product called dioxin. Scientists, testing it in dosages of parts per trillion, find that even in this infinitesimally small amount it is carcinogenic and mutagenic to animal organisms.[11] Pfeiffer illustrates the concept of minutest quantities in his *Bio-Dynamic Farming and Gardening* by showing that copper sulfate in a solution of 1 part to 1,000,000,000 will hurt the spirogyra algae, that 1 part per 700,000,000 hinders wheat from sprouting and so on.[12] One must not think of the preparations in the same terms as one does about trace minerals or radioactive substances. They are simple, common substances that have been potentized, or dynamized, much like homeopathic medicine where the healing information in the substance is released by repetitive shaking and stirring.

In three of the preparations, horn-dung, horn-quartz, and valerian, homeopathic portions are given into water, which is stirred rhythmically as previously described. This stirring sensitizes the water and makes it receptive to imprints even if the substance dissolved therein is very minute. That matter can be sensitized is shown in phonograph records, magnetizing metals, etc. Theodor Schwenk shows in his research how extremely receptive and impressionable water is that has been kept in rhythmic motion.[13] Water in rhythmic motion becomes sensitive and open to the influences of the planets.[14] This is also one of the reasons for stirring one's liquid manures (Russian tea, chicken manure, nettle, seaweed, comfrey, shepherd's purse, and cabbage ferments) at certain times, such as on the day of the full moon. It is likely that the constant motion of blood through the body, and of currents and tides in large bodies of water, have a similar effect of opening up the water to cosmic forces and potencies of dissolved substances.

A Closer Look at the Herbs in the Preparations

All of the herbs used in the preparations are of known medicinal value and, in the system of the older science of signatures, they are associated to planets by virtue of their physiognomy of growth, the color of the flowers, the geometric arrangement of the leaves and petal placement, and other criteria. Of course, all of the planets, and indeed the entire cosmos, work in every plant, but in some, one or the other planet's signature predominates.

> **Yarrow:** In this herb, Venus predominates; Culpeper assigns it to Venus and in the Middle Ages it was known as *supercilium veneris*, the eyebrows of Venus. From the fragrance and fine lacy leaves, one can tell that the sulfur process penetrates yarrow so that "as a medicine it is drying and binding. A decoction of it . . . is good to stop the running of the reins in men and whites in women."15 Reins (kidneys) and bladder are of course under the rule of Venus, so it is no wonder that the hart's or elk's bladder is used. The hart excretes large amounts of potassium in his urine, an element found in large amounts in yarrow. The astringent, drying action of yarrow is indicated in its Latin name, *Achillea*, named after the Greek warrior Achilles because warriors used the herb to staunch the bleeding of wounds. An old English divination relates to the venereal aspects of yarrow in the following way:
>
>> Thou pretty herb of Venus tree,
>> Thy true name is Yarrow
>> Now who my bosom friend may be
>> Pray tell thou me tomorrow.

The answer would come in a dream. Sexuality has to do with the relating of the astral to the etheric, and in a wider sense we can expect this function to be fulfilled by the yarrow as a compost preparation.

> **Chamomile:** This tough little herb with flighty, lacelike foliage and a strong smell is recognized as one of the most potent medical herbs. The Anglo-Saxons called it *Maythen* and included it in the nine magic herbs wielded by Woden, the shamanic god of healing.[16] It grows on compacted, alkaline soils. Culpeper assigns it to the sun; and apparently so did the Germanic tribes who "dedicated it

to their sun god Baldur because to them the chamomile's yellow center and white petals around it seemed to convey sun forces."[17] Chamomile helps relieve pain, stop inflammations, and soothes troubled intestines. Its name *matricaria* (Latin *mater*) refers to its use during childbirth to soothe labor pains. In the preparations, the herb is given into cow's intestines, where its Mercury processes are called upon to keep the ethereal inflow and harmonize the astral.[18]

Stinging nettle: The nettle is truly a plant of Mars, ready to inflict a jab at anyone who dares touch it, forming a special relation to iron, so that it can be used as medicine for iron deficiency anemia. It is a good spring tonic when eaten like cooked spinach, an excellent hair rinse, and brings "martian" heat to joints and muscles plagued by arthritis and rheumatism. Placed into liquid manure pits, it helps the slurry break down fast and smoothly. Its needles contain histamines, toxalbumins similar to snake poisons, as well as small amounts of formic acid found in ants. In other words, it contains so much animalistic astrality that it does not need an animal organ as a sheath in the preparations.

Oak: The common oak, variously called the English oak or French oak, is a Mars or Jupiter tree, but its bark contains so much calcium (78 percent ash content), that the bark can be assigned to the moon. This "lunar" calcium, a residue of living processes deposited in the bark of the tree, is alchemically activated in the skull cavity of a domestic cud-chewing animal. The finished preparation is added to the compost to help the plants be resistant to a number of diseases. In naturopathic medicine, oak bark has been used to counter ulcers of the stomach and other forms of internal bleeding, for it is astringent due to the tannin content. In ancient Europe, each farmstead or village had a sacred oak to protect against sorcery and lightning. Plant fungi and parasites, which appear by the excess of lunar forces, will be stayed by the use of the oak bark preparation.

Dandelion: The feathery, crystalline fruiting body (pappus) of this herb bears the signature of Saturn, and the milky latex that of the moon. However, this plant is mainly under the rule of Jupiter as indicated by its yellow flower head, its long taproot penetrating deeply into the soil, and its medicinal use against jaundice and liver ailments. Dandelion salad is a good spring tonic, activating digestion and metabolism within the human microcosm. In a similar way, the dandelion preparation facilitates the radiation of the formative forces of the upper planetary region into the metabolic processes of the compost.

Valerian: The last of the compost preparations, valerian, is assigned to Saturn for its warmth-generating ability.[19] The roots can be made into a sedative, anxiolytic tea and Valium is a synthetic analogue of the active ingredients of the valerian root. If grown in the garden, it attracts earthworms. Sprayed over the finished compost, this preparation regulates the "phosphorus processes," making it possible for the spiritual archetypes to penetrate and structure the amorphous mass (*prima materia*) of the compost.[20]

Having briefly discussed the herbs that go into the compost, we obtain a greater appreciation of what compost is, and what goes on in it. The compost is a great digester; it breaks down substances completely and builds them up into a different form. It takes old, decaying, diseased, organic biomass of plant and animal origin, breaks them down and returns them to a state of chaos (unformed matter), and then rebuilds and organizes them into complex, life-carrying molecules. In contemplating composting, we are touching upon the mysteries of life and death. In the breaking-down process and in the building-up process, the wider cosmos is involved; the planets accompany each step. This is outlined beautifully in the book called *The Workings of the Planets and the Life Processes in Man and Earth,* written by the Dutch physician Bernard C. J. Lievegoed. (The book is no longer available, but can be downloaded in the Internet.)

Whenever matter is returned to chaos, it becomes once again impressionable to new influences; this is so even microcosmically when people's lives are in shambles and they become open to numerous suggestions and influences. With his preparations the biodynamic gardener provides anchoring places for the working of the planets. Inserted into the compost the biodynamic preparations become focal points, through which the planetary forces can enter chaotic matter and work into the etheric, astral, and even spiritual aspects of soil, plant, animal, and eventually man. We see that the use of the preparations is much more encompassing than mere compost starters.

We can understand the compost in another light; it can be likened to an extremely generalized organism, more generalized than an algae or a jellyfish, whose life activity is diffused throughout its substance. Just like worms and starfish, some roots and leaves can be cut in half and each part regenerates, because nowhere is life focused into specific vital organs, so one can divide the compost, seeing it as the most primitive of such generalized organisms.[21] A continuum could be set up, starting with the compost at one pole, going through the lower plants and animals all the way to the mammals (including humans), the latter with their highly specialized life organs. Although such highly specialized life organs are not found on the lower end of the scale, all the life functions of respiration, metabolism, circulation, secretion, reproduction, etc. are successfully carried on. In primitive non-differentiated life forms the organs are there as rudiments or predispositions, commonly referred to as *anlagen* or *primordia*. Cosmic rhythms, tides, temperature cycles, light rhythms, and other factors work macrocosmically on these primordia, or anlagen. In the case of the compost, the biodynamic preparations enliven and animate the anlagen, allowing the compost to resonate with and become more receptive to the various cosmic impulses. Instead of the seven major sets of endocrine glands that send hormones throughout the body regulating body chemistry, growth, calcium usage, reproduction, etc., the preparations create the proclivity for this. The preparations themselves function as anlagen for the major organs: the yarrow becomes the "kidney" and "bladder" with their Venus function, the oak bark becomes the "brain" with its moon function, the nettle becomes the "red blood" with its Mars function, dandelion becomes the "liver" with its Jupiter function, and so on. The structuring influences of the planets can flow into our food sources again, into our fields and gardens, something that the use of artificial fertilizer salts prevents. This is why the quality of biodynamically raised produce is excellent, because the formative forces can flow into the plant unimpeded. In a deeper sense, then, the biodynamic gardener is creating a helpful being by creating a compost and fitting it out with "organs" and skin, letting it live through its three stages, and then sacrificing it to the earth where it fertilizes and imparts its macrocosmic strength.[22] In the same vein, Karl Koenig proposes that the compost preparations bring about a living process, where the compost heap is a "becoming being" endowed with a physical and etheric body.[23] What it comes down to is that the gardener is the magician who provides a basis upon which the archetypal plant can more fully manifest itself.

The preparations are difficult to make, but once they are made they will last a long time. It is best if each farmer and gardener can make his own in order to develop that personal relationship to his farm-garden organism. Often biodynamic interested farmers and gardeners of an area will get together and jointly make the preparations on a weekend, such as at fall equinox, and dig them up together in the spring, perhaps at spring equinox. Such get-togethers are festivals, good for community building and for exchanging practical know-how. Each participant then receives a portion to take home to the farm-garden organism for which he or she is responsible. In my opinion, the preparations, as any medicine, should not be bought and sold. Most traditional healers, medicine men, and even the great doctor Paracelsus considered medicines to be gifts of the gods for the blessing of creation, not for making a profit. Such blessings should be freely given.

A less complicated way of preparing the herbs used in biodynamic preparations has been developed by Miss Maye Bruce of England. She suggests simply cooking the biodynamic herbs in honey and then applying them to the compost. Miss Bruce's method of composting is called the Quick Return and the herb extracts are known in England as Humofix.[24] Simple comparative experiments carried on in the Aigues-Vertes garden in Switzerland showed no immediate differences in the quality of the composts thus prepared; however that does not mean that there is no long-range effect, which might be indicated by more involved studies.

Other Herbal Preparations

All medicinal plants have potential for use in the garden. A number of fermentations have already been discussed in the chapter on composting. Ferments can be made from comfrey, shepherd's purse, cabbage, nettle, thistles, and many common weeds. The ferments should be stirred every once in a while to open them up to the air and to sensitize, or potentize, the water. Each gardener should carry on his or her own experiments with these substances. The common bracken fern *(Pteridium aquilinum)* can be made into a tea that will drive off red mites and as mulch it will provide potassium to the potatoes and other crops.

Chapter 18

Biodynamic Cooking, Nutrition, and Food Preparation

By eating wholesome food we inform ourselves with cosmic order.
—Fritz Albert Popp, physicist

Now that we know a little bit how happy, healthy vegetables are grown, we should know how to turn them into good food without losing food value.

When it comes to eating, human beings have lost the sureness of instinct that the animals have. This is so because the human being has evolved out of the intimate connection with nature that characterizes beings still closely tied to the macrocosm. Native people seem to have much more sense when it comes to eating. This is so because food practices are regulated by complex traditions, taboos, and rituals that were evolved at a time when human consciousness was much more closely tied to its spiritual origin, the macrocosm. Modern human beings, if they rely on their "instincts," overeat and become obese, become hyperactive, and rot their teeth due to excess sugar, damage their nerves and circulatory system by taking too many stimulants, create sluggish stool by eating too many soft, processed foods, and help no one except their doctors. Growing a nice garden is not enough; we must become conscious of what we should do with the produce.

What is food? All foods are derived from *living* organisms. Man, with all of his technology and long years of research, has not been able to create one single lettuce leaf. All food, including animal substances, is based upon plant life. "You live because we live!" the plant admonishes us in a quiet way every time we take a bite to eat or draw a breath of air.

What is it that the plant does in that it becomes food for other living beings? One can set up the equation of assimilation and photosynthesis in which twelve parts water (H_2O) and six parts carbon dioxide (CO_2), in the presence of sunlight, warmth, and certain catalytic minerals yield sugars ($C_6H_{12}O_6$) which can be converted to starches and lipids, and yield oxygen (O_2) and water. A more goetheanistic way of looking at this is to see how the plant organism can take up the "dead" elements earth (minerals), water, air (carbon dioxide), and fire (light and warmth), and, in combining them, *vitalize* (L. *vita* = life) them. The energies that bring these elements together giving them an orderly form are *cosmic energies*, as they come to us primarily from the sun, but also from the moon, the planets, and the stars. Thus when we eat a plant (and all food is ultimately plant), we are eating the entire universe, that is, the elements as they are arranged by cosmic impulses. One can say that the plant captures celestial life and fixes it into a material, physical form. When we eat, we take that celestial life and cosmic information into ourselves, and it becomes our own life.1

Actually, eating food is only one form of nutrition available to us. Breathing fresh air nourishes us, as do all the impressions that pass our senses. A garden is a source of health not only because of the nutritious food it provides, but also because of the fresh air, and the sights and sounds that nourish and delight body and soul.

We *transform* the macrocosmic, celestial, and terrestrial impulses by means of the process of digestion, into microcosmic impulses. Our digestion breaks the substances down completely and releases the etheric forces and information that had been fixed into it. Animals use these forces for running, springing, frolicking, sexuality, and giving expression to their astrality or soul life. The human being does this, too, but takes it a step further by using the energy to think and reflect, to intuit and imagine, to speak and to love. The human being has the free will to decide what to use these energies for that the plants have given us; to do good or to do works of evil (selfishness), to give of ourselves, like the plant, or to self-indulge.

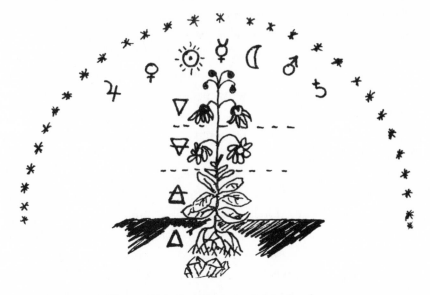

Figure 18.1. Cosmic energies in food

In order to have the cosmic energies available to carry on a healthy culture and sustain the life of our body, soul, and spirit on Earth, we must see to it that we have the right kind of food . . . food which comes from plants that have been grown on living soil under the best natural conditions and which is eaten with only minimal loss of vitality through cooking and preparing. Inadequately grown food and badly cooked food will not only harm the body but also make it impossible to think, feel, and will in a holistic manner.

Pfeiffer, in his foreword to the *Agricultural Course* by Steiner, relates a conversation he had with Dr. Steiner about the shortcomings and faults so typical in all sorts of spiritually oriented, esoteric movements. Pfeiffer asked: "How can it happen that the spiritual impulse, and especially the inner schooling for which you are constantly providing stimulus and guidance, bear so little fruit? Why do the people concerned give so little evidence of spiritual experience, in spite of all their efforts?" Why, he continued his questioning, are people having such trouble carrying out their intentions without being pulled off the right path by personal ambition, illusions, and petty jealousies? The thought-provoking and surprising answer that

Steiner gave was: "This is a problem of nutrition. Nutrition as it is today does not supply the strength necessary for manifesting spirit in physical life. A bridge can no longer be built from thinking to will and action. Food plants no longer contain the forces people need for this."[2] Elsewhere Steiner stated that if current developments continue, the time would come when people will starve at a fully decked table, which seems entirely possible with the de-natured, processed, not to mention genetically mutilated foods that fill supermarket shelves.

With this as a background, we can see how biodynamics has vital consequences for the future of humanity. In order to have the right kind of food that fully supports our thinking, feeling, and willing functions, we must have foods full of vitality. This starts, for one thing, with healthy, living soil as Are Waerland, J. I. Rodale, and Jethro Kloss also have realized.[3] But the proper soil and growing techniques are not enough; our cooking must not devitalize the food. Loss of vitality can be incurred during:

1. Storage
2 Processing
3. Cooking
4. Eating habits
5. Seasoning

Freshness

The fresher the food, the better, the more etheric properties are available. Leaf crops are best harvested in the morning hours, as the vitality rises with the sap into the plant in the morning hours in its daily rhythm. Root crops are best harvested in the early evening hours, as the vitality draws into the roots in the "inbreathing" phase of the daily rhythm.[4] Plants, as living organisms, are constantly changing and growing. They are never exactly the same. Alan Chadwick stated that a fruit is ripe only for one moment; before that it is still green and ripening and after than, it is already starting to decompose. Thus, vegetables, especially fruits, must be picked at the right moment. Plants that have been picked a long time previously usually wilt and rot, and even if artificially preserved, will not transmit vitality well.

Processing

The Swiss nutritionist Werner Kollath emphasizes *wholeness* and *freshness* as criteria for good food.[5] By that criterion, a fresh carrot is better than carrot juice, and whole wheat is better than white, processed flour.

> **Fresh Whole Vitalized (Alive)**
> Ripe Apple + +
> Fresh Carrot + +
> Carrot Juice + -
> Preserves - -
> Refined sugar - - Mineralized (Dead)

The further away one gets from freshness and wholeness, the closer one gets toward mineralization, the stage at which substances fall out of the cycle of living matter. We have seen this falling out of the living cycle in our study of composts and manures, which are normally full of etheric and astral life; and mineral fertilizers are lifeless in comparison, these salts are dead end processes fallen out of the living cycle. Studies with rats show that whole-wheat grain keeps the animals healthy, ground wheat is not quite as good, and modern processed flour will eventually lead to the animals' demise. Modern milling techniques remove bran and germ, leaving the flour so de-natured that synthetic nutrients have to be added to create fortified flour. In earlier times, it was possible to keep prisoners healthy on bread and water alone, but today, because of the mismanagement of the soil and the processing of the flour, the poor prisoners would starve. Like flour, sugar is devitalized by excessive processing, causing tooth decay and a host of other problems. Good sweeteners are honey, malt, molasses, date sugar, or fruits.

Loss of wholeness results from unnecessary peeling, skinning, and grinding of the vegetables. Often most of the vitamins are in the rinds and skins.

Canning has become a popular way to preserve foods for the winter months. It goes along with the pioneer mystique that many modern "folksy" people try to recapture and it is a lot of work and ruins many of

292 • Practical Aspects of Gardening

the nutrients. Rather than canning, winter gardening and storage of whole foods, roots, and tubers in the root cellar is perhaps a better way to go. As far as fruits go, drying preserves more nutritional value than canning. In the Rogue Valley region of southern Oregon, for example, it is possible to have a full diet of garden vegetables all winter long and not have to eat the same vegetable for two weeks. (See Appendix1: Winter Gardening in Oregon.) Variety on the winter plate includes cabbages, Brussels sprouts, kale, collard greens, mustard greens, turnips and turnip greens, rutabagas, Swiss chard, beets and beet greens, leeks, parsnips, Hamburg parsley, carrots, oyster plant, Jerusalem artichokes, celeriac, Florence fennel, and others. Most of these plants can be kept in the ground over the winter with minimal protection of mulch or plastic tents. Potatoes should be dug up and stored separately from other vegetables because their respiration causes others, especially apples, to rot more quickly.

In the winter months, tasty salads need not be lacking. Sugarloaf, a frost hardy, fleshy type of chicory that grows into a football-sized head of tightly packed, blanched leaves, was developed in Switzerland. It can be eaten as a lettuce or a cooked vegetable. As a lettuce it can be garnished with frost hardy corn lettuce *(Valerianella)*. Witlof (also witloof) is another type of chicory, which can be used as a cooking vegetable or for salad. Witlof is grown all summer long in the field and in the fall the leaves are cut and fed to animals or composted, while the roots are placed in cool storage. The former hot bed that has been emptied of its by now well-rotted manure can be used for such storage. After the winter solstice, at periodic intervals, the roots of the witlof can be planted by fitting them tightly next to each other in a container with soil. The container or box is then put into a warmer room, such as a basement, a barn with cows, or a heated garage. A mixture of sand and peat or sawdust is placed over these planted roots to a depth of about one foot. The witlof responds to the warmth and watering by growing a thick, white terminal bud. When the bud starts to peak out above the sand-peat mixture, it is time to harvest this delicious vegetable.

Greens and herbs growing in the fallowed beds can augment these winter lettuces. (Onions and boiled eggs also complement them very well, as they are not as sweet as summer lettuces.) Added as spices and flavoring,

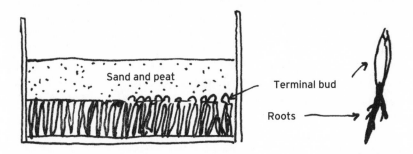

Figure 18.2. Witlof box

the herbs include: ground ivy *(Glechoma hederacea)*; chickweed *(Stellaria media)*; plantain *(Plantago maior, P. lanceolata)*; wild mustards *(Brassica arvensis, B. albus, B. nigra)*; winter cress *(Barbarea vulgaris)*; sheep sorrel *(Rumex acetosella)*; dandelion *(Taraxacum officinale)*; and others. The number of greens increases toward the spring.

Of course, pumpkins, squash, onions, and a number of fruits can be stored for the winter also.

Given all of these plants, one can achieve a good, wholesome variety in one's winter diet without relying on processed, canned, or imported foods. The heat of canning destroys some of the nutritious value. Perhaps the only canning that needs to be done is to save some of the good summer fruits such as strawberries, raspberries, and blackberries, which make a delicious winter treat. Fruits, such as berries, apple chips (slices of apples), and other fruits can be dried for the winter on racks near the stove; this is the best way to preserve them and still retain their nourishing value.

Eating the fruits and vegetables in their due season keeps us aware of the rhythms of the macrocosm, supplying us with the etheric energies we need at specific times of the year. The experience of a stronger connectedness with the forces that pervade our garden will be ours if we follow the plant cycle in our diet. In the fall and winter, as the sun is at its lowest point and the plants retreat into root, bud, and seed, one would eat mainly tubers, roots, buds (cabbage, witlof, etc.), grains, and forest mushrooms. In the spring it is time to enjoy the tonic of fresh greens; summer and autumn follow with ripe fruit and seed crops. Although as humans we have greatly emancipated ourselves from the dictates of the cosmos in the course of evolution, we still respond to the seasonal cycles, such that we become more inward, reflective, and indoor oriented in the winter and we become more open to the outer world when the days lengthen. The recognition of our soul's response to the changing rhythms of the earth is expressed in the meditations given in Rudolf Steiner's *Calendar of the Soul.*

Cooking

It goes without saying that cooking is one of the most important parts of food preparation. It is proverbial that food should be cooked with love in order to become us well. The Chinese in the countryside, with family farms of a few acres, not only grow their food intensively, but also know to not ruin the food through excessive cooking. They steam and quick-fry with very little flavor or nutrient loss.

Steaming is one of the best ways to prepare vegetables. The water collected from the steaming pan should be saved, for it contains most of the water-soluble vitamins. This water can be used for soup, flavored with minced herbs, butter, egg, grated cheese, soy sauce, nutritional yeast, or whatever is preferred.

Different processes of food preparation unlock different nutrients. In Aigues-Vertes this was taken into account by steaming or cooking two-thirds of the vegetables and quick-frying the other third in vegetable oil. The cooked and quick-fried vegetables were always served around a *staple* such as rice, millet, barley, and other grains or potatoes. Salads made of lettuce and of raw vegetables provided the fresh greens with the meal, or were served as *hors d'oeuvres* along with sprouts (wheat, lentil, bean, radish, or alfalfa) in the winter. A diet of this nature, along with an assortment of herbal teas, kept the people of the village extraordinarily healthy.

The idea of a staple is important. A staple (Anglo-Saxon *stapol* = main post, or pillar) is a total food containing all the nutrition needed by human beings; it is the "daily bread," the "staff of life," the food wherein all of the elements are balanced according to macrobiotics. All cultures have had their staples, and for most societies it has been a grain, though for some people in the southern hemisphere the staple has been a tuber (yam, taro, manioc, potato). The great civilizations of the East depended on rice, the Native Americans on corn (maize), Africa largely on millet, West Asia and the Mediterranean basin mainly on wheat, while the colder countries depended on barley, rye, and oats. The grain plant, rooting firmly in the earth, stretching its ears toward the sun, and sacrificing abundant leaf and flower development, is truly the nutritional foundation of human civilization. Modern people, especially twenty-first-century Americans, tend to forget this and prefer the trimmings (meat, vegetable, fruit) to the staple. This can have an unstabilizing effect on human health.

One can indicate the distance of a food from the staple by a continuum in the following manner:

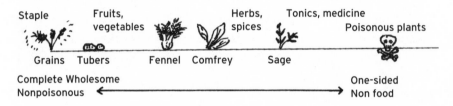

Figure 18.3. Food continuum

Any grain, such as wheat, barley, rye, etc., can be soaked overnight for softening (lunar processes) and then slowly cooked, simmered to simulate a continuing ripening process (solar process). Other foods are served in combination with this.

Some of the cooks in Aigues-Vertes made sure that the "whole plant," meaning some root, some leaf, and some fruit or seed was eaten every day, in order to provide wholeness for the human organism. The rule of thumb is that roots stimulate the head and nervous system, leafs the respiration and blood circulatory system, and the flowers and fruits mainly the metabolic and limb system, whereas the staple has an overall balancing effect.[6]

Foods should not be overcooked, which leads to loss of vitamins and decreased salivating due to lack of chewing, which in turn creates weak digestion, constipation, and eventually loose teeth. Overcooking also causes loss of flavor, creating a need for strong seasoning, too much salt and pepper, with the possible effect of constipation and kidney damage.

Good Food Habits

A meal must look, smell, and taste good for it to be becoming and worthy of the long process of growing. We do not just eat with our taste buds, but our eyes have a part in the feast. Our other organs "taste" the food also. It is just that this "tasting" does not reach the threshold of consciousness. If the other organs do not like the food, they make themselves noticed in the form of heartburn, indigestion, fatigue, and even sickness. An aesthetic atmosphere with flowers, a tablecloth, and pretty serving dishes aids in this sensible enjoyment of the meal. Traditionally, a prayer before and after the meal has created a sacred temporal space at mealtimes. A brief meditation of following with one's mind's eye the path of the food from where it came to how it got on the plate and what was involved connects the meal with the greater parts of the universe. Course choices and variety (i.e., raw food appetizer, soup, main meal, and dessert) are provided by the many cultural traditions of food preparation.

SEASONING
Locally grown *herbs* can substitute for harsh spices. They create a delicate palate of flavors that go excellently with biodynamically grown vegetables. Harsh spices (which numb the taste buds to more delicate flavors after prolonged use), or overseasoning with salt, pepper, sugar, ketchup, or soy sauce, is usually more due to the lack of flavor in chemically grown foods as it is to processing, overcooking, and long storage. For organically grown foods one needs merely to accentuate or complement the innate flavors.

Herbs used as seasoning aid digestion, causing better salivation, pepsin, and gall and pancreas secretion. They also help to balance certain one-sidedness in foods. Heavy cabbage is made more digestible with caraway seed; dill balances cucumbers; the watery nature of sauerkraut is aided by the fragrant, fiery nature of juniper berries; chervil and caraway are good with "moony" cheese; beans are accentuated by savory; and tomatoes are complemented by sweet basil and parsley. What good would the Christmas goose be without a stuffing flavored with mugwort? Most spices bring cosmic forces (the quality of the upper planets) into the terrestrial-lunar nature of some vegetables. Spices of the carrot family (*Umbelliferae*) show especially the effect of light and warmth ether in their delicate, lace-like, filigree foliage and aromatic seeds. The *Labiatae,* or mint family members, retain much of the aromatic flowering processes within the realm of the leaves, leaving them savory and full of essential oils. All of these herbs can be grown locally in the home garden.

Umbelliferae	Labiatae	Others
Anise	Sweet basil	Borage
Chervil	Oregano	Chives
Fennel	Mints	Horseradish
Dill	Sage	Tarragon
Caraway	Marjoram	Mugwort
Celery	Thyme	Cress
Coriander	Rosemary	Rocket
Parsley	Savory	Salad burnet
Lovage	Tulsi	Garlic, Mustard

STORAGE

The problem of storage involves finding the best way to keep the ether body of the plant connected with its physical substance. One should use only the best vegetables for storage. They should not have received any substantial nitrogen fertilization late in the season. They should be harvested in dry weather and in the waning moon. Specific factors involved in storage are *optimal temperature, ventilation* and *humidity.*

- Temperature: Sweet potatoes, pumpkins, and squash are warm storers (around 50° F). Cool storers (around 35° F) are potatoes, cabbages, carrots, beets, turnips, celery, oyster plant, parsnips, kohlrabi, leeks, and endives. Some of the latter can be left *in situ* in the garden in regions where it does not freeze too much and where rodents, such as field mice or voles, are no problem.
- Ventilation: The root or vegetable cellar should not be completely airtight.

- Humidity: Onions, sweet potatoes, pumpkins, squash, and fennel bulbs should be stored in dry places. Onions can be braided and hung in cool, dry rooms such as an unheated attic. Fennel must be stored in a dry, cool place to prevent rotting. Other vegetables prefer to be stored in a somewhat moist environment (75 to 90 percent) as is provided by a root cellar.

One can leave root crops (parsnips, salsify, Hamburg parsley, carrots, beets) directly in the ground where they grew and cover them with thick mulch of straw or leaves. Mustard, spinach, cabbages, endives, corn salad, leeks, kale, Brussels sprouts, and sugar hat can also be left in the ground and a plastic tent can be built over the beds to protect from heavy freezes. Root crops, potatoes, and cabbages can be placed into *mound storage*. To do that, the crops are placed on a wire mesh, bedded into straw, and a layer of sand and earth is put over them. They are dug out as needed. One has to be careful that this doesn't turn into compost. Cabbages can be uprooted and stored upside down in trenches, which are covered with leaves or straw.

Whatever kind of storage place one may choose, simple comparative tests will show that organically grown vegetables keep much longer that those grown with chemical fertilizers. The latter are usually not stored in a live form, but must be frozen or canned in order to keep.

Empty hot beds make good underground storage. They can be covered by boards and mats and are easily accessible.

Other forms of storing fruit are *drying* (fruits, beans, tomatoes), *pickling* (beans, cucumber, pumpkins), *souring* (cabbage, beets, radish) and last and least, *canning*. A number of good publications are available on all of these techniques.

Figure 18.4. Using empty hot beds to store food

Chapter 19

Seeds and Tools

Good huswives in summer will save their owne seeds
Against the next year, or occasion needs:
One see for another, to make an exchange,
With fellowly neighbourhood, seemeth not strange.
　　　　—Thomas Tusser, Five Hundreth Points of Good
　　　　　　Husbandry, 1573.1

Now sets do ask watering, with pot or with dish,
New sown do not so, if ye do as I wish:
Through cunning with dibble, rake mattock and spade,
By line, and by level, trim garden is made.
　　　　—Thomas Tusser, 1573.2

In many instances, it is worth one's while to raise one's own seeds. At the
cost of seed in inflationary times, it saves money; but it also brings one
closer to an appreciation of the mystery of life as the plant moves into and
out of manifestation in continuous rhythms. It is still a miracle how the
tiny seed, this little round microcosm, can become the focal point of the
forces that build up the stately plant. Some seeds are easy to save, while
others are tricky, requiring much skill and patience. Like keeping bees, it is
something for which one must almost have a special predilection.

Seed Selection

Pick the very best of the plants, such as the lettuce plant that bolts last, the spinach that has the lushest leaves, the corn that has the first and largest ears, or the cabbage that forms the tightest head. These plants should have been grown on organic, biodynamic soil so that the greatest vitality can assist them and the least amount of seed degenerations results.

Let the seeds ripen on the plants as long as possible. As they are about to mature, paper bags can be tied over the heads to prevent them from being eaten by birds or falling on the ground. The entire stalk is then cut, the seeds shaken off or thrashed in the bag and then winnowed. Some, like peas, beans, and corn, can be left to dry in the shells or husks. Let fleshy fruits, such as tomatoes, squash, cucumbers, or eggplant overripen on the vine, then scrape the seeds out of the fruit, soak for a couple of days in water until they ferment slightly, free the seed from the pulp by washing and rubbing, and then dry on paper blotters or on screens.

Seed potato tubers are usually cut into sections and then planted; each section will form a new plant. Genetically such a new potato plant is a clone of the older plant. If one's potatoes seem to degenerate from season to season, being prone to scabs or other problems, then one might consider letting them sexually reproduce. This would allow a reshuffling of the genes and allow new cosmic impulses to manifest. To do so, one lets the plant flower and extracts the seeds from the berries much as one would with other fleshy fruits, as mentioned above. The potato seeds are planted in the seedbed, where they will produce a relatively small plant with small tubers in the first year. The next year one uses these tubers as seed potatoes. Whatever the outcome, usually one will be surprised. Often the new variety will have a different shape, color, or other characteristic than the parent. Often one is lucky and has a vital new strain of potatoes, adapted to local conditions.

Seed Storage

It is useless to save seeds if one does not label, date, and store them correctly. The seeds should be thoroughly dried and then placed in cool, dry storage, so that they will not become moldy or mildewed. Glass containers (i.e., small jars) or snuff boxes (i.e., Copenhagen lids) that are sealed airtight with wax and contain traces of tobacco, which discourages seed-eating bugs, are the best for storing.

GERMINATION TEST

If one would like to be sure that the seeds are viable, especially after long storage, one can do a germination test to determine the *germination ratio*. Ten to twenty seeds are counted out and then laid on a moist blotter paper or on a sheet of cotton and covered. The number of seeds that sprout versus the number that are dead gives the percentage of the germination ratio. For example, if one out of twenty does not germinate, the ratio is 95 percent, and if only ten out of twenty sprout, the ratio is obviously only 50 percent. From this percentage, one can determine if it is worth sowing the seed out, or how thickly one must sow for an even stand.

Some seeds are *quick sprouters*, such as cress, beans, sunflowers, mustards, lettuce, and most members of the brassica family. *Slow sprouters* include most of the umbellifers (carrots, parsnips, parsley, celery, turnip-rooted chervil), New Zealand spinach, and most herbs. These can take from three weeks to over a month to germinate.

Most vegetable seeds sprout soon after they have been dried; some, however, have to be cured for some time before they will germinate. The umbellifers need at least a month before they are ready to grow, and the germination ratio of red beets and Swiss chard is increased if the seeds are stored for a couple of years.

Some seeds, such as many weed species, might not sprout and grow even when moisture, temperature, and soil conditions are right. This is known as *seed dormancy*. Dormancy might be caused by chemical inhibitors, which have to wear off the coat (they prevent tomatoes and squash from sprouting while within the fruit); it might be related to lunar and planetary positions as suggested by Maria Thun for many weeds; it might need the corrosive effect of a symbiotic fungus on the seed coat; or the seed might need to go through a cold period before it germinates. Some weed seeds last for several decades in this way while buried in the soil.

SEED VIABILITY

Is it necessary to grow seeds or to buy them in a store each year? No, some seeds have very long viability. For example, one can keep cucumber and endive seeds for over ten years; celery and celeriac seed lasts seven to eight years; beets, eggplant, melons, and squash last six years before the germination ratio starts to drop off; most cabbages (including cauliflower, kohlrabi, broccoli, and kale), lettuce, pumpkin, spinach, and turnips are viable up to five years; asparagus, carrot, mustard, pepper, and tomato last for four years; beans, leeks, parsley, and peas can be stored for three years; and it is best to replenish corn, onions, oyster plants, and parsnips every other year.

Hybrids

For raising one's own seeds, unless one is really fanatic about it, it is best to use standard varieties, which will breed true. Hybrids contain latent and recessive genes, which become manifest in the next generation, so that at least three-fourths of the next crop will deviate considerably from what one expects.

Nowadays most seed companies have been taken over and are owned by international oil or pharmaceutical companies, even though some have kept their traditional names. The consequence of this is that many locally adapted varieties seeds have disappeared and that the vegetable species have an ever-diminishing genetic basis. Of course, these seed corporations are interested that the farmer or gardener becomes dependent on them to buy their seeds anew each year. They create this dependence with hybrids and with so-called "terminator" seeds, which are genetically programmed to self-destruct. To be independent and self-sufficient it is a good idea to grow one's own seed, as farmers and gardeners have done for centuries. Local seed swap groups, garden clubs, and organizations like the Seed Saver's Exchange are a good source of various untreated, non-GMO varieties.

Pollination

Pollination comes about when the haploid pollen combines with the haploid gametes of the female flower (gynoecium) to form a new diploid seed. Wind and insects pollinate some plants, while others are *self-pollinating*. Self-pollinated vegetables include tomatoes, beans, peas, and corn, which makes it extremely easy to save seed from them, because they tend to come out true and they are not easily *cross-pollinated*. Lettuce tends to self-pollinate but can be crossed with a nearby wild growing, tough, spiny compass plant or wild lettuce *(Lactuca scariola)*. Oyster plant, chicory, and dandelion can be self-fertilized although bees and other insects do cross them with others of their own species. Their seeds should be shaken into bags every few days to keep the finches from eating the ripe seed. Most other plants are fertilized mainly by insects.

Peppers must be watched because the sweet peppers can cross with the hot peppers. Cucumbers, melons, and cantaloupes will not cross, but different species of squash and pumpkins, both of the genus *Cucurbita*, can cross into strange combinations resulting in weird looking crook-necked squash-zucchini-pumpkins. Beets, Swiss chard, sugar beets, and mangles cross-pollinate each other by means of wind. The cabbages, which all belong to the species *Brassica oleracea* (cabbage, cauliflower, collard, kohlrabi, kale, Brussels sprouts) are cross-pollinated by bees and butterflies creating throwbacks that are of little use to the gardener. Carrots cross easily with their wild relative, Queen Anne's lace; leeks cross with onions; celery with celeriac; and parsnips with wild parsnips in the neighborhood. For any vegetables that are threatened with the loss of desired characteristics because of cross-pollination, extreme caution and care must be taken. Either the plants grown for seed are placed in pots far removed from their cousins (a quarter of a mile), or the flowers have to be hand pollinated by using a soft-haired brush to transfer the flower dust from the stamen to the pistils of the female flowers. All the while a paper bag is tied over the flowers to prevent unwanted pollen from fertilizing the pistils. The bags can be removed when the fruit is starting to set.

Collecting Seed from Annuals, Biennials, and Perennials

Annuals complete their life cycle and produce seed within a single season's span. Annuals include beans, peas, corn, fava bean, tomatoes, peppers, eggplant, cucumbers, melons, squash, lettuce, spinach, rocket, radish, Chinese cabbage, broccoli, orache, cress, and New Zealand spinach.

Biennials, on the other hand, like cabbages, carrots, parsnips, celery, or burdock, take two seasons to produce seed. The first year's growth is vegetative, producing a food storage organ; a winter rest-period intervenes before the seed formation occurs in the second year at the end of which the plant dies. In tropical countries where there is no winter freeze, the plants will remain in their vegetative state and not flower and go to seed. In the relatively mild climate of the Northwest coastal region, chosen biennial plants can be left in the ground over the winter and let to go to seed the next summer. In climates with cold, icy winter, these plants must be carefully removed from the field and put into cold storage by being packed into peat moss and put into a root cellar; in the spring they can be replanted and allowed to go into flower. Fennel and oyster plant often make seed in the first year. It is best, however, to obtain seeds for the next crop from those plants that have gone through the biennial cycle.

Perennials live more than two years and often need permanent beds. They include asparagus, chives, dahlias, garlic, Good King Henry, hops (young shoots make an excellent spring vegetable), Jerusalem artichoke, some onion varieties (such as the Chinese onion or Japanese scallion), sorrel, seakale, skirrett, and others; eggplant and potatoes are also perennials, as are strawberries, fruit trees, and berry bushes.

Other Means of Propagation

Not all plants in the garden are propagated by means of seeds. With potatoes and Jerusalem artichokes, tubers are cut and the eyes planted to produce the next season's crops. With strawberries and many herbs such as nettle, mints, or tansy, runners are cut and replanted; while for others, such as comfrey, horseradish, valerian, or rhubarb, cuttings of the roots multiply the number of plants.

Gardening Tools

While the technology of intensive gardening is simple, the techniques are sophisticated. The opposite can be said of an agriculture, which is dependent upon complicated and expensive machinery and chemicals, but simplifies the technique to the point of crating boring, alienating work routines and at the same time harmfully simplifies the ecology (monocultures, destruction of a wide range of fauna and flora).

The tools of gardening are ancient, not having changed substantially since the early Neolithic, when the first crops were deliberately planted and sowed. Even then the digging stick used as an all purpose tool for furrowing the ground for seeding, poking the ground for planting, weeding, and eventually harvesting tubers had a precursor in the ancient dibble stick with a fire-hardened tip, as used by Mesolithic hunters and gatherers as an extension of their fingers. The digging fork, spade, trowel, and eventually the plow derived from this ancient simple tool. The hoe, too, is an ancient tool found in nearly all horticultural societies, used for weeding, cultivating, aerating, and dry mulching the soil. Shells, bones, flat stones, and deer scapulae preceded the use of metal in the making of hoes. Rakes for smoothening the beds (and later harrows derived from the same principle) and blades (sickles, scythes, and knives) for harvesting and pruning are nearly as ancient and universal for gardeners and still make up the core technology of intensive horticulture.

The Tools One Needs for Successful Gardening

1. A *digging fork* for double digging, harvesting potatoes, carrots, salsify, etc.; for turning compost; and also for loosening the soil in the beds at the beginning of each season

2. A *spade* for double digging, trenching, chopping compost material, etc.
3. A *hoe* for weeding, clearing, cultivating. The triangular hoe makes it possible to work close to the individual plants, and the stirrup, or pendulum, hoe, which can be dragged forwards and backwards between rows, reduces some of the toil. The ordinary hoe is also used for furrowing and for mounding up potatoes, peas, beans, leeks, fennel, corn, and tomatoes.
4. A *rake* for smoothing the newly prepared beds and for sowing (making furrows, covering the seeds with earth, and pressing the soil firmly onto the seeds)
5. *Pegs, line,* and *measuring tape* (or a *yard stick*) is used for marking the beds, rows, and paths. A nylon line will not rot.
6. A *trowel* for transplanting seedlings (make sure that seedlings have been watered about thirty minutes before transplanting and that the hole dug for the seedling is deep enough so that the roots of the young transplants are not bent)
7. A *pitchfork* is handy for pitching compost material, manure, and mulch.
8. A *wheelbarrow* is needed for transporting earth, compost, mulch, lime, or tools.
9. A *sickle* or *scythe* for harvesting grains, mowing grass, and cutting mulching and composting material. Working rhythmically with a well-sharpened scythe, one can smoothly and quickly mow large areas. It is definitely more relaxing and less costly that a fume-spewing, noisy lawnmower.
10. *Barrels* for collecting and brewing Russian tea, nettles, comfrey, and other liquid fertilizers and preparations. Wood or crockery barrels are preferable to plastic or metal containers. Metal tends to chemically interact with the brews while plastic is not durable.
11. *Watering equipment* includes a *watering can* with a sprinkler spout for the seedbeds, *hoses, drip irrigation* or *soaker hoses* for those plants that do not like water on their foliage (tomatoes, beans, and some other warm weather lovers), and *overhead sprinklers*. This might be the most expensive investment for the garden.

12. *Hand* or *knapsack sprayers* for foliar feeding and application of preparations (such as horn-dung, horn-quartz, or valerian preparations)
13. *Plastic tents* and their frames (easily made from willow or pine saplings or a PBC pipe) for covering early or late beds. Old plastic can be used to cover composts to prevent them from leaching and to trap the sun's heat for the compost.
14. A *hatchet* might come in handy for cutting, sharpening, and driving bean poles, tomato stakes, and fence posts for pea and cucumber fences.
15. A wooden *mallet* for driving in fence posts
16. A *pocketknife* comes in handy for cutting ropes, sharpening pegs, pruning, and harvesting.
17. A *thinking cap*! Ever wonder why the garden gnomes and dwarves always wear pointed caps? Proper concepts are as important as tools made of wood and steel.

As we see, garden technology is simple, quiet, and ancient. It does not lend itself readily to capital intensity, being invented and used long before money was ever even thought of. Usually it is only the gimmicks that cost a lot, and they are not really necessary. Advanced horticultural technology such as rototillers, mini-tractors, electrical compost tumblers, and compost shredders can be useful but are not absolutely necessary. This is true especially in smaller gardens where costs outweigh the benefits. Stalks, twigs, and haulms that are usually shredded can be chopped up with a spade and composted for a longer time, or they can be placed into the bottom of a newly double dug bed where they will have ample time to decompose. Double digging and raised beds generally preclude rototillers.

The work with ordinary garden tools is quiet and rhythmical, an activity conducive to achieving an open, receptive frame of mind. One can hear oneself think, so to speak, and one can meditatively apprehend the aliveness of the soil, the plants, and the many creatures with whom we share a garden. This frame of mind is necessary to be in empathy with the biological and ecological needs of the garden. By contrast, loud machinery and commotion close the gardener's chakras off from this important contact.

Gardens where people with simple tools but sophisticated techniques predominate instead of expensive machinery recreate a human environment for young and old. In Africa hoe-agricultural societies, the fields are filled with song rather than motor din and fumes, as many people work the soil as a social activity.

TOOL CARE

Gardening tools are not expensive. However it is advisable to not buy the very cheapest ones, for often bargain basement tools break very quickly, whereas better wrought tools might last a lifetime. Though we live in a throwaway culture, replacing tools is going to cost more as our resources become more expensive. Like our forebears we should, once again, learn to respect and care for what we have and to make it last. Garden tools, for example, should not be left laying in the field over night. Exposure to rain or dew inevitably weakens the handles as microorganisms digest wood fiber and unprotected, moist metal rusts. Tools should be put into a tool shed clean and dry. The handles should be treated occasionally with boiled linseed oil so they will last; the metal tools should be greased before winter storage. Garden hoses and plastic tents should be put out of the sun and the elements when they are not in seasonal use, as should stakes, posts, and poles. Garden hoses should not be dragged in a way that kinks develop which will eventually weaken and crack them. After some time it is possible to even develop a fondness for one's long worn tools with their sweat stained handles, much as one has a liking for a favorite coffee cup or cooking pot. Here, too, it is possible to establish a personal, soul-filled relationship with one's world. The ancient Europeans even gave personal names to their favorite tools.

Chapter 20

Social Implications

> O goddess Earth, O all-enduring wide expanse! Salutation to thee.
> Now I am going to begin cultivation. Be pleased, o virtuous one!
> Tilling, tapping and whatever other injury I have inflicted on thee,
> Pray pardon me for all that and yield me a rich harvest.
> Thou alone art declared to be the mother of all beings
> Therefore be gracious to me.
> O goddess Earth! And bring me a boundless reward.
> —Ancient Sanskrit prayer offered before plowing,
> attributed to the sage Kashyapa.[1]

Growing food is not just a matter of biology, or even economics, but of the interrelationships among people, the use of their time, energy, and resources. It is a social concern. Any use of land, any method of growing food, assigning work, and distributing products includes the human element. It requires a social arrangement.

These social arrangements, until recently in history, had been safeguarded by religious instructions, rituals, and traditions. From anthropological studies of simple, precolonial horticultural societies we know how carefully these social arrangements were handled; they were, as it was believed, embedded in the very nature of the universe.

In most of these societies, women belonging to the same blood-kin group, lineage, or clan did the work of planting, hoeing, and harvesting. The land was the property of the clan, not of the individual, and the highest level of social organization was the autonomous village unit. War, hunt, and the heavier work of clearing land were the domain of the men within a ritually prescribed gender division of labor. These simple societies did not hover on the edge of starvation. Ethnologists point out that even with the simplest hand tools they were able to create a comfortable standard of living. The surpluses regularly produced were consumed in redistributive rituals and special festivals. These gardening tribes sometimes kept animals, such as pigs and chickens, in Melanesia and Southeast Asia.

Rites and traditions, still tied into bloodlines and kin groups (such as extended families or matrilineal clans), continued to be the structuring principle of primitive gardeners and swidden farmers for a long time. As opposed to simple horticultural societies, later agricultural societies utilized more animal power, used irrigation, and the plow replaced the dibble stick and hoe. In these emergent peasant societies women still worked in the fields, planting, hoeing, and harvesting; they also gardened, in what would later become the kitchen vegetable gardens, while the men generally took over the heavier tasks, such as clearing the land, plowing, and taking care of the herds. It was a natural division of labor. This farming was still a communal affair, carried out in a fairly autonomous village and community context; it was not yet a system of individual entrepreneurs competing in a moneyed market system. Surpluses, redistributed through barter, secured the services of specialists such as potters, tanners, weavers, cartwrights, and the like.

This pattern of plow agriculture proved very successful and became standard as a basis of the great civilizations of the West, Middle East, India, Far East, and later, in the Americas. The land, the countryside, was not only a place of production, but also the place where the majority of the population lived. These people were tied personally and spiritually to the land that nourished them and took their dead into its bosom. Indeed the earth, which brought forth its fruit each year, was regarded as sacred; it was the embodiment of the Great Earth Goddess. This profound tie to the land assured more or less that the life-sustaining ecology was kept intact, that love and care was lavished on it and not just profit extracted.

For the city dweller, the land was always a place of refuge in war, social chaos, and pestilence. This was partially true even in the United States where during economic depressions the family farm, or close relative's farm, was a place to weather the difficulties.

Loss of the Sacred Land

With the coming of the modern international market economy, these traditions and sympathies connected with the land held ever less. As our anthropological studies indicate, they are everywhere becoming decadent and fading rapidly. The Industrial Revolution with its end of the commons, its turning of peasant communities *(Gemeinschaft)* into proletarian societies *(Gesellschaft),* widened the gap between the rich and poor. The concurrent implementation of colonialism and the plantation system (whether raising beef for foreign landlords in Ireland, sugar cane in the West Indies, or cotton in Egypt or the antebellum South), the decline of crafts with the coming of imported, cheaply manufactured goods, and the consequent alienation from land and meaningful work put an end to functional village life and changed the relationship of humans and their environment. All of this has been lamented, studied, and documented, and numerous attempts at solutions have been proposed. Attempts to return to an idealized past often revealed themselves as effete romanticism, if not authoritarian sectarianism.

Great thinkers have tried to deal with these fundamental problems all along. Thomas Jefferson, eager to throw off vestiges of feudalism with its special privileges and stifling rigidness, envisioned the new United States as the place where the dignity of each individual was to be guaranteed by the establishment of an independent, self-reliant people based firmly on yeoman agriculture and tied into a network of functional town communities. Private ownership would guarantee the dignity of labor and that responsibility and personal interest pervade the management of the land. Freedom to experiment and universal education would ensure continual progress and betterment of the people. Stifling centralized control and exploitative hierarchy were to be avoided, being replaced by grassroots democracy where voting guaranteed that the voice of each household was made known.

Jefferson could not have foreseen the impact of industrialization and its implicit centralization of power and control. He could not have foreseen that the principle of private initiative was to be misused by monopolies working against the interest of society as a whole, merely for self-aggrandizement and profit, while passing the costs (pollution, resource depletion, urban sprawl, and other pathologies) on to the public as a whole.

A century later, Marx, realizing the scope of the Industrial Revolution, analyzed the phenomenon of alienation, the condition of a humanity cut off from its roots, its meaning, where the worker has neither a relation to his tools nor his products and experiences himself as a commodity, while the owner is alienated from the actual process of labor and involved in abstract notions of capital and ownership. Marx foretold that a rectifying revolution would come about of historical necessity, in which people would regain the dignity of their work and become socially responsible again. He did not foresee the effect of unions, automation, the mechanisms of co-option, and the adaptability of the world-spanning corporations.

The mechanisms of the world market and the Industrial Revolution rambled on, creating masses of dispossessed peasants and reducing others to cheap labor sources for commodity production, while the mounting pressures of an international economy with global networks of markets, resources, and power stiffened the competition and increased the monopolistic hold of the corporations or centralized state structures.

In recent years, corporations began opting for control of food production. Dow Chemical, ITT, Coca-Cola, Gulf & Western, Kaiser Aluminum, Aetna Life Insurance, Goodyear, Tenneco, Ralston-Purina, Monsanto, and other main players in the industrial agricultural complex have continually increased the acreage of land in their possession.[2] In the course of this development, some five million family farms were eliminated in the United States since the 1930s. In 1935 the number of farms stood at 6.8 million. In the 1970s government policies in favor of large corporations forced farmers to abandon their farms at the rate of one hundred thousand per year. I remember the many empty farm buildings in rural Ohio where I grew up; each empty house and dilapidated barn spoke of a family tragedy. At the time of this writing (2012) there were, according the census of the

Department of Agriculture, only two million agricultural production centers left. However, of these two million only about one-fourth (500,000) could be considered real family farms, owned and worked on by families, who have a personal stake and a lifestyle invested in the soil. The death of family farming continues. The farm population is aging and literally dying out; the average age of farm residents being currently fifty-seven.[3] The result of this development is that small rural communities are vanishing, that the social fabric of wide areas of the country is being destroyed.

Corporations envision a worldwide network of supply and demand, as already seen in huge shipments of wheat, soy beans, fertilizer, raw fiber, coffee, tropical fruit, latex, and other commodities around the globe. Already in the 1970s radical anthropologists pointed out that mechanized production of genetically engineered vegetables in northern Mexico for the tables of North America left substantial portions of poor *campesinos* deprived of land and hungry. The selling of the rich Peruvian catches of anchovies to U.S. chicken batteries and cattle feedlots for fodder caused not only the Peruvian *Indios* to suffer protein deficiency, but also the guano fertilizer industry to be shut down because the seagulls that feed on the anchovies and produce the guano were starving.[4] Already at that time Purex and United Brands owned about one-third of the U.S. green leaf vegetable production, and Green Giant about 25 percent of the canned pea and corn production.[5] Year after year, five crops of heavily chemicalized, mechanically grown iceberg lettuces were produced in Salinas Valley, California, amounting to about a quarter of the iceberg lettuce sold in supermarkets across the country. These trends and developments continue, pleasing the stockholders, but ultimately putting whole nations into a state of utter dependency and threatening food security.

The attempt by a few international corporations to seize total control of land and food production has accelerated since. As Dr. Vandana Shiva says, "Seeds controlled by Monsanto, agribusiness trade controlled by Cargill, processing controlled by Pepsi and Philip Morris, retail controlled by Walmart—is a recipe for food dictatorship. Indeed we are in a phase where the state has merged with corporations and holds power over the lives of the people. This is a return to feudalism and this corporate feudalism is not compatible with democracy."* Vandana Shiva, fighting for cultural and biological diversity, sees it as a crime that seeds have been colonized and patented. According to her, Roundup and other potent herbicides amount to ecocide, killing bees and soil organisms. Nature responds to these poisons with new super weeds and to genetically modified Bt crops with new super bugs. It is time to end this greed and nonsense. Shiva is able to show that corporation agriculture is not as productive as it claims; on the contrary, loving care and organic methods are more productive. "We need more people on the land," she says.5

The Land of Cockaigne

The last few decades were a time of material abundance, especially in the Western world. One felt secure and it seemed that nothing could stop progress. Ever more sophisticated machines took over hard work for us, pesticides and herbicides held food competitors in check, and antibiotics and miracle drugs kept disease at bay for us and our domesticated animals. The medieval dream of the Land of Cockaigne,[6] where there is a chicken in every pot, seemed to have turned into reality in our well-stocked supermarkets and shopping malls. A worldwide net of commerce and, especially, the energy of cheap fossil fuel in the form of crude oil made this miracle possible.

But then, toward the end of the millennium, dark clouds appeared on the horizon. Suddenly it was recognized that agricultural chemicals are increasingly poisoning the soil and the water. We are suffocating in our garbage, chemical poisons, and plastic waste. A world full of humming and buzzing machinery and electronics causes ever more debilitating stress; antibiotic miracle drugs have lost their punch and brought forth, through selection pressure, potent new microbes. Even the optimists gradually have come to realize that our resources—oil, coal, minerals, metals, uranium, and even fresh water—are limited. When fossil oil becomes scarce and subsequently ever more expensive, how can the basic needs of the world's population be met? How can social peace be ensured?

The world leaders are presently trying to alter course. In times when resources are running ever shorter, the prospect of reducing consumption must be made palatable. A new behavioral codex is being formulated, for example, the trend toward vegetarian nutrition for the masses. Forget the image of the "sacred cow" or of "good old Bess" in the barn. Bovine "livestock units" are being redefined as food competitors; besides they burp methane, a global warming gas. The attempt is made to bridge coming energy shortages by furthering renewable energy, such as solar panels, water turbines, wind turbines, and crops that produce oil bearing fruits. But there is a hook: corn and sugar cane cultivation for the sake of ethanol production competes with food crops; oil palm plantations are instrumental in destroying the last tropical forests left on earth. Population control is a further proposed priority. China shows the way with its one-child-per-family policy, but that leads to severe distortions of the social structure. Meanwhile the masses are distracted with the virtual "bread and circuses" of the media, with the cult of superstars and supermodels, and a neverending "sex, drugs and rock 'n' roll revolution." At the same time sophisticated surveillance systems are being installed. But will this be enough to buffer the social restructuring without leading toward chaos and collapse? Many are doubtful; some fantasize about "terraforming" other planets—settling them, as though they were a new frontier, even though we apparently don't even know how to live on this planet! Others lose themselves in "last days" scenarios—and wasn't there something about some ancient Mayan calendar?

America was always the country of optimism; the future was seen with confidence. "Progress is our most important product," was a mantra chanted by Ronald Reagan each week in the General Electric Theater on TV in the affluent fifties. But on my last visit in 2011 to my folks in Illinois and Wyoming there was hardly any of this confidence left. Despite the promises of industrial agriculture, some were even worried about a possible coming food collapse.

Monsanto and a handful of other corporations monopolized food production. They have created genetically "improved" plants and animals and a market for high yielding profitable terminator seeds. Terminator seeds of corn and other main edibles have been modified so that they do not bring forth viable seed and they do not germinate; farmers and gardeners cannot use the seeds from the previous crop and are forced to buy new ones from outside sources every year. The gene-manipulated species (GMOs), which are the bases of our food system, stand on a dangerously thin genetic foundation. A new virus, a germ, a fungus—and the next starvation catastrophe is imminent. In Ireland, in the middle of the nineteenth century, the fungus *Phytophthora* infested the potatoes and decimated the harvest. Seed potatoes are basically clones, which are planted year after year. The Irish potatoes were clones from one kind of potato. They therefore had a very narrow genetic basis and were easy prey for this parasitic fungus. Ireland's population was halved: between one and two million starved and another two million emigrated to America. Another weakness of our food system is that GMOs and modern hybrids need a complex support system of fertilizer, herbicides, and irrigation—all based on cheap energy, mainly oil.

Small, Decentralized, and Local Is Beautiful

It has been shown that large-scale corporate farming is not as efficient as labor-intensive small-scale family farming or gardening. In the last analysis, industrial farming does not result in better and cheaper produce, or even in more production per acre.[7] Studies conducted by the Rodale Society, among others, show that nowhere is production more energy efficient than on small, intensively and lovingly cultivated parcels of land. This was shown after the Second World War in Europe when citizens were allotted small garden plots on the outskirts of the cities and along the railroad tracks where they could grow their own vegetables and spuds as well as a few extra to sell. Small farms and gardens are more tuned to the specific needs of the land, allowing better ecological stewardship of the land, upon which all increased production ultimately depends.

More recently, in Johannesburg, on April 2008, the International Assessment of Agricultural Knowledge, Science and Technology for Development (IAASTD), an intergovernmental process under the co-sponsorship of FAO, GEF, UNDP, UNEP, UNESCO, World Bank, and WHO, came to a similar conclusion when it compared different types of agriculture. The report states that hunger and poverty can best be countered on the local level. In ecologically less favored regions, small peasant family farms are able to produce substantially more food than would be possible by means of high-tech industrial farming.

The giant collective farms (*kolkhoz*) and the state-owned "factories in the fields," the *sovkhoz*, were even less efficient than the corporate farms in the United States. It was mainly because of food shortages due to centrally planned gigantism and economic incompetence that the former Soviet Union collapsed. If the people had not been able to retreat to their privately owned household plots or *dachas* (Rus. "small country house"), ranging in size from six-tenths of an acre up to one and one quarter acres, it would have been worse. On small, private plots, where personal judgment and responsibility could be exercised, the Russian peasant significantly outproduced the government supported kolkhoz and sovkhoz. The total area covering these personally owned gardens made up in total only 1 percent of the arable land of the Soviet Union. Thirty percent of the food was produced on this 1 percent. By contrast, on the other 99 percent of the arable land and pastureland a highly subsidized and mechanized agriculture produced the remaining 70 percent of the food.[8]

Currently, in the West, in Europe and America, it is a policy of subventions, tax write-offs, government favoritism, exploitation of migrant workers, and monopolistic practices that put the corporate farmers at an advantage, not more efficiency. If one were to calculate the ecological damage to the soil; the destruction of natural habitats of beneficial animals; the genetic impoverishment of crop varieties; the unbridled squandering of fossil fuel energy in the making and using of labor-saving machinery, insecticides, fertilizer, and herbicides; the processing, packing, transporting, and storing; not to mention the social costs and health costs throughout the world of people deprived of meaningful employment; the creation of slums and urban sprawl as a result of rural depopulation—then one can see that this kind of industrialized farming is not progressive at all, but the tool of unsocial, special interests. Government subsidies of around thirty billion dollars a year mask much of the high cost of this kind of food production. Even now, individual farm income continues to drop while, at the same time, food prices are rising.

The rapid depletion of fossil fuel brings humanity to the point of making a decision whether to continue the trend toward ever larger corporate and industrial farming, or whether to evolve into a different direction. Organic and biodynamic farming and gardening can be seen in this regard as a vote for human dignity and independence.

For Americans, it is time to reconsider the ideas of local ecological farming and gardening coupled with grassroots Jeffersonian democracy. In the 1970s a number of thinkers such as Wendell Berry,[9] Robert Rodale,[10] and Charles Walters Jr.,[11] urged a reconsideration of this approach. E. F. Schumacher's ideas on intermediate technology go into the same direction.[12]

Wendell Berry gives convincing evidence that our social problems, urban riots, idle, drifting youth, unemployment, and lack of meaning in our lives are related to the loss of our Jeffersonian foundation, our alienation from the land. He points out that agribusiness has succeeded in replacing some forty million people from the land between 1920 and 1970, to be absorbed into the sprawling city and its slums, where due to automation jobs are increasingly difficult to get. Why not make it possible for people to get back to the land, if they want to, where meaningful work can be done? Why not revitalize local skills and crafts? Why not use local energy, such as animal and human energy, wind, solar, wood, water, and methane energy wherever applicable? That would be an alternative to costly polluting fossil fuel, which is finite and creates international tensions, or nuclear fuel, which is unbelievably expensive and so toxic that life-destroying wastes will have to be guarded for hundreds of thousands of years.

Berry cites the Amish community, which shows no mental breakdowns, alcoholism, alienation, sexual problems, crime, or pollution, as an example of local economic independence. The large households of extended families are independent economically in gardening, cooking, simple technology, and energy, while at the same time, highly responsible to the community as a whole. There are no neglected poor, sick, and old, and the young are given community support to start out on their own. In case of fire or catastrophe, the entire community is there to give assistance. Amish fields are per acre as productive as any energy intensive, mechanized, and electrified corporation farm. Yet, because of true horsepower, simple windmills, and plenty of elbow grease, they achieve this with 87 percent less energy input.

Reclaiming Our Garden

Of course, in our modern times we cannot turn ourselves into Amish farmers—no more than we can turn ourselves into hunters and gatherers or swidden gardeners again. But we are still not necessarily hopelessly vulnerable.

Even a small family garden can make a big difference in times of rising food prices. Learning about wild edible plants can also be very beneficial. With a garden of some five thousand square feet and less than 250 hours of work, a four-person family can provide its yearly need of vegetables, lettuces, and potatoes. Garden expert Gerhard Schönauer13 did the math on this: with an even bigger area of some thirty thousand square feet, a family can even have their own eggs, meat, and honey if rabbits, doves, chickens, and bees are taken into the garden's biotope. On a bigger parcel one can have a couple of sheep, goats, or a pig; these animals produce valuable fertilizer, which can be composted. With a little more than a hectare (about two and a half acres), one can even have a cow and a fishpond.

Such measures should be considered. Who can guarantee that our transportation and energy systems will stay intact in the coming years? Currently government food reserves, stocked in case of national disaster, are down from two years to only a few days. This is due to a U.S. Government decision in 1996 to end its holding of food stocks, a decision strongly endorsed by the multinational agribusiness because it makes speculation and price manipulation easier.[14]

People seem to be sensing that if nothing is done there might be trouble ahead. There is an increasing attempt by individuals to attain some degree of self-sufficiency and to decentralize food. The boring lawns that surround suburban homes covering hundred of thousands of acres are increasingly being turned into vegetable gardens, into so-called *survival gardens*. Mini-farming, i.e., optimizing the use of small areas, is becoming ever more popular. The people who are propagating this nowadays are not the dropouts, dreamers, or civilization-weary members of the "alternative" culture of the 1960s and 1970s, but "normal" mainstream citizens. It has hardly escaped their attention that food prices are constantly rising—17 percent in the year 2011—while salaries are stagnating. At the same time, the cost of industrial food production and transport is rising. It is also not escaping people's attention that the foods in the supermarkets look good at first glance, but are low in actual nutritional value and laced with of herbicide and pesticide residues.

Getting control over one's own life by turning lawns into sustainable organic gardens is a good start. Brett L. Markham, an engineer by profession, is one such fore-rider in suburban "mini farming." On an area of some ten thousand square feet he has invested roughly two hundred dollars to establish a garden that provides his family with 85 percent of their food; in addition he earns up to seven thousand dollars a year selling surplus vegetables.[15]

Another trend is to attempt to set up *local food systems*. This helps avoid the costly endless continental and transcontinental transport of livestock and produce. A Swiss friend of mine, a five star cook, calls this locally grown food "church-bell food," meaning that ideally one's potatoes, fruits, and vegetables should come from an area no wider than the radius of the sound of the bells ringing from the village steeple. This, he says, would guarantee absolutely fresh, unprocessed foods. It would imply more control of local people over their affairs and economy; it would also imply that one eats vegetables that grow in their own season. Eating *seasonal food* lets one live in harmony with the rhythms of nature. The idea of buying and growing local foods is good for other reasons also. Food co-ops and farmers' markets will play a role in distributing the produce and thus stimulate the local economy.

Besides Vandana Shiva, who is helping people to take back control over their food, their land, and their lives, and Percy Schmeiser, a farmer from Saskatchewan fighting for the right of farmers to reuse their own seeds (www.percyschmeiser.com), there are many known and even more unknown courageous persons working on solutions. Besides the biodynamic movement, there is the *permaculture* movement initiated by the

Australians Bill Mollison and David Holmgren; the movement for *natural farming* by Masanobu Fukuoka; there is Sepp Holzer, the Austrian "rebel farmer," an innovative permaculture activist; there is the movement for *community supported agriculture* (CSA), known as *Teikei* in Japan, which is a network bringing locally grown organic or biodynamic foods in form of *food boxes*, which are delivered directly from the producers each week to the consumers. Also interesting is WWOOF (Worldwide Opportunities on Organic Farms, originally "working weekends on organic farms) initiated by Sue Coppard at the biodynamic farm at Emerson College in Sussex, England (www.emerson.org.uk). "Many hands make light work" is the motto of WWOOF.

The movement of locally grown, organic food and of nontoxic herbal medicine that can be grown in one's garden or gathered in nature is gaining momentum at the grassroots level. It is developing in the shadow of the mega-industrial food-complex and the equally dehumanized medical and pharmaceutical establishment. A whole network of survival knowledge is developing in a quiet and unspectacular way and without a lot of media support. As the inspired poet and visionary Friedrich Hölderlin put it in his poem *Patmos*:

> But where there is danger,
> A rescuing element grows as well.

Biodynamics is certainly a part of this renaissance. It is, however, as we have seen, not just concerned with survival or good nutrition. Biodynamic agriculture has a deeper significance; it regards itself as a service of love to the earth and its creatures.

Winter Gardening in Oregon

With occasional exceptions, Oregon has the kind of relatively mild winters that make winter vegetable gardening possible. European gardening practices, developed for the most part in northwestern Europe, were carried to the East Coast and eventually to the Midwest of this continent. Each of these geographical regions has in common a climate of distinct spring, summer, fall, and winter. In the winter the earth is frozen and covered by snow and only a fool would think of gardening at that time. With the coming of spring and summer, it is time to "put in a garden," and after it has grown during the summer, by the fall equinox (traditionally called "Michaelmas") it is time to harvest, to dry fruits and vegetables, can them, and put them up for winter use. The garden gets a dressing of manure and lies fallow until the spring comes again and a new garden is put in. Thus we have a different gardening tradition, which makes sense in the regions where it developed, but in Oregon (as well as California and the southern United States), it is possible to do things differently.

The famous nutritionist Bircher-Benner concludes that food is always most nutritious when it is *whole* and *fresh*. If we can eat vegetables that are whole and fresh from the garden in the winter then we can save a lot of canning and preserving, except for some favorites such as berries or peas.

There are so many fresh vegetables that can be enjoyed in the winter that there is no need to worry about having the same dish day after day. Here is a list of vegetables that like cooler weather and grow well in Oregon winter gardens:

I. The following should be planted in *cold frames* during the waxing moon of July, or August at the latest. This will permit them to grow strong before the days get cooler and darker and their growth will slow down. The cold frames should be specially prepared with the following mixture:

- Two parts good garden loam
- One part equally mixed peat and sand
- One part very ripe (humified) compost

The seeds should be kept moist and a lattice (burlap, cheesecloth) should shade the young seedlings. They are transplanted when they are about six inches tall.

- *Cabbages*: Just about all cabbages like cooler weather. Kale and Brussels sprouts even taste better after nipped by frost. Bok choy can be grown also.
- *Swiss chard.*
- *Leeks*: Leeks can take very cold weather.
- *Endives*: Curly endive (frisée), broad leaf endive, the reddish radic-chio, and other members of the chicory tribe are not put off by light frosts.
- *Sugarloaf*: This member the chicories forms tightly packed heads the size of a football, of tender, slightly bitter leaves that can be eaten all winter in salads. It can take severe frost; with the out-side leaves frozen, it will still be good inside.

II. The following should be sown into their own beds directly as they do not transplant easily. Since in July and August germination can be a problem, they should be kept moist; this holds true especially for the umbellifers (parsnips, carrots, Hamburg parsley). The umbellifers should be companion planted in alternating rows with members of the lily family (leeks, onions) for symbiotic effects.

- *Parsnips.*
- *Hamburg parsley*: This is grown mainly for its carrot-like root. The greens can be used like regular parsley.

- *Skirret* or crummock: This sweetish tasting perennial root vegetable belonging to the carrot family can take extreme cold.
- *Tournip-rooted chervil:* This nearly forgotten hearty root vegetable of the carrot family can be stored as a winter crop.
- *Turnips:* The fresh tops are good winter greens.
- *Rutabagas* also called Swedish or yellow turnips: (In Ireland and Scotland lanterns with faces—"tumshie heads"—were carved at Halloween out of these turnips to scare off evil spirits.)
- *Beets:* Besides the root one can also eat the young tops as winter greens.
- *Carrots:* Companion plant with leeks.
- *Oyster plant* or salsify: A root vegetable from the composite family, oyster plant smells like oysters when cooked.
- *Mustard greens.*
- *Corn salad,* also called *mâche,* lamb's lettuce, fetticus *(Valenianella olitoria):* This delicious, tender salad plant can be eaten by itself or in combination with endive or sugar hat, or with hard-boiled eggs as the Swiss like it. It should be sown out in August or September. It is sensitive to heat and grows all winter long.
- *Rocket:* This member of the mustard family, also known as garden rocket, arugula, or rucola, is best sown in September.
- *Spinach:* Popeye's power plant likes cool weather.
- *Florence fennel:* This fennel is sown late in July or early August, kept moist, and cultivated until the large, bulbous eatable leaf bases the size of a hand can be harvested by the first frost. When harvested, the foliage, which can be dried as a culinary herb, is cut off; the leaf bases are stored in a dry, airy environment and will keep until the new year.
- *Celeriac,* or root celery: These umbellifers are started in the cold frame in the spring, and then transplanted. They like wood ashes for their potassium needs and much water, and they need the entire growing season to make their bulbous hypocotyl (the so called "root"). Leeks are good companions and can also be planted in the spring, when they can make the best use of the growing season.

- *Witlof* or *witloof*: The Dutch name meaning "white leaf" refers to a kind of chicory that is sown in the spring and harvested for its roots in the fall. The roots are put into dormancy in a cool, somewhat dry storage. When needed, they are placed into good soil in wooden boxes in a warmed cellar or garage. A foot of sand/peat or sand/sawdust is added on top. When they are watered, they will send the terminal bud growing through this light mixture. When this blanched terminal bud becomes visible, the witlof-endive, a superior winter salad and cooking vegetable, is ready for the table. The root itself is then discarded (composted, fed to livestock or chopped, dried, ground, and roasted as a coffee additive (especially cherished in France).
- *Jerusalem artichokes*: This nutritious tuber from the sunflower family is an alternative to the potato. It can be served cooked or eaten raw in salads.

The list could go on to include some of the herbs such as horseradish, comfrey, mint, and other plants, such as Chinese cabbage *(michihili)* and New Zealand spinach, that continue for some time if it does not freeze too harshly.

On colder, freezing days, the plants in the winter garden should be protected by covering them loosely with straw, or by putting plastic tents over them. The plastic tunnels can fit the beds easily and are cheaply constructed with PBC pipe as supports. Doubling the plastic creates dead air spaces that help insulate.

Beginning in February, a new impulse for growth exists in nature: by this time it is advantageous to have put many of the root crops into a root cellar to prevent them from becoming woody (leeks, parsnips, Hamburg parsley, turnips, beets, carrots, celeriac, oyster plant, and rutabagas). By this time, free beds are needed for early peas, snow peas, fava beans, onion sets, spinach, etc.

Oregon has garden weather the year round and can provide fresh vegetables in their respective seasons.

Appendix II

A Summary of the Agricultural Lectures of Rudolf Steiner

Truly, the farm is a living organism.
—Rudolf Steiner, *Agriculture,* Lecture 8

The biological movement in farming and gardening had its beginning with Steiner's agricultural lectures and with the enthusiasm and dedication engendered among the participants of this course. Even though the lectures were admittedly hard to understand, experimental circles of farmers, gardeners, and scientists were immediately formed.[1] Even after nearly a century, we can appreciate the newness of what was said at the time. It required study, not mere reading, and a background of practical agricultural experience to come to terms with the course and this is still true today.[2]

To summarize the contents, as is attempted here, is a difficult, if not impossible undertaking if one means to do these lectures justice. The reader first confronted with the course will perhaps have as hard a time of it as the first listeners did because, essentially, a new worldview has to be grasped. The lectures begin to make sense when the worldview expressed in them is understood.

In the first lecture, Steiner points out that we must proceed from a holistic point of view that takes all factors into account. Cosmic and tellurian factors are at work in all phenomena. The Earth and the planets belong to the same system. Plants and animals are permeated by cosmic rhythms, as are human beings—but in humans, the cosmic rhythms do not follow the cosmic phenomena directly, but have emancipated themselves by degrees (fever curves, menses, etc.).

He points out that there are two aspects of agricultural production: that of *quality* involving nutrition, aroma, and clear metamorphic stages of fruiting and flowering; and that of *quantity*, related to the production of mass, bulk, and also reproduction. Chemical fertilizer application supports only the latter process of creating bulk at the expense of quality. Quality is the result of the influence of the distant planets (Mars, Jupiter, Saturn), which work though the medium of quartz (silica) of the earth's crust. Forty-eight percent of the earth's crust is composed of this "inert" element. Quantity results from the workings of the lower planets (Mercury, Venus, the moon) through the medium of calcium, potassium, sodium, and their relatives in the earth. The faster-moving lower planets work more strongly into the annual plants, whereas the slow-moving, distant planets affect the perennial plants.

After opening with such a wide and unfamiliar perspective of linking the planets to the life of the earth, Steiner follows in the second lecture with the concept of the *integrated farm organism* (we would say ecosystem or biome today), where plants and animals, soil and man operate like integrated organs within the total organism.

In a similar fashion, the earth, with its connection to the sun, moon, and other planets, is seen as an extended "organism". The soil, the surface of the earth, absorbs cosmic forces and, by the use of silica, reflects them back into plant growth. Calcium pulls the atmospheric forces into the ground, affecting quantity production. The soil can be seen as a diaphragm of the earth organism involved in these various exchanges. Clay works as a medium for the forces streaming in both directions. Earth, water, air, and warmth are perceived to have different qualities when found above or below this diaphragm, the soil. Above the soil, air and warmth are "dead," while they are "alive" below the soil. By contrast, earth and water are considered to be "living" when above the soil and "dead" below it. At first glance, these might be confusing concepts, but when one observes nature, one can see that warmth and air, fixed by the plant, enter the soil as living roots or as larva and worms; whereas mineral earth and water taken up from below the ground become part of living plant tissue above the ground.

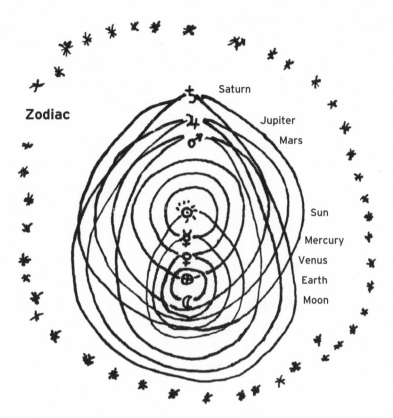

Zodiac

Saturn
Jupiter
Mars

Sun
Mercury
Venus
Earth
Moon

**Figure II.1. The distant and nearer planets seen in
their geocentric and heliocentric orbits[3]**

The crystallizing forces radiate into the earth (soil) and water from
the cosmos most strongly during the period from mid-January to mid-
February, when, in the northern hemisphere, at least, the earth and water
are the "deadest" and most receptive to the imprinting of cosmic forces.
During this time, the plants, slumbering in thick-skinned seeds and tightly
packed buds, are neutral and self-contained. But when the highly complex
proteins of the seeds later become "chaotic" and fall apart in germination,
these forces stream into the plants and imprint their form into the plants
as these plants build up their living substance with the aid of humus. The
cosmic forces reappear in the geometry of plant architecture, in their color
and quality aspects.

In a profound foreshadowing of ecological thinking fifty years later, Steiner states that specific animals belong to specific regions of the earth and that they are in symbiosis with other life forms there. In providing the manures, they are tied into the soil processes with their digestive organs and, in turn, affect the vegetation. Thus, a healthy farm-garden organism must have just the right number of animals (cows, horses, sheep, fowl, etc.) to produce the right amount of manure to aid humus formation and maintain a healthy soil. Plant, animal, and soil are an interacting unity.

The third lecture can be a breath of fresh air or a shaking of foundations for the biochemist, as Steiner discusses the life elements—carbon, oxygen, hydrogen, nitrogen, and sulfur—in nature's household. Our current materialistic conceptions of these elements are inadequate. They are like snapshots of a person, not like the living person itself. The mesh of our conceptual net is too crude to capture the subtleties of these elements. Again, Steiner uses a comprehensive approach that goes beyond charting the cycles in nature of these elements. He tries to apprehend their essence, to meet the person, not the snapshot, by characterizing each element in the sum of its multifold appearances.

Carbon, that "black chap," is the *form-giving* element in organic nature. Using the carbon from the carbon dioxide taken in by photosynthesis, the plants build up their carbon framework (C-C-C-C-C-C) upon which the other elements become attached. Basically plants have a carbon skeleton. When one burns a plant, its rigid structure disintegrates as the carbon is oxidized and the sun energy bound up with it are released as heat and light. Carbon's form-bearing potential is seen in the mineral world in diamonds. In animals and man, a calcium phosphate skeleton instead of a carbon framework provides structure. In order to be free of the rigidity that characterizes the plants, animal organisms constantly expel CO_2 through their lungs.[4]

Carbon, the form-giving element, is permeated by *oxygen*, the universal *carrier of life* (etheric). Without the carbon framework, the etheric would have no carrier. Underneath the soil of the earth and inside living organisms, the "dead" atmospheric oxygen becomes alive, activating light and warmth through oxidation. (The fact that our modern instrument-laden robots on the moon and Mars are searching for traces of oxygen is an acknowledgement of its function as life-carrier.)

Nitrogen, the element of universal *sensitivity*, is seen by Steiner as a bridge between the life forces and the spiritual archetypes. It is the link between the etheric and spirit plane. It is the element that provides the anchor for astrality (soul workings) in animals and man. In plants, whose tissues as carbohydrates, cellulose and lignin contain little nitrogen; the astrality works mainly from the outside. Nitrogen, the carrier of feeling, sensitivity, and movement, works in the soil in such a way that the soil can "sense" what is going on in the planet sphere, in the atmosphere and biosphere. The supposedly dull-witted peasant often knows intuitively what his plants or his soil need, for he picks up the nitrogen wafting up from a freshly ploughed field through his nostrils and comprehends, below the level of consciousness, what is needed for the farm. Like oxygen, nitrogen is "dead" in the air, but it becomes "alive" in the earth and inside organisms.

Whereas *sulfur* (L. *sol* = sun, *ferre* = to carry) has the function of carrying the spiritual forces into the physical medium, a process akin to sunlight being fixed into the plant, Steiner indicates that *hydrogen,* the lightest of the elements, dissolves forms, dissipates and carries substances back into the spiritual, non-manifest form. All these elements are supported by the working of "greedy" calcium that pulls oxygen and etheric forces into the ground, silicon that rays outward cosmic forces, and clay that works as a mediator between them. He goes on in this lecture to point out how each plant species has a specific function on the earth organism regarding these elements. For example, legumes are the organs for the inhaling of nitrogen; they are supported by "greedy" calcium as shown by the fact that legumes need an alkaline soil.

The fourth and fifth lectures, the median point of the course, deal with central issues of farming and gardening, and the maintenance of fertility. It is established that fertilizing is not a process of feeding the plant, but it means making the soil more alive so that the plant is not put into a dead medium. There should be no sharp division between the plant and the living earth. How does one achieve this enlivening of the earth? For one thing, raised beds are suggested, which are more easily penetrated with etheric forces. He likens trees to these raised beds, with each leaf and bud forming a separate plant. This principle has been made use of by master gardener Alan Chadwick whose raised beds are also double dug so that the "dead" air can enter the soil where it becomes alive. Steiner rejected mineral fertilizers in favor of compost, which is rich in etheric and astral elements. Mineral fertilizer cannot quicken the earth; it works only on the water. Lady Balfour would agree, claiming "mineral fertilizer amounts to the art of making water stand upright."

Composts, made up of plant and animal residues, can be properly described as generalized living organisms, which do not have specific organs but have vital energies circulating around within them. Like all living organisms, they should have a protective skin; they should not stink. If they do stink, a loss of life quality is implied, much as when sick animals develop bad odors. Slight amounts of lime should be added to the composts to soak up the excess etheric. It is the aliveness, the quickness of the compost that is then imparted to the soil, whence it works into the plants and animal fodder, leading to the overall health of the farm organism.

At this point in the lectures, a special preparation from cow manure is described as an enlivening measure. Cow manure because of its rich etheric and astral forces is especially suited for composting. A cow horn, filled with fresh cow manure, is buried in good soil over the winter. In the following season, homeopathic portions of its contents are stirred rhythmically in a bucket of water and then sprayed over the fields to aid root growth and foliage development. The horn is effective because the cow, with its elaborately developed digestive system, uses horn and hoof to ray back and intensify the etheric energies released from the fodder during digestive processes. Horn and hoof work as capacitors or condensers of these energies. Another preparation made from pulverized quartz, placed into a cow horn and buried in the ground over the summer, has the effect of making the plant more responsive to light and aiding the fruiting and flowering processes. This, too, is to be made by stirring a homeopathic portion in a bucket for an hour. Ideally, both preparations are stirred by hand with a birch broom instead of by a machine; this helps to create the personal relationship that Steiner felt was so necessary to develop between the human being and the land.

In the fifth lecture, Steiner also points out that is useless to inoculate the compost, manure, or earth with microorganisms, for they are not so much the cause of fertility as a symptom that life forces are present. Not substances or bacteria are to be given to the soil, but primarily forces are to be transmitted to the earth and plants made receptive to them. These forces are not found by isolating substances in experimental situations and analyzing them microscopically, but are found by studying the wider connections of macrocosmic processes. In the rest of this lecture, Steiner prescribes preparations that can be placed into the amorphous body of the living compost like organs, to regulate its chemistry and make the compost especially receptive to the workings of the planets. These preparations are made from chamomile, yarrow, dandelion, stinging nettle, oak bark, and valerian.[5] It is in this lecture that the possibility of the transmutation of elements within the realm of living chemistry is suggested and the implication is made that the chemistry of living organisms transcends that which can be ascertained in the test tube.

The sixth lecture deals with the problem of weeds, pests, and so-called plant diseases. He discusses how strong lunar forces working through the water can influence weed germination and how, by passing the weed seeds, or insects, through a fire process and preparing a "pepper" of ashes which is sprinkled over the land, pests will be discouraged. Cyclical recurrence of insect infestations is discussed. As regards plant disease, he points out how astrality can "slide down into the plant" impinging too heavily on it, causing mildew and insect damage. A strengthening of the plant's etheric through the use of the biodynamic herbal preparations as "medicines" can restore vigor. Sickness is something very different in the animal than in the plant organism, for in the latter, astrality works from without, while in the former, it works from within. Most illness is due to an imbalance between the astral and the etheric. Composts will strengthen the ether body in plants. When influences of the lower planets press too strongly onto the plant, spore-forming mildews and fast-breeding aphids are likely to appear, somewhat like premature fruiting and pollen production. These forces can be held at bay by the use of silica-rich horsetail (equisetum) tea spray.

The seventh lecture can be considered a classical statement on the ecological interconnections within the household of nature. We must see the plant, animal, mineral, insect, and bird worlds as belonging together in one sophisticated organic system. They do not work on each other in crude causality, but there are multitudes of subtle forces (warmth, odors, pheromones, resonance phenomena, etc.) to which the farmer and gardener must be sensitized. He must use all of his senses. She must become clairsentient in respect to smelling. Animals, insects, and birds must be understood as the expression of a landscape's astrality. The loss of one species in an area has many unfortunate consequences. He further points out the ill effects of monocropping and the importance of forest, hedges, and mushroom-harboring meadows to the farm organism. None of this can be successfully studied in the laboratory or on experimental parcels, for the effects must be understood in their entirety, the whole being greater than the sum of its parts.

The eighth and final lecture deals with feeding. Livestock need more than just bulk food that produces calories and fat. What the animal takes in with his senses as smells, the air it breathes, and sunlight and warmth constitute just as much a "food." All these have as much an effect on the animal as the fodder it eats. When these senses are satisfied and the cow is allowed to eat that which its instincts command in the way of herbs and shrubbery-browsing, then the animal dung will have a special guiding and organizing effect on the plants. The manure will be of better quality, aiding the whole farm organism. The animals themselves will be healthier and more fertile. Animal dung should come from local animals where the same atmospheric and terrestrial conditions prevail, and beast and plant are geared for each other. The cow, horse, sheep, or goat receives messages from the earth via the fodder, and they answer with their dung, as a message to the soil.

Though the course seems unusual in a number of aspects, it truly represents a pioneer work that has been a reliable guide to the many farmers and gardeners who have taken it seriously. The proof of the value of the outlook presented lies in the healthy and happy livestock, the steady high-yield and high-quality production of biodynamic farms and gardens worldwide.

NOTES

Introduction

1. Somewhat later, an agronomist from Oberlin College who had just spent nine months on a research tour of all the countries engaged in the "Green Revolution" came to visit an old friend at the village. I introduced myself as a fellow academician, eager to tell him about biodynamic agriculture and the promise that it holds. He was just as incredulous as I had been at first, and after hearing about companion planting, lunar cycles, and medicine for the soil, he refused to even look at the garden. "I don't want to see it," he exclaimed. "Organic gardening—I know all about it. It doesn't work! But I do hope you will publish your findings and expose this sort of quackery."

Chapter 1: Historical Sketch

1. See Carl O. Sauer, *Agricultural Origins and Dispersals* (New York: American Geographical Society, 1957).

2. For a good description of the development of agriculture in the Western world, see Sir Albert Howard, *The Soil and Health* (New York: Schocken Books, 1972), Ch. 3.

3. Quite a lot is known of the cloister gardens through the writings of such renowned individuals as Abbot Walafried Strabo, whose poem *de cultura hortorum*, 842 AD, describes many of the gardening procedures. Abbess Hildegard of Bingen writes extensively of plant cultivation and medical uses. Albertus Magnus, mid-thirteenth century, writes of composts and of peasant folk sayings. In the twelfth and thirteenth centuries, many Greek and Roman astrological, metrological, and agricultural writings become available via the Arabs and are translated into Latin. Much of these treasures has not yet been translated into modern languages and made available to us.

4. St. Swithin (July 15) in England:

   St. Swithin's Day, if thou dost rain,
   For 40 days it will remain.

> St. Swithin's Day, if thou be fair
>
> For 40 days 'twill rain na mair (no more).

5. *Baer's Agricultural Almanac* (New York: Grosset & Dunlap) is one of the few Farmers' almanacs that still provide the name of the saint for the day.

6. Nicolas Culpeper (1616–1654), a British physician, has in his *Culpeper's Complete Herbal* recorded for posterity what planets govern the various plants. His book was and remains a classic on medicinal herbs. If one were to attempt to apply these principle to the situation in southern Oregon, for example, one would come up with the following analysis: The predominant vegetation in the Grants Pass area is oak, coniferous trees, manzanita, madrone, poison oak, and St. John's wort. Oak is ruled by Mars; coniferous trees are ruled by Saturn; poison oak, a *rhus*, is ruled by Jupiter, a lunar Jupiter at that; manzanita and madrone, as *ericaceae*, belong to the sun, as does St. John's wort. Decomposed granite, high in silicon content, belongs to the supra-solar planets. Thus, given the vegetation and the soil, one can say that the upper planets, the forces of Mars, the sun, Jupiter, and Saturn, are predominating, as opposed to the sub-solar forces. For the gardener, this would mean that what he or she grows will be highly nutritious, the seeds will be of good quality, and he or she will have to aid the sub-solar and lunar forces with the application of some lime and liquid manure. As far as the elemental spirits are concerned, the medieval observer would note that during the dry, hot summer months, the fires spirits and sylphs predominate; while in the rainy season the nymphs, who are not even there to make dew in the hot season, make a strong comeback and the mosses and lichens are very much moon. The gnomes, who are associated with the crystal formation of the winter, are not very strong. The archangel Michael does not manifest his being with lightening storms, but shows his presence by an occasional falling star that is a spark from his sword as he fights the great dragon. Such a way of looking at nature, quite foreign to us in modern times, nevertheless has an attractive, imaginative quality, satisfying the soul and not just the intellect.

7. Albert Hauser, *Bauernregeln* (Zürich: Artemis Verlag, 1973). Also Jerry Mack Johnson, *Country Wisdom* (Garden City, NY: Anchor Press/Doubleday, 1974).

8. Eric Sloane, *The Seasons of America Past* (New York: Funk & Wagnalls, 1958).

9. Ibid., 32.

10. Elliot Wigginton, *The Foxfire Book* (Garden City, NY: Anchor Books, 1972).

11. Groundhog Day has its roots in an ancient Celtic holiday marking the reappearance from the underworld of the white spring goddess and her companion bear. It was a day of oracle: if the bear, coming out of his den would see his shadow, he would retreat, indicating that the winter would stay forty more days. The Church co-opted this sacred day as the Holy Candlemas, dedicating it to the Virgin Mary, who replaced the heathen goddess. The peasants, however, continued to watch for the bear's, and later for the badger's appearance in order to predict the coming weather. In the New World, the Pennsylvania Dutch and other early settlers replaced the badger with the native American woodchuck.

12. Recorded by William Shampine of Williams, Oregon.

13. See Gordon J. Cook, *Our Living Soil* (New York: The Dial Press, 1960), Ch. 1.

14. In the early 1950s, DDT was dusted and sprayed in every barn against flies, in swamps and canals against mosquitos, and in households against all kinds of bugs. The use of DDT in the United States peaked between 1950 and 1955, a time period that coincides exactly with the peak of the polio-myelitis epidemic. There is ample scientific evidence that this chlorinated hydrocarbon insecticide is a vector in the outbreak of polio beyond the exposure to the poliovirus. Cf. Wolf D. Storl, *Healing Lyme Disease Naturally* (Berkeley, CA: North Atlantic Books, 2010), 80–82.

Chapter 2: Voices of Concern and Reform

1. Paavo O. Airola, *Health Secrets from Europe* (New York: ARC, 1970).

2. F. H. King, *Farmers of Forty Centuries, or Permanent Agriculture in China, Korea and Japan* (Mineola, NY: Dover Publications, Inc., 2004).

3. John Paul, *Journal of Organic Systems* "China's Organic Revolution" (Hobart, Univ. of Tasmania, 2007), 2 (1) 1–11.

4. A lot has been publicized since that time about the mismanagement of collective farms, centrally planned by bureaucrats, who knew only abstract economic priorities and nothing about local ecological con-ditions, as well as the ecological distortions and soil depletion in the so-called "free world" and the accompanying dehumanization of the workers in the plantation systems located in tropical countries. Instead

of offering solutions, the market pressures of today's global economy and corporate agribusiness dominating America as well as the European Union seem to intensify the problem.

5. In Britain, Lady Balfour wrote *The Living Soil* (1943) and launched the famous Haughly Experiment. Friend Sykes, using his 750-acre organic farm as a basis, wrote *Food and Farming of the Future* (1950). Together they formed the Soil Association. The works of Dr. Hans Mueller and Dr. R. Bircher, who is incidentally the creator of the "Bircher-Muesli," make for important reading in Switzerland; in Germany, the writings of Prof. Alwin Seifert, Ewald Könemann, N. Remer, and others deserve mention. In the United States the research of soil scientist William A. Albrecht, soil bacteriologist Selman Waksman, and biodynamic researcher E. Pfeiffer, as well as the literary works of E.H. Faulkner, L. Bromfield, and others, provide interesting reading on the subject.

6. The American bald eagle is one of a number of top carnivorous birds that were brought to the verge of extinction by chlorinated hydrocarbons, which interfere with the calcium processes of eggshell formation. In 1973, a delegate of American Indian Tribes was sent to Europe to procure eagle feathers, necessary in the sacred ceremonies, because there were hardly any more eagles to be found in the United States.

7. At the time, in 1964, I was enrolled in a course of entomology at Ohio State University. The professor doubled as a pesticide researcher for a major chemical corporation and as a university teacher. When confronted with Rachel Carson's book, he scoffed at the ideas expressed as those of a hysterical woman. For him, it was matter of total warfare: insects compete with *Homo sapiens* for scarce resources (carbohydrates, proteins, etc.), and one or the other would eventually be decimated.

Chapter 3: The Pioneers of Organic Agriculture

1. Charles Darwin, *The Formation of Vegetable Moulds through the Action of Worms*, 1882. Darwin estimated that ten tons per acre passed through the earthworms annually, the resultant castings being much richer in P, K, and Ca than the surrounding soil.

2. Sir Albert Howard, *The Soil and Health*, fn. page 74.

3. Ibid., 72–75.

4. J. I. Rodale, *Encyclopedia of Organic Gardening* (Emmaus, PA: Rodale Books, 1973), 802.

5. In the wake of the social chaos following the First World War, Steiner picked up the slogan of the French Revolution, "Liberty, Equality, and Fraternity." He applied these concepts as principles in the three realms of social life; these three realms in turn are based upon the image of the human being as a whole composed of body, soul, and spirit. *Liberty* or freedom should be guaranteed for the cultural and spiritual life; there should be no dictates regarding science, education, art, or religion. *Equality* should be practiced in the legal realm; before the law, everyone has equal rights. *Fraternity* or brother/sisterhood, un-coerced solidarity should apply to the economic realm.

6. Koepf, Petterson, Schaumann, *Bio-Dynamic Agriculture* (Spring Valley, NY: Spring Valley Press, 1976), 14.

7. Rudolf Steiner, *Agriculture* (London: B-D Agricultural Association, 1974).

8. Books that give some indications of this tradition of Old World folk healers and herbalists include the popular *Of Men and Plants* by Maurice Mességué (New York: MacMillan Co., 1973); *Witchcraft Medicine* by Claudia Müller-Ebeling, Christian Rätsch, and Wolf D. Storl (Rochester, VT: Inner Traditions, 2003); and *The Herbal Lore of Wise Women and Wortcunners* by Wolf D. Storl (Berkeley, CA: North Atlantic Books, 2012).

Chapter 4: Basic Concepts

1. E. J. Holmyard, *Alchemy* (Middlesex, England: Penguin Books, 1968), 21.

2. Agrippa of Nettesheim, *De Occulta Philosophia. Magische Werke* (Meisenheim Glan:

A. Hain, 1530), 49–51.

3. Theodor Schwenk describes in his excellent work *Sensitive Chaos* water in its sensitive, all-pervading form as the sense organ of the earth. In the complementary dualism (yin-yang) of East Asian philosophy, water, being cool, sensitive, and receptive, is considered a perfect expression of yin. Its opposite, fire, being dry, hot, and penetrating, is an expression of yang.

4. The alienation from the immediate phenomenological perception and from confident personal judgment is instilled into the school child at the earliest age in our modern society: children are taught that their

perception is wrong when they think the sun rises and sets and that, except for mountains, the earth is essentially flat. Instead, the child is told that the earth is a ball that orbits around the sun. The latter is intellectually and scientifically sound and is the basic factor that makes rockets and space satellites possible, but phenomenologically and on the level of down-to-earth decisions, it is *not* true. For the plants in the garden, the sun does actually rise in the morning in the east and set in the evening in the west, and the starry or sunlit heaven is above and the dark moist earth below. R. Steiner would say that both perspectives are necessary and one is not more "right" than the other.

5. Benjamin Franklin was so impressed by Chladni's demonstration of beautiful symmetries brought about by the rhythmic interplay sound resonance that he invited Chaldni to demonstrate this for scientists in Paris. The anthroposophically oriented physicist Hans Jenny (1904–1972) continued the research on the effect of sound vibrations on fluids, powders, and liquid pastes under the name of "cymatics" (www.cymatics.org).

6. L. Kolisko, *Agriculture of Tomorrow* (London: Kolisko Archinves, 1939).

7. Ehrenfried Pfeiffer, *Sensitive Crystallization Processes: A Demonstration of Formative Forces in the Blood* (Anthroposophic Press, 1975). Also see Christian Marcel, *Sensitive Crystallization* (Edinburgh, Scotland: Floris Books, 2011). Such tests are also conducted at the Research Center at the Goetheanum in Switzerland.

8. Theodor Schwenk, *Sensitive Chaos* (New York: Schocken Books, 1976).

9. P. E. Schiller, "Untersuchungen an der freien schallempfindlichen Flamme" (Akustische Zeitschrift, 1938).

10. This anthropological insight is expressed in the Hebraic-Babylonian account in Genesis of the creation of Adam from the mud (substance) and the breath (spirit) form the *imago Dei*, in contrast to the other creatures that came into existence by the fiat: "Let there be . . . !"

11. Nineteenth-century philosophy and, for that matter, western philosophy in general after Descartes, believed the two regions to be entirely separated and "never the twain shall meet." The outer world of nature takes its separate, mindless course, unaffected by the inner world of human thinking, feeling, and willing—so the university professors thought. For Kant, thought and even perception were subjective; the *Ding-an-sich*

(G. "the thing in itself") i.e., the objective world, could not be known in its essence. Of course, shamans, Native American medicine men and women, African *Ngangas* ("witch doctors"), as well as Shakespeare's witches and other traditionalists would not agree. They always acted as though there were sympathies between people's state of soul and nature, such as between the inner climate and the weather in nature, and they held that one could affect the other and vice versa. Sir James Frazer, in his *Golden Bough,* cites numerous examples of such primitive "sympathetic" and "contagious" magic. But the enlightened world has split the subjects of study at the universities into sciences and humanities, and the two have ever since had a difficult time communicating. Modern anthropology, as originally conceived by Sir James Tylor and Franz Boas, attempted to heal the breach, but it, too, soon fell apart into the specialties of cultural and physical anthropology. Rudolf Steiner's anthroposophy has tried to do the same with more success, showing that the inside and the outside are metamorphoses of the same forces and beings.

12. Frances Yates, *Giordano Bruno and the Hermetic Tradition* (New York: Vintage Books, 1964).

13. For example, small children have a better idea about where the baby brother or sister comes from when they are told of the stork that flies to the swamp and picks up the baby from among the water lilies and drops it through the chimney of the house. Included in this true imagination are numerous symbolic elements that satisfy the curiosity of the child without violating its sense of truth, and that avoid abstract notions of microscopic sperm, ova, zygotes, DNA-RNA, etc., which the child is incapable of comprehending at that age. The stork, a white bird, symbolizes the transcendent origin of the human being; the long, red beak, the depositing of the infant in the family hearth include beautiful imaginations of human sexuality; the primal swamp indicates the frog-like nature of the embryo in the watery environment of the womb, etc.

14. A microcosmic version of the tree is seen in the backbone along which the vital organs, with their different faculties, are arranged, starting with the unconscious, wormlike intestinal apparatus and ending on top with the head from which thoughts arise and arrive like flocks or birds. In the Nordic *Völuspa,* the tree, which spans nine universes, is called the Yggdrasil, roughly translated as the "I-Carrier."

15. Max Scheler, *Man's Place in Nature* (New York: Noonday Press, 1962). Scheler, a mentor of philosophical anthropology, sees in the ability of *Homo sapiens* to say "No" to his drives and passions indications of spirit.

16. The many experiments of subjecting soils or plants to electric currents in order to induce more rapid growth are recorded in Tompkins and Bird in *The Secret Life of Plants*, ch. 10 and 11.

17. In using the terms *imagination* for perceiving etheric plane, *inspiration* for contact with the astral plane, and *intuition* for realizing the spiritual plane, I have been following the anthroposophic terminology as used by Rudolf Steiner in his writings, such as *Macrocosm and Microcosm* (London: Rudolf Steiner Press, 1968), 206 n. Varying terminology employed for the supersensible worlds:

    • Theosophy: Physical Plane, Astral Plane, *Rupa-Devachan* or Lower Mental Plane, *Arupa Devachan* or Higher Mental Plane

    • Tantric: everyday waking consciousness, dreaming consciousness, catatonic consciousness, super-consciousness (See Wolf D. Storl, *Shiva,* 2004)

    • Renaissance and Rosicrucian theosophy: Physical World, Imaginative World, World of Inspiration or Harmony of the Spheres, World of True Intuition

    • Other occultists: Little World, World of the Elements, World of Spirit or Heavenly World, World of Reason, World of Archetypal Images

18. Alfred C. Hottes, *Garden Facts and Fancies* (New York: Dodd, Mead, & Co., 1949), 63.

19. P. Tompkins, and C. Bird, *The Secret Life of Plants*. A comprehensive overview is given in ch. 9, The Harmonic Life of Plants.

20. Ethnologically, it is of interest to note that in most horticultural societies, especially in Africa and East Asia, the dead, the ancestors, are thought of as working to bring about fertility in field and garden. One feeds the dead food offerings, shows deference with flowers and sacrifices, and they, in turn, working from the macrocosm onto the earth, help grow and ripen fruits and flowers, grain and seed and assure a good crop. American Indian horticulturists, such as the Iroquois, believed the dead travelled

the long road along the Milky Way and lived in villages located somewhere in the fixed stars, where they tend corn, beans, and squash. Mircea Eliade notes, "Hippocrates tells us that the spirits of the dead make seeds grow and germinate and the author of the *Geoponica* says that the winds (souls of the dead) give life to plants and everything else" (*Patterns of Comparative Living*, (New York: Meridian Books, 1963), 351. Ancient Germanic tribes offered sacrifices to the dead in the spring as sowing began and also at harvest time. The folklore surrounding "old corn man" or "old corn mother" among European peasantry has retained the nature and appearance of ancestor reverence. That we decorate our graves with flowers and that, in popular Christian conception, the dead are seen sitting on clouds, playing harps, or singing with choirs of angels, is a crude image of what used to be perceived as the plane of the Harmony of the Spheres.

21. Franz Hartmann, *Paracelsus: Life and Prophecies* (Blauvelt, NY: Rudolf Steiner Publications, 1973), 156.

22. This again offers interesting insights into the customs of primitive societies regarding sacred stones. The theophany of stones is shown in Bethel, the Rock of Ages, St. Peter, (Gk. *Petros* or Peter means "rock"), the Muslim's Ka-aba, etc.; see Mircea Eliade, *Patterns of Comparative Religion*.

23. Books by Rudolf Steiner that are an aid in this endeavor include: *Knowledge of the Higher Worlds and its Attainment*; *An Outline of Occult Science, Theosophy*; *Macrocosm and Microcosm*; *Nine Lectures on Bees*; *Agriculture*; *Man as a Symphony of the Creative Word*; *Spiritual Science and Medicine*, and others which are available from the Anthroposophic Press, Spring Valley, NY, or from the Rudolf Steiner Press in London.

24. Paul Hawken, *The Magic of Findhorn* (New York: Harper and Row, 1975).

Chapter 5: Transmutation, Destruction, and Creation of Matter

1. Here belongs the idea that the fetus growing in the watery womb receives the impression of the horoscope. Here, too, belong baptism and immersion rituals that rearrange people's souls in a new way.

2. The words *holy, whole* and *healing* have the same etymological root.

3. Rudolf Hauschka, *Heilmittellehre* (Frankfurt/Main: Vittorio Klostermann, 1965).

4. Rudolf Steiner, *Agriculture* (London: Rudolf Steiner Press, 1974), 98.

5. Ibid., 99.

6. Ibid., 48.

7. Rudolf Steiner, *Man as a Symphony of the Creative Word*. London: Rudolf Steiner Press, 1970.

8. "It is a mistaken notion when from anthroposophical sides it is claimed that the biodynamic fertilizing techniques, as they were developed by Rudolf Steiner and so successfully carried out by his followers, are something completely new, something that has not existed heretofore. Those who claim this simply do not know about alchemy and its essence, for otherwise they would know that the problem of fertilizing, of putrefaction, decomposition and combustion is actually the essential problematic of alchemy." Alexander von Bernus, *Alchemie und Heilkunst* (Nuremberg: Verlag Hans Karl, 1969), 47.

9. James Christian, *Philosophy* (San Francisco, CA: Rinehart Press, 2011), 384.

10. E. Kolisko and L. Kolisko, *Agriculture of Tomorrow* (London: Kolisko Archives, 1939).

11. Rudolf Hauschka, *The Nature of Substances* (London: Vincent Stuart, Ltd., 1966) (German original, *Substanzlehre.* Stuttgart, 1950).

12. P. Kammerer, *Das Gesetz der Serie* (Stuttgart: Deutsche Verlag Anstalt, 1919).

13. Henri Spindler, *Bull. Lab. Maritime de Dinard XXVIII* (1946), and *Bull. Lab. Maritime de Dinard XXXI* (1948).

14. Pierre Barranger, *Science et Vie* No. 499, April, 1959.

15. Louis C. Kervran, *Biological Transmutations,* trans. M. Abehsera (Binghampton, NY: Swan House Publ. Co., 1972), 94.

16. Ibid., 114.

17. Tompkins and Bird, *The Secret Life of Plants*, 246.

18. Ehrenfried Pfeiffer, *Bio-Dynamic Farming and Gardening* (condensed version by B. Rateaver) (Pauma Valley, CA, 1973), Ch. 14.

19. Theodor Schwenk, *Sensitive Chaos* (New York: Schocken Books, 1976), and *Grundlagen der Potenzforschung* (Stuttgart: Verlag Freies Geistesleben, 1972).

20. G. Piccardi, *The Chemical Basis of Medical Climatology* (Springfield IL: Thomas, 1962).

Chapter 6: Goetheanistic Science

1. See Theodore Roszak, *Where the Wasteland Ends* (New York: Vintage Books, 1969).

2. Rudolf Steiner, *Goethes Naturwissenschaftliche Schriften* (Stuttgart: Verlag Freies Geistesleben, 1972).

3. A similar understanding underlies the spagyric medicines (*medica spagyrica*) of earlier centuries; to be effective a medicine had to made new each time to fit the specific case of illness, the specific astronomical situation, the character of the individual: all these factors were considered relevant. Doug Boyd, in *Rolling Thunder* (New York: Random House, 1974), mentions similar considerations taken by native American Indian healers in regard to relevant and irrelevant factors: "Rolling Thunder offered us the idea that experiments do not cause things to happen. Events are caused by their natural causes. There is no experiment other than the real situation . . . How can 'science' make any valid test of American Indian medicine if it is too 'scientific' to include all the conditions of the real situation . . . the real situation includes the need for an unordinary result and the belief that the need will bring that result. It includes a certain attitude toward the sun and the earth and all of nature . . . Absent from the situation are skepticism and judgment . . ." (10).

4. If the assumption of an order in nature is rejected as an unproven *a priori*, so can the assumption that chaos, or chance, dominates in nature be considered an equally unproven *a priori*.

5. Gerbert Grohmann, *The Plant* (London: Rudolf Steiner Press, 1974), 51.

6. The mutually enhancing effect of a great variety of organisms within a garden environment is part of the success of the Biodynamic/French Intensive Method as taught by Alan Chadwick and John Jeavons and their students. Chadwick, an English gardener teaching in California, was himself a student of Rudolf Steiner.

Chapter 7: Evolution

1. The three views need not be contradictory if their claims are examined in the right light. Two somewhat different accounts of the creation are given in Genesis chapter 1 and Genesis chapter 2. The first verses in chapter 1 deal with the creation of the elements (physical world), then with

the creation of the etheric, or plant world (1:11, 12) and, finally, the last to appear is the archetypal human being conceived in the image of God. All this marks the first phase of creation, the creation of the macrocosm and the Idea of man. Genesis 2 speaks of the second phase of creation, the forming of the microcosm out of the elements and the in-breathing of the Spirit. Alchemists and kindred minds perceive in the process of evolution, the taking hold of the primal matter (*chaos, hyle, prima*) by the creative Spirit (*eidos, forma*) and penetrating it with formative forces, which leads to the creation of primitive life (Pre-Cambrian); as the penetration proceeds, the astral forces appear amidst the ocean of etheric forces (Paleozoic to Cenozoic); and, finally, the Spirit recreates itself microcosmically in the form of the human being (Pleistocene). As the scientist examines his evolutionary data stretching from the soft-bodied marine organism to *Homo sapiens*, he is witnessing the involution-evolution of the microcosm out of the macrocosm.

2. Michael Landmann, *Philosophical Anthropology,* trans. D. J. Parent (Philadelphia: Westminster Press, 1974).

3. Theodore Roszak, *Unfinished Animal.* (New York: Harper and Row 1975), Ch. 6, "The Occult Evolutionists."

4. See Rudolf Steiner, *Outline of Occult Science.*

5. An interesting etymological aside: the words *think* and *thing* are related. In the physical world we are "thinging" as we bring objects into consciousness.

6. The *prima materia,* which was predispositioned in the earliest phase of supersensible cosmic evolution on "Old Saturn" by the highest hierarchies, is now subjected to the organizing, ordering forces of the next hierarchy of the "Old Sun." A small picture of this is provided by *Chladni's figures*: Ernst Chladni "mounted a thin metal plate on a violin, scattered sand on the plate and found that when the bow was drawn across the strings, the sand arranged itself into beautiful patterns . . . By juggling around with powders of different densities and by playing notes with a wide range of frequencies, it is possible to induce a pattern to take on almost any form. It is interesting and perhaps significant that Chladni's figures most often adopt familiar organic forms." Lyall Watson, *Supernature* (New York: Bantam Books, 1974), 90.

7. African mound birds (megapodes, incubator birds) solve the problem by building a compost out of plant scraps and letting its heat hatch the eggs.

8. Theodor Schwenk, *Sensitive Chaos*. In this outstanding work, Schwenk shows how in human and animal organs, the archetypal movements of fluids (water, air), recreate themselves in a solid form. The vortex-like structure of the heart, ear and intestines remind one of the vortices of ocean currents, and these, in turn of the great macrocosmic vortex of the planetary system (84–93).

9. As Teilhard de Chardin would have it, the level of "phyletization"(the formation of new species) has been completed and the level of "cephalization" is commencing. See Chardin, *Man's Place in Nature* (New York: Harper and Row, 1956).

10. The relation of plants and the form-giving forces of sunlight is illustrated by the disorderly, serpentine growth of potato sprouts in a dark cellar, by the diffuse amorphous irregular webs formed by the mycelia of fungi in the ground, or by the rather disheveled appearance of blackberry vines in deeply shaded corners. Sunlight is, as physicists attest, the ordering principle of life.

11. When an animal sleeps, its awareness and movement decrease and, in that, it becomes more plantlike. One can say that the astral body leaves the physical and ether body during sleep, a condition that is more or less permanent in plants.

12. Rudolf Hauschka, *Heilmittellehre* (Frankfur/Main: Vittorio Klostermann, 1965), 194–198.

13. The word *plantlike* or *vegetative* designates an essential orientation toward the outside . . . In the case of plants, therefore, an ecstatic feeling or impulse is spoken of in order to indicate that they completely lack the capacity of animals to report organic states back to a center. Thus they lack completely a turning back of life upon itself, even the most primitive capacity of "reflection" or an ever-so-dim inner "conscious" state. See Max Scheler, *Man's Place in Nature* (New York: Noonday Press, 1062), 11.

14. William A. Jensen and Frank B. Salisbury, *Botany: An Ecological Approach* (Belmont, CA: Wadsworth Publ. Co., 1972), 507.

15. Wilhelm Pelikan, *The Secrets of Metals* (Spring Valley, NY: Anthroposophic Press, 1973), 74.

16. Mircea Eliade, *Patterns of Comparative Religion*, 274–275. Eliade also mentions the Hebrew Tree of Life, the *Otz Chiim*, which is an inverted tree, and Australian witch doctors who plant magic trees, daubed with human blood, upside down (symbolizing the human being). In the *Bhagavad Gita* (ch. 15) one reads: "The rishis tell us of the tree Asvattha, heaven-rooted, trunk below. Each leaf sets forth the Veda. Who knows this, knows all."

17. For a detailed discussion of the correspondence between the thrice-partitioned human psychosomatic entity and the threefoldness of the archetypal plant, see Wolf. D. Storl, *The Herbal Lore of Wise Women and Wortcunners* (Berkeley, CA: North Atlantic Books, 2011).

18. Gerbert Grohmann, *Die Pflanze als Lichtsinnesorgan der Erde* (Stuttgart: Verlag Freies Geistesleben, 1962). When the plant photosynthesizes, it replaces the O_2 of the CO_2 with sunlight, letting the oxygen go. Thus, the plant fixes the sunlight, which when we eat a plant turns into inner light, by releasing it through oxidation.

19. This is expressed in the Greek legend of Persephone, the beautiful daughter of Zeus (the sky god) and Demeter (the mother earth), who is captured while picking flowers by Pluto, the dark lord of the underworld and forced to marry him. Hermes (Mercury) frees her but, by having eaten a pomegranate seed, she has to return each year to the underworld where during half the year she reigns with Pluto over the regions of the dead. Persephone (the Roman Proserpina) is thus the goddess of vegetation, spanning the polarity of light (summer, sun; unfolding in foliage and flower) and dark (earth, winter; concentrating in seed and bud).

Chapter 8: Heredity

1. Rudolf Steiner, *Agriculture*, 164.

2. Sir Albert Howard, *Soil and Health*, 10–11.

3. Ibid., 75.

4. Ibid., 84.

5. William A. Albrecht, *The Albrecht Papers*, ed. Charles Walters (Raytown, MI: Acres, USA, 1975), 258.

6. Ibid., 374.

7. C. J. Pank, *Dirt Farmer's Dialogue* (Sparkers, NY: B-D Press, 1976), 127.

8. Aside from the biodynamic preparations, Steiner gave indications for revitalizing potatoes by cutting single eyes with as little degenerate parent substance as possible, growing them in good humus, and planting them at the correct lunar phase.

9. Questions can be raised whether the excessively protein-fed, artificially inseminated, and overbred cattle will still be able to supply health-restoring manures for the soil.

10. Theodosius Dobzhansky, "On Genetics and Politics" in *Heredity and Society*, ed. A. S. Baer (New York: Macmillan Co., 1973), 31.

11. Wilson Clark, "U.S. Agriculture is Growing Trouble as Well as Crops," Smithsonian, January, 1975, 64.

12. Ibid., 64.

13. Marguerite Gilstrap, *Seeds. 1961 Yearbook of Agriculture*, USDA, Washington DC, 26, 1962.

14. E. Pfeiffer, *A Condensation of Bio-Dynamic Farming and Gardening*, 39–41.

15. Possibly we can understand the concept of the splendid isolation of genes from a sociology-of-knowledge view point, as a projection of the isolated and powerful position of researchers and ivory tower academicians of social prestige, who like to see themselves as effective in the world but not affected, as objective and not subject. Emphasis of "adaptation" to existing conditions, and a "survival" of the best adapters, seems to fit this line of thought that reveals itself as a projection of ideology into the biochemical realm.

16. Mutagens, besides radiation, include a number of new chemical compounds, such as the fungicide Captan, the plant growth inhibitor maleic hydrazide, the sweetener cyclamate, the food preservatives sodium nitrite and sodium nitrate, certain antibiotics, insect chemo-sterilants such as triethylene phosphoramide and trietheline melamine; agents used in methylating and ethylating phenols, amines and other compounds are ingested by organisms including humans beings by way of air and water pollution, food preservatives, soft drinks, residual pesticides, and medications. See James V. Neel and Arthur D. Bloom, "The Detection of Environmental Mutagens" in *Heredity and Society*, ed. A. Bear, 44. The phenoxy herbicide 2, 4, 5-t sprayed widely on forests, cropland, and roadsides to kill dicots, containing dioxin, effective in parts per trillion, has such

mutagenic effects. See W. Boly, "Sweet Dioxin," *Oregon Times Magazine* Sept. 1977, 39–42.

17. Arthur Koestler, *The Case of the Midwife Toad* (New York: Vintage Books, 1973), 130.

18. Ibid., 131.

19. Arthur Koestler, *The Ghost in the Machine* (New York: Macmillan Co., 1967), 127.

20. Theodore Roszak, *Unfinished Animal* (New York: Harper & Row, 1975), 98.

21. Koestler, *The Case of the Midwife Toad*, 133.

22. Ibid., ch. 4 and 5.

23. Ibid., 19.

24. See the publications and blog of Dr. Vandana Shiva. Also Marie-Monique Robin, *Le monde selon Monsanto. De la dioxine aux OGM, une multinationale qui vous veut du bien* (Paris, France: Editions La Découverte, 2008), ch. 15.

Chapter 9: Terrestrial Factors: Soil

1. John Fletcher, *Russia: Past, Present and Future* (London: New Knowledge Books, 1968), 3. When the burden of carrying wicked humanity becomes too heavy to bear, Mother Earth asks that she may be allowed to swallow them up. Christ answers:

   > O, Mother, Moist Mother Earth,
   > Of all creatures thou art most in pain
   > By the sins of humanity thou art stained
   > Have patience yet a little while until I come again
   > Then thou, O Earth, shalt rejoice and skip
   > Thou shalt shine forth whiter than snow!
   > I shall change thee into a marvelous garden
   > Where beautiful flowers of Paradise shall bloom for thee!
   > O ye, my chosen souls, rejoice.

2. As, for example, found in the Grants Pass, Oregon, area where I gardened and where this was written.

3. In the theory of atoms, a *cation* positively charged atom or group of atoms. Its opposite, a group of atoms with a negative charge, is called an *anion*.

4. This on one of the reasons, besides the direct health danger to man and

beast, why spraying stands of forest with defoliants, as is done to rid the economically important conifers of their "competitor" species, is ecologically disastrous. The spray will likely kill off the mycorrhizae, which are very sensitive. The conifers, weakened by the loss of this symbiotic association, will become subject to insect (bark beetle, for example) damage, since the insect's function in the life cycle is to destroy unhealthy tissues. The result will be the necessity of spraying not only artificial nutrients on the forests, but resorting to the use of insecticides. All of this spells profits for chemical companies, but on the other hand, ecological disaster.

5. See Ehrenfried Pfeiffer, *Biodynamic Farming and Gardening*, 91–103 and Bargyla and Gylver Rateaver, *The Organic Method Primer*, 80–88.

6. Charles Darwin, *The Formation of Vegetable Mold*, 1881.

7. T. J. Barrett, *Harnessing the Earthworm* (Boston: 1950). Dr. Barrett estimates that with eight to ten earthworms per square foot, and five hundred thousand per acre, one can optimally count on eighteen to thirty tons of transformed earth.

8. John Jeavons, *How to Grow More Vegetables*, is a valuable guide in the application of the double-dig method.

Chapter 10: Nutrients and Fertilizer

1. Albrecht D. Thaer, *Grundsätze der Rationalen Landwirtschaft* (1809).

2. Justus v. Liebig, *Chemie und ihre Anwendung auf Landwirtschaft und Physiologie* (1840).

3. This fear still exists today in the minds of most agronomists. Seen from a comparative socio-cultural perspective, one can understand how an age under the spell of the second law of thermodynamics that feared that the sun would eventually burn itself out, would have similar fears in other areas. We are surely dealing with projected fears generated in a culture that operates on rapid consumption of a non-renewable fossil energy base, coal then, and oil now.

4. Frank B Salisbury and Cleon Ross, *Plant Physiology* (Belmont, CA: Wadsworth Pub. Co., 1969), 192.

5. The concern with essential and inessential plant nutrients has its analogy in the Darwinian postulation concerning inessential vestigial organs, or "survivals" of earlier evolutionary phases. One hundred eighty-seven

such survivals have been identified for *Homo sapiens* (toes, wisdom teeth, appendix, tonsils, nipples on male breasts, etc.). By now, the list of inessential organs has drastically diminished. Hospitals no longer have a "tonsil day" on Friday afternoons for the youngsters.

6. Ross Salisbury, *Plant Physiology*, 193.

7. Ibid., 201.

8. Justus v. Liebig, *Chemische Briefe* (1859).

9. Tomkins and Bird, *The Secret Life of Plants*, 197.

10. C. J. Pank, *Dirt Farmer's Dialogue*, 78.

11. Elstrup Rasmussen, "Lebendige Erde," 5/1962 (Darmstadt).

12. Ibid., 78.

13. My own experience with bagged steer manure bought at a gardener's supply store in Oregon confirms this. When placed in a barrel of rainwater to make "Russian tea" for fertilizing heavy feeders during the growing season, the "organic manure" immediately colored the water an unnatural brown, indicating that the substance had been artificially colored to make it look like good compost. Needless to say, it did not ferment as it was probably laced with antibiotics and pesticides. When I tried to make a compost of this "manure" it took more than two years to start to break down.

14. Koepf, Pettersson, Schaumann, *Bio-Dynamic Agriculture*, 117.

15. This is probably why blackberries grown along dusty country roads are the sweetest; they are dusted with fine particles of silicone.

16. Due to excessive chemical fertilization the amount of silica in plants, especially in cereal grains, has diminished by about 30 percent ash content analysis in the last ninety years. The result is poorer keeping and baking quality in bread and a decline in the nutritional quality of bread. Thatch roofs, common for farmsteads around the North Sea, once lasted about thirty years; now because of the poor quality of the straw, they last at most fifteen years. cf. Nicolas Remer, *Lebensgesetze imn Landbau* (Dornach, Switzerland: Philosoph.-Anthropo. Verlag, Goetheanum, 1968), 38–62.

17. Koepf, Pettersson, Schaumann, *Bio-Dynamic Agriculture*, ch. 9.; also, Manfred Klett, "Untersuchungen von Licht- und Schattenqualität" (Darmstadt: Biologisch-*Dynamischer Land und Gartenbau* II, 1973), 178.

18. A horse gives nine tons of manure per year; a cow, eleven tons; a pig, three tons; a sheep one-half ton; one hundred hens give seven tons, which equals 280 pounds of N, 250 pounds of P, and 140 pounds of K. The NPK ratio of rabbit manure is 2.4/0.62/0.05; of chickens, 2.3/1.8/1.8; of turkeys, 1.3/0.31/0.41; cow urine, 5./.05/8.4, and cow solid waste, 5./5./1.6.

19. These spores are sold commercially at garden supply centers.

20. Some gardeners feel that legumes are hard on the soil. This is due to the fact that increased yields also lead to increased consumption of P and K, which are not supplied by the legume.

21. Dorman J. Steele, *A Fourteen Weeks Course in Chemistry* (New York: A. S. Barnes & Co., 1868).

Chapter 11: Cosmic Influences

1. Biblical support of these beliefs is given by Genesis 1:14, "And God said: Let there be lights in the firmament of the heaven to divide the day from the night; and let them be for signs and for seasons and for days and years." Also, Eccl. 3:1–8, "To everything there is a season and a time for every purpose under the heaven. A time to be born and a time to die; a time to plant and a time to pluck up that which is planted . . ."

2. An interest in astrological influences in the garden since the 1970s is evidenced by books such as Louise Riotte, *Planetary Planting* (New York: Simon and Schuster, 1977).

3. Some anthroposophically oriented astrologers feel that this system is justified, for at the time of the birth of Christ, the human soul had evolved out of its immediate relationship with the external universe, so that the astrological data refer to the microcosmic universe with its inner constellations, not to the macrocosmic universe with its outer constellations.

4. Between these cardinal points, which form the solar cross of the year, the ancient Celts marked four other festivals in between. The full moon of November (Old Irish. *Samhain,* Halloween) celebrating the end of the year, the hunt and the departed ancestors; the full moon in February (O.Ir. *Imbolc,* Candlemas) celebrating the melting of the snow, the birth of lambs, the reawakening of nature; the full moon in May (O. Ir. *Beltane,* May Day) celebrating the beginning of summer and the marriage of the sun god to the vegetation goddess; the full moon in August (O. Ir.

Lughnasadh), the hottest time of the year, celebrating the harvest of the grain cereals and the gathering of healing herbs. These festivals, too, were tied to nature and the cosmic rhythms.

5. The spring point itself is in retrograde (called the precession of the equinox), so that it is moving approximately every 2,200 years into a new zodiac sign. It is now moving from Pisces into Aquarius, which is why hippie visionaries were singing ago about the "Age of Aquarius." Jesus was born at the beginning of the age of Pisces, and before that was the Age of the Ram (Aries), coincidentally, a historical epoch when sheep were considered to be proper sacrifices. Before that, during the age of the Egyptian pharaohs, it was the time of the cosmic bull (Taurus) etc. The Platonic World Year (a cycle of about 26,000 years) is defined as the movement of the spring point through all the twelve signs of the zodiac.

6. The twelve-year cycle of the East Asian calendar of years is based on this Jupiter period. These twelve years are known as the year of the rat, ox, tiger, rabbit, dragon, snake, horse, sheep, monkey, cock, dog, and boar.

7. Peasants regard the lunar nodes at which eclipses occur as unfavorable and only the most important work is done at this time. My own experience concerns a lunar eclipse in Scorpio on May 28, 1975. While watching the spectacle, the temperature dropped so that the beans and tomatoes froze. The temperature drop was not necessarily causally related to the reddening, darkening moon in Scorpio, but it did occur synchronically.

8. Benjamin Lee Whorf, *Language, Thought, and Reality* (1956; rpt. Cambridge, MA: MIT Press, 1964).

9. Ritchie R. Ward, *The Living Clocks* (New York: Alfred A. Knopf, Inc., 1971), 48.

10. Günther Wachsmuth, *Erde und Mensch* (Dornach, Switzerland: Philosophisch Anthroposophischer Verlag, 1945), ch. 6.

11. Frank A Brown, "Hypothesis of Environmental Timing of the Clock" in *The Biological Clock* (New York: Academic Press, 1970).

12. Ibid., 32.

13. The entomologist and electronics specialist Philip Callahan distinguishes chemo-receptors for olfaction, located mainly in the mouth parts and legs of insects, from the sensilla of the antennae that function like dielectric antenna that are receptive to electromagnetic wavelengths ranging

from radio waves through infra-red, visible, ultra-violet, past X-rays, to the high energy gamma rays. The dielectric antennae of insects are perfectly constructed to receive and amplify such short wave radiations as light, infrared, and short-millimeter radiation bands. There is no reason to assume that they are not affected by cosmic influences. *Insects and How they Function* (New York: Holiday House, 1971), ch. 10.

14. Agnes Fyfe, *The Signature of the Moon in Plants (Die Signatur des Mondes im Pflanzenreich)*. (Stuttgart: Verlag Freies Geistesleben, 1967).

15. Ostrander and Schroeder, *Psychic Discoveries Behind the Iron Curtain*, ch. 26.

16. Ellsworth Huntington, *Mainsprings of Civilization*, "Cycles, Rhythms and Periodicities" (New York: Mentor Books, 1962), ch. 24: 495.

17. The impressionability of water to cosmic influences has also been shown by the research of Theodor Schwenk in his book *Sensitive Chaos*. The sensitivity of water to subtle stimuli has been repeatedly investigated by homoeopathic researchers. Interesting in this respect are the water crystallization experiments by Masaru Emoto.

18. G. Wolber, and S.Vetter, "Samenjahre der Rotbuche und Planetenstellung im Tierkries," in *Sternkalender* (Dornach, Switzerland, 1972), 73–74.

19. Kolisko, *Agriculture of Tommorow* (1939), 72.

20. Ernst Michael Kranich, *Die Formensprache der Pflanze* (Stuttgart: Verlag Freies Geistesleben, 1976), 168.

21. Organic forms can be explained not only from inner concentric forces, but also, by outer tangential forces. Just as a sphere can be explained in geometry as the end point of all radii, it can equally well be seen as having been molded plastically from without by all the possible tangent planes. These tangent planes that fill the universe invisibly can be labeled "etheric," or "counter space." In a similar fashion, the sun, which is usually seen as a radiating center, can be seen as its opposite as a suction force, as the center of a vortex around which the planets rotate. Mathematics in this direction have been done by L. Locher-Ernst, *Projective Geometry*, (1940); George Adams, *The Plant between the Sun and Earth*, (Stourbridge, 1952); and Olive Whicher, *Projective Geometry* (London: Rudolf Steiner Press, 1961).

22. See also, Nathan Cabot Hale, *Abstraction in Art and Nature* (New York: Watson-Guptill Pub., 1972).

23. The Fibonacci sequence is also found in the logarithmic spirals of the chambered nautilus, the curvature of mountain sheep horns, elephant tusks, winter rosettes of plants, and other organic phenomena.

24. The Golden Ratio (*section aurea*), a key to the universe since Pythagoras, is found in the intervals of music (monochord), mollusk shells, the genealogy of drone bees, as well as in works of art such as the proportions of the sculptures of Phidias, the ratios of the pyramid of Cheops and others. Gustav Fechner found this ratio in windows, architecture, books, the Christian cross, playing cards, and other objects that are intuitively held to be well balanced and harmonious.

25. Joachim Schulz, "Blattstellungen im Pflanzenreich als Ausdruck kosmischer Gesetzmässigkeiten," *Lebendige Erde*, Bd. II, (Darmstadt, 1973), 267.

26. Ernst Michael Kranich, *Die Formensprache der Pflanzen* (Stuttgart: Verlag Freies Geistesleben, 1976).

27. These observations also coincide with older color schemes, which attribute the colors of the rainbow to the superior planets. The colors range from the red of Mars, through the yellow of Jupiter, to the blue of Saturn. Green, the color of the vegetative plant is the color of Venus in connection with the sun. Mercury is said to not have a color as such, but consists of a sheen. The moon is identified with the subterranean color of silver, and the sun with gold, both beyond the range of the rainbow.

28. Hermann Poppelbaum, *New Light on Heredity and Evolution* (Spring Valley, NY, 1977), 15.

29. George Adams, *Physical and Etheric Spaces* (London: R. Steiner Press, 1965), 23.

30. Grohmann, *Die Pflanze als Lichtsinnesorgan der Erde* (Stuttgart: Verlag Freies Geistesleben,1962), 34.

31. Alan Chadwick, Biodynamic conference in Los Angeles, 1974, recorded by Steve Dinkowitz.

32. Lilli Kolisko, *Agriculture of Tomorrow*.

33. Traditional correspondences are as follows:

 Aries (ram), the head, is barren, dry, fiery and masculine.
 Taurus (bull), the neck, is fertile, moist, earthy and feminine.

Gemini (twins), the arms, is barren, dry, airy, and masculine.
Cancer (crab), the breast, is fruitful, moist, watery, and feminine.
Leo (lion), the heart and back, is barren, dry, fiery, and masculine.
Virgo (virgin), the bowels, is barren, moist, earthy, and feminine.
Libra (scales), the hips, is semi-fruitful, moist, airy, and masculine.
Scorpio (scorpion), the loins, is fruitful, moist, watery, and masculine.
Sagittarius (archer), the thighs, is barren, dry, fiery, and masculine.
Capricorn (goat), the knees, is semi-fertile, moist, earthy, and
  feminine.
Aquarius (water carrier), the calves, is barren, dry, airy, and masculine.

34. Maria Thun, "Kosmische Wirkung in Boden und Pflanze im siderischen Mondrhythmus" (Dornach, Switzerland: *Sternenkalender* 1974); *see also Work on the Land and the Constellations* (Peredur, G. B.: Lanthorn Press, 1977).

Chapter 12: Atmospheric Factors

1. Simple hygrometers are made from a human hair with a weight for a pointer suspended from it. Peasants in Europe used a little "weather house," which shows Hansel and Gretel when the weather is fair and an old witch when the weather is poor. Other devices include frogs in jars with a ladder to climb up and down on, twisted ropes that coil and uncoil with changes of humidity, and fir twigs.

2. Simple, homemade weather monitoring instruments are recorded in *Weather* (New York: Life Science Library, Time Inc., 1965), 160–170.

3. When the French invaded Holland, Quatremer Disjonval was incarcerated in a spider-infested dungeon in 1787; here he made an intensive scientific study of these creatures. He could verify the rules concerning the weather related behavior of arachnids.

4. Christ reveals himself, for example, as the master of the macrocosm and microcosm when he calms the storm on the Sea of Galilee and the fear in the hearts of his followers.

5. On the Howerth farm in Grants Pass, Oregon, a rain dance was held when the waxing February moon was in Pisces, a good water sign, to alleviate the severe 1977 drought. A chanting, praying, dancing group gathered for the conjuring. Indeed, despite the weather bureau's prediction for continuation of the dry weather, it rained the next day.

In the 1920s, the distinguished British anthropologist, W. H. R. Rivers, asked natives of Melanesia to perform a rain dance.

"Oh, no sir," they replied, "the missionaries have forbidden such things."

"I'll grant you permission to do it just one more time," he replied, for he was eager to study their customs. They put on their grass skirts, danced, and chanted, and to his surprise, it promptly started to rain. In order not to compromise his reputation of being an objective scientist, he never published this fact. But he did record it in his private diary.

6. The atmospheric factors of light and warmth in combination with water bring out the colors of the rainbow. In a way, this is also the case when flowers blossom; that too is the expression of the mediation of the light (cosmic forces) and dark (terrestrial forces).

7. It is the difference in air moisture that accounts for the fact that in the desert one can go into the shade to cool off, whereas in the humid Midwest, the shade offers no relief from the heat. Though it takes four to five times the heat to warm a quantity of water by one degree than it takes for an equal amount of air, the water will hold the warmth much longer.

8. John Jeavons, *How to Grow More Vegetables*.

9. Two wonderful books on mulching are Toby Hemenway, *Gaia's Garden: A Guide to Home-Scale Permaculture,* Second Edition (Burlington, VT: Chelsea Green, 2009) and Ruth Stout and Richard Clemence, *The Ruth Stout No-Work Garden Book* (Emmaus, PA: Rodale Press, 1971).

Chapter 13: Composts and Liquid Manures

1. King, *Farmers of Forty Centuries*, 212.

2. Hauser, *Bauernregeln*, illustration 64.

3. J. I. Rodale, ed., *The Complete Book of Composting*, 137.

4. Sources for the B-D compost starter can be found in the Internet, or is available at the Pfeiffer Foundation, Threefold Farm, Spring Valley, New York.

5. Pfeiffer, *Condensation of Bio-Dynamic Farming and Gardening*, 22.

6. Remer, *Lebensgesetze im Landbau, 19.*

7. Pigs are denatured if not allowed to root or if rings are put through their

snouts to prevent this behavior. In France, the rooting ability is put to good use by training pig to dig up truffles. In other parts in the world, such as the highland of New Guinea, pigs are used to plow the swiddens; they turn the soil, dig up stumps, eat grubs and weeds, and fertilize the new fields at the same time. After the pigs have finished, they are taken out of the plot and then the garden is planted. Permaculture has picked up on pig plowing. Well known is the Round River Farm in Finland, Minnesota, where bush land is successfully transformed by rooting pigs into farmland without the use of heavy equipment such as bulldozers or caterpillars. In Europe (Austria), the permaculture guru Sepp Holzer uses pigs to plow his gardens and fields. Not only does one save fossil energy this way, claims Holzer, you can't beat the taste of the bacon of these naturally raised happy hogs.

8. Herds of sheep grazed the large peppermint plantations of Oregon until herbicides and chemical fertilizers replaced them. After the sheep were gone, the mint fields started to degenerate and many had to be eventually abandoned.

9. It is not just our superior agrarian technique that makes bumper crops in the wheat belt possible as the USDA ethnocentrically suggests, but the stored up fertility of soil where the buffalo ranged for millennia creates bigger crops than are attainable on soils exploited agriculturally for up to four thousand years.

10. Marvin Harris, *Cows, Pigs, Wars and Witches* (New York: Vintage Books, 1975), 19.

11. In a lecture held in Dornach, Switzerland, on January 13, 1923, Rudolf Steiner stated that "when these gentle vegetarian beings are fed meat . . . they will go crazy." This indeed happened some seventy-five years later with the mad cow disease. Cf. Rudolf Steiner, *Health and Illness, 1983.*

12. Gardeners at the abbey at Fulda, Germany, suggest using this comfrey slurry to fertilize tomatoes. Cf. Abtei Fulda, *Comfrey, was ist das?* 1972.

13. As it is no coincidence that the words *human* and *humus* are related, and the Bible reminds us that from dust we came and to dust we shall return, we can appreciate the significance of the analogy of three stages of human life, childhood, adolescence and adulthood, to the three stages of humus development. In the first stage, the compost breaks down and completely

rebuilds its substance. Humus is a new product, not just rotted organic material. In an analogous fashion, the child, during its first seven years will completely exchange its inherited physical substance to build up a new body, signaled by the loss of the milk teeth. The next seven years of the child are a ripening out process until puberty, and the years from puberty to the legal age of twenty-one at which stage the child is considered mature (Latin: *matures* = ripe). The "salt of thinking" then developed, is analogous to the nitrate salts of the compost.

14. Rodale, *The Complete Book of Composting*, 91–93.

15. King, *Farmers of Forty Centuries*, 19.

16. Ibid., 257.

17. Ibid., 194.

18. *The Findhorn Garden*, The Findhorn Community (New York: Harper and Row, 1975), 15.

19. John Todd, "A Modest Proposal: Science for the People." In *Radical Agriculture*, Richard Merrill, ed. (New York: Harper and Row, 1976), 272.

20. Clarence G. Golueke, *Biological Reclamation of Solid Wastes*. (Emmaus, PA: Rodale Press, 1977), 106.

21. Ewald Könemann, *Düngerstaetten, Kompost und Düngersilos* (Berlin: Siebeneicher Verlag, 1941).

22. Maria Linder, "Compost" in *Acres, USA*. (Austin TX: April, 1975) Vol. 4, No. 5, 18.

Chapter 14: Companion Planting, Crop Rotation, and Weeds

1. Pfeiffer, *Condensation of Biodynamic Farming and Gardening*, 91.

2. Philbrick and Gregg, *Companion Plants* (New York: Devin-Adair Co., 1966, new edition 2008).

3. L. Riotte, *Carrots Love Tomatoes: Secrets of Companion Planting for Successful Gardening* (North Adams, MA: Storey Publishing, second edition 1998; originally published Charlotte, VT: Garden Way Publ., 1975). *The Organic Gardening and Farming magazine* has published several lists of companion plants, including in the Feb. 1977 issue. William H. Hylton writes of "The Companionable Herbs" in the *Rodale Herb Book*. Other good sources for companion plants lists are B. and G. Rateaver, *The Organic Method Primer*, John Jeavons,

How to Grow More Vegetables (Berkeley, CA: Ten Speed Press, 2004), Koepf, Schumann, and Petterson, *Bio-Dynamic Agriculture*, 1976.

4. B. and G. Rateaver, *The Organic Method Primer*, ch. 5, 78.

5. Pfeiffer, *Condensation of Biodynamic Farming and Gardening*, 95.

6. Joseph A. Cocannouer, *Weeds, Guardians of the Soil* (New York: Devon Adair Company, 1964).

7. William H. Hylton, "The Companionable Herbs" in *The Rodale Herb Book*, 225.

8. King, *Farmers of Forty Centuries*.

9. Clifford Geertz, "Two Types of Ecosystems" in *Environment and Cultural Behavior*, ed. A. P. Vidya (Garden City, NY: Natural Historical Press, 1969), 14.

10. Roy A. Rappaport, "The Flow of Energy in an Agricultural Society," in *Scientific American 225*, 1971, 121.

11. Edgar Anderson, *Plants, Man and Life* (Boston: Little, Brown, and Co., 1952) 137.

12. Ibid., 140.

13. John Jeavons, *How to Grow More Vegetables*, 4–5.

14. Pfeiffer, *Weeds and What They Tell*, (Stroudsburg, PA: BD Farming and Gardening Assoc., 1976).

15. Monocots or monocotyledons are one of two major groups of flowering plants. Monocots, such as grasses or lilies, sprout only one seed leaf (cotyledon), usually with parallel veins. Dicots, on the other hand, have typically a pair of seed leaves usually with netted veins.

16. The great Roman poet Tulli became known as Cicero because of a prominent wart the size of a chickpea (L. = *ciser*).

17. The French call dumb people "haricots" (beans), the Germans say that a dullard is a "dumb as bean straw" and the English label the same "full of beans." The *Bean Feast*, held in England, France and the rest of Europe on the Twelfth Day of Christmas, was a fest of merriment and foolishness. On that day, whoever found the bean or pea hidden in the cake was chosen the "bean king," the king of fools. Even now, Mr. Bean is the name of a popular British buffoon.

18. For reference on poisonous plants, see Walter Conrad Muenscher, *Poisonous Plants of the United States* (New York: Macmillan Company, 1958).

19. The Japanese have developed a delicious burdock root vegetable called *takinogawa* or *gobo*. It ranks among their favorite vegetables. Seeds are available at The Seed Saver's Exchange and various seed companies including Nichol's Garden Nursery in Oregon. When one lets this plant mature, it is easy to obtain the seeds oneself.

20. Edwin Rollin Spencer, *All About Weeds* (New York: Dover Publications, Inc., 1974), 83.

21. Eugene N. Koxloff, *Plants and Animals of the Pacific Northwest* (Seattle: University of Washington Press, 1976), 184.

22. Jules Janick, *Horticultural Science* (San Francisco: W. H. Freeman & Co., 1963), 259.

23. Pfeiffer, *Weeds and What They Tell*, 11–17.

24. Maria Thun, *Work on the Land*, 21. "There is very high weed germination from a soil that is worked on when the moon is in Leo."

25. Rexford Daubenmire, *Plant Communities* (New York: Harper & Row, 1968), 170.

26. Robert Rodale, "Making Enemies into Friends," *OGF Magazine* Feb. 1977, 58.

27. Rateaver, *Organic Gardening Primer*, 91.

28. Ben Harris, *Eat the Weeds* (New Canaan, Conn: Keats Publ., 1995).

29. P.V. Glob, *The Bog People* (New York: Ballantine Books, 1975).

Chapter 15: Insects and Other Beasties

1. V. G. Dethier, *Man's Plague: Insects and Agriculture* (Princeton, NJ: Darwin Press, 1976), 86.

2. For example, that a single pair of flies, if unhampered, would have enough offspring that it would form a tightly-packed sphere of flies ninety six million miles in diameter thick (more than the distance to the sun) within a year's time, is reported in the Life Nature Library, *The Insects* (New York: Time Life Books, 1968), 108.

3. Dethier, *Man's Plague*, 73.

4. Ibid., 73. It goes without saying that insects can cause consternation when

one sees entire trees defoliated by moths and grasshoppers eating the garden bare. Epidemic diseases have certain insect vectors: fleas are links to bubonic plague, mosquitos to malaria, lice and mites to typhus, flies to typhoid and dysentery. Our aim, however, must be to not rush into a hysterical reaction at the sight of a few bugs.

5. Ibid., 57.

6. For example, in Exodus 10:12–19, Jehovah commands Moses to stretch out his hand over the land of Egypt, "for the locusts, that they may come upon the land of Egypt and eat every herb of the land, even all that the hail hath left." When the Pharaoh finally repents "the Lord turned a mighty strong west wind, which took away the locusts and cast them into the Red Sea; there remained not one locust in all the coasts of Egypt." In this account in Exodus we read of lice plagues (8:16), fly plagues (8:21), frog plagues, red algal blooms, and human and animal deaths; in other words, we have an account of ecological disaster in the Nile Valley.

7. For example, Cynthia Wescott in *The Gardener's Bug Book* (Garden City, NY: Doubleday, 1964).

8. W. D. Storl, *Shamanism Among Americans of European Origin* (Univ. of Berne, Switzerland: Dissertation, 1974), 112.

9. Hauser, *Bauernregeln*, 407–8.

10. Frazer, *The Golden Bough*, 614–16.

11. Ibid., 616.

12. Dethier, *Man's Plague*, 105.

13. From J. L. Cloudsley-Thompson (New York: St. Martin's Press, 1976), 7.

> Baby bye, here's a fly,
> We will catch him you and I,
> How he crawls up the walls
> Yet he never falls.
> I believe with six such legs
> You and I could walk on eggs
> There he goes on his toes
> Tickling baby's nose.

Or

> Buzz-buzz was a jolly fly, full of life and gay,
> You could hear his merry dance at the dawn of day,
> Up and down the windowpane, in the soup tureen,
> Buzz-buzz was the dearest fly you have ever seen.

> I myself remember visiting farms in Europe as a child where the flies settled as thick as raisins on the cakes. The farmer's wife just shooed them away when serving the delicious yeast cakes and no one seemed to mind.

14. Apparently, since pre-Christian times, folk belief had it that one could transfer one's illnesses upon the ladybug—providing, one knew the right spell. One such magical chant has survived as a children's rhyme:

> Ladybird, ladybird, fly and be gone.
> Your house is on fire and your children at home.

15. Allantoin is also present in comfrey, making this herb an important wound healer.

16. Philbrick, *Bug Book*, 120.

17. F. Lawson, cited in Rodale's *Organic Plant Protection*, 56.

18. Sudden outbreaks of bark beetles that leave dead trees in the forests of Oregon and keep the foresters puzzled are the result of radical disturbance of the etheric forces. I have observed that such insect damage always occurs after logging and spraying, and after bulldozers and gangs of pre-commercial thinners with chain saws had gone through the forest. Here again, the beetles were not the cause of the trees dying, but merely an indication that the life forces had declined. Similarly, the electromagnetic radiations (EMR) emitted by cell phone towers and radar stations not only threaten the bees, so that they do not find their way back to their hives, but also cause stress for the plants. The subsequent weakening their etheric life forces of trees exposed to EMRs has intensified the problem of insect infestations in the forests worldwide. Dr. Ulrich Warnke of the Institute of Biology and Bionics in Saarbrücken, Germany, compiled the scientific evidence of this and presented it at the Joint Hearing of the Council of Europe's Committee on the Environmental, Agricultural and Local and Regional Affairs September 17, 2010.

19. Cloudsley-Thompson, *Insects and History*, ch. 9, "Famine, Hysteria and the Dancing Mania," 178.

20. For example, the Brückner Cycle averaging thirty-five years, associated with disturbances in weather, including warm, wet winters and dry, cool summers, coincides with cycles of insect pest maximums (for Europe 1700, 1740–43, 1780–83, 1815, 1850–53, 1880–83, 1920–4), which in turn coincides with peak immigration periods due to ruined crops (i.e., three wet years led to the fungus-favoring conditions of the Irish potato famine). Cf. Ellsworth Huntington, *Mainsprings of Civilization* (New York: Mentor Books, 1962) 461–3.

21. A Norwegian legend connects pestering insects with the fire element in the following way: Long ago, there existed a terrible dragon that flew over the land breathing fire and spewing fumes. His body was made of shiny, slippery scales. The archangel Michael in the form of the knight St. George fought the dragon and slew him. However the scales of the monster's body began to turn into flies, lice, fleas and other pests that fly in the air, while out of the flesh maggots and grubs crawled into the ground. The legend clearly associates the pests with the Dragon of Chaos, and with the devouring element of fire.

22. A Muslim legend tells of a locust that fell to the feet of the prophet. Upon its wings was written: We are the army of the Great God and we lay 99 eggs; if the number of these is completed to 100, we shall eat the world and what there is in it.

23. Dethier, *Man's Plague*, 119.

24. According to Dr. Patricia Muir, (professor at the Dept. of Botany and Plant Pathology, Oregon State University, October 28, 2011) insecticides are not as effective as claimed. In the United States, between 1945 and 1989 losses due to insects increased twofold (doubled from 7 percent loss to current 13 percent) in spite of a tenfold increase in both the amount and toxicity of the insecticides used.

25. *Organic Plant Production*, Yepson, ed., 22.

26. Ibid., 26.

27. Texas A&M University, "Monarch butterflies down again this year as decline continues." *ScienceDaily* (March 21, 2012), accessed October 23, 2012.

28. One is reminded of a science-fiction movie of the 1950s showing an invasion from outer space by ominous-looking space capsules that land

offshore. The air force quickly bombs the invaders, but the strikes are of no avail. The capsules open and robot-like creatures invade the land. They seem to get more energized after every attack against them. Just as it is about to be decided to drop nuclear weapons on them, it is realized that these invaders are not to be destroyed by force. Every use of force against them increases their power. It is with flowers and songs that the monsters are finally vanquished.

29. Donald J. Borror and Dwight M. DeLong, *An Introduction to the Study of Insects* (New York: Holt, Rinehart & Winston, 1971), 657.

30. Flowers also attract bees, whose positive astrality disposes the astrality of "pests" which, as far as the gardener is concerned, is not so positive. Bee-keepers find that beehives near the gardens tend to keep the pest population lower than expected.

31. William H. Hilton, "The Companionable Herbs" in *The Rodale Herb Book*, 254.

32. *Organic Plant Protection*, ch. 12, 145.

33. The need to understand ecological networks is illustrated by a slug infestation in our Swiss garden. Clean cultivation was practiced for a number of years and the slugs and snails posed no problem. We even enjoyed the presence of the pretty yellow-black striped garden snails (*Cepaea*) and the beautiful "escargot" snail (*Helix pomatia*), well knowing that they eat carrion, keeping the garden healthy, and that the trails of slime they leave behind have a good effect on the soil. When the little milk slug (*Agriolimax reticulatus*) or the red slug (*Arion ater*) ate too many holes into the salad, they could be hand-picked; the rest was taken care of by birds, frogs, toads, hedgehogs, beetles, and salamanders from the pond. But then suddenly, over a period of three years the slugs became unmanageable. What had happened? The highly invasive Spanish slug (*Arion vulgaris,* syn. *A. lusitanicus*) had reached Switzerland in the early 1970s. The voracious, reddish brown to bright orange invader had crossed the Pyrenees in the late 1950s with vegetable transport trucks and spread across all of Western Europe. (In 1998 it made its first appearance in the United States.) By coincidence, this Spanish mollusk arrived in our vegetable garden at the same time that city water had been made available at reduced rates, and consequently an elaborate overhead sprinkling system was installed to

make the watering easier. The continual ground moisture not only aided the slugs, but watering during the heat of the day weakened the plants and made them more susceptible. Not only that, a Frenchman working in the garden delighted at the presence of the escargot or Burgundy snail, and set about diligently collecting jars of them to turn them into gourmet delights. After decimating the Burgundy snails, the slugs became ever worse, practically unmanageable. The escargot snails eat the white, translucent eggs of the slugs whenever they find them. By this time the problem was out of hand and the gardener resorted to poisons, which were immediately effective, of course, but apparently killed the hedgehogs that lived in the hedge on the garden's edge. Slugs are one of the favorite foods of the hedgehog. The head gardener concluded that slugs, like fate, are something about which nothing can be done; he packed his bags and went elsewhere.

What should have been done instead? The watering should have been managed better, using mulch to preserve the soil moisture, instead of continuous overhead sprinkling. The escargots should have been spared. Providing mulch might have given the slugs something to eat besides the plants on the clean cultivation plots. But then, on the other hand, mulch provides a good hide out for the gastropods. The hedgehogs should have been encouraged to frequent the garden with saucers of milk. Wooden planks should have been laid in the rows as traps under which the slugs hide by day and can then be easily picked and removed from the garden. Deep containers filled with beer could have been used as lures into which the slugs would fall and drown.

34. Helen and John Philbrick, *The Bug Book* (Charlotte, VT: Garden Way Publ., 1074).

35. *Organic Plant Protection*, 113.

Chapter 16: The Garden Calendar

1. A number of good books on the market are worth consulting for helpful hints on how to attract and care for garden visitors, including *An Illustrated Guide to Attracting Birds,* by the editors of *Sunset* magazine (Menlo Park, CA: Lane Books, 1990).

2. In order to find organic seeds, to help preserve and maintain thousands

of heirloom vegetable varieties, and avoid the GMO-seeds of the multinational companies, consult the websites of *Seed Saver's Exchange* (SSE, Decorah, Iowa), the *Organic Seed Alliance* (OSA, Port Townsend, Washington), *Saving our Seeds* (Charlottsville, Virginia), or contact local seed swap groups.

3. *Encyclopedia of Organic Gardening*, ed. Jerome Olds (Emmaus, PA: Rodale Books, 1975), 201–5.

4. Peruvians placed stones in the ground to increase the number of potatoes, and many peasant societies, including some Europeans, honored the last potato as the "Potato Mother."

5. "A dragon springs therefrom which, when exposed in horse's excrement for 20 days, devours his tail till naught thereof remains." From a Greek alchemical poem, recorded in Holmyard, *Alchemy*, 159.

6. See *The Rodale Herb Book* for exact instructions.

7. A hint from an old gardener on how to tell if a watermelon is ripe: "Thump it. If it sounds like when you thump your head, it is too green, if it sounds like your gut, it is too ripe; but if it sounds like your chest, it is just right."

Chapter 17: Teas, Preparations, and Biotic Substance

1. John Soper, *Studying the Agricultural Course* (Biodynamic Agricultural Association, 1976), 43.

2. I was reminded of the Russian story of a young heir to a run-down, indebted estate. The young man, at a loss about what to do, consults an old wise woman who gives him a bag of magical sand. "If you want your land to prosper," she advises him, "traverse your property each morning and strew a few grains of this magic sand on the fields and into each barn." He takes the advice to heart and in a few years the estate is prosperous and healthy again. Why? To the normally lazy workers, the new master appearing in fields and barn early each day seemed to be a man who meant business. Not wanting to be shamed, they worked hard. Thus, from a psychological perspective, one could interpret much of the spraying, dusting, and burning that goes on in agriculture, not so much in view of its rational effectiveness, as from its psychological effect.

3. See Koepf, Pettersson, Schaumann, *Biodynamic Agriculture* (1976) and Kolisko, *Agriculture of Tomorrow* (1939).

4. For a simple introduction, see A. P. Shepherd, *A Scientist of the Invisible* (London: Hodder and Stoughton, 1954).

5. Steiner states in the fourth lecture of *Agriculture:* "You see, by burying the cow horn with the manure in it, we preserve in the horn the etheric and astral force that the horn was accustomed to reflect when it was on the cow. Because the cow horn is now outwardly surrounded by the Earth, all the Earth's etherizing and astralizing rays stream into its inner cavity. The manure inside the horn attracts these forces and is inwardly enlivened by them. If the horn is buried for the entire winter—the season when the Earth is most inwardly alive—all this life will be preserved in the manure, turning the contents of the horn into an extremely concentrated, enlivening and fertilizing force." L. Kolisko, in *Agriculture of Tomorrow*, sees in this a key to the treatment of the dreaded hoof-and-mouth disease.

6. G. Pat Flanagan, *Pyramid Power* (Camarillo, CA: De Vorss & Co., 1975).

7. Sheila Ostrander and Lynn Schroder, *Psychic Discoveries Behind the Iron Curtain* (New York: Bantam Books, Inc., new ed. 1984), ch. 27.

8. Karl Koenig, *On the Sheath of the Preparation* (England: Glencraig Printery, 1968).

9. For similar reasons, Preparation 501 is sprayed out in the morning for then, too, as Wachsmuth noted, the centrifugal forces are a work, shooting sap into stems and leaves, with maximum secretion and assimilation occurring. The cow dung Preparation 500, is, for the opposite reason, sprayed on the ground in the late afternoon as the earth goes into its daily "in-breathing" phase.

10. Anyone interested in exact measurements can contact the Biodynamic Association or consult the book *Bio-Dynamic Agriculture* (Koepf, Pettersson, and Schaumann).

11. William Boly, "Sweet Dioxin" in *Oregon Times Magazine*, Sept. 1977, 39.

12. Pfeiffer, *A Condensation of Bio-Dynamic Farming and Gardening.*

13. Schwenk, *Sensitive Chaos* and *The Basis of Potentization Research.*

14. Schwenk, "Wassernot und Wasserrettung" *Soziale Hygiene* (Stuttgart: Freies Geistesleben, 1973).

15. *Culpeper's Complete Herbal*, 397.

16. Recorded in the "Anglo-Saxon Lay of the Nine Herbs" (*Nine Worts Galdor* or *Lacnunga*), written down in the eleventh century AD.

17. *Rodale Herb Book*, 389.

18. B. C. J. Lievegoed, *The Working of the Planets and the Life Processes in Man and Earth* (Stourbridge, Worcs.: Broome Farm, 1972).

19. Culpeper assigns it to Mercury, probably because of its many medical uses; in England the herb is occasionally referred to as "heal-all."

20. Lievegoed, 31.

21. Humans also start as very generalized clumps of cells. Because of this, as we recapitulate phylogeny, human embryos can be split easily at an early, generalized stage, creating twins, triplets or other multiple offspring.

22. The creation of such a compost reminds one of the homunculus of the alchemists as described by Paracelsus when he talks of "the being developed without the aid of the female organism by the art of the experienced *spagyricus*," which is treated by a mysterious *arcanum sanguinis hominis*, kept in hot horse manure for forty weeks, and so on. (Hartmann, *Paracelsus*, 174).

23. Karl Koenig, *On the Sheaths of the Preparations*, lecture 4, 4–5.

24. M. E. Bruce, *Common Sense Compost Making* (London: Faber and Faber, Ltd., 1946).

Chapter 18: Biodynamic Cooking, Nutrition, and Food Handling

1. The research of the physicist Fritz Albert Popp provides evidence that there might be more to the idea of cosmic light as a source of information for living organism than mere esoteric talk. Popp, picking up on pioneer research done by the Russian physicist Alexander Gurvich (1923) on ultra weak photon emissions of biological organisms, developed a method of precisely measuring such bio-photon emissions. The source of these bio-photons is ultimately the sun. These bio-photons are stored in the DNA of living cells and emitted at different rates following biological rhythms; they show coherence, that is, they have an organizing, ordering effect, and they transmit information within and between cells. Popp was able to show conclusively that there is a difference between organically grown food and food grown conventionally using pesticides and chemical

fertilizers. Organically grown food contains more "light," keeps longer and oxidizes less rapidly than non-organic food. According to Popp, such food contains more organizing information for the human or animal organism. This information is more important than mere caloric content, or mineral constituents contained in nutriments. Using his bio-photon measuring device, he was also able to differentiate eggs from happy free ranging chickens from those of battery hens, making it difficult for cheats who want to sell conventional eggs as organic eggs. He also could show that in ill people the rhythm and coherence of light emissions is weakened; cancer cells contain less light. The relevant scientific publications and literature concerning of Fritz Albert Popp concerning bio-photons can be viewed in en.wikipedia.org/wiki/Fritz-Albert_Popp

2. Ehrenfried Pfeiffer in preface to Steiner's *Agriculture*, (London, 1947), 7.

3. Jethro Kloss, *Back to Eden* (Santa Barbara, CA: Woodbridge Press, Pub. Co., 1975).

4. Wachsmuth, *Erde und Mensch*, ch. 6.

5. Werner E. Loeckle, *Bewusste Ernährung und Gesunde Lebensführung* (Freiburg im Breisgau: Verlag Die Kommenden, 1970), 105.

6. Arthur Hermes, one of my teachers in matters concerning biodynamics, used a method he called "planetary cooking:" On Sunday, there should be something white on the plate for the light of the sun, some "solar" vegetable like cauliflower, corn or Jerusalem artichoke; on Monday some—preferably violet, purple—"lunar" vegetables like squash, cabbage, leeks, or eggplant; on Tuesday some red "martian" vegetable such as carrots, artichokes, peppers, red beets, or tomatoes; on Wednesday something multicolored for Mercury, some "mercurial" vegetables such as fennel, mallow, or okra; on Thursday a yellow "jupiterian" vegetable such as parsnips, or chicory; on Friday green fruits or vegetables for Venus such as peas, beans spinach, or asparagus; and on Saturday something dark or bluish for "saturnian" vegetables such as Swiss chard, black radish, and the like. Grains were always there as the "sun" and other foods as planets that periodically went into conjunction with it. Quaint as it may seem, this provided an interesting nutritional variety. Of course, in order to cook like this, one must know the old Renaissance system of planetary signatures and correspondences.

Chapter 19: Seeds and Tools

1. Thomas Tusser, *Five Hundreth Points of Good Husbandry,* 1573, (cited in Rosetta E. Clarkson, *The Golden Age of Herbs & Herbalists* (New York: Dover Publications, 1972), 63.

2. Ibid., 155.

Chapter 20: Social Implications

1. D. Raghavan, *Agriculture in Ancient India.* (New Delhi: 1964), 37.

2. Michael Perelman, "Efficiency in Agriculture: The Economics of Energy" in *Radical Agriculture* (New York: Harper & Row, 1976), 71.

3. www.sustainabletable.org

4. E. N. Anderson Jr., "The Life and Culture of Ecotopia" in *Reinventing Anthropology,* ed. Dell Hymes (New York: Vintage Books, 1974), 268.

5. Perelman, "Efficiency in Agriculture" in *Radical Agriculture,* 71.

6. The Land of Cockaigne (Fr. *pais de cocaign;* Dutch *Luilekkerland;* G. *Schlaraffenland;* Sp. *pais de cucaña,* Swed. *Lubberland*) was the collective dream of medieval European peasants, offering an escape from want and backbreaking toil. It was a land where people are forever young and sexy, where roasted pigs wander about with forks and knives in their backs for easy carving, where wine flows from the fountains, grilled pigeons fly directly into one's open mouth, where the weather is always pleasant, etc.

7. Ibid., 62, 82.

8. "The household plots . . . continued to be a major source of food for the nation. In 1956 this private sector produced over 80 percent of the eggs, 46 percent of the vegetables and 60 percent of the potatoes consumed in the Soviet Union. In 1963, 45.6 percent of meat and milk products came from private husbandry . . . The Party wanted to abolish private plots, but as no formula had been found to produce adequate food supplies through the kolkhoz and sovkhos farms alone, such drastic action could not be taken." From Ian Gray and Editors of Horizon, *History of Russia* (New York: American Heritage, 1970), 392.

9. Wendell Berry, *The Unsettling of America* (San Francisco: Sierra Club Books, 1977).

10. Robert Rodale, head of the Rodale Institute and publisher of the *Organic Gardening magazine* (Emmaus, PA), which presents articles and editorials that are in line with grassroots American tradition.

11. Charles Walters, who died 2009, is the founder of the farming journal, *Acres, USA*, a major voice for eco-agriculture.

12. E. F. Schumacher, *Small is Beautiful: A Study of Economics as if People Mattered* (London: Blond Briggs, 1973).

13. Gerhard Schönauer, *Zurück zum Leben auf dem Land* (Munich: Goldmann, 1985).

14. Geoffrey Lawrence, Kristen Lyons, and Tabatha Wallington (eds.), *Food Security, Nutrition and Sustainability* (London: Earthscan Publ., 2009), 233.

15. Brett L.Markham, *Mini Farming: Self-Sufficiency on ¼ Acre* (New York: Skyhorse Publ., 2010).

Appendix II: A Summary of the Agricultural Lectures of Rudolf Steiner

1. *Landwirtschaftlicher Impuls und seine Entfaltung*, ed. F. C. L. Schmidt (Birnenbach: W. Müller Verlag, 1973).

2. John Soper, *Studying the Agricultural Course* (London: Bio-Dynamic Agricultural Association, 1976).

3. *Sternenkalender* (Star calendar), 1971–72, Dornach, Switzerland, 58.

4. Steiner suggests that the mysterious "Stone of the Wise" of the alchemists is related to carbon respiration, where carbon has to do with the ability to translate images into form. Yogic breathing exercises include the retaining of the breath for a longer period of time than is normal, in order that the yogi may realize certain images more concretely than when breathing unconsciously.

5. These preparations are discussed in detail in the second part of this book in chapter 17, "Teas, Preparations, and Biotic Substances."

BIBLIOGRAPHY

Adams, George. *Physical and Etheric Spaces*. London: Rudolf Steiner Press, 1965.

_____ *The Plant Between the Sun and the Earth*. Broom Farm, Clent, Stourbridge, Worcester London: Blond Briggs, 1973s: 1952.

Agrippa of Nettesheim. *De Occulta Philosophia—Magische Werke*. Meisenheim Glan: A. Hain, 1530.

Airola, Paavo O. *Health Secrets from Europe*. New York: ARC, 1970.

Albrecht, William A. *The Albrecht Papers*, ed. Charles Walters. Raytown, MO: Acres, USA, 1975.

Allaby, Michael and Floyd Allen. *Robots Behind the Plow*. Emmaus, PA: Rodale Press, 1974.

Anderson, Edgar. *Plants, Man and Life*. Boston: Little, Brown & Co., 1952.

Anderson Jr., E. N., "The Life and Culture of Ecotopia" in *Reinventing Anthropology* (Dell Hymes ed.), New York: Vintage Books, 1974.

Attracting Birds to Your Garden. Editors of *Sunset* magazine. Menlo Park, CA: Lane Books.

Baer's Agricultural Almanac. New York: Grosset & Dunlap Publishers.

Balfour, Lady. *The Living Soil*. Soil Association Organic Classics, 2006.

Barranger, Pierre. "Science et Vie" No. 499, April, 1959.

Barrett, Thomas. J. *Harnessing the Earthworm*. Ontario, Canada: Bookworm, 2010.

Barthélemy de Glanville. "Le Propriétaire des Choses." Lyon, France: Mathieu Huss,1487.

Basic Book of Organic Gardening, ed. R. Rodale. New York: Ballantine Books, 1974.

Bernus, Alexander V. *Alchemie und Heilkunst*. Nuremberg: Verlag Hans Karl, 1969.

Berry, Wendell. *The Unsettling of America: Culture and Agriculture*. San Francisco: Sierra Club Books, 1977.

Boly, William. "Sweet Dioxin." *Oregon Times Magazine:* Sept. 1977.

Borror, Donald J. and Dwight M. De Long. *An Introduction to the Study of Insects.* New York: Holt, Rinehart & Winston, 1974.

Brown, Frank A. "Hypothesis of Environmental Timing of the Clock" in *The Biological Clock.* New York: Academic Press, 1970.

Bruce, M. E. *Common Sense Compost Making.* London: Faber & Faber, 1946.

Callahan, Philip. *Insects and How They Function.* New Year: Holiday House, 1971.

Chardin, Teilhard de. *Man's Place in Nature.* New York: Harper & Row, 1956.

Christian, James. *Philosophy.* San Francisco: Rinehart Press, 2011.

Clark, Wilson. "U.S. Agriculture is Growing Trouble as Well as Crops." Smithsonian January, 1975.

Cloudsley-Thompson, J. L. *Insects and History.* New York: St. Martin's Press, 1976.

Cocannouer, Josef A. *Weeds, Guardians of the Soil.* New York: Devin Adair Co., 1971.

Cook, Gordon J., *Our Living Soil.* New York: The Dial Press, 1960.

Culpeper, Nicholas. *Culpeper's Complete Herbal.* London: Wordsworth Editions Ltd., 2007.

Darwin, Charles. *The Formation of Vegetable Moulds Through the Action of Worms,* 1882.

Daubenmire, Rexford. *Plant Communities.* New York: Harper & Row, 1968.

Dethier, V. G. *Man's Plague: Insects and Agriculture.* Princeton NJ: Darwin Press, Inc., 1976.

Dobzhansky, Theodosius. "On Genetics and Politics" in *Heredity and Society,* ed. A. S.

Baer. New York: MacMillan Co., 1973.

Eliade, Mircea. *Patterns of Comparative Religion.* New York: Meridian Books, 1963.

Emoto, Masaru. *The Message of Water.* Tokyo: Hado Kyoikusha, 2000.

Encyclopedia of Organic Gardening, ed. Jerome Olds. Emmaus, PA: Rodale Books, Inc., 1975.

Farmer's Almanac 1978. Dublin, NH: Yankee, Inc., 1977.

Flanagan, G. Pat *Pyramid Power.* Camarillo, CA: De Vorss & Co., 1975.

Fletcher, John. *Russia: Past, Present and Future.* London: New Knowledge Books, 1968.

Frazer, Sir James. *The Golden Bough*. New York: McMillan Co., 1951.

Fulda Abbey of St. Mary. *Comfrey, Was ist das?* Fulda: Abtei Fulda, 1972.

Fyfe, Agnes. *The Signature of the Moon in Plants (Die Signatur des Mondes im Pflanzen-reich)*. Stuttgart: Verl. Freies Geistesleben, 1967.

Geertz, Clifford. "Two Types of Ecosystems" in *Environment and Cultural Behavior* edited by A. P. Vayda. Garden City, NY: Natural History Press, 1969.

Gilstrap, Marguerite. *Seeds*. Yearbook of Agriculture. Washington DC: USDA, 1961.

Glob, P. V. *The Bog People*. Translated by Rupert Bruce-Mitford. New York: The New York Review of Books, 2004.

Golueke, Clarence G. *Biological Reclamation of Solid Wastes*. Emmaus, PA: Rodale Press, 1977.

Gray, Ian, and eds. *Of Horizon History of Russia*. New York, NY: American Heritage, 1974.

Greene, Sheldon L. "Corporate Accountability and the Family Farm," in *Radical Agriculture*. New York: Harper & Row, 1976.

Grohmann, Gerbert. *The Plant*. East Troy, WI: Biodynamic Farming and Gardening Assoc., 2009.

____*Die Pflanze als Lichtsinnesorgan der Erde*. Stuttgart: Verlag Freies Geistesleben, 1962.

Hale, Nathan Cabot. *Abstraction in Art and Nature*. New York: Watson-Guptill Publ., 1993.

Harris, Ben. *Eat the Weeds*. New Caanan, CT.: Keats Publ., Inc., 1995.

Harris, Marvin. *Cows, Pigs, Wars and Witches*. New York: Vintage Books Edition, 1989.

Hartmann, Franz. *Paracelsus: Life and Prophecies*. Blauvelt, NY: Rudolf Steiner Publications, 1973. (Reprint Kessinger Publishing's Rare Reprints, 2010.)

Hauschka, Rudolf. *The Nature of Substances*. London: Vincent Stuart Ltd, 1966; reprint, Sophia Books, 2008.

____*Heilmittellehre*. Frankfurt/Main: Vittorio Klostermann, 1965.

Hauser, Albert. *Bauernregeln*. Zurich: Artemis Verlag, 1973.

Hawken, Paul. *The Magic of Findhorn*. New York: Harper & Row, 1975, reprint 1988.

Hemenway, Toby. *Gaia's Garden: A Guide to Home-Scale Permaculture,* Second Edition. Burlington, VT: Chelsea Green, 2009.

Hightower, Jim. *Hard Tomatoes, Hard Times.* Cambridge, MA: Schenkman Publ., 1972.

Holmyard, E. J. *Alchemy.* Middlesex, England: Penguin Books, 1968.

Hottes, Alfred C. *Garden Facts and Fancies.* New York: Dodd, Mead & Co., 1949.

Howard, Sir Albert. *An Agricultural Testament.* New York and London: Oxford University Press, 1949. (Special Rodale Press edition, 1972).

_____ *The Soil and Health.* New York: Schocken Books, 1972. Reprint 2007.

Huntington, Ellsworth. *Mainsprings of Civilization.* New York: Mentor Books, 1962.

Hylton, William H. "The Comparable Herbs" in *The Rodale Herb Book.* Emmaus, PA: Rodale Press, 1974. New edition 1983.

Insects. Life Nature Library, New York: Time-Life Books, 1973.

Janick, Jules. *Horticultural Science.* San Francisco: W. H. Freeman & Co., 1973, new edition, 1986.

Jeavons, John. *How to Grow More Vegetables.* Palo Alto, CA: Ecology Action of the Midpeninsula 1974. (New edition: Berkeley, CA: Ten Speed Press, 2004)

Jensen, William A. and Frank B. Salisbury. *Botany. An Ecological Approach.* Belmont, CA: Wadsworth Publ. Co., 1972.

Johnson, Jerry Mack. *Country Wisdom.* Garden City, NY: Anchor Press/Doubleday, 1974.

Kammerer, Paul. *Das Gesetz der Serie.* Stuttgart: Deutsche Verlagsanstalt, 1919.

Kervran, Louis C. *Biological Transmutations.* Binghampton, NY: Swan House Publ. Co., 1973, new edition 1998.

King, F. H. *Farmers of Forty Centuries.* Mineola, NY: Dover Publications, Inc., 2004.

Klett, Manfred. "Untersuchungen von Licht- und Schatten Qualität." In *Biodynamischer Land und Gartenbau* II. Darmstadt, W. Germany: Lebendige Erde, 1973.

Kloss, Jethro. *Back to Eden.* Twin Lakes, WI: Lotus Press, 2004.

Koenig, Karl. *On the Sheaths of the Preparations.* Glencraig England: Glencraig Printery, Reprint, 1968.

Koepf, Herbert, Bo Pettersson and Wolfgang Schaumann. *Bio-Dynamic Agriculture.* Spring Valley, NY: Anthroposophic Press, 1976, new edition 1990.

Koestler, Arthur. *The Case of the Midwife Toad.* New York: Vintage Books, 1973.

_____ *The Ghost in the Machine.* New York: MacMillan Co., 1967, new edition 1990.

Kolisko, Lilli. *Agriculture of Tomorrow.* London: Kolisko Archives, 1939, new edition 1982.

Könemann, Ewald. *Düngerstaetten, Kompost und Düngersilos.* Berlin: Siebeneicher Verlag, 1941.

Koxloff, Eugene N. *Plants and Animals of the Pacific Northwest.* Seattle, WA: U. of Washington Press, 1976, new edition 2003.

Kranich, Ernst Michael. *Die Formensprache der Pflanze.* Stuttgart: Verlag Freies Geisteleben, 1976.

Landmann, Michael. *Philosophical Anthropology.* Philadelphia, PA: Westminster Press, 1974.

Lawrence, Geoffrey, Kristen Lyons, and Tabatha Wallington (eds.). *Food Security, Nutrition and Sustainability.* London: Earthscan Publ., 2009.

Liebig, Justus von. *Organische Chemie und ihre Anwendung auf Landwirtschaft und Physiologie.* Braunschweig: 1840.

_____ *Chemische Briefe.* Leipzig: Winter'sche Verlagsbuchhandlung, 1859.

Lievegoed, C. B. J. *The Working of the Planets and the Life Processes in Man and Earth.* Clent, Stourbridge, Worcs.: Broome Farm, 1972.

Linder, Maria. "Compost," in *Acres USA,* Austin TX: April, 1975, Vol. 4, No. 5.

Lindholm, Dan. *Wie die Sterne Entstanden.* Stuttgart: Verlag Freies Geisteleben, 1973.

Loekle, Werner E. *Bewusste Ernaehrung und Gesunde Lebensfuehrung.* Freiburg i. B.: Verlag Die Kommenden, 1970.

Markham, Brett L. *Mini Farming: Self-Sufficiency on ¼ Acre.* New York: Skyhorse Publ., 2010.

Mességué, Maurice. *Of Men and Plants.* New York: MacMillan Co., 1973.

Milton, Schurmann. *People's China*. New York: Vintage Books, 1974.

Muenscher, Walter Conrad. *Poisonous Plants of the United States*. New York: Mac-Millan & Co., 1958.

Müller-Ebeling, Claudia, Christian Rätsch, and Wolf-Dieter Storl. *Witchcraft Medicine*. Rochester VT: Inner Traditions, 2003.

Myers, Robin. "The National Sharecroppers Fund and the Farm Co-op Movement" in *Radical Agriculture*. New York: Harper and Row, 1976.

Neel, James V. and Arthur D. Bloome. "The Detection of Environmental Mutagens" in *Heredity and Society*, ed. A. Baer. New York: MacMillan Co., 1973.

Ostrander, Sheila and Lynn Schroeder. *Psychic Discoveries Behind the Iron Curtain*. New York: Bantam Books, 1973, new edition 1984.

Pank, C. J. *Dirt Farmer's Dialogue*. Sparkers, NY: B-D Press, 1976, new edition 2009.

Pelikan, Wilhelm. *The Secrets of Metals*. Great Barrington, MS: Lindisfarne Books, 2006.

Perelmann, Michael. "Effeciency in Agriculture: Economics of Energy," *Radical Agriculture*. New York: Harper & Row, 1976.

———— "The Green Revolution: American Agriculture in the Third World," *Radical Agriculture*. New York: Harper & Row, 1976.

Pfeiffer, Ehrenfried. *A Condensation of Bio-Dynamic Farming and Gardening*, ed. B. Rateaver. Pauma Valley, CA: Bio-Dynamic Farming and Gardening Press, 1973.

———— Preface in *Agriculture* by Rudolf Steiner. London: 1974.

———— *Weeds and What They Tell*. Stroudsburg, PA: Bio-Dynamic Gardening & Farming Assoc., 1973, new edition 2008.

Philbrick, Helen and Richard Gregg. *Companion Plants and How to Use Them*. New York: Devin-Adair Co., 1966, new edition 2008.

Philbrick, John and Helen. *The Bug Book*. Charlotte, VT: Garden Way Publ., 1974.

Piccardi, Giorggio. *The Chemical Basis of Medical Climatology*. Springfield, IL: Thomas, 1962.

Poppelbaum, Hermann. *New Light on Herdity and Evolution.* Spring Valley, NY: St. George Publ., 1977.

Raghavan, D. (ed.) *Agriculture in Ancient India.* New Delhi: Indian Council of Agricultural Research, 1964.

Rappaport, Roy A. "The Flow of Energy in an Agricultural Society," *Scientific American,* 225.

Rasmussen, Esltrup. "Lebendige Erde" Darmstadt: 5/1962.

Rateaver, Bargyla and Gylver. *The Organic Method Primer.* Pauma Valley, CA, 92061, 1973.

Remer, Nicolaus. *Lebensgesetze im Landbau.* Dornach, Switzerland: Phil-Anth. Verlag, 1968.

Riotte, Louise. Carrots Love Tomatoes: Secrets of Companion Planting for Successful Gardening. Charlotte, VT: Garden Way Publ., 1975. New edition 1998.

Robin, Marie-Monique. *Le monde selon Monsanto. De la dioxine aux OGM, une multinationale qui vous veut du bien.* Paris, France: Editions La Découverte, 2008.

Rodale, J. I. *Encyclopedia of Organic Gardening.* Emmaus, PA: Rodale Book, Inc., 1973, new edition 2009.

Rodale, J. I., ed. *The Complete Book of Composting.* Emmaus, PA: Rodale Books, Inc. 1975, new edition 2000.

Rodale, Robert. "Making Enemies into Friends," *Organic Gardening and Farming magazine,* Feb. 1977.

Roszak, Theodore. *Unfinished Animal.* New York: Harper & Row, 1975.

_____ *Where the Wasteland Ends.* New York: Vintage Books, 1969, new edition 1995.

Salisbury, Frank B. and Cleon Ross. *Plant Physiology.* Belmont, CA: 1969, new edition 1991.

Sauer, Carl O., *Agricultural Origins and Dispersals.* New York: American Geographical Society, 1957.

Scheler, Max. *Man's Place in Nature.* New York: Noonday Press, 1962.

Schiller, P. E. "Untersuchungen an der freien schallempfindlichen Flame," *Akkustische Zeitschrift,* 1938.

Schmidt, F. C. L., *Landwirtschaftlicher Impuls und seine Entfaltung*. Birenbach: W. Mueller Verlag, 1973.

Schoenauer, Gerhard. *Zurück zum Leben auf dem Land*. Munich: Goldmann, 1985.

Schumacher, E. F. *Small is Beautiful: A Study of Economics as if People Mattered*. London: Blond Briggs, 1973.

Schulz, Joachim. "Blattstellungen im Pflanzenreich als Ausdruck kosmischer Gesetzmaessigkeiten," in *Lebendige Erde*, Bd. II. Darmstadt, 1973.

Schwenk, Theodor. *Grundlagen der Potenzforschung*. Stuttgart: Verl. Freies Geistesleben, 1972.

_____ *Sensitive Chaos*. Forest Row, East Sussex: Rudolf Steiner Press, 2004.

Shepherd, A. P. *A Scientist of the Invisible*. Rochester, VT: Inner Tradtitions, 1990.

Sloane, Eric. *The Seasons of America Past*. New York: Funk & Wagnalls, 1958.

Soper, John. *Studying the Agricultural Course*. London: Bio-Dynamic Agricultural Association, 1976.

Spencer, Edwin Rollin. *All About Weeds*. New York: Dover Publ. Inc., 1974, new edition 2011.

Spindler, H. Bull. Lab. Maritime de Dinard XXVIII, and Bull. Lab. Maritime de Dinard XXXi, 1948.

Steele, Dorman J. *A Fourteen Weeks Course in Chemistry*. New York: A. S. Barnes & Co. 1868.

Steiner, Rudolf. *Agriculture*. London: Rudolf Steiner Press, 2004.

_____ *An Outline of Occult Science*. London: Rudolf Steiner Press, 1997.

------- *Goethes Naturwissentschaftliche Schriften*. Stuttgart: Verlag Freies Geistesleben, 1972.

_____ *Health and Illness*. Great Barrington, MA: Anthroposophic Press, 1983.

_____ *Macrocosm and Microcosm*. London: Rudolf Steiner Press, 1968.

_____ *Man as a Symphony of the Creative Word*. London: Rudolf Steiner Press, 1970.

_____ *Nature's Open Secret*. London: Rudolf Steiner Press, 2010.

_____ *The Social Future*. New York: Anthroposophic Press, 1972.

_____ *The Threefold Social Order*. New York: Anthroposophic Press, 1972.

Sternenkaledar 1971–72. Dornach, Switzerland: Verlag am Goetheanum, 1970.

Stone Soup, Ltd. *The Green World, A Guide and Catalogue*. New York: A Berkeley Windhover Book, 1975.

Storl, Wolf D. *Shamanism Among Americans of European Origin*. Unpublished Dissertation. University of Berne, Switzerland, 1974.

_____*Healing Lyme Disease Naturally*. Berkeley, CA: North Atlantic Books, 2010.

_____*The Herbal Lore of Wise Women and Wortcunners*. Berkeley, CA: North Atlantic Books, 2011.

_____*Shiva: The Wild God of Power and Ecstasy*. Rochester, VT: Inner Traditions, 2004.

Stout, Ruth. *The Ruth Stout No-Work Garden Book*. Emmaus, PA: Rodale Press, Inc., 1979.

Thaer, Albrecht. D. *Grundsätze der Rationalen Landwirtschaft*. Berlin: Realbuchhandlung, 1809.

Thompson, William I. (ed.) *The Findhorn Garden*. New York: The Findhorn Community, Harper & Row,1975.

Thun, Maria. "Kosmische Wirkung im Boden und Pflanze im siderischen Mondrhythmus" in *Sternenkalender 1974*. Dornach, Switzerland, 1973.

_____ *Work on the Land and the Constellations*. Peredur, GB: Lanthorn Press, 1977.

Todd, John. "A Modest Proposal: Science for the People," in *Radical Agriculture* ed. Richard Merrill. New York: Harper & Row, 1976.

Tompkins, Peter and Christopher Bird. *The Secret Life of Plants*. New York: Harper & Row, 1989.

Wachsmuth, Guenther. *Erde und Mensch*. Dornach, Switzerland: Philos. Anthro. Verlag, 1945.

Walters Jr., Charles. "The Case for Eco-Agriculture," *Acres, USA*, Rayton, MI, 1975.

Ward, Ritchie R. *The Living Clocks*. New York: Alfred A. Knopf, Inc., 1971.

Watson, Lyall. *Supernature*. New York: Bantam Books, 1974, new edition 1999.

Weather. New York: Life Science Library, Time, Inc., 1965.

Wescott, Cynthia. *The Gardener's Bug Book*. Garden City, NY: Doubleday, 1973.

Whicher, Olive. *Projective Geometry*. London: Rudolf Steiner Press, 1975.

Whorf, Benjamin Lee. *Language, Thought, Reality*. Cambridge, MA: The MIT Press, 1964.

Wigginton, Eliot. *The Foxfire Book*. Garden City, NY: First Anchor Books, 1972.

Wortman, Sterline. "Agriculture in China." *Scientific American*: June, 1975.

Yates, Frances. *Giordano Bruno and the Hermetic Tradition*. Chicago: The University of Chicago Press, 1991.

Yepsin, Roger (ed.). *Organic Plant Protection*, Emmaus, PA: Rodale Publications, 1979.

INDEX

ABOUT THE AUTHOR

Wolf D. Storl, PhD, is an ethnobotanist and the author of some two dozen books on herbalism, alternative medicine, ethnobotany, and shamanism. Born in Saxony, Germany, he received his PhD in ethnology from the University of Berne, Switzerland. His early post-doctorate career included research in a Swiss biodynamic farming community, teaching anthropology and organic gardening at Rogue College in Oregon, participant-observer research at a traditional Swiss farm, and two years in India as a visiting scholar at the Benares Hindu University.

Always interested in local gardening practices in his travels around the world, twenty-five years ago Dr. Storl was able to put his learning to the test when he and his family moved to a mountain farmstead in southern Germany. There he maintains a year-round vegetable garden and continues to teach, also appearing on television in the United States and many countries in Europe as a spokesman for natural horticulture.